The New English Grammar

LESSONS IN ENGLISH AS A FOREIGN LANGUAGE
MORE LESSONS IN ENGLISH AS A FOREIGN LANGUAGE

By R. A. CLOSE

British Council Representative, Athens

PARTS ONE AND TWO

PARTS THREE AND FOUR

PUBLISHERS' NOTE: All four parts have been combined into one volume, but for the sake of economy no attempt has been made to change the pagination or to alter the text in any way.

London
GEORGE ALLEN & UNWIN LTD
RUSKIN HOUSE   MUSEUM STREET

FIRST PUBLISHED IN 1964
SECOND IMPRESSION 1967
COMBINED ONE VOLUME EDITION 1971

© George Allen & Unwin Ltd, 1964, 1971

ISBN 0 04 425021 5

PRINTED IN GREAT BRITAIN
by Photolithography
BY JOHN DICKENS AND CO LTD
NORTHAMPTON

PREFACE

This book provides the essential grounding that all students of English need before they can understand and use the language properly. In its material, it includes important features of the English of today that are not dealt with in traditional textbooks. In its method, it avoids definitions, pedantic or specialist terminology and dubious 'rules', and concentrates on putting example into practice. Such new material and methods are already widely known and are rapidly replacing the old. This book makes them into a comprehensive course covering pronunciation, spelling, grammatical forms, sentence structure and idiom, and exercising essential vocabulary. An original contribution to English language teaching is made in the exercises on the articles, prepositions and tenses, following principles explained in the author's *English as a Foreign Language*.

Part One lays a basis for good pronunciation (including stress and intonation) and accurate spelling. Part Two deals with nouns, articles, adjectives, adjuncts, pronouns, verbs, tenses, adverbs, prepositions, the construction of the simple sentence, and word-order. Parts Three and Four follow.

This book was begun at Wedmore in Somerset, whose significance in the early history of the English language is a reminder that the roots of modern English are old and deep. It was finished on an island off the coast of Greece, in an atmosphere of clarity which I hope has penetrated into these pages. Certain obscurities in the typescript were removed through the painstaking efforts of Mr Andrew Bonar. I am responsible for those that remain. The passage quoted in Exercise 252 is from Ethel Mannin's *The Flowery Sword* (Hutchinson) and that in Exercise 253 from a broadcast talk by Dr J. Welch on 'The Foundations of Western Values' (*The Listener*).

R. A. C.

EXPLANATION AND ADVICE TO TEACHERS

What is 'the new English grammar'?

To know and be able to speak and write any language well, we must have a perfect control of its grammar, by which I mean its own particular *system* of communication. Imagine the system as an intricate machine capable of conveying an immense variety of meanings, and making very subtle *distinctions* in meaning. The system is built up of a comparatively small number of words, parts of words, and speech-sounds, modified by stress, pitch and tone of voice. To understand and use the language, we must also know many other words that fit into the system, or that feed the machine and enable it to transmit and receive messages for a great variety of occasions.* The system works as a set of *conventions*, i.e. habits—in this case habits of speech or writing—adopted in a community by common consent. When we learn our mother tongue, we pick up these habits unconsciously, and they become engrained in us. In learning another language, we must—unless we have exceptional opportunities or powers of imitation—be taught them with the direct or indirect aid of a grammatical systematisation or *scheme*, i.e. the product of an attempt to trace and describe the system and to classify and label its component parts.

All that is true of English. Yet people often say that English is unsystematic; that grammar, as far as English is concerned, has practically disappeared, and that as a method it does not really help us to *learn* the language. That will appear to be true also, so long as we go on applying to English the kind of grammatical scheme that was meant to describe the underlying system of, say, Latin or Anglo-Saxon. But modern English can be systematised in its own right. It will then be found to have plenty of grammar of its own kind. If the teaching of English through grammar has failed, there are two reasons for it. First, much of what has been taught as English grammar is dead wood, or dogma passed on by one generation of pedagogues to another, while significant features of the living language have been overlooked. Secondly, we have paid too much attention to *knowing a scheme*, with its definitions, rules and terminology; and too little to gaining *control of the system*. What the great majority of students want and need is not so much to know the grammar as to speak and

* It would be a waste of time for a student to try or be expected to learn a large assortment of words without being able to control the system on which their effective use depends; and it would help the student if he realised from the beginning that he can and need only learn a limited amount of the vocabulary of a major language, according to his requirements.

write grammatically. They want to be able to work the machine, not merely to learn a design of it.

The 'new English grammar', therefore, might refer to the significant features of modern English; or to the natural arrangement of them in a system; or to a logical systematisation of them. Many of them are survivals from the past; others may be recent developments; all must belong to the English of the twentieth century. The term 'new English grammar' might also refer to a teaching method that keeps definitions and rules in the background and concentrates on training in conventional usage.

This is a textbook for the teaching of the new English grammar in this modern way. It is designed as a course of training in the handling of a complex system of communication; and it supplies a stock of vocabulary that we shall often want to feed into the machine for purposes of social intercourse and scientific statement.

For Whom is this Course Intended?

The course is intended for two main categories of student:

(a) intelligent beginners able and wishing to become proficient in both the spoken and the written language, for their general education or for some special purpose; and

(b) more advanced students (including prospective and practising teachers) who want or need a reference book or a remedial course broadly covering the fundamentals of their subject.

Beginners will require a tutor to explain meanings; and both categories of student should have a tutor (or a good recording of at least the first part of the course) to give reliable models of pronunciation. Notes, and a key to certain of the exercises, are provided for teachers. The notes and key can also be used by students working on their own.

Its Aims

Students using the course are expected to think, to think what they are doing, and to think in English from the start. Their *ultimate aim* should be to give their undivided attention to *meaning*, to comprehend what they hear and read in English, and to express themselves effectively in it. To achieve that aim, they must understand how the grammatical system works and learn to operate it correctly and unconsciously. Their *immediate aim* should therefore be to become so automatically proficient in the mechanics of the language as to be able to concentrate on meaning and style. It is very hard to think of the meaning and the mechanics at the same time.

EXPLANATION AND ADVICE TO TEACHERS

What do we Mean by 'Correct'?

Users of this course are expected to speak and write 'correctly'. But what do we mean by that? In this course, 'correctness' should be seen primarily as a matter of *effective communication*, i.e. a process through which the hearer (or reader) understands precisely what the speaker (or writer) intends to convey. Whether a word or construction is 'correct' depends on (*a*) just what the speaker has in mind and tries to express, and where he wants to place his emphasis; and (*b*) his choosing the precise form of expression conventionally associated with his particular shade of meaning. A hearer or reader understands correctly when he sees exactly what the speaker or writer means. In order to speak or write English correctly ourselves, the essential thing is that we should express our meaning in such a way that our audience or our readers understand it fully and precisely if they know English perfectly and are relying on no other medium.

In taking part in this process of communication, either as sender or receiver, we must know and use the conventions of which the system we are handling is composed. Without strict observance of these conventions, a language would soon cease to function as a means of social intercourse. The conventions either have meaning in themselves, or help us make a distinction in meaning, so that if we ignore or mis-use them we may not succeed in expressing our exact meaning effectively.* Moreover, mis-use of them will turn our audience's attention towards our mistakes and away from our meaning: it may even alienate people's sympathy so that they refuse to listen to what we have to say. For these reasons, conformity with the current conventions of the language we are learning is not only desirable but is also more or less essential to complete comprehension.

'Correctness' should therefore be seen as a matter of effective communication, and that is dependent on conformity with widely adopted habits of speech and writing. 'Incorrectness' is then a matter of failure in the communication of meaning, and this may result from ignorance or mis-use of the conventions. The teacher should realise that there are degrees of seriousness in 'mistakes', depending on the degree of the student's failure to make his exact meaning clear to somebody relying entirely on English.

---

* For example, the habit in English of using the word *the*, as in *Give me the paper*, is a convention expressing the meaning 'that specimen, or those specimens of paper, or that object of a special kind made of paper, which the speaker assumes the hearer can identify'. This convention would be used quite unconsciously by people whose mother-tongue is English, but not so by a Russian, Chinese or Japanese, for whom at first it would be a mystery.

Now there may be more than one widely adopted habit in the pronunciation, spelling or function of an English word, and consequently there are **varieties** of English. All important varieties follow the same basic patterns, since they are all recognisably 'English'. If you master the system of one of the major varieties, you should have no difficulty in making the comparatively minor adjustments necessary to understand another variety and to make yourself understood in it. Learners with limited time for studying English need to concentrate on one of its more widely accepted varieties, and even that must be standardised for purposes of study. This book reflects a standardisation, by a student and teacher of grammar, of the kind of English with which he happens to have grown familiar.* He expects his readers *not* to assume that other widely accepted forms of English are 'wrong', or in any sense less desirable than his own. He would regard as 'wrong' a linguistic specimen which is supposed to be English, which has some of the characteristics of it, but which would not be fully accepted as English in any one of its generally adopted forms. However, an accepted expression which is peculiar to one form of English may be 'unsuitable' when it occurs in a context of a different style.

Make sure you can do all the exercises in this course yourself, and get them right. Your pupils can learn more from your example, for good or ill, than from the book.

Rules

'Correctness' should not necessarily be taken to mean 'obedience to stated rules'. You must not conclude from this that in English we can do what we like: we are bound by the necessity of expressing our meaning effectively: and, in doing that, of conforming to the conventions. But the conventions of English are not defined as rules laid down by any authority. The only real authorities for English usage are tradition and common consent, whose rules are found reflected in what people actually say and write. Your best guide to 'correct' English is not a book of 'rules' but the example of authentic English, in a full context, spoken or written by people who can express themselves effectively, and who follow widely adopted practice. Teachers and textbook writers often **invent** rules, which their students and readers repeat and perpetuate. These rules are usually statements about English usage which the authors imagine to be, *as a rule*, true.

* The writer was born and educated in southern England, and has spent most of his adult life in academic or administrative circles, either in London or in international communities abroad where English has been a common tongue.

But statements of this kind are extremely difficult to formulate both simply and accurately. They are rarely altogether true; often only partially true; sometimes contradicted by usage itself. Sometimes the contrary to them is also true.* They must therefore sooner or later be supplemented and supported by a patch-work of sub-rules and exceptions. Learning rules of this kind can be largely a waste of time: it must not be mistaken for learning English or even for learning its grammar.

Instead of trusting to so-called rules, the student should be encouraged to rely on:

(*a*) typical *examples* of English usage, particularly when those follow *patterns* of a high degree of usefulness and when they occur or can be used in real situations or context; and

(*b*) *advice* on what to do in certain circumstances. Definite pieces of advice are much safer than sweeping generalisations and should not be converted into them. They should be based on a clear understanding of the language and should not be issued or learnt in the abstract. They should be related to specific examples and put into practice as soon as they are given.

Warning: This book gives information and advice. It is not the author's intention to lay down a code of laws.

Explanations

Certain explanations are given in this book, especially in the Notes, for the guidance of teachers and advanced students. Teachers should resist the temptation of passing these explanations on to pupils in the early stages: let learners give their attention chiefly to the examples and the exercises. In any case, beware of explanations, as of rules. It is extremely difficult, perhaps impossible, to explain *why* we say what we do; and it is by no means easy even to define the circumstances in which we say it. The time devoted to abstract (and often unsatisfactory) explanations of usage can often be much better spent observing usage in an interesting context, and imitating it in practice.

None the less, teachers will always want to give *some* explanation of usage, if only because students will always demand it; and every textbook writer assumes *to a certain extent* that he can provide it. The present writer is no exception; and readers will find in his *English as a Foreign Language* the assumptions on which many of the exercises in the following pages have been based. The writer does not expect everyone to agree with those assumptions; but at least

* See *English as a Foreign Language* by R. A. Close (George Allen and Unwin, London, 1962).

they provide a carefully laid foundation on which to place his examples: and *it is the examples that the pupils should learn, practise and imitate.*

Choice of Material

In learning a language it is important to maintain a proper *balance* of its main elements in the cultivation of the different skills required. This consideration has determined the choice of material in these pages and the order of its presentation. Students should follow this order strictly, working through each exercise in turn, even though they may 'know' it, or think they do.

The *vocabulary* used is primarily *structural*, i.e. consisting of words required for the construction of sentences of various kinds, whatever the subject-matter. Secondly, it consists of *content* words in very frequent use, or words of lower frequency but of a high degree of usefulness. The choice of vocabulary has been influenced particularly by *A General Service List of English Words* (Dr Michael West, Longmans Green, London, 5th Edition, 1960), and by the lists worked out by Mr C. K. Ogden and Professor I. A. Richards in their fundamental researches into words and meanings.

The selection of the *syntax patterns* introduced in this course and the order of their presentation were determined by the scheme outlined in the Contents. This was done solely because the present writer decided to deal with the problem in that way: which for practical purposes and in the present state of our knowledge is perhaps an adequate reason.

The Exercises: Practise Language like Music

The exercises are not, of course, meant for translation, but for *practice in English.* Their technique has been influenced by the work of several modern British and American linguists, and by the author's feeling that learning to operate the machinery of language is like learning to play a musical instrument. Like music, language has rhythm and tune and is made up of sounds and symbols which have no meaning unless they are put together in certain arrangements. Both are composed of a great variety of patterns and variations on them. Each requires several skills which must be synchronised and executed automatically, so that the performer can give his full attention to expression and meaning. For both, it is not the theory but the performance that counts; and each therefore demands constant practice.

Focus attention in each exercise on its main purpose. However, even a short sentence, like a bar of music, may contain several patterns that cannot be separated. While you are concentrating on one pattern, you may also be using others which have either occurred in previous exercises, or not. In other words, you will incidentally be reviewing, or previewing. Reviewing is essential to language learning, and it is often best done incidentally. Previewing is also important. It prepares us for the future, so that a new lesson supplies something we are waiting to hear.

What Else do You Need?

Any course such as this must be accompanied by conversation and reading where the words and constructions introduced in the course are used in a genuine context. Only in context can we see the full meaning of words, and discover their exact *field* of meaning. This course is, after all, only a preparation for real English, i.e. not the simplified and standardised language of the language lesson, but English that is spoken and written by native speakers of it in normal communication. The student will soon reach a point where progress can be made not by doing more and more 'grammar', but by reading and using real English in pursuit of what interests him. In any case, not until he experiences grammar, and puts it into practice, in a genuine and interesting *context*, can his command of it stand a chance of becoming perfect.

You will, of course, need a good dictionary, not only to explain meanings but also as a guide to spelling, pronunciation and established usage. You will find that works such as the *Pronouncing Dictionary* of Professor Daniel Jones, the *Advanced Learner's Dictionary of Current English* by Hornby, Gatenby and Wakefield (Oxford University Press), the *Concise Oxford Dictionary* and *Webster's Collegiate Dictionary* contain much of the information you will need about the language as you proceed with your studies.

R. A. C.

The use of the accents, which indicate stress and intonation, should become quite clear as one works systematically through the book, following the notes and paying particular attention to the explanation given on page 166.

CONTENTS

CONTENTS

Contents

PART ONE

THE SYSTEM OF PRONUNCIATION AND SPELLING

1. THE SOUND AND SPELLING OF ENGLISH WORDS

The Sounds of English

TABLE 1

The English Vowels

Number	Key Word	Number	Key Word
1	see	13	day
2	this	14	time
3	pen	15	boy
4	that		
5	car	16	house
6	hot	17	home
7	horn		
8	look	18	here
9	moon	19	hair
10	sun	*Where the key word is in*
11	burn	*heavy type, pronounce the*
12	(bèt)ter	*vowel* long.

EXERCISE 1. *Learn and practise Table 1.*

2. *LISTEN; then give the number of each* **vowel** *sound:*

(a) one, two, three, four, five, six, seven, eight, nine, ten, eleven, twelve, thirteen, fourteen, fifteen, sixteen, seventeen, eighteen, nineteen, twenty.

(b) Do you speak English? No, but I am learning it.

(c) I want to learn English. You are learning it now.

(d) I am, you are; I was, you were; boy, girl.

(e) man, men; woman, women; child, children.

(f) Learn and practise Table One. The English vowels.

(g) Number, key word. Exercise two. Listen to each sound.

(h) This is number eight. Is this number ten?

19

(*i*) No it is not. It is nought. Very good. Thank you.
(*j*) Please sit down. Say that after me. Say it again.

3. *LISTEN; then give the number of each vowel sound:*

(*a*) live, leave. Where do you live? In this street.
(*b*) feel, fill. Feel this wood. Is it rough or smooth?
(*c*) still, steel; sheep, ship; heat, hit, head, hat.
(*d*) bed, bad, board, bird; run, ran; angry, hungry.
(*e*) sharp, shop, shot, short, shut; weak, ankle, walk, uncle.
*(*f*) work, word, wide; high, low; law, order.
(*g*) was, wars; day, die; why, way; wait, wet.
(*h*) nice, nose, noise; he hears; we wear. Good idea.
(*i*) full moon, soon; two chairs; three cheers.
(*j*) How many cups? Thirteen. How much water?
(*k*) Not much. Have you a match? Only one, no more. [100]

TABLE 1a

| 20 (or 7) | **more** | 22 | **fire** |
| 21 | **tour** | 23 | **power** |

---

4. *Practise Table 1a. Then listen, and give the number of each vowel sound:*

(*a*) twenty-one, twenty-two, twenty-three, twenty-four.
(*b*) door; why, wire; too, poor; town, tower; tie, tired.
(*c*) mine, yours, ours, theirs; floor, flower; fly, flyer.
(*d*) tyre, burst, car, crash, iron, crush.

5. *Listen again to the words in Exercises 2, 3 and 4. Then say and REPEAT them clearly.*

6. *Practise pairs of vowels which you find difficult.*

7. *Learn and practise Table 2.*

8. *Listen to each* **word** *or syllable; then say the sound of the* **cönsonant** *(or the number of the vowel) at the beginning of it, and give the key word for that sound. Examples:* good:— g, garden; wood:— w, we; write:— r, run:

(*a*) What is your name? Write that on paper.
(*b*) Our next lesson is tomorrow at ten. Don't be late.
(*c*) What is the key word for vowel number seven?
(*d*) Whose is this thing? Did you say 'sing' or 'finger'?
(*e*) right, wrong; light, dark; raw, rice; law, rule.

TABLE 2

The English Consonants

(single sounds)

Soft		Hard	
Sound	Key Words	Sound	Key Words
b	burn	— p	pen
m	moon		
w	we		
v	voice	— f	full
th(soft)	this	— th(hard)	thing
d	day	— t	table
n	no		
l	look, pull		
r	run		
z	zoo, pens	— s	see, books
[ʒ]	measure	— sh	ship
y	yes		
g	garden	— k	cake
ng	long		
h	here		

(f) loud shout; soft voice; town, village; down there.

(g) good girl; fair, hair; he thinks; she speaks; one, do.

(h) warm air; fine weather; vine, wine; heat, sheet; sort, short.

(i) think, sink; thought, fought; sure, sugar; no use.

(j) push, bull; bush, pull. He shows, she sews.

9. **Twelve** (*one syllable*). **Twenty** (*two syllables*). *Listen to each word. Do you hear one syllable, or two? Is the last sound a consonant, or a vowel? What consonant or vowel is the last sound?*

(a) rub, rubber; stopper, stop; some, summer; love, lover.

(b) leave, leaf; bath, bathe, bather; ride, write, rider, writer.

(c) rice, rise; place, plays; runner, run; bag, pack.

(d) crash, garage; study, student; live, lived; stop, stopped.

(e) song, sing; singing, singer; strong, stronger; English; ended.

10. *Listen to each group of words in Exercises 8 and 9, then say and repeat it correctly.*

11. **Pràctise:** pull, bull, tàble, pèople (1), sỳllable (2), lìttle, pèncil, gèntle, gèntlemen, sìngle, doùble (10), bìcycle (14), ùncle, ànkle,

pòssible, tèrrible (3), còmfortable (10); sun, sèven (3), listen, òften, lèsson, gàrden, cùshion (8), attèntion, stàtion (13), translàtion.

TABLE 3

The English Consonants
(compound sounds, and clusters)

First sound soft		*First sound hard*
jump	—	chair
drink	—	tree
blue	—	please
brown	—	print
		flat
		front
		three
glad	—	cloud
green	—	cream
		twelve
		quick

	First sound hard	
small	swim	street
speak	snow	scout, sky
split	sleep	square
spring	stop	screw

---

12. *Practise Table 3. Then* **listen** *and* **repèat:**

(a) John, George; Charles, church; Mary, Jane; English language.
(b) sleep, dream; slip, slope; dry, try; train, drain.
(c) bright blue; below, blow; play, pray; please, police.
(d) present, past; pleasant journey; fly, fry; three, free.
(e) great crowd; clean glass; green grass; grease-proof.
(f) twice twenty; quite quiet; exercise six; throw, threw.
(g) sweet smile; speak slowly; stand still; sneeze, splash.
(h) sport, support; straight line; strong tea; strange people.
(i) skin, scratch; lost, found; count, most; thank, thanks..
(j) jumps, jumped; round table; bags, packs; men's clothes.

13. *Listen, and* **pronöunce** *all these words with the sounds y + 9:*

(a) you, use, ùseful, unìted, univèrsity;
(b) beaùtiful, pure, mùsic; view, few; due, dùty, new tune, Tùesday, stùdent; excùse, hùmour, hùman, huge.

Syllables: Accented and Unaccented

14. *Listen, and repeat:*

(a) Ĕng-lish; nŭm-ber; prăct-ise; lĭs-ten, ĕx-er-cise.

(b) beaŭ-ti-ful; mŭs-ic; to-dày; to-mòr-row; yĕs-ter-day.

(c) mòrn-ing; äf-ter-nòon; ĕven-ing; Mòn-day; Tùes-day.

(d) Wĕdnes-day; Thùrs-day; Frì-day; Sàt-ur-day; Sùn-day.

(e) thĭr-tèen; thìr-ty; fŏur-tèen; fòr-ty; fĭf-tèen; fĭf-ty.

(f) phò-to-graph; pho-tò-graph-er; phö-to-gràph-ic; äp-par-à-tus.

(g) ex-plàin; ëx-plan-à-tion; pro-nòunce; pro-nŭnc-i-à-tion.

(h) know; knòw-ledge; àc-cid-ent; äc-cid-ènt-al-ly.

(i) còm-fort-a-ble; ärm-chàir; ràd-i-o; të-le-vì-sion.

(j) rè-cord; re-còrd; òb-ject; ob-jèct; im-pòrt-ant, nèc-ess-ary.

How English Words are Written

TABLE 4
The English Alphabet

Printed		Written		Pronunciation
Capital	*small letter*	*Capital*	*small letter*	
A	a	𝒶 or 𝒜	𝑎	ay (*as in* say)
B	b	ℬ	𝑏	bee
C	c	𝒸 or C	𝑐	see
D	d	𝒟	𝑑	dee
E	e	𝑒	𝑒	ee (*as in* see) .
F	f	𝒻	𝑓	ef
G	g	𝑔	𝑔	jee
H	h	𝐻 or H	𝒽	aitch
I	i	𝑔	𝒾	i (*as in* time)
J	j	𝒿	𝒿	jay
K	k	𝒦	𝓀	kay
L	l	𝓁	𝓁	el
M	m	𝑀 or 𝑀	𝓂	em
N	n	𝒩	𝓃	en
O	o	𝒪	𝑜	o (*as in* home)
P	p	𝒫	𝓅	pee
Q	q	𝒬	𝓆	kyoo
R	r	𝑅	𝓇 or 𝓇	ar
S	s	𝒮 or 𝒮	𝓈	es

23

TABLE 4: The English Alphabet—*continued*

Printed		Written		Pronunciation
Capital	small letter	Capital	small letter	
T	t	𝒯	𝓉	tee
U	u	𝒰	𝓊	yoo
V	v	𝒱	𝓋	vee
W	w	𝒲	𝓌	double-yoo
X	x	𝒳	𝓍	eks
Y	y	𝒴	𝓎	wy
Z	z	𝒵	𝓏	zed

15. *Learn the English* **àlphabet.** **CÖPY** (6) *the wrïtten* (2) *lètters. Then copy the key words in Tables 1, 1a, 2 and 3 in English wrìting* (14). *Say each word as you copy it. Do the same with Exercise 14, but join all the letters of one word together, without hỳphens* (14).

16. **SPELL:** table (tee, ay, bee, el, ee), see (es, double-e), look, better, why, house, fire. *Learn the* **spelling** *of all the words in Tables 1, 1a, 2, 3 and 4.*

TABLE 5

The Spelling of English Vowel Sounds
(standard)

1	see, sea, me, these	13	say, rain, date
2	pin, *y* in vèry (3)	14	why, fine, high, I
3	pen	15	boy, noise
4	hat	16	house, how
5	car	17	note, coat, no, toe
6	not	18	cheer, here, hear
7	horn, law	19	chair, care
8	look	20	more, door
9	too, June, blue, new	21	pure, fewer
10	sun	22	fire, higher
11	her, first, burn	23	our, flower
12	*Second syllable in* bètter, àctor, còllar		

Reading: English Vowels

17. *Learn Table 5: THIS IS A SCHEME FOR THE SPELLING OF ENGLISH VOWEL SOUNDS AND THE PRONUNCIATION OF VOWEL LETTERS. Then* **READ** *the following:*

THE SOUND AND SPELLING OF ENGLISH WORDS

(a) Free, meet, need; speak, read, teach; he, she; complète, scene, scheme.
(b) Big, fish, ship; hàppy, fùnny. Bètter, best, sell, well.
(c) Cat, flat, match, stand. Arm, bar, hard, sharp.
(d) Dog, got, lot, top. Short, sort, sport; law, raw, saw.
(e) Book, cook, hook, took. Soon, spoon, food, school, shoot, smooth; tune; true; few, view.
(f) But, bùtter, cup, cut, shut. Bird, girl, shirt; turn, hurt.
(g) Lètter, nùmber, vìsitor, gràmmar; addrèss, alòne, accòunt.
(h) Day, may, play; wait, pain, plain; face, make, late.
(i) Dry, try, fly; bite, hide, nice; bright, light, night.
(j) Toy; coin, point, spoil. Loud, mouth, shout; now, down, town.
(k) Bone, nose, stone; boat, road, soap; go, so.
(l) Beer, steer; ear, dear, near, tear, year. Fair, hair, stair.
(m) stare, share, spare. Shore, tore, wore; floor.
(n) Cure, endùre. Higher, hire, wire. Flour, flower, power, tower.

18. *Important exceptions to the scheme in Table 5. Read the words in this Exercise with the vowel sound indicated by the number on each line:*

		Key Word	Other examples
a	5	fàther	àfter; half; dance, branch, ànswer, can't, plant; ask, class, glass, grass, pass; last, past, fàsten, nàsty; bath, path, ràther. (*See note*)
(w)a	6	want	was, wash, watch, what; *also* wand, wànder; quàlity, quàntity.
al, (w)ar	7	all, war	ball, hall, small, tall, wall; alrèady, àlso, àlways; salt, talk, walk; ward, warm, quàrter.
ea	3	bread	brèakfast, dead, deaf, death, head, health, lèather, mèasure, plèasure, ready.
	13	great	break, steak.
ear, ⎫	11	èarly	earn, earth, learn.
ere ⎭	19	wear, where	bear, pear, tear; there.
o	9	do	to, two, who.
	10	come	bròther, còlour, còmfortable, còmpany, còver, done, front, Lòndon, love, Mònday, mòney, month, mòther, none, nòthing, one,* òther, some, son, stòmach, ton, tongue, won, wònder.

* *Pronounce as* [wun].

25

		Key Word	Other examples
oo	8	good	foot, room, wood, wool.
(w)or	11	word	work, world, worm, worse, worst, worth.
ow	17	know	grow, show, snow, sow (seed), throw; bow.
u	8	full	bull, bush, pull, push, put.

19. *Read the following* sèntences. *Then copy them, saying each word as you* write *it:*

(a) Be here at five. Do not be late. Don't (17) be late.
(b) Please stand up. Sit down again. Wait for me.
(c) Stop talking. What is your name? I can't hear.
(d) How old are (5) you (9)? I am sïxtèen, not sìxty.
(e) What is the key (1) word for vowel number two?
(f) Show me your book. What does (10) this word mean?
(g) I don't know. I can't ünderstànd. Explàin it to me.
(h) We want to learn Ènglish (2). Learn this by heart (5).
(i) My bröther is a stùdent (y + 9). He is stüdying (10) làw.
(j) Göod-býe (8 + 14). I hope you have (4) a plëasant (3) joùrney (11). Come back soon.

Reading: English Consonants.

20. *Pronounce and learn the examples below. THESE EXAMPLES, COMBINED WITH THOSE IN TABLE 2, PROVIDE A SCHEME FOR THE PRONUNCIATION OF WRITTEN CONSONANTS.*

Letter	Sound	Examples
c	$\begin{cases} k \\ s \ (before \ e, \ i) \end{cases}$	cat, come, cup. cent, cìty (2).
cc	$\begin{cases} k \\ ks \ (before \ e, \ i) \end{cases}$	occàsion (13), accòunt, occùr. accèpt, àccident.
ch	ch	chair, cheese, chin, choose.
ck	k	quick, lock, luck.
g	$\begin{cases} g \\ j \ (before \ e, \ i, \ y) \end{cases}$	game, good, gun. gèneral, gìnger, Ègypt (1 + 2).
gh	Silent*	high, light, night; straight; through (9), though (17).
gu	g	guard, guess, guest, tongue.
h	h	hair, he, here, hit, house, hunt.
kn	n (k silent)	knee, knife, know (17), knòwledge (6).
ph	f	phòtograph, phỳsics (2).

* Except at the beginning of a word, when it is pronounced g, as in ghost (17).

26

Letter	Sound	Examples
pn	*p silent*	pneumònia (*see note*).
ps	*p silent*	psychòlogy (*see note*).
qu	*kw*	quàrter, queen, quiet (22).
s	*z in*	boys, girls, pens, pèncils, goes.
	s in	shops, hats, books, puts.
-sion	[ʒ] + *n in*	occàsion, tëlevìsion (*after a vowel*).
	sh + *n in*	pènsion, tènsion (*after a consonant*).
th	*th, soft*	the, this, that, then, there; fàther, mòther, bròther, òther; bathe, breathe (1), smooth, with.
	th, hard	thank, thick, thin, thing, think; bath, path, breath (3); nòthing.
-tion	*sh* + *n*	attèntion, addìtion, cömposìtion, stàtion.
wh	*w in*	what, when, where, which, why.
wr	*w silent*	write, wrong, wrap, wreck, wrist.

Exceptions:

b	*silent in*	climb (14), comb (17), debt, doubt, dumb, thumb.
ch	*k in*	school, stòmach, chàracter (4), àrchitect, chèmistry, psychòlogy.
	sh in	machìne (1).
g	*g in*	get, give, gift, girl.
gh	*f in*	laugh (5), cough (6), enòugh (10), rough (10).
gu	*gw in*	lànguage.*
h	*silent in*	hònest (6), hònour (6), hour.
s	*sh in*	sùgar (8), sure.
s	[ʒ] *in*	plèasure, mèasure, ùsual (9).
sc	*s* (*c silent*) *in*	science (22), scissors, scene.
t	*silent in*	lìsten, fàsten, càstle, whìstle, *and commonly in* òften.
w	*silent in*	two, ànswer, sword (7).
wh	*h in*	who, whose (9), whole.

21. *Listen. Read: then* **learn by heart** *and write out from* **memory:**

There are fïve pëople (1) in our fàmily (4) | —Fáther, Móther, my bróther, my síster and mysèlf. We lïve (2) in a smàll hóuse | jüst outsïde the tòwn. Söme people lïve in flàts, or apàrtments. We have a lärge gárden, | with früit (9)-trees and flòwers. My fäther and bróther

* *Pronounce as* [làngwidge].

27

| gö to wörk in an òffice. My sïster göes to schóol, | and I gö to the ünivèrsity. Möther stäys at hòme äll däy.

22. *Listen. Repeat each sentence, or part of a long sentence, without looking at the book. Then read:*

(a) Göod mòrning. Höw àre you? Dïd you slëep wéll?
(b) I am vëry wëll, thànk yoú. I feel müch bètter.
(c) Whëre is your (7) bröther Hènry todäy? Is he at hóme?
(d) I have nö idèa (14 + 18). I thïnk he has göne (6) òut.
(e) Dïd you sëe mäny (3) pëople at the cóncert?
(f) Yès. I saw äll my öld schòol frïends (3) agäin.
(g) Coüld (8) you cöme to my höuse for téa on Thürsday?
(h) With plèasure. I will mäke a nöte of it nòw.
(i) Whät tìme is it? Nëarly hälf pàst èight (13).
(j) It is töo èarly to go höme yét. I have some möre wòrk to dö.
(k) Whö is thère? Spëak ùp. I cän't hëar your vòice.
(l) I wänt to büy (14) some bréad, méat, végetables, sált, sùgar.
(m) Whëre is the Töwn Hàll? Sträight ón, | thën türn lèft.
(n) Drïve through the gáte, | and pärk in the sìde strèet.
(o) Bë quìet. Stöp làughing. Öpen your bòoks. Ġo on wòrking.
(p) Wríte càrefully. Is thïs wörd ríght or wròng?
(q) Gïve (2) me äll your attèntion. Änswer my quèstion.*
(r) My fäther säw the àccident. He gäve an accòunt of it to the polìce (1). He sáid (3), 'I säw whät hàppened.'*
(s) Ìs this störy trúe? I'm quïte sùre it is. There's nö döubt abòut it.
(t) Höw much möney do you ëarn in a mònth? Nòthing yét, I'm önly (17) a stùdent.

23. *Prepare Exercises 19, 21 and 22 for* **dictàtion.**

24. *Read the words in Exercises 2, 3, 4, 8, 9, 11, 12 and 13. Read the words in Exercise 14, first very carefully, syllable by syllable, then more fluently.*

Stressed and Unstressed Words in a Sentence

25. *Listen, and repeat, first deliberately, then fluently. Give the words in italics a weak* **pronünciàtion.**

	strong	weak	
a	13	12	Thïs is *a* pèn.
an	4	12	Thïs is *an* àpple.

* *In* question, *pronounce* -tion *as* ch + n. Happened, *two syllables.*

	strong	weak	
is	2 (+ z)	s only	Thät *is* a bòok. (That's . . .)
is	2 (+ z)	z only	Hëre *is* a pèncil. (Here's . . .)
the	1	12	Thät *is the* dòor. (That's . . .)
the	1	2	Whät *is the* ànswer?
to	9	12	Gö *to the* wìndow.
to	9	8	Gö *to* a dòctor.
am	4	12, *or m only*	}I *am* göing *for* a wàlk. (I'm . . .)
for	7	12	

it is	2, 2 + z	2 + s	} It *is* làte. We *must* gò. (It's . . .)
must	10	12	
but	10	12	*But* it's töo èarly *to* lëave yét.
are	5	12	Wë *are* göing *to* swìm. (We're . . .)
us	10 (+ s)	12 (+ s)	*Are* yoü cöming wíth *us*,	
them	3	12	or göing with thèm?
After let, s *only*			Lët *us* sèe (Let's . . .)
and	4	12	Häts *and* cóats, shöes (9) *and* sòcks.
can	4	12	Ĭ *can* sëe a shìp. *Can* yoú sëe it? Yës, I càn.
than	4	12	Yoü *can* see bëtter *than* Ĭ can.
some	10	12	Söme people lïve in flàts. Hëre *are some* lètters.
at	4	12	Büy stämps *at the* pòst-öffice (17, 6, 2).
have	4	12 (*or simply v*)	Häve you äny (3) stámps?
has (z)	4	12 (*or simply z*)	Ĭ *have* nòne (I've none), nör *has* Jòhn (6). (Nor's John.)

26. *Repeat fluently:*

This is a pen. This is an apple.
That is the door. What is the answer?
I can see a ship. We are going to swim.

Make up sentences on thẹse patterns, replacing the last word of each sentence by one of the following:
book, page, word, desk, chair, floor, cèiling (1), wall, window; arm, egg, òrange (6 + 2), umbrèlla; question, number, time; sleep, work, leave, stop.

Rhythm

27. Listen; practise, and learn by heart:

(a) Bëtter läte *than* nèver (3). (*Proverb*)
(b) *The* ëarly bïrd cätches *the* wòrm. (*Proverb*)
(c) *A* bïrd in *the* hánd | is worth twö in *the* bùsh. (*Proverb*)
(d) Täke *the* büll by *the* hòrns. (*Idiomatic saying*)
(e) Thïs little pïg went *to* márket,
Thïs little pïg stayed *at* hòme. (*Nursery Rhyme*)
(f) Is thïs *the* fäce that läunched (7)* *a* thöusand shíps? (*Marlowe*)
(g) *To* bé, or nòt *to* be, | — | thät is *the* quèstion. (*Shakespeare*)
(h) If Wïnter cómes, *can* Sprïng be fär behínd? (14) (*Shelley*)
(i) My heärt (5) is lïke *a* sïnging bìrd. (*Christina Rossetti*)
(j) Is there änybody (3) thére? said *the* Träveller (4),
Knöcking on *the* möonlit dóor. (*Walter de la Mare*)

Pitch and Ïntonàtion: (1) Falling Tone

Examples

28. (a) (What is that?)   Food.   ◖   (stàtement)

(b)   Wait!   ◖   (commànd)

(c)   Why?   ◗   (quèstion)

Say the following on a falling tone:

(a) Bread. Rice. Fruit. Milk. Tea. Yes. No. Now.
(b) Stop! Run! Walk! Jump! Laugh! Cough! Help!
(c) What? Who? Whose? Where? When? How?

29. Practise the following examples with the intonation indicated at the beginning of each line:

Wàter (7) ◖ ,   Garden. City. Study. Student. English.
Question. Answer. Thirty. Forty. Fifty. Sixty.
Monday. Tuesday. Wednesday. Thursday.
Listen. Read it. Write it.

Beaùtiful ◖ ● ●   Exercise (3, 12, 14). Yesterday. Saturday.
Accident. Traveller. Comfortable. Look at it.
All of it.

* *Pronounce as* [lornsht].

30

A bòok . ⟨symbol⟩ A hat. A coat. It's mine. The door. The wall. Some tea. Alone. Address. Towards (7).

Some wàter . ⟨symbol⟩ . A student. A lawyer. My father. Your mother. Some people. An answer. I'm looking.

A phòtograph . ⟨symbol⟩ . . An exercise. A fountain-pen. A bicycle. An accident. Impossible.

It's a càr. . , ⟨symbol⟩ At the door. I'm alone. In the room. I'm surprised.

It's a plèasure. . . ⟨symbol⟩ . I'm a student. He's a lawyer. She's attractive (12, 4, 2). In the garden.

30. *Phrases and sentences with more than one stress. Practise the examples with the intonation indicated:*

Gö hòme. ⟨symbol⟩ Don't (17) wait. Why not? Stand still. Thirteen. Ármchair.

Gö awày. ⟨symbol⟩ Come at once. Afternoon. Thirty-three. Forty-four. What is this?

Còme to my ròom. ⟨symbol⟩ How do you do? Tell me the truth (9). What is the time? Why are you late?

Còme quìckly. ⟨symbol⟩ Hot water. Young children (2). Old people. Speak slowly.

Whät a pìty! ⟨symbol⟩ What's the matter? Bring some water. Do it quickly.

Höw wònderful! ⟨symbol⟩ What time is it? Take care of it.

I dön't knòw. ⟨symbol⟩ I can't see. An old man.

Whëre are you gòing? ⟨symbol⟩ Why are you leaving?

31

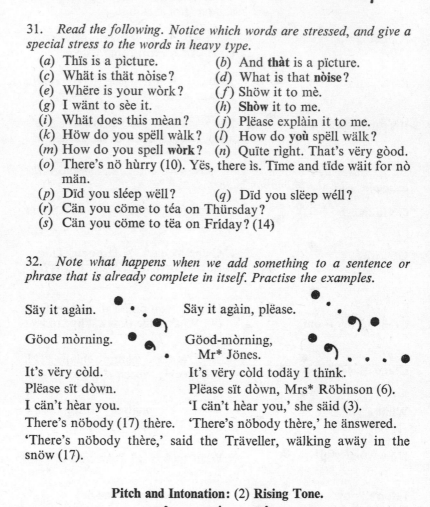

Bĕtter lāte than nèver.   English words are easy.

The ëarly bïrd cätches the wòrm.

31. *Read the following. Notice which words are stressed, and give a special stress to the words in heavy type.*

(a) Thïs is a pìcture.

(b) And **thàt** is a pïcture.

(c) Whät is thät nòise?

(d) What is that **nòise**?

(e) Whëre is your wòrk?

(f) Shöw it to mè.

(g) I wänt to sèe it.

(h) **Shòw** it to me.

(i) Whät does this mèan?

(j) Plëase explàin it to me.

(k) Höw do you spëll wàlk?

(l) How do **yoù** spëll wälk?

(m) How do you spell **wòrk**?

(n) Quïte rìght. That's vëry gòod.

(o) There's nö hùrry (10). Yës, there ìs. Tïme and tïde wäit for nò män.

(p) Dïd you sléep wëll?

(q) Dïd you slëep wéll?

(r) Cän you cöme to téa on Thürsday?

(s) Cän you cöme to tëa on Fríday? (14)

32. *Note what happens when we add something to a sentence or phrase that is already complete in itself. Practise the examples.*

Säy it agàin.   Säy it agàin, plëase.

Göod mòrning.   Göod-mòrning, Mr* Jönes.

It's vëry còld.   It's vëry còld todäy I thïnk.

Plëase sït dòwn.   Plëase sït dòwn, Mrs* Röbinson (6).

I cän't hèar you.   'I cän't hèar you,' she säid (3).

There's nöbody (17) thère.   'There's nöbody thère,' he änswered.

'There's nöbody thère,' said the Träveller, wälking awày in the snöw (17).

Pitch and Intonation: (2) Rising Tone.

33. (a) (*statement*) One,   two,   three, . . .   (I have not finished)

* Mr: *pronounce* [mìster]; Mrs: *pronounce* [mìsses].

(b) (command) Wait! ✔ (There is more to come)

(c) (question) Food? ✔ (I wonder. Is it true?)

What? ✔ (I want more information)

Tired? ✔ (Answer 'Yes' or 'No')

Say the following on a rising tone:

(a) four, five, six, seven, eight, nine, ten, . . .
a, b, c, d, e, f, g, h, i, j, k, l, m, n, o, p, q, ..
(b) Stand! Look! Turn!
(c) Rice? Salt? Wood? Iron?* Yes? No? Who? Whose? When? Why? How? Where? Right? Wrong? Hot? Cold? Wet? Dry?

34. *Repeat and learn the following, saying each word on a rising intonation except the last. Drop the voice on the last word.*

(a) twénty, thírty, fórty, fífty, síxty, séventy, éighty, nínety, | öne hùndred.

(b) fírst, sécond (3), thírd, fóurth (7), fífth, síxth, séventh, éighth, nínth (14), ténth, eléventh, twélfth, | thïrtèenth.

(c) fóurtëenth, fífteenth, síxteenth, séventeenth, éighteenth, níneteenth, | twèntieth.

(d) twënty-fírst, twenty-sécond, thírtieth, fórtieth, | hùndredth.

(e) 1st, 2nd, 3rd, 4th, 5th, 6th, 7th, 8th, 9th, 10th.

(f) 21st, 22nd, 23rd, 24th, 25th.

(g) Mónday, Túesday, Wédnesday, Thúrsday, Fríday, Sáturday, | Sùnday.

(h) Jánuary,† Fébruary,† Márch, Ápril (13), Máy, Júne, Julý, Aúgust (7), Septémber, Octóber (17), Novémber, | Decèmber.

(i) Spríng, súmmer, áutumn (7), | wïnter.

Raise your voice on the last word of the group, except at the end:

(j) a hündred and óne, a hundred and twó, a hundred and thrée, a hundred and twénty, | twö hùndred.

(k) It's öne o'clóck, fïve pást one, tén past, quárter past, twénty past, twenty-fíve past, hálf past, twënty-fïve to twó, twënty tó, quárter to, tén to, fíve to, | twö o'clòck.

* iron (22: *r usually silent*).
† January (4, y + 8, 12, 2). February (*you need not pronounce the first r*).

35. *Practise the following with the intonation indicated:*

Wáter?		Eighty? Really (18)? Never?
Beaútiful?		Yesterday? All of it? None of us?
A bóok?		Some tea? Alone? Today?
Some wáter?		The doctor? You're going?
In the róom?		Is it true? Has he gone?
In the gárden?		In the morning? In the evening?
Is it a récord?		Was it an accident?
Is it Sáturday todäy?		

36. *Sentences with more than one stress. Practise:*

Thïrtéen?   Last night? Go home?

Thïrty-thrée?   Can't you see?

Cän't you ünderstánd?   May I have some tea?

Is thät chäir cómfortable?

Ïs this ëxercise dífficult?

37. *Something added to a sentence. Practise:*

Äre you thére?   Äre you thére, Mr Jönes?
Mäy I häve some téa?   Mäy I häve some téa, plëase?
Is thïs your ráin-cöat?   Is thïs your ráin-cöat, Jöhn?
'Is thïs chäir óccupied (6, y + 8, 14)?' 'Is it óccupied?' I
äsked.
'Is there änybody thére?' said the Träveller.
'Is there änybody thére?' said the Träveller, knöcking on the
möonlit dóor.

38.   *Use a rising tone at the end of a phrase or clause when it is not the end of a sentence. Practise:*

We gö to wörk in the mòrning.   We gö höme in the èvening.
In the mórning, | we gö to wòrk.   In the évening, | we äll gö hòme.
Ïf it is wét, | we stäy indòors.   We stäy indöors if it is wèt.
Thïs little pïg went to márket, | thïs little pïg stäyed at hòme.
Plëase excùse me. Excüse mĕ, | cän you tëll me the tíme?

39.   *Use a falling-rising tone as a sign of politeness. Practise:*

Normal, plain, abrupt	*Polite, encouraging*
Göod nìght.	Göod nĭght.
Thànk yoü.	Thànk yoú.
Göod mòrning.	Göod mŏrning.
Whät is your nàme?	Whät is your năme?
Whät tìme is it?	Whät tĭme is it?
Whät does this mèan?	Whät does this mĕan?
Whëre is the bùs stöp?	Whëre is the bùs stóp?
Plëase sït dòwn. Dön't gò.	Plëase sït dŏwn. Dön't gŏ.

Pünctuàtion

Füll stòp . Còmma , Quèstion märk ? Hÿphen - Invërted còmmas, " " (or quötation märks). Ëxclamàtion Märk !

40.   *Do Exercises 21 and 22 (a to d) as dictation, putting in the pünctuàtion märks.*

REVISION

41.   (*a*) *Read Exercises 2, 3, 4, 8, 9, 11, 12, 13, 14.*
(*b*) **Count** *from 1 to 20; count in tens from 20 to 100.*
(*c*) *Say* **the days of the week, the months of the year,** *and* **the four seasons.**
(*d*) **Tell the time** *in ïntervals of five minutes from eight o'clock till ten.*
(*e*) **What is the date?** January 16th 1965. (*Say:* Jänuary the sïxtéenth, nïneteen sïxty-fìve). *Say:* February 21st 1642; April 22nd 1770; May 1st 1880; July 8th 1969.

TESTS

42.   (*a*) *Arrange the following words in rhyming pairs:* are, bed, break, burn, buy, car, care, come, debt, do, done, dumb, earn, friend, front, get, give, go, good, great, gun, hair, head, near, here, high,

35

hunt, know, live, make, my, not, nought, pleasant, present, run, send, son, sort, there, through, tongue, wait, wear, what, who, why, wood, you, young. [50]

(*b*) *Read correctly:* accept, account, answer, attention, brother, certain, character, comfortable, cover, doubt, exercise, ginger, give, have, hour, house, know, knowledge, laugh, law, listen, man, many, mother, one, only, photograph, photographer, photographic, pleasure, pronounce, pronunciation, right, school, straight, student, study, sugar, through, throw, tomorrow, two, university, walk, want, what, where, who, work, write. [50]

(*c*) *Read Exercise 22, pronouncing the vowels and consonants correctly, and using the intonation indicated.*

Dictation, to test correct hearing and spelling.

(*d*) eat, heat, hit, it, heater; man, men, bed, bad, bird.

(*e*) short, sort, shot, not, nought; head, had, hard, hurt, hut.

(*f*) ear, hear, hair, air, dear; he, see, she, sheet, seat.

(*g*) boat, vote, bush, push, pull; right, long, light, wrist, wrong.

(*h*) the, fee, thing, sink, down; one, two, free, present, pleasant.

(*i*) some, day, summer, soon, runner; ride, writer, lighter, race, lays.

(*j*) three, four, thirteen, forty, eighteen; want, wash, watch, work, walk.

(*k*) Don't shout. Turn left. Write neatly. Where are your friends?

(*l*) What does 'high' mean? How much do these flowers cost?

(*m*) I have only seventy cents. Is that enough? Not quite. [100]

PART TWO

WORDS SERVING DIFFERENT PURPOSES, AND HOW THEY ARE COMBINED

2. WORDS REFERRING TO THINGS AND PEOPLE, THEIR KIND, QUALITY AND CONDITION

Nouns and Articles: (1) Màss-Wörds

43. *Learn these* **nouns** *as mass-words:*

earth	rice	cloth	smoke	time
stone	meat	pàper (13)	heat	space
air	salt	ink	light	plèasure
wàter (7)	sugar	glass	sound	pain
life	flesh	wood	music	work
health	blood	mètal (3)	thought (7)	play
grass	skin	iron (22)	feeling	money
corn	bone	steel	knòwledge (6)	love
food	hair	oil	science (22)	peace
bread	wool	fire	art	power [50]

Mass-words, with no article

44. **Whät is ràin? Räin is wàter.**

Use these patterns to ask and answer questions about: meat, mud, music, science, lèather.

What is bread? Brëad is a kïnd of fòod.

Use these patterns to ask and answer questions about: rice, gold, còtton, milk, silk, sìlver, wheat, soup (9), màrble, elëctric lìght. [15]

45. **Cöal is blàck. Snöw is whìte.**

Complete: (*a*) Ice is cold, — is hot. (*b*) — is green, — — red, — — blue. (*c*) — — brown, — — yellow. (*d*) — — hard, — — soft.
Use the same pattern with: (*e*) wet, dry. (*f*) hèavy (3), light. (*g*) sweet, bitter. (*h*) rough, smooth. (*i*) sòlid (6), lìquid (2). (*j*) cheap, expènsive. [20]

37

46. (a)   Whät is ìron lïke? Ïron is hárd and hèavy.
Whät cölour is sùgar? Sügar is whíte or bròwn.

Ask and then answer one of these questions about: paper, ink, tea, còffee, coal, ash, smoke, steam, soap, sand. [10]

(b)   Lead (3) is heavy. Whät èlse is hëavy? Ïron is älso hëavy.

Use these patterns with: white, grey (13), red, yèllow, brown, hard, soft, cold, ùseful, nècessary (3). [10]

47.   We ëat fòod. We can sëe lìght.

Complete: (a) Söme pëople ëat brèad; öther people ëat —. (b) Söme drïnk —, öthers — —. (c) Some — wear —, others — —. (d) — like —, others — —. (e) We all want — and —. (f) We can see —. (g) We can hear —. (h) We — feel —, touch (10) —, taste (13) — and smell —. (i) We can cut —, break —, mëasure —, weigh (13) —, count —, and wrap — in —. (j) We wash with s— and w—. [30]

48.   Whät is thìs? Pàper. This is pàper. It is pàper.
What is that? Ïnk. That is ìnk. It is ìnk.

Repeat each of these patterns 10 times, but use a different word from Exercise 43 every time. Choose words referring to things you can see, feel, taste or smell.

49.   Thïs tëa is hòt. This is höt tèa. It's höt tèa.
That soup is cold. That is cold soup. It's cold soup.

Hot, cold, *etc. are* **adjectives.** *Make a list of all the adjectives in 45 and 46, and add:* good, bad; clean, dirty; new, old; fresh, stale; long, short; thick, thin; warm, cool; strong, weak; bèautiful; ìnteresting; nàtural (4), ärtifìcial (2; *ci* = *sh*). *Then use one of the patterns at the head of this exercise, and a different adjective every time, with 20 nouns from Exercises 43 to 46.*

50.   Thïs is hòt mïlk; thät is còld mïlk.

Make up 10 sentences on this pattern using different mass-words and making a contrast between the two adjectives every time.

51.   This is nöt sált, it is sùgar.

Form 10 sentences on this pattern, making a contrast between the two nouns every time.

Mass-words with some

52. **Plëase gïve me some wàter. Hère is some wäter. Hère is söme.**
Repeat these patterns with 10 different mass-words.

Nouns and Articles: (2) Unit-Words

53. *Learn these nouns as unit-words:*

pèrson	hat	knife	plant	mark
man	coat	fork	tree	sign*
wòman (8)	dress	spoon	branch	point
boy	shoe (9)	cup	leaf	line
girl	house	glass	vègetable	sùrface
fàmily	gàrden	plate	flower	curve
fàther	wall	coùntry (10)	ànimal (4)	àngle
mòther	room	rìver (2)	bird	square
bròther	door	hill	ìnsect	cìrcle
sìster	wìndow	mòuntain	pìcture*	nùmber
bòdy (6)	chair	field (1)	book	wheel
face	table	ìsland*	page	ball
head	desk	town	word	box
eye (14)	bed	shop	name	stick
ear	watch	òffice (6 + 2)	mìnute*	part
hand	clock	school	hour	mèmber
arm	pen	tool	day	side
leg	pencil	hàmmer	week	slope
foot	key (1)	machìne*	month	edge
step	lock	car	year	end

[100]

Unit-words with a (indèfinite àrticle).

54.
Whät is thìs?
- A lìne. — Thät is a lìne.
- An angle. — That is an angle.
- A circle. — Thät is a përfect cìrcle.

Repeat with: chair, desk, watch (6), match (4), egg, apple, òrange, step, square, curve, sträight lìne, bënt stìck, bröken glàss, ëmpty bòttle, old hat, new dress, clean shirt, dïrty plàte, little bird, dead fly. [20]

* ìsland (14: *s silent*); machìne (*see* 20, *Exceptions*); pìcture: *pronounce* -ture *as* [cher]; mìnute (2, 2,); sign (14; *g silent*).

39

55. Whät is
- a màn?   A män is a pèrson.
- a bròther?   A bröther is a mëmber of a fàmily.
- a mònth?   A mönth is a pärt of a yèar.
- a hàt?   A hät is an ärticle of clòthing (17).
- a dèsk?   A dësk is an ärticle of fùrniture.*
- an àpple?   An apple is a kind of fruit.

Ask the question, and answer it with one of these patterns, about the following, using words from 53: ant, banàna (5), bee, branch, car, càrpet, chàpter, cow, dog, dress, fìnger (ng + g), fly, glove (10), hammer, horse, leaf, minute, potàto (13), room, root, rose, thumb, shirt, wall, wheel. [25]

56. **Whät shäpe is a whëel? A whëel is ròund. Whät èlse is röund?**

Give 5 different answers to the second question.

Draw: a long line; a tall tree; a short, fat man; a tall, thin man; a thick wall; a square house; a low chair and a high table; a narrow window; a wide door; a mountain with a flat top.

57.   **A knïfe has a shärp èdge.**

Use this pattern to answer the following questions: (*a*) What has a flat surface? (*b*) What else has a flat surface? (*c*) What has a sharp point? (*d*) What else? (*e*) What has a high top? (*f*) a tall trunk. (*g*) a long tail. (*h*) a soft wing. (*i*) a steep slope. (*j*) a round handle. *Use the same pattern to say something about:* (*k*) a needle. (*l*) a ràzor (13). (*m*) a cat. (*n*) an old tree. (*o*) a broom. [15]

58. **Ï häve a bròther. I am a stùdent. I wänt to bë a dòctor.**

Make up 10 sentences using the above patterns and the following words: sìster, fàther, mòther, son, dàughter (7), uncle, aunt (5), nèphew, niece (1), gràndfäther, gràndmöther, làwyer, ënginèer, scìentist, wrìter, àrtist, tèacher, àrchitect, fämous (13) màn, göod frìend.

59   **We gó, cóme, or móve sömething, TÒ a pläce.**
We stäy ÁT or ÌN a pläce.
We püt something ÖN a súrface, but ÏN a spàce.
We dö something WÏTH an ìnstrument.
We cüt brëad with a knìfe. We ëat with a knìfe and fòrk.

* Furniture: *pronounce* -ture *as* [cher], *as in* picture.

To, at, in, on, with *are* prëposìtions

Complete: (*a*) I write with — —. (*b*) We can write with — — or — —. (*c*) We put food on — —. (*d*) We keep milk — — bottle. (*e*) We boil water — — kettle. (*f*) We make tea — — pot. (*g*) We drink from — — or — —. We buy (14) food at — —. (*i*) We work at — — or —. (*j*) We sit on — — but sleep in — —. (*k*) We live in — —. [15]

60. A. I wänt a pèncil. B. Thère is a pëncil | över thère.

Repeat with: knife, fork, spoon; cup, sàucer (7), plate, glass; brush, comb; ènvelope, stamp; match; watch; àpple, òrange; hànd-kerchief, nèedle, bùtton; nail, screw. [20]

   B. But you hàve* a pëncil: there is a pëncil in your pòcket.
   A. It's äll rïght. I hàve* a pëncil: there is a pëncil on my dèsk.

Use one of these patterns with: fork in your hand; spoon by your plate; plate under my sàucer; chair in your room; little table by my bed; watch on your wrist; apple in my bag; handkerchief in my pocket; water (*see Ex. 52*) in your glass; sugar in your tea; milk in my coffee; tèlephone (3) in my office; ink in your pen; needle in your coat; paper in your drawer (20). [15]

                    a piece of bread, a drop of water.

61.

	a pïece (1) of brèad (sòlid)
	a bit of bread
	a loaf (of bread)
	a drop of water (lìquid)
Thïs is	——
That is	a slice of bread (a pïece cüt flàt)
Here is	a ball of string
There is	a bar of chòcolate (6)
Get me	a blade of grass
Give me	a block of ice
Show me	a grain of rice
Bring me	a heap of earth
	a lump of coal
	a roll of cloth
	a sheet of paper
	a stick of chalk
	a strip of cloth (a löng, thìn pïece)

Draw a slice, ball, bar, block, blade, grain, heap, lump, sheet, stick, strip. *Learn the phrases in the right-hand column at the head of this*

* Or, *informally*, you've got a pencil, I've got, *etc.*

41

exercise. Form complete sentences using one phrase from the left-hand column and one from the right. Then form complete sentences on the same pattern using the following words: cake, corn, dust, fruit, glass, ink, iron, land, meat, milk, oil, rubber, salt, skin, soap, snow, stone, wheat, wood, wool. [20] *Use* piece *and* bit *once only.*

62. **A cüp of còffee. A bag of flour. A pound of butter.**

Contàiner	Mèasure	Lìquid	Sòlid
glass, pot,	pound	water, milk,	meat, fruit,
bottle, bowl (17),	ton	tea, wine,	sugar, fat,
bàsin (13), bùcket,	pint (14)	beer, soup,	corn, coal,
kettle, bag,	gàllon	oil, ink,	cheese,
sack, box, tin		paint	chalk (7)
(*or* can)			

Using these words, form 20 phrases on the pattern given at the head of this exercise.

63. **I wänt a pïece of pàper. Hère is a pïece.**

Repeat these patterns 20 times, using different words from Exercise 61 instead of piece *and* paper.

64. **a stamp, one stamp**

    A. Plëase gïve me a stàmp. B. Hère is öne.
    A. I want önly *òne* stämp—there are *twò* hére.
    Hère are twö stàmps.
    ***Öne* stämp is úsed (*zd*) and *öne* is tòrn.**

Repeat with 10 different unit-words instead of stamp, *and with suitable adjectives.*

Nouns used as mass-words or unit-words

65. **Söund trävels (4) at 365 yärds a sècond.**
    Be quiet. Don't make a sound.
    Nöise is a nùisance (y + 9). Don't make such a noise.
    Metal is heavy. Iron is a metal (i.e. a kind of metal).
    Stöne is a härd sùbstance. There is a stöne in my shòe.

Fill each gap with a mass-word without a, *or a unit-word with* a *or* an, *using one of the following words:* life, light, fire, time, space, food, fuel, pleasure, pain.

    (*a*) — travels faster than sound. There is — by my bed.
    (*b*) We have — in our house in winter. Take care: danger* of —.

            * danger: *pronounce* [dane-jer].

(c) — is èndless. There is — for work and — for play.
(d) Men can now travel through —. A room is — in a house.
(e) We like — and fear —. I have — in my stòmach.
(f) You have — ïnteresting —. Yes, but — is sömetimes very hard.
(g) We burn —. Coal is — .Oil is —: it is also —.
(h) Good-bye. It was — to see you. [20]

66. *Fill each gap with a mass-word alone, with* some + *a mass-word, with* piece of —, *or with* a + *unit-word, using one of the following words:* glass, cloth, iron, paper, money, work, play, job, game, ïnformàtion, advìce, prògress, fùrniture.

(a) Write your name on a —. We can burn —: we cannot burn stone. I want to make a fire: bring me —. I want to see the news: bring me —.
(b) We can see through —. Waiter! There's a — in my soup. Bring me — of milk instèad.
(c) An iron bar is a long, flat —. We press clothes with —.
(d) We make clothes from —. A handkerchief is a —. We are going to have dinner: put — on the table.
(e) Can you lend me — pleasc? — is made of metal or paper.
(f) I've fïnished (2) my wòrk: let's have — of tènnis. I wörk in a fàctory: I have a very interesting —. — is üsually* harder than —.
(g) I wänt to knòw sömething. Can you give me —? That is an interesting —.
(h) You need help. Let me give you —. This is a useful —.
(i) This room looks empty: it needs —. A chair is a —.
(j) Very good. You are making —. [25]

Unit-words: Singular and Plural

67. *Learn this SCHEME FOR THE PLURAL OF NOUNS:*

	Singular†	Plùral (8)	
(a) Words ending in vowel or soft consonant	tree, boy, girl pen, pencil	trees, boys, girls pens, pencils	s soft
(b) Ending in hard consonant	cup, hat, book	cups, hats, books	s hard
(c) Ending in hissing sound	piece, rose, vìllage, dress, match, box	pìeces, ròses, vìllages, drèsses, màtches, bòxes	extra syllable (iz)

* usually: *pronounce the* s *as z or* [ʒ].
† *Pronounce* 2, y + 8, 12; *and sound the* g *after the* ng, *as in* single.

43

Note that the words in (c) *have an extra syllable in the plural. This happens after a hissing sound—s, z, j, ch, x.*

68. *Learn these exceptions to the scheme in 67:*

Singular	Plural
(a) house (*ending in sound s*), bath, path, mouth (*hard th*)	houses (*ending in z + iz*), baths, paths, mouths (*soft th + z*)

(*In the above words the exception is in the pronunciation only.*)

(b) bàby (13), coùntry, làdy (13) *and all other words ending in* y *when the letter before the* y *is a consonant.*	bàbies, coùntries, làdies (*In these words, the exception is in the spelling only.*)
(c) hèro (18), potàto (13), tomàto (5 *or* 13) *and other words ending in* o, *but not certain words borrowed from other languages, or abbreviations,* e.g. piànos (4), dỳnamos (14), phòtos (17).	hèroes, potàtoes, tomàtoes. (*In these words, the exception is in the spelling only.*)
(d) leaf, thief (1), self, shelf, half, calf, wolf (8), knife, life, wife, loaf.	leaves, thieves, selves, shelves, halves, calves, wolves, knives, lives, wives, loaves. *Pronounce all these words with one syllable each, ending in -vz.*

(*In the above, the exception is in both pronunciation and spelling.*)

(e) man, gèntleman, wòrkman, *etc.* wòman (8 + 12), child (14), foot (8), tooth (9), mouse, goose (9, *s*), sheep.	men, gèntlemen, wòrkmen, *etc.* wòmen (2 + 2), chìldren (2), feet, teeth, mice, geese, sheep. (*These are old forms, still used*).
(f) pèrson	pèrsons (*sèparate*), pèople (*togèther*)
fish	fìshes (*sèparate*), fish (*togèther*)
pènny	pènnies (*sèparate*), pence (*togèther*)

(g) *Use* clothes, tròusers, scìssors *only in the plural, and say* Clothes are . . . *etc.* News *is plural in form, but treat it as singular and say* News is . . . *The same applies to* mäthemätics *and* phỳsics (2). Lens *is singular: the plural is* lenses, *as in 67. Treat* polïce (1) *as plural and say* The police are . . .

69. *Say and then write the plural of:*

person; man, woman and child; lady and gentleman; hüsband and wife; boy and girl; eye and ear; mouth, tooth and lip; knee and foot; niece and nephew; shoe and stocking; hat and coat; house and garden; tree, leaf, branch; sheep and goat; dog and wolf; rat and mouse; fox and goose; loaf and fish; day, week, month; country, city, village, place; church, box, penny; hero; knife and fork; photo, lens; half, life; pocket, handkerchief; library (14), shelf; key. [60]

Unit-words, plural, with no article

70. **Birds fly. Books are made of paper. I like apples.**

Fill the gaps with unit-words in the plural: (*a*) — walk. · (*b*) — swim. (*c*) — eat grass. (*d*) — drink milk. (*e*) — like bones. (*f*) — are made of wood. (*g*) — are made of glass. (*h*) — are made of steel. (*i*) — are made of cotton. (*j*) — are made of leather. (*k*) Men wear — and —, women wear —. (*l*) We keep wine in —. (*m*) We put food on —. (*n*) Some people work in —, others work in —. (*o*) In geömetry (6) we study — and —. (*p*) In mäthemätics, we study —. [20]

71. **Whät are thèse? Lìnes. Thöse are lìnes. They are lìnes.**

On this model do Ex. 54 in the plural. The adjectives, perfect, *etc.,* *remain unchanged.*

Wë are stùdents. We wänt to be dòctors.

Repeat these sentences 10 times, replacing doctors *by the plural of words in Ex. 58, adding* sóldiers,* sáilors, *and* airmen.

72. **Unit-words, plural, with** some

A. **Plëase gïve me some (12) stàmps.**
B. **I hàven't any stämps.**
C. **There are some stämps in that tìn.**
D. **Hëre you áre. Nòw you häve söme (10).**

Repeat with 10 different unit-words instead of stamps *and* tin.

Unit-words with the (dëfinite àrticle)

73. **Hëre are twö hàts. Öne is mìne, öne is yòurs.** **Whìch one is yòurs? Thìs öne—the òld öne.**

* soldier: *pronounce* sòld-jer.

45

Which one is mine? That one—the new one.
The öld hat is yóurs, the nëw hat is mìne.

Repeat with 10 different unit-words instead of hat *and with suitable adjectives.*

74. Here are twö different thìngs. A whïte cóat and a bläck umbrèlla.
Whïch is yòurs? The umbrèlla—the bläck umbrèlla?

Repeat with 6 different pairs of words instead of coat *and* umbrella, *and with suitable adjectives.*

75. Hëre is a kéy: thëre is a lòck. Püt the këy in the lòck.

Repeat 20 times: each time choose one word from the left-hand column and one from the right:

book, pen, letter, pòstcard (17), | ènvelope, lètterbox, lìbrary (14),
match, screw, picture, film, cake, | drawer, càmera (4), hole, frame,
button, dress, sùitcase (9), car, | box, cùpboard,* car, òven (10),
egg, apple, flower, plant, bird, | bùttonhole, bowl, bàsket, vase,*
spoon, coin. | garage,* nest, saucer, garden,
 | purse. [20]

76. Whëre is the kèy? Whïch òne? The këy in Ëxercise 75.
Thät key is nöw in the lòck. It is ïn the lòck.
Thère is the këy. Thère it ïs.

Repeat with the other 40 words in Ex. 75.

77. Where is the sun? It's in the sky.

Repeat with: moon, sky; sea, world; world, ùniverse (y + 9).

78. Hëre is a ròom. Thïs is the dóor, the wíndow, the flóor, the céiling (1), the lìght.

Repeat with: (a) hòuse; kítchen, díning-room, bédroom, báthroom, róof, gárden, gáte, ròad. (b) tòwn; márket, bánk, póst (17)-öffice, théatre,† stàtion (13). (c) plànt; róot, stèm. (d) trèe; róot, trùnk. (e) bòx; tóp, bóttom, báck, frónt, míddle, léft sïde, rìght sïde.

79. I cän't fïnd (14) the dòor. Thère is the döor. Thère it ïs.

Repeat with: handle, light, switch, kitchen, dìning-room, bàthroom, làvatory (4), lift, wäy ìn, wäy òut, bùs stöp, pòst-öffice, stàtion, bank, polìce-stätion.

* cùpboard (10 + 12: *p silent*); vase (5, *or* 13); gàrage (4 + 5) *or* garàge (12 + 5)—*in either case, pronounce the second g as* [ʒ].
† thèatre: *pronounce* [thèer-ter], hard *th*.

80. (a) Here are twö réd böoks | and twö grèen böoks. The rëd books are mìne. *Complete:* — — — — yours.
(b) Hëre are some rëd péncils | and some bläck pèns. The pëns are yòurs. *Complete:* — — — —.
(c) Hëre are some létters: thëre are some ènvelopes. Püt the lëtters in the ènvelopes.
Repeat with: matches, pictures, dresses, flowers, suitcases *instead of* letters, *and find suitable substitutes for* envelopes.
(d) Where are the lettérs? Which ones? The letters in 80(c). Those letters are in the envelopes. They are in — —. There are the letters. There they are.
Repeat with: matches, pictures, etc.

81. **Here is a face. Here are the eyes and the ears.**

Repeat with: (a) mouth, lips, teeth; (b) body, shóulders (17), arms, hands, fingers, legs, feet; (c) house, walls, windows; (d) town, streets, shops; (e) country, mountains, rivers, fòrests (6).

Unit-words without an article.

82. *Learn:*

(a)   *See Ex. 78.*   *Idiomatic Expressions.*

Go { to the door. / to the bank. / to the station. / to the post-office. / to the theatre. / to the shops.

Go { to bed. / to school. / to church. / to hòspital. / to prìson (2). / home.

Stay { in bed. / in school. (*or* at) / in church. / in hospital. / in prison. / at home.

(b) We travel by bícycle (14), by bus, by car, by train, by boat, by ship or by áeroplane (19) (*or* by plane); or we go on foot.
(c) I like lemon in my tea—but not a whole lemon, please.

Mass-words with the definite article.

83.   **Wäter can be bóiling or nòt boiling.**
The wäter in this säucepan (7) is bòiling.
Whàt water is böiling? The wäter in that sàucepan.

Repeat this sequence with the following words, filling in the gaps:
water, hot, —, pipe; earth, wet, —, pot; ink, clean, —, —; fruit, —, not ripe, —; ïnformätion, ínteresting, ùnïnteresting, — ; —, —, ùn-

hëalthy, tünnel; —, good, —, rëstaurant; light, too strong, too —, —; fürniture, —, expènsive, —; work, hard, èasy, —. [10]

84. **We are häving a mèal. There is some brèad on the table. Päss the brèad, plëase.**

Repeat with: bùtter, salt, pèpper, sùgar, milk, fruit, jam, màrmalade, sauce (7), vìnegar (2).

85. **The water in these saucepans is boiling.**

Repeat Ex. 83 putting saucepan, pipe, pot, etc. into the plural.

Descriptive Adjectives

86. **A nïce pèrson. A bräve màn. A beaütiful wòman.**

Supply an adjective for each of the words in Ex. 53, choosing one of the words below. Say a (or an) — —. Then use each of the words below with a suitable unit-word (with a) or mass-word (without a):

(a) *What is your imprèssion of the person or thing?* good/bad; nice/nàsty; pléasant (3)/ùnplëasant*; prétty (2), beaútiful/ùgly; big, great/little.

(b) *mèasurement:* large/small; long/short; wide/nàrrow; thick/thin; fat/thin; high/low; tall/short; deep/shàllow; héavy/light; young (10)/old; fast/slow; éven (*number*)/odd (*number*); expénsive/cheap; rich/poor.

(c) *shape:* straight/bent; cròoked,* curved*; square/round; flat/sloping, steep; sharp/blunt; even/uneven.

(d) *còlour:* dark/light; black/white; red/green.

(e) *fèeling:* hard/soft; dry/wet; hot, warm/cool, cold; smooth/rough; tight/loose*; (*hearing*) loud/soft (e.g. a loud noise).

(f) *taste:* good/bad; sweet/sour, bìtter.

(g) *quàlity:* good/bad; real, nátural/ärtifìcial, unnatural; true/untrue, false; hard, dífficult/èasy; ínteresting/ùnínteresting.

(h) *condition:* good/bad; new/old; clean/dìrty; full/èmpty; whole, pérfect/bròken, torn; fresh/stale; strong/weak, hèlpless (*person*); safe/unsafe; happy/sad; héalthy/ùnhëalthy; quiet/noisy; tídy/ùntïdy.

(i) *behàviour* (13): good/bad, nàughty (7); kind/unkind, cruel; gentle/rough; políte/rude; quiet/noisy; cáreful/càreless; tidy/untidy; cléver/stùpid (y + 8); thoughtful/thoughtless; helpful/unhelpful.

* *Pronunciation:* an ünplëasant vòice, *but* Thïs is not pléasant, it's ùnplëasant; crooked: *two syllables* [crook-id]; curved: *one syllable* [curvd] (*see Table* 26); loose (9 + *hard s*).

87.   *Nouns*   *Adjectives*
         dirt, mud, stone   **dìrty, mùddy,* stòny***

The adjective dirty *is formed by adding a süffix to the noun.*
Spell the adjectives formed from bone, dust, flower, fun, hair, health,
hill, ice, leaf, oil, noise, rain, salt, sand, skin, sleep, soap, sun, wind,
wool.* *Use 10 of these adjectives as in 86.*

88. *Learn:*

Nouns	*Adjectives*
fool; beaùty	fòolish; beaùtiful*
care, help, pain, thought	careful, helpful, etc.
	careless, helpless, etc.
father, mother, friend	fatherly, motherly, etc.
dànger, pòison, mòuntain	dàngerous, pòisonous, etc.
rèason; sense	rèasonable; sènsible*
mùsic; science (22)	mùsical; scïentìfic (22, 2, 2)

Adjectives	*Nouns*
(*a*) good, kind, sweet,	gòodness, kìndness, swèetness,
càreful, càreless	càrefulness, càrelessness
(*b*) warm, true, strong,	warmth, truth (9), strength,
long, deep, wide, high	length, depth, width, height (14)
Examples: a true story.	Tell me the truth.

89.   **Thïs is a blàck tïe. I wänt a whìte öne.**

Repeat 40 times to make a contrast with each of the following:
a bad egg, a big box, a blunt needle, a cheap präsent, a crooked stick,
a dark room, a dirty cloth, an expensive seat, a full bottle, a hard
cushion, a hard question, a heavy süitcase, a high stool, a hot drink,
a light colour, a light weight (13), a loose cöllar, a noisy hotël, an
odd number, an old rëcord, an old horse, a rough surface, a rough
manner, a rude waiter, a sad story, a short chain, a short man, a slow
train, a soft bed, a soft voice, a stale loaf, a stùpid boy, a thin face, a

✗ ***** *Important Spelling Instructions*
   1. *Whenever a stressed syllable (e.g.* rùn, begìn) *ends in a single consonant letter*
preceded by a single vowel letter, double the final consonant before an ending that
begins with a vowel letter (e.g. rùn, rùnning, rùnner; stop, stopped; begìn, begìnning,
beginner). However, woolly may have double l in spite of the two o's.
   2. *When a word ends in mute e (e.g.* come), *omit the e before an ending that*
begins with a vowel sound (e.g. come, coming).
   3. *When a word ends in y preceded by a consonant, change the y to i before any*
ending (beauty, beautiful) except an ending beginning with i itself (try, trying).

49

thin blänket, a tight knot, an ugly view, a warm shirt, a wet towel (16), a wide belt, the wrong answer. [40]

Adjuncts

90. Thïs is a wàll. It is mäde of stòne. It's a stöne wàll.

On the same pattern, make 40 combinations from the following:

What is it?	What is it made of?
bag, ball, band, belt, box, brick, building, can, coin, fence, jèrsey, pie (14), rail, ring, rod, sàlad (4), sheet, shirt, wall, watch	apple, brick, cemènt, copper, cotton, fruit, gold, iron, leather, metal, mud, paper, rubber, silk, silver, steel, tin, wire, wood,* wool*

91. The wïndow in my bédroom | is my bëdroom wìndow.
The döor to the kítchen | is the kïtchen dòor.
A chäir üsed in a díning-room | is a dïning-room chàir.

Answer on the same pattern:

What is a cärpet for a dràwing-room; the desk in my office; the gate to your garden; a doctor in a village; the clock at the station; the hall in our school; the walls round the city; an exäminätion in a üniversity; an offïcial† in a gòvernment (10); a road over a mountain; an evening in winter; a mörning in Octòber (17)?

Compound Nouns

92. (a) Whät kïnd of shïp is thàt? It's a spàce shïp.
(b) Whät kïnd of brùsh is thät? It's a tòoth-brush.
(c) Whät kïnd of knìfe is thät? It's a pènknife.
(d) Whät is a störy abòut lòve cälled? A lòve-störy.
(e) Whät is a böx for màtches cälled? A màtch-box.

Ask and answer questions on this pattern of a, b and c to form:

(*a*) flòwer shöp; shèep färm; alàrm bëll; bùs tïcket; ràilway brïdge; gòld mïne; quèstion märk; tràde märk; dànger sïgn; fïre stätion.

(*b*) tèa-cup; ègg-cup; soùp-plate; tèa-pot; frùit-tree; ràin-coat; hànd-bag; màtch-box; hàir-oil; fàce-pöwder; tòoth-paste (13); stòre-room; rìght-ängle; wàsh-bäsin; dòor-bell; hànd-brake; fòot-

---

* *Use the adjectives* wöoden *and* wöollen *in the third sentence.*
† offïcial (2: *ci* = *sh*).

pump; light-bulb; picture-frame; finger-nail; finger-mark; pocket-book; sèa-water; silk-worm. *Note:* ärm-chàir.

(c) fòotball; snòwball; bàthroom; bèdroom; hairpin; sùnlight; mòonlight; firewood; dùstpan; blàckboard; bòokcase.

Now ask and answer questions on the pattern of (d) and (e) about:

(d) a lesson about science; a book about physics*; a field for football.

(e) a book for notes; a brush for teeth; a box for tools; a bowl for fingers; a peg for clothes*; a basket for eggs; juice from lemons; a shop for newspapers; leather for shoes.

93.　　　**Whät is the wàter† like? Ìcy.**
　　　　　Whät kind of bòx is thät? An ìce-box.

In the following sentences, fill the gaps with either an adjective formed from the noun in brackets, or with an adjunct:

(a) (sun) In — weather, I wear — glasses.
(b) (rain) In — weather, I wear a — coat.
(c) (wind) On a — day, we can measure the force of the wind by a — instrument.
(d) (soap) Soap is made in a — factory. Don't drink — water.
(e) (sand, stone) Vegetables grow in — soil but not in — ground.
(f) (beauty) We see — girls in a — competition.
(g) (music) I take — lessons, because I am —.
(h) (danger) There is a — sign. We are coming to a — corner.
(i) (science) Not all — teachers are —.
(j) (poison) This stuff is —. Keep it in a — bottle.

Order of words before a noun. Noun phrases.

94.　　**The nëw bröwn lëather glöves in the häll are mìne.**
　　　　Whöse is thät bïg bläck Amërican (3) càr at the döor?

The words new, brown, leather, *and in the hall* all describe the noun gloves *and help to identify the gloves that are mine. What can we say about* big black *etc.? Put such words in the following order:*

First—a, or the, some, this, that, these, those, my, your, etc.
Second—descriptive adjectives; but—
Third—put adjectives of colour after others, except—
Fourth—adjectives referring to places.

* *See* 68 (g). *Do not put* physics *and* clothes *into a singular form.*
† What water? (*See Ex.* 83.) The water in the swimming pool, for example.

51

Fifth—Put adjuncts after adjectives and immediately before the noun; and

Sixth—put phrases after the noun.

Arrange the words in brackets below in order according to the models and instructions above, and then read and write out each complete sentence:

(*a*) This is (sand, yellow, soft). (*b*) I want (bread, white, fresh, some). (*c*) Look at (the, sea, blue, deep). (*d*) Bring me (that, warm, in the basin, water). (*e*) Where are (my, glasses, sun, black)? (*f*) Here is (a, wall, stone, low, grey). (*g*) George is (a, engineer, radio, young). (*h*) (That, long, in my drawer, envelope) is for you. (*i*) Sit on (cushion, comfortable, air, this). (*j*) (The, vase, on the table, Chinese,* green, beautiful) is broken.

Predicate and Attribute

95. **(a) I wash a cup and put it on the shelf.**
    (b) The cup is now clean.
    (c) The clean cup is on the shelf.

In sentence (b) we say that 'the cup' is the sùbject of the sentence, and 'is clean' the prèdicate. We are therefore using the adjective 'clean' predicatively. In sentence (c) we say that the cup now has the quàlity or àttribute of clean-ness, and the adjective 'clean' is here used attrìbutively.

Predicative	*Attributive*
Thïs böx is hèavy.	Thïs is a hëavy bòx.
Thïs böx is for ìce.	Thïs is an ìce-box.

Using the patterns in the left-hand column, say the following sentences in a different way (see 91 and 92):

(*a*) This is an interesting story. (*b*) This is a war story.
(*c*) This is a Chinese cupboard (*d*) This is a china cupboard.
(*e*) This is sweet juice. (*f*) This is grape juice.
(*g*) This is a broken bottle. (*h*) This is a beer bottle.
(*i*) This is an honest official. (*j*) This is a government official.

96. *Learn:*

Attributive	*Predicative*
Tom is a healthy boy;	but he is not well today.
His father is a sick man.	He is often sick (or ill).

* Chìna (14, 12); Chinèse (14, 1).

WORDS REFERRING TO THINGS AND PEOPLE

A lïving (2) crèature.	Is it lïving (or alìve (14))?
The Sleeping Beauty.	She is sléeping (or aslèep).
—	She is not awàke yet.
A closed shop.	The shops are closed (or shut).
An expēnsive matèrial (18).	Silk is expensive (or dear).

Avoid using well, ill, alive, asleep, awake *and* shut *attributively. On the other hand, do not use adjuncts predicatively in the same way as adjectives (see 95).*

97. (a)   Adjective without a noun

Thïs is nöt a rìpe pëach: gïve me a rìpe öne.
I want the ripe peach: give me the ripe one.
Thëse are nöt rìpe pëaches: gïve me some rìpe önes.
I want the ripe peaches: give me the ripe ones.

Repeat all four lines with:
sweet orange, fresh loaf, clean handkerchief, cheap card, sharp knife.

(b) *Note* the living, the dead, the sick, the blind (16), the deaf, the dumb, the poor, the rich, the young, the brave, the old, *meaning* living people in general, living people as a class, *etc. Examples:*

Speak well of the dead. Take care of the sick.
Help the blind. Nöne but the bräve desërves the fàir.

A handful
98.   My pöcket is fùll. It's füll of sàndwiches.*
I have a pöcketful of sàndwiches.

Form sentences on these patterns, using:
handful, armful, mouthful, spoonful, bagful, basketful, bucketful.

Plural of adjunct + noun and of compound nouns
99. *Learn:*

Singular	Plural
flower shop, egg-cup	flower shops, egg-cups,
football, handful	footballs, handfuls

Excèptions:
| fàther-in-läw, etc. | fàthers-in-läw, etc. |
| pässer-bỳ | pässers-bỳ |

* *Pronounce* sandwich *as* [san-widge].

53

Give the plural of:

apple-tree, rose-garden, fountain-per, arm-chair, railway, railway station, writing-table, number plate, mother-in-law, brother-in-law, bucketful, book-shelf, tooth-brush, match-box, fig-leaf. [15]

Proper Nouns

100. *Proper Nouns, i.e. names of people and places, do not normally take an article. But note the following exceptions:*

(*a*) (*countries: names formed from a unit-word, e.g. state, union, island*) The Unïted Stätes of Amèrica; The Ünion of Söviet Söcialist Repùblics; The Phìlippine Islands.

(*b*) (*rivers, seas, mountain ranges, ships, newspapers*) The River Nìle (*or simply*, The Nile); The Red Sea; The Atläntic Òcean (17: ce = sh) (*or simply*, The Atlantic); The Rocky Mountains (*or simply*, The Rockies); The *Quëen Elìzabeth*; *The Times*.

(*c*) (*family or group of people with the same name*) The Smiths.

(*d*) *Note: we can say:* The Ünivèrsity of Óxford, *or* Öxford Ünivèrsity; The äirport at Àthens (4), *or* Äthens Àirport; The rädio station at Cáiro (14), *or* Cäiro Ràdio (Station).

I cöme from Utòpia.* I am Utòpian. My fëllow-coüntrymen are Utòpians. I speak Utopian (or the Utöpian lànguage).

Supply the name of your own country instead of Utopia in the above sentences. Note that when the name of the nationality ends in a hissing sound, we say: My fellow-countrymen are (*for example*) Brìtish, Chinèse, Dànish (13), Ènglish, French, Japanèse, Portuguèse, Singalèse, Spànish (4), *or* Spàniards, Welsh. *Note:* The Japanese (in general: *see 97b*) use the same kind of writing as the Chinese.

TABLE 6
Summary of the Use of the Articles

Exercises **Use no article—**

44–51   (*a*) *with a mass-word, to suggest:* (*i*) *a thing in general;* (*ii*) *an indefinite example of it;* (*iii*) *one thing and not another; e.g.*

(i) Grass is green. (ii) This is grass. (iii) It is grass not corn.

* Utòpia: *pronounce* (y + 8, 17, 18).

70–71   (*b*) *with a unit-word in the plural, to suggest:* (*i*) *the objects in general;* (*ii*) *indefinite examples of them;* (*iii*) *one class of object and not another; e.g.*

(i) Birds fly. (ii) Those are birds. (iii) They are birds, not àeroplanes (19).

82   (*c*) *with a unit-word in the singular;* (*i*) *in conventional expressions, which refer to the general idea of a thing rather than a particular example of it; or* (*ii*) *to suggest the substance of a thing rather than the thing as a whole, e.g.*

(i) We go to school by bus. (ii) I like lemon in my tea.

(*d*) *with names of persons and places, e.g.*
Shàkespeare, Àthens, Austràlia (6, 13, 18)

Use the indefinite article, a

54–60   (*e*) *with a unit-word,* (*i*) *to suggest that an object is an example of a class bearing a certain name; or* (*ii*) *to suggest one indefinite example of a class, e.g.*

This is a book (*emphasis on class*). Give me a book (*one example*).

(*For* one, *see 64; and for* some, *see 52, 72.*)

Use the definite article, the

73, 80a   (*f*) *with a unit-word, as a sign that you are referring to one or more examples of a class and that you assume your hearer knows which example or examples you mean, e.g.*

Here are three books of different sizes: the biggest book is yours, the smaller books are mine.

74, 80b   (*g*) *with a unit-word, as a sign that you are referring to a particular class of thing, and are distinguishing it from another class or other classes, e.g.*
The teacher teaches. The learner learns.

75–79   (*h*) *with a unit-word, as a sign that you are referring to one*
80c, d, 81   *or more known or identifiable members of a class, when you are not concerned with the existence of other members of that class, e.g.*

Go to the door. Open the window.
The sun and the moon are in the sky.

83–85   (i)   *with a mass-word, in the singular only, as a sign that you are referring to a known or specified part of the mass, e.g.*

Please pass me the bread—I mean the bread on the table.

100   (j)   *with place names, when they are formed by unit-words or when they specify which sea and which river (see 100b); e.g.*

The United States of America. The Soviet Union. The River Rhine (*or* the Rhine). The Atlantic (Ocean).

100   (k)   *with names of people, when referring to two or more people of the same name, e.g.*

The Smiths (*i.e.* Mr and Mrs Smith, or the Smith family).

Passages for reading and dictation

101. Our höuse ständs by the sïde of a wïde ròad. It has a smäll gärden in frónt of it | and a lärge gärden behìnd. There are flöwers in the frónt gärden, | and früit-trees and vëgetables at the bàck. In wärm wëather, we häve our mëals öutsìde. Whën it is hót, | the ëarth gëts vëry drỳ. Thén, | in the évening, | we must wäter it with a hòse-pïpe.

The höuse has a flät róof | and whïte wàlls. The frönt döor lëads into a lïttle hàll, | where we häng our häts and còats. On the lëft of the háll | is a dìning-röom, | where we üsually häve our mèals. On the rïght is the dràwing-röom, | where we recëive (1) vísitors, | or réad, | lïsten to the rádio (13), | or wätch the tëlevìsion. Fäther älways türns on the rädio to hëar the nèws. The kïtchen is at the bàck of the höuse.

Üpstáirs | there are thrëe bëdrooms and a bàthroom. From my bëdroom wìndow I can see snöwy mòuntains, | fär awày. Whät a wönderful vìew!

102. We lïve nëar a bïg tòwn. It has some fïne öld bùildings (2) | and mäny nëw cóncrete önes | füll of òffices. Fäther wörks in öne of thëse grëat blòcks. He sïts at a désk, | wrïtes létters | and änswers the tèlephone. I dön't knöw whät èlse he döes (10).

My bröther häs a jöb in a fàctory. He drïves thére in a sëcond-händ càr. I thïnk it is dàngerous. The tÿres are älmost (7, 17) wörn òut, | and the ëngine is älways gïving troùble (10). He drïves töo fàst. There are töo mäny cärs on the ròads, | töo mäny pëople in the närrow strèets, | and töo müch nòise.

Fórtunately, | our schöol büilding is in a quïet ärea (19 + 18) awäy from the tràffic. It has lïght, äiry cláss-röoms, | and a lïbrary (14) with sëveral (3) thöusand bòoks. The schöol ständs on the ëdge of a lärge fìeld (1) | where we pläy gämes twïce a wèek. We have lëssons ëvery (3) däy excëpt Sŭnday, | and we have thrëe mönths' höliday (6) a yèar.

103. The pëople who lïve nĕar us | are our nèighbours (13). The pëople who lïve nëxt dŏor to us | are our nëxt dòor nëighbours. Our nëxt döor nëighbours are the Frèemans. Döctor Frëeman is the profëssor of physics at the Ünivèrsity. His wïfe is the pràctical mëmber of the fämily. They have twö sóns, | Jöhn (6) and Geórge, | and twö dàughters, | Jäne and Màry (19). Jöhn is twënty-òne, | and is clëver, quïet and cäreful, lïke his fàther. Geörge is sïxteen | —cǎreless, | üntïdy, | but vëry amùsing (y + 9). Jáne, | who is nïnetéen, | is prètty, | like her mòther. Märy is önly twèlve. She is a räther wèak chïld | and öften ìll, | but ëverybody is fònd of her.

104. A cómpass (10) | is an ïnstrument with a néedle | that älways pöints in the säme dirèction. The chief diréctions, | or pöints of the cómpass, | are nórth, sóuth, éast and wèst. The sün rïses in the éast in the mörning, | and sëts in the wést in the èvening. At mïd-däy, we sëe it in the söuth, if we lïve in the nórthern hëmisphere (3, 2, 18), | and in the nörth if we lïve in the soùthern (10) hëmisphere. At nïght, the stàrs appëar (18).

Coüntries (10) in Eürope (y + 9, 12) have a cöld clïmate (14) in wínter, | and a cöol or a wärm clïmate in sùmmer. Öne däy it is fïne and ëven (1) hŏt, | the nëxt day it mäy be cöld, wïndy and wèt.

105. A tÿpewriter is a machïne that wrïtes. It has about fïfty kèys (1), öne for ëach lëtter of the ălphabet, | öne for ëach nümber from nöught to nïne, | the rëst for dïfferent sïgns and pünctuàtion märks. It has a härd rübber röller at the bàck. To tÿpe a létter, | you put a shëet of päper behïnd the röller, | and türn the röller untïl the töp of the päper cömes betwëen the röller and an ïnky rìbbon. Whën you toùch (10) a këy with your fínger, | it räises a lïttle hàmmer. At the ënd of this hämmer there is the förm of a létter, fígure (2 + 12) or sìgn. The hämmer hïts the ríbbon | and lëaves a märk on the pàper.

TESTS

106. **What is truth? What is a box? What are bees?**
What is the moon?

Use one of these patterns with each of the following, and then answer the question: ants, blood, bottle, branch, brothers, cow, corn, èlephant (3), finger, flour, flower, fruit, glove, grapes, hour, Ìndia, ink, jam, Lòndon, match-box, needle, orange, rain, ràzor, sea, stick, stone, thumb, wheat, world. [30]

107. **Whät beaütiful wèather! Whät a fïne dày!**

Put what *or* what a (an) *before:* good idea, kind man, hard work, interesting story, narrow streets, soft hand, dirty hands, stüpid boy, dängerous thïng to dò, peace! [10]

108. *Put* a, an, the, some, one *or nothing, before the words in brackets:*
   (a) We put (water) in (bath), (matches) in (box), and (beer) in (barrels).
   (b) (Fire) is red, (ash) is grey. (Smoke) from this (fire) is black.
   (c) We put (ash) from (cigarette) in (ash-tray).
   (d) (Sheets) are made of (cotton), (blankets) of (wool).
   (e) (Car) is (machine). (Carpet) is (article) of (furniture).
   (f) I want (loaf) of (bread), (milk) and (biscuits*).
   (g) Please go to (post-office) and buy me (stamps).
   (h) I must get (new hat). I want (good one).
   (i) Here are two (hats). Which one is yours? (brown one).
   (j) What (hot day)! All (food) in our (ice-box) is bad.
   (k) I go to (school) by (bus) and come (home) on (foot).
   (l) At (school) we study (science) and (mathematics).
   (m) (Students) study (law) and (medicine) at (university).
   (n) Please give me (ink). There is (ink) in (bottle) on that table.
   (o) When I write (letter), I put (date) at (top) of (paper).
   (p) What (wonderful weather)! There is not (cloud) in (sky).
   (q) It's dark in this (room). Turn on (light). I can't find (switch).
   (r) Manïla is (cäpital) of (Phìlippine Ïslands).
   (s) (river Ganges†) rises in (Himalayas†) and flows into (Bay of Bengàl).
   (t) In physics we study (heat), (light) and (sound).
   (u) We have quite (good knowledge) of (English). We are making (progress). [70]

* *Pronounce* biscuit *as* [bìskit].   † *Pronounce* [gàn-jees] [hïmmer-làyers].

109. *Put all the nouns (but not the mass-words or adjuncts) into the plural, and make other changes that then become necessary:*

(a) A city is a big town; a village is a small place.

(b) On a summer evening, we have a meal in the open air.

(c) A book-shelf is a long board or sheet of metal.

(d) A knife is an instrument with a sharp blade.

(e) Put this match and this leaf in that box.

(f) Write an answer to the following question.

(g) In the picture, we see a man, a woman and a child.

(h) A mother-in-law is the mother of a husband or wife.

(i) There is a lady and gentleman outside.

(j) There is a sheep in the field, and a wolf in the forest. [30]

110. (a) *Give 20 examples of the pattern* a (piece) of (paper), *but do not use the words in brackets.*

(b) *Give 10 examples of the pattern* a (stöne wàll), *and 10 of the pattern* a (tèa-cup), *but do not use the words in brackets. Then put all the examples into the plural.*

(c) *Form adjectives from:* sun, rain, noise, beauty, help, friend, danger, reason, music, science; *and nouns from:* good, kind, sweet, warm, true, strong, long, high, wide, deep. [20]

3. IDENTITY, QUANTITY AND DEGREE

Pronouns

111. 'He' *refèrs to a person or animal that we think of as a male*—a man, a father, a son, a waiter, an actor, a bull. *The word* 'he' *is* màsculine (4, 8, 2). 'She' *refers to a person or animal that we think of as a fèmale* (1, 13)—a woman, a mother, a daughter, a wàitress, an àctress, a cow. *The word* 'she' *is* fèminine (3, 2, 2). A child, a friend, a neighbour, *can be male or female.* A child, *etc. therefore can be* 'he' *or* 'she'. 'It' *refers to a thing; or to a person or animal that we do not specially think of* | *as male or female. The word* 'it' *is* neùter (y + 9). 'They' (13) *refers to things, persons or animals in the plural—masculine, feminine or neuter.* He, she, it *and* they *are* pèrsonal prònouns.

Which pronoun would you use in refèrring to: John, Anne, a tree, an oak, James, Elízabeth, an uncle, an aunt, a húsband, a wife, a flower, a rose, William, Márgaret, a proféssor, a públisher, an ènginéer, notebooks, a teacher, a nephew, a niece, a néwspaper, the Daïly Póst, gloves, an actress, a sécretary, hándkerchiefs, shirts, whïte háir, a wàlking-stïck? [30]

112. *Read the following as dìalogues. Then repeat each dialogue three times, using words from the last exercise instead of those in italics.*

A says:	*B says:*
(a) Whät is thàt? Whät ìs it?	It is a *star*. It's* a *star*.
What *star* ìs it?	I don't know its* name.
And what one is that?	Oh, that's *Venus*.
(b) Who is that? Who is it?	It's *George* Freeman.
That's his name, but who is he?	He's my *neighbour*.
And what is he?	He's a *student*.
(c) *George* Freeman is a *student*.	I can see six *students*. Which is *George* Freeman?
He's the one with *glasses*.	
(d) Who's that?	It's *Mary* Baker.
That's her name, but who is she?	She's my *coùsin* (10).
And what is she?	She's a *nuŕse*.
(e) Whose are these five *keys*?	One is yours, three are mine.
Which is my *key*?	This is. Which *keys* are mine?
Those are. And the other one?	
Whose is it?	I don't know whose it is.

* *Notice the difference between* it's (*i.e.* it is) *and* its.

[*Note:* What, which, whose + *noun are interrogative adjectives.*
What, which, whose *alone are interrogative pronouns.*
Who *is only used as a pronoun.*
This, that, these, those *are demonstrative adjectives or pronouns.*]

113. *Read and repeat the following as a conversation, with three people, A, B and C:*

A says:	*B says:*	*C says:*
(a) I have a *pencil.*	Ĭ have öne, | tòo.	Sö have Ĭ.
(b) But I haven't a *pen.*	Ĭ haven't öne, | either.*	Nör have Ĭ.
(c) There's some *nöte-paper* on the *dèsk.*	Ĭs there äny *nóte-paper?*	Yès, | there ìs söme.
(d) But we haven't any *ink.*	Ĭs there äny *ínk?*	Nò, | there ìsn't äny.
(e) Thcre are some *ènvelopes.*	Äre there äny *énvelopes?*	Yès, | there àre söme.
(f) But we haven't any *stamps.*	Äre there äny *stámps?*	No, | there àren't äny.
(g) Where's my *pencil?*	It's in your hand.	Yoù häve it.
(h) Where's the *note-paper?*	It's on the *desk.*	Hère it ĭs.
(i) Where are the *envelopes?*	They are in the *drawer.*	Thère they äre.
(j) Where are the *stamps?*	We haven't any.	There àren't äny.
(k) Who's that?	Your *father.*	It's your *father.*
(l) Where's my *father?*	Över thère.	He's över thère.
(m) Where's my *mother?*	At home.	She's at home.
(n) Where are your *brothers?*	At school.	They're at school.
(o) Where are your *sisters?*	In the garden.	They're in the garden.

Now use the same patterns with the following words instead of those in italics: knife, fork; bread, table, butter; sàusages (6), eggs; cùpboard; uncle, aunt, nèphew, nieces.

* either (14 or 1).

61

TABLE 7

Personal Pronouns; Possessive Adjectives and Pronouns

Singular

1st Person	I am		I have my book.		mine.
2nd „	You are	a student.	You have your book.	It is	yours.
3rd „	He is		He has his book.		his.
	She is		She has her book.		hers.

Plural

1st Person	We are		We have our books.		ours.
2nd „	You are	students.	You have your books.	They are	yours.
3rd „	They are		They have their (19) books.		theirs.

114. *Learn Table 7 by heart.*

The Possessive Form

115. **Whose house is this? That's mỳ house. It's mine. It's my òwn (17).**

Repeat with all persons, singular and plural, and with the following words: garden, field, farm, trees, sheep (*plural*); lùggage, handbag, sùitcases, tìckets, car. [10]

116. **Thät cämera belöngs to Jòhn. It's Jòhn's cämera. It's Jòhn's.**
This belongs to my brother. It's my brother's.
These belong to your friends. They are your friends'.
This belongs to James. It is James's.
This belongs to Mr Church. It is Mr Church's.

(*a*) *Use the pattern with apöstrophe* s *or* s *apòstrophe, to express the relation between:* Mr. Rose and his umbrella; your mother and her bìrthday; your sisters and their admirers; the Prësident (3) and his wìfe; the söldiers and their bòots. [5]

(*b*) *Use the same pattern for:* a dog and its tail, a cat and its paw, an elephant and its trunk, a lion (22) and its roar (20), a tïger (14, g) and its spòts. [5]

* *Pronounce* [a|pos|tro|phee], *4 syllables.*

62

117. (a) **I have mäny frïends. Fränk is òne. He's a frïend of mïne. Fränk has sëveral coùsins. Hënry is a coüsin of Frànk's.**

Repeat four times, beginning: You have —, Märgaret has —, We have —, Dävid (13) and Joan have —, *and replacing* cousins *by* students, clients (22), pàrtners, ènemies (3).

(b) **Thïs is the wäll buïlt (2) by Hàdrian (13). It's Hädrian's wàll.**

Repeat with: the hat worn by Napòleon (17); the theatre used by Shakespeare; the bïrthday of the Prèsident; the bïrthplace of Dànte (4 + 2); a play about the death of Caèsar.*

(c) **I am going to my brother's, to the baker's.**

Repeat with: my sìster-in-läw, the dòctor, my tàilor, the gròcer (17) the bùtcher (8), Mr and Mrs Tàylor (Mr and Mrs Taylor's).

118. *Read the following as a dialogue. Then cover up the right-hand column, read the sentences on the left, and repeat those on the right from memory:*

A says:	B says:
(a) Thïs is a jöb for a bòy.	That's a bòy's jöb.
(b) These are clothes for a girl.	Those are a gìrl's clöthes.
(c) These are clothes for girls.	Those are gìrls' clöthes.
(d) This is work for a man.	That's a màn's wörk.
(e) This is work for men.	That's mèn's wörk.
(f) These are toys for children.	Those are chïldren's töys.
(g) The place for a woman is at home.	A wöman's pläce is at hòme.
(h) Look at that boy: his coat is torn to pieces.	Thät böy's cöat is törn to pìeces.
(i) This is the office of one of the secretaries.	That's a sècretary's öffice.
(j) This is the office of the secretary.	That's the sècretary's öffice.
(k) These are the offices of the secretaries.	Those are the sècretaries' öffices.
(l) These are the offices of the bànk mänager.	Those are the bànk mänager's öffices.
(m) This is the office of my brother-in-law.	That's your bròther-in-läw's öffice.
(n) That's the daughter of the King of Spain.	That's the Kïng of Späin's dàughter.†

* Caesar = [Sèezer].
† *A reference to an old song, but a useful pattern for modern English.*

119.   **An höur's lèsson. A day's peace. Twö wëeks' wòrk.**

Use this pattern to express the length of time taken by: a joùrney (11), a hòliday (6), a walk, thought, sìlence (14), àbsence, a rest, a drive, sleep, ìllness.

The relation between the part and the whole

120.   **A part of a thing. The back of a chair.**

Use this pattern to express the relation between: the stairs, the top; the sea, the bottom; the table, the middle; the term, the beginning; this month, the end; my house, the side; your tie, the colour; that box, the weight (13); this road, the length; that building, the height (14). [10]

121.   **The sïde of the röad is the ròad-sïde.**

Repeat with: side, sea*; side, river; side, mountain; bank, river; top, hill; top, tree; top, roof; end, week*; handle, door; holder, pen.

122.   **A man's hand. The hand of a clock. The road-side.**

Use one of these patterns to express the relation between: my wife and her relàtions; Thomas and his addrèss; this table and its legs; a mountain and its top; the wall and its colour; a cow and its horns; a pärcel and its wèight; a child and its pàrents (19); a speaker and his sùbject; a book and its tìtle (14). [10]

other, same, next, only

123. *Read, filling the gaps:*

(*a*) Write down a number. Write down another number. Now another one; and another; and one more.

(*b*) Here are five numbers: 16, 18, 23, 41, 16.

(*c*) The first number is —, the second is —, the third — —, the fourth — —, the fifth — — again.

(*d*) The first is —, the next number is —, the next — —, the next — —, the last — —. The first is the same as the —.

(*e*) The — and the — are the same. The other numbers are different. The third is not — — — — —.

(*f*) The second is 18. The third is not the — number, it is a — one.

(*g*) The — is the only number over 25: — — is the only one over 25. The — and the — are the only numbers under 18. There is only one number — —. There are only two numbers — —.

* See note.

Use other, same *and* next *as adjectives and pronouns. Use* only *as an adjective, not as a pronoun. If a noun is omitted, say* the only one.

124.

Adjective	Pronoun
another number, another one	another
other numbers, other ones	others
the other number, the other one	the other
the other numbers, the other ones	the others

Form 7 sentences using another, other *and* the other *as adjectives, then* another, others, the other, the others *as pronouns.*

125. *Learn Table 8.*

TABLE 8
WHOLE and PART

Höw müch of a màss? Whät **amòunt**?

The whòle amöunt	—ALL
Part: a cèrtain amöunt; not all, not none	—SOME
: an ùncertain amöunt	—ANY
Nò amöunt	—NO, NONE*

Höw mäny ùnits? Whät **nùmber**?

		More than two	Two only
1 1 1 1 1 1 1	—The whòle nümber	—ALL	BOTH
1 1 1 1 1 1 1	—The sëparate ünits, äll pòsitive	—EVERY*	EACH
|1|1|1|1|1|1|1|	—The units, one by one	—EACH	
1	—A certain one	—ONE	ONE
1 1 1 1	—A certain (plural) number	—SOME	
???????	—An uncertain one or number, chosen from all	—ANY	EITHER*
XXXXXXX	—Every öne nègative	—NOT ANY	NOT EITHER
———————	—The whole number negative	—NO, NONE	NEITHER*

* *Use* no *and* ëvery (3) *as adjectives only. Use* none, ëvery òne, ëach òne, *as pronouns. Use all the other words in this table as both adjectives and pronouns. Pronounce* ëither *and* nëither *with vowel 14 or 1.*

65

126. *Suppose the seven units in Table 8 are cards with numbers, 1 to 7. Practise and learn the following dialogue:*

A says:	B says:
(a) I have all the cards.	I have no cards, I have none.
(b) I have every card—1, 2, 3, 4, 5, 6 and 7.	I haven't any—1, 2, 3, 4, 5, 6, or 7.
(c) I put each card on the table, one by one. Count.	One; two; three; four; five; six; seven.
(d) I give three or four cards to you. Don't look. How many have you?	Three or four. I don't know exactly how many.
(e) I still have some cards. I don't know how many, either. But have I a fixed number?	Of course you have.
(f) In any case, I have some. Have you some cards too?	Yes, I have some too.
(g) Are any of the cards on the floor—1, 2, 3, 4, 5, 6 or 7?	Not one. Every card is on the table.
(h) Now take two cards, 1 and 2. Where are the two cards?	Both are in my right hand.
(i) Put one card in each hand.	I have one in each hand.
(j) Is either of the cards on the table, either 1 or 2?	No, neither of the cards is on the table, neither 1 nor 2.

127. *Study Table 8 again. Then read and study the following examples:*

A. How much of a mass?

(i) ALL water is wet, but not all water is fresh. All the water in this tank—all of the water in it—is fresh. All of it. It is all fresh.

(ii) ANY water is wëlcome (3, 12) to a very thirsty man. Have you any milk? I'm sörry (6) we haven't any. But any of the wine here is good—drink what you want. Thank you, but I don't want any of it.

(iii) SOME water is salty—not all. Will you have some water? Thank you, I have some. Some of the milk in the ice-box is sour. Some of it is still fresh.

(iv) These flowers have no water—they must have some. Now they have none.

B. How many units? What number? More than two.

(v) ALL men are hùman (y + 9), but not all sing. All the men in this room sing. All of them sing. They all sing.

(vi) EVERY word in this book is in the dictionary. Every word is there. You can find every one. But not every word in the dictionary is in this book.

(vii) Write EACH new word, one by one, in your notebook. Write each one on a sëparate (3) line. Use a separate line for each.

(viii) I go to the library every day. Come to the library one day—ANY day you like. Have you any books on space travel? We haven't any yet.

(ix) We have ONE book now, only one. SOME day we'll have more.

(x) SOME people never answer letters. Are there some letters for me?—I am expëcting four or five.

(xi) There is NO answer: NONE. There are no letters for you: none, not one. None of the letters are for you.

C. Which of two?

(xii) Here are two keys. BOTH the keys—both of them, both—are good. Both keys, both my keys, can open my drawer.

(xiii) Here are the two keys. I have one key in EACH hand.

(xiv) EITHER key can open my drawer; either of them.

(xv) But NEITHER key can open my safe: neither of them.

D. How much of a unit?

(xvi) Some people will ünderstand all of this book—the whole book. Others will understand some of it. Others will not understand any of it: they will understand none of it.

(xvii) *Note:* We work all day, sleep all night and breathe all the time.

128. *Fit the following words into the patterns in 127:*

A (i) earth, solid, hard, garden, soft; (ii) food, hungry, bread, fruit, eat; (iii) fruit, sweet, corn, this field, ripe, green; (iv) plants, no soil; B (v) boys, swim, class; (vi) name, list, tèlephone böok; (vii) addrèss, addrèss böok; (viii) and (ix) club, evening, places for new members; (x) send, prèsents; (xi) nèwspaper todäy; C (xii) straps, light, hold my camera, my suitcase; D (xvi) can (can't) transläte, page.

129. *Study; then cover up the right-hand column, look at the left, and repeat the right from memory:*

Instëad of—	we can say:
(*a*) all things; all the things here	èverything; ëverything hère
(*b*) all the other things	ëverything èlse

(c) all people; all the other people everyone (or èverybody);
                                      everyone (etc.) else

(d) any thing; any other thing ànything; änything èlse

(e) any person, any other person ànyone (or anybody); anyone
                                        (etc.) else

(f) some thing; some other thing sòmething; something else

(g) some person; etc. sòmeone (or somebody); etc.

(h) no thing; etc. nòthing; etc.

(i) the hat of some other person sömebody èlse's hät

(j) These are mine. They belong to These are mine. They are nobody
    no other person else's

TABLE 9

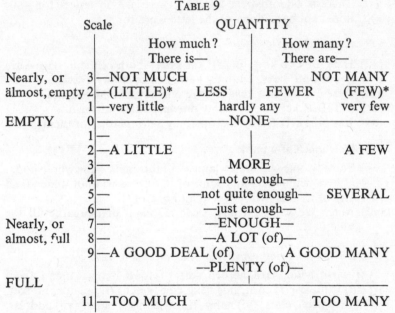

Scale		QUANTITY		
		How much? There is—		How many? There are—
Nearly, or	3	—NOT MUCH		NOT MANY
älmost, empty	2	—(LITTLE)*	LESS	FEWER	(FEW)*
	1	—very little	hardly any	very few
EMPTY	0	—————————NONE—————————		
	1	—		
	2	—A LITTLE		A FEW
	3	—	MORE	
	4	—	—not enough—	
	5	—	—not quite enough—	SEVERAL
	6	—	—just enough—	
Nearly, or	7	—	—ENOUGH—	
almost, full	8	—	—A LOT (of)—	
	9	—A GOOD DEAL (of)		A GOOD MANY
		—PLENTY (of)—		
FULL				
	11	—TOO MUCH		TOO MANY

From 3 to 0 there is a dècrease (1) in quäntity. From 0 to 11, an increase. Use the words on the left only for amòunt; the words on the right only for number; the words in the middle for both.

Little and *few* = älmost nòne; *a little* and *a few* = more than none; *too much, too many* = möre than nècessary.

All these words except *none* (see Table 8) can be used with a noun or without. If *a lot, a good deal* and *plenty* are used with a noun, say *a lot of water*, etc. Without a noun, omit *of*.

* See note.

130. *Learn Table 9.*

131. *Imagine the line down the left-hand side of Table 9 is a scale marking the amount of a liquid or solid, or the number of objects, in a container. Suppose the container is the petrol tank of a car. The tank holds 10 gallons. We are going on a journey and need about 6 gallons. Read the following:*

(a) When there are only two gallons in the tank, there is not **much**.
(b) When there is only one gallon, there is **very little**, or **hardly any**.
(c) When the tank is empty, there is **none**.
(d) Start filling the tank. There is **a little** in it now.
(e) There is **not enough** yet, **not quite enough**.
(f) Now there is **just enough**. **Enough**. **Quite enough**.
(g) There is **a lot**. There is **plenty**.
(h) The tank is full. Stop. Now there is **too much**.

Imagine the container is a packing-case for books (units). Begin: 'When there are only two dozen . . .' and continue. Again, imagine it is a sack of rice (mass), and begin: 'When there are only two pounds . . .'. Then, imagine it is a box to hold packets of cigarettes, and begin: 'When there are only two packets . . .'. Now repeat the whole exercise inserting the noun after the expressions in bold type and making the necessary changes, e.g. there is not much petrol, there are not many books, enough petrol, etc.

132. *Read. Then cover up the right-hand side, look at the left, and say the right from memory. Then cover up the left, etc., and begin the sentence putting the second part first.*

(a) When there are only 5 gallons in it, | the tank is half empty.
(b) When there is still half a gallon, | it is not quite empty.
(c) When there is only half a gallon, | it is almost empty.
(d) When there is none left, | it is quite empty.
(e) When there are 5 gallons in, | the tank is half full.
(f) When there are 9 gallons in, | it is almost (or nearly) full.
(g) When there only 9 gallons in, | it is not quite full.
(h) When there are 10 gallons in, | it is quite full.
(i) When there are only 4 or 5 gallons in, | it is not nearly full.
(j) When there are 5 gallons, no more, no less, | it is just half full, exactly half full.

(k) When there is a little more than
    5, or a little less,   it is about half full.
(l) Don't guess. Tell me the ăctual
    amöunt in the tànk.   Five and three-quarter gallons.
(m) What is the ăctual fìgure?   5¾ (five and three-quarters).

TABLE 10

Order of limiting adjectives before a noun

(a) a lot of, plenty of, a little, all, any, hardly any, enough, much, not much, more, most, no	white bread ⎫ hot water ⎬ (mass) good advice ⎭
any, each, every, no, some	young person— (unit)
a lot of, plenty of, a few, all, enough, many, more, most, several, some	young people— (units)

(b) all, both, half, twice,		the this	
all, both, half; any, hardly any, a few, few, a little, little; each one, every one; either, neither; enough; much, many, more, most, none; several, some; plenty	of	that these those my your his our their John's	white bread hot water good advice young people

---

133.   **We have no hot water. We have plenty of fresh eggs.**
       Both the new suits in that cupboard are mine.
       Some of John's English books are missing.

*Notice how these examples follow the scheme in Table 10. Use Table 10 to make up 20 sensible sentences using **either** a phrase from column 1 (at the beginning of the sentence), **or** a phrase from column 4 (at the end), plus one word or group of words from column 2, and one group of words from column 3:*

1	2	3	4
I want	all, both, each,	that brown paper	is broken
You can have	each one of,	those red apples	is torn
There is	every,	hot water	are broken
There are	every one of,	old photographs	are true
	a few, a lot of,	my big suitcases	is useful
	more, most,	John's good advice	are useful
	some, some of,	plate on this table	
	several,	the money in my	
	several of	purse	

How much, how many, how old, how long, etc.

134. *Read, and fill the gaps:*

(a) I have a certain amount of money. What amount? Much or little? How much?

(b) What is the price of this material? How much does it cost?

(c) What is the value of it? How much is it worth?

(d) I have a certain — of books. What —? Many or —? How —?

(e) What is your age? Are you old or —? How — are you?

(f) What is the size of this room? It is big or little? How — — —? Is it large or small? How — — —?

(g) What is its length? How — — —?   (h) its width? How — — —?   (i) its height? How — — —?   (j) the weight [13] of this parcel? How — — —?   (k) the depth of this river? How — — —?   (l) the strength of this steel? How — — —?   (m) the thickness of this rope? How — — —?   (n) the distance from x to y? How far — —?   (o) the length of this pèriod (18)? How — — —?

135.

Question	Negative	Affirmative
How much water is there in the tank?	Not much, not very much.	A lot; plenty; a good deal.
How many eggs are there in the basket?	Not many, not very many.	A lot; plenty; a good many.
How far is it to the station?	Not far, not very far.	A long way.
How long is it till Christmas?*	Not long, not very long.	A long time.

Make up 5 questions on each of these patterns and answer each question, first in the negative, then in the affirmative.

* Chrìstmas (2: ch = k).

136. (a) **I want a piece of wire 8 inches long. This piece is seven and a half inches. It is not long enough: it is too short. That piece is nine inches: it is too long. Ah, this piece is just long enough.**

Repeat with: pole, 8 mètres* high; piece of tape, one inch wide (half an inch, one and a half inches, or an inch and a half); a cushion, ten cëntimetres thìck; a piece of meat weighing three kìlos (1, 17).

(b) **I want a piece only eight inches long. I don't want a piece as long as that. I don't want it so long. I don't want such a long piece.**

Repeat with the examples given in (a).

137. *Learn Table 11.*

TABLE 11

Degrëe and Compàrison (4)

Tèmperature	Wèather	Temperature	Weather
0 degrèes	very cold	30	very hot
5 ,,	cold	25	hot
10 ,,	not so cold	20	not so hot
	not very cold		not very hot
15 ,,	warmer	15	cooler
20 ,,	warm	10	cool
25 ,,	hot	5	cold
30 ,,	very hot	0	very cold

Notes: 1. *not so cold* = not cold to the same degree (as before), or not cold to an extrëme degrèe.
 2. *not very cold* = not cold to an extreme degree.
 3. 30 degrees is *the highest* temperature on this scale; 0 is *the lowest*.

---

138. *Look at the scale in Table 11. Then read the sentences below, answer the questions, fill the gaps and follow the instructions in (m):*

(*a*) Which are the high numbers? Which are the low ones?

(*b*) 5 is lower than 10; therefore 10 is — — 5.

(*c*) 25 is a lower number — 30; therefore 30 — — — — — —.

(*d*) Which is the lower number, 15 or 20? And which is the —?

(*e*) Which is the lowest number on the scale? And which is the —?

(*f*) Three times three (3 × 3) is more than twice four (2 × 4).

(*g*) Three times five is less than four — —.

* mètre: *pronounce as* [mèeter].

(*h*) Four twos (4 × 2) are —— three threes (3 × 3).

(*i*) (3 × 4) is as much as (2 × 6): one amount is ëqual (1) to the other.

(*j*) (3 × 5) is not as much as (2 × 9); (*k*) (4 × 6) is twice as much as (3 × 4); (*l*) (3 × 6) are half as much as —.

(*m*) Compäre: (4 × 5) and (3 × 7); (6 × 3) and (2 × 9);
(8 × 2) and (3 × 5); (8 × 3) and (5 × 5);
(8 × 4) and (3 × 11).

(*n*) Which is the greater, (6 × 8) or (7 × 7)?

(*o*) Which is the smaller, 6 plus 8, or 23 minus* 9.

(*p*) What is the highest mountain in the world?

(*q*) John (6) has 14 dollars, Pëter (1) has 13, James has 15. Peter has — money than John and also — than James. John has —— Peter, and —— James. John has as — money as Peter, but not ——— James. Who has the most (17)? ——— least?

(*r*) Many people drink coffee, but ëven (1) möre drïnk tèa. In fact, most people drink tea today.

(*s*) We have mäny impörtant thïngs to dò. This is more important than that; therefore that is less important — —. In fact, this is the most important thing of all, and that —— — —.

(*t*) Thank you very much. You are most kind; and you tell a most interesting story. (That is to say, you are kind to the highest degree, and your story is interesting to the highest degree).

139. *Learn Table 12, and study these notes on it:*

(*a*) near, nearer, nearest: *use this form of the comparison for words of one syllable.* Near, nearer, nearest *refer to distance.* Next (*123*) *refers to order.*

(*b*) longer, longest; stronger, strongest; younger, youngest: *Pronounce* ng + g *in all of these words.*

(*c*) big, bigger; late, later: *see 87, footnote.*

(*d*) clever, cleverer, cleverest: *use this form of the comparison for words of two syllables when the first is stressed and the second consists of a simple sound such as consonant plus vowel, or l or n, as in* gentle, common.

(*e*) useful, more useful, most useful: *use this form for all other adjectives of more than one syllable.*

(*f*) *Note the irregular forms.* Little, less, least *refer to quantity (see Table 9). Do not use the comparative or superlative for* 'little' *meaning* 'small' *but say* smaller, smallest.

(*g*) *Use* farther, farthest *only for distance:* e.g. The North and South

* mïnus (14).

73

TABLE 12

Compärison of Àdjectives

Degrèe				
1. Pòsitive (6)	near	long	big	late
2. Compàrative (4)	nearer	longer	bigger	later
3. Supèrlative	nearest	longest	biggest	latest

èarly	clèver	nàrrow	còmmon
èarlier	clèverer	nàrrower	còmmoner
èarliest	clèverest	nàrrowest	còmmonest

ùseful	fòolish	ìnteresting
more useful	more foolish	more interesting
most useful	most foolish	most interesting

Irregular

good	bad, ill	much, many	(a) little	far
better	worse (11)	more	less	{ farther { further
best	worst (11)	most	least	{ farthest { furthest

Poles are the farthest points from the equàtor (13). *Use* further *for distance, or to mean 'one more'; e.g.* 'a further question' *means* 'one more question'.

(*h*) *The comparison of* old *is regular, i.e.* older, oldest. *In referring to comparative ages in a family group, use* elder *and* eldest, *but attributively only* (*see 96*). *Examples:*

Attributive	*Predicative*
John is George's elder brother.	John is older than George.
Dr Freeman is the eldest member of the family.	

140. *Give the comparative and superlative of:*

àngry, bad, beaùtiful, cèrtain, cheap, còmmon, dàngerous, deep, èarly, far, fat, fèeble, fèrtile, frèquent (1), good, great, hàppy, hèalthy, ìnteresting, kind, little, long, loud, much, nàrrow, nàtural, nècessary, old, pàinful, poor, pùblic, prìvate (14), quick, quiet, règular, respònsible, sad, safe, sènsible, sèrious (18), shàllow, straight, strong, thin, üncèrtain, ünhèalthy, weak, wet, wise, young. [50]

141. *Read; then cover up the right-hand column, look at the left and repeat the right from memory:*

If something is very cold,	we say it is as cöld as ìce.
,, ,, ,, ,, dry,	,, ,, ,, ,, as dry as dust.
,, ,, ,, ,, hard,	,, ,, ,, ,, as hard as iron.
,, ,, ,, ,, soft,	,, ,, ,, ,, as soft as silk.
,, ,, ,, ,, heavy,	,, ,, ,, ,, as heavy as lead.
,, ,, ,, ,, light,	,, ,, ,, ,, as light as a feather.
,, ,, ,, ,, sharp,	,, ,, ,, ,, as sharp as a knife.
,, ,, ,, ,, old,	,, ,, ,, ,, as old as the hills.
,, a child ,, ,, quiet,	,, ,, ,, ,, as quiet as a mouse.
,, ,, ,, ,, good,	,, ,, ,, ,, as good as gold.

Passages for Reading, Study and Dictation

142. A letter to a friend

Dëar Jàck,

Mäny thänks for your pòst-card. I'm sörry I can't gö to the màtch with yoú. I have a mönth's hòliday | and am spènding it at my coüsin's färm in the coùntry. Coüsin Röbert (6) is märried (4) and his wïfe is a vëry göod hòusewïfe. He thïnks her cöoking is the bëst in the wòrld. They are as häppy as sànd böys, | and I'm gläd to be with them.

My röom is at the töp of the hòuse, | and it is müch quïeter hère than at hòme. This is jüst whät I wànt. I have a löt of rèading to dö, | and there is sö lïttle öpportünity (y + 9) for it düring the tèrm. There are töo mäny òther thïngs to dö. Wòrk nëxt tèrm will be fär möre dìfficult, | and nöw I have tïme to thìnk abòut it.

The pëople hére | gët üp at fíve | and stärt their däy èarly. I dön't gët öut of bëd tïll sèven. Thën I gö for an hòur's wàlk, | üsually alöng the rìver-bänk | and häve a swìm—if the wäter is nöt töo cóld. Äfter brèakfast, | I rëad äll the mòrning, | and dön't sëe ànybody. Äfter lúnch, | I explöre the coùntrysïde, | and ëvery ëvening we äll drïve över to the nëxt vìllage | to pläy gölf with some frïends of Ròbert's. There's nöthing ëlse to dò; | but I enjòy it.

All the best,
John

143.   A bùsiness* lëtter

24, Öxford Ròad,
Frèetown.
16th October, 196–.

Dear Sir,

Thank you for your letter of yesterday's date in answer to mine of October 14th about furniture for my new office. I am now able to send you a firm order.

Please supply:

1. a desk, of the same size, quality and price as the larger one in your shòw-room, and a chair to match;
2. two of your bëst quälity lëather ärm-chàirs;
3. a low round wooden table;
4. two steel cupboards (lockable), each six feet high, three feet wide, and two feet six inches deep, and each with four rows of shelves, of equal height; colour, either black or brown.

I am not ordering any cúrtain matërial (18), as I think I have enoügh for the prèsent (3). But please send me at least twelve different sàmples of matërial, | in cäse I decïde to örder söme làter.

Yours fáithfully,
T. B. Morris

Messrs. William Harris and Sons,
4, Nórth Street,
Freetown.

TESTS

144. *Put one word in each gap, and make sense of the whole dialogue. Count a word followed by apostrophe s as one.*

(a) — is that noise?   There is — at — door.
(b) — is it?   — the postman.
(c) Good. There — — letters.   There — — — tèlegram (3).
(d) — is — important?   — telegram, of course.
(e) Not — telegrams — —.   I agree, but — are; and — one is
                                     — —. Read —. Is there —
                                     answer?
(f) No, there is — answer.   Now look at — letters. — writing
                                     is that?
(g) That is —.   And — is Charles?

* *pronounce* [bìznis].

(*h*) — is a good friend — —. In
fact, he is my — friend. — is
— — — men in — photo-
graph.

— one is he?

(*i*) — first on the left in — front
row (17).

And — is the name of the —
man?

(*j*) I don't know — name. Let
me read — —.

All right, I won't (17) ask —
more questions.

(*k*) Good. Now bring me — to
drink.

Tea? Coffee? Or anything —?

(*l*) It doesn't matter. Bring me
— liquid.

Here is — lëmonàde, as cold as
—.

145. *We can say* 'This cup is clean' *or* 'This is a clean cup'. *We can
say* 'What is your age?' *or* 'How old are you?' *There is very little, or
no, difference in meaning between one expression and the other, although there may be a difference in emphasis. Say the following in a
different but acceptable way, using only the patterns given so far in this
book:*

1. What is that letter?
2. What boy is that?
3. Whose towel is this?
4. That is her towel.
5. The name of your father.
6. The address of your parents.
7. The trunk of an elephant.
8. The side of the road.
9. The work of an evening.
10. I haven't any idea.
11. All the people are happy.
12. Any person can tell you.
13. Ask some other person.
14. There is hardly any time.
15. There are hardly any plates.
16. But there is a lot of bread.
17. There is nothing in the basket.
18. The box is not quite full.
19. This is not the same box.
20. But is it just as big?
21. Answer the question after
this.
22. It is not so warm today.
23. Lead is heavier than tin.
24. (2 × 3) is half as much as
(3 × 4).
25. This is the same length as
that.
26. I am the same age as you.
27. How large is this room?
28. Give me one more.
29. Where are the other people?
30. My two sisters are married.
31. Their husbands are doctors.
32. The life of a doctor is a busy
one.
33. His day is not long enough.
34. This chair is too low.
35. It is higher than the next one.
36. Peter is older than Harold.
37. Harold is Peter's younger
brother.
38. My work is not so good as
yours.
39. Mine is not so bad as his.
40. Yours is the least untidy.
41. I can understand only some of
this.

42. The room is only half full.
43. Here is a further example.
44. This is not public property.
45. This is mine, nobody else's.
46. I don't like tea as weak as this.
47. I don't like such strong coffee.
48. Mr Porter is a teacher of music.
49. Ralph is one of his students.
50. I can't sleep on such a hard bed.

4. STATEMENT, COMMAND AND QUESTION

TABLE 13
Parts of a Sentence

SUBJECT	PREDICATE		
noun (with ádjective) or prònoun	verb	còmplement	òbject	àdverb
Bïrds	flỳ.			
My yoünger bröther	is	an àrchitect.		
He	dräws		plàns.	
The pëople in this coüntry	wörk			hàrd.
It	is	làte.		
Yoü	sït			dòwn!
(You)	Stànd!			

146. *Study Table 13, and make up other sentences on the same patterns. Give every sentence a* **subject** *and a* **verb**. *The verb must be* **finite** (14, 14), *i.e. either in the* **indícative** (2) *form or the* **impèrative** (3)*: see Tables 14–17.*

TABLE 14
The verb TO BE

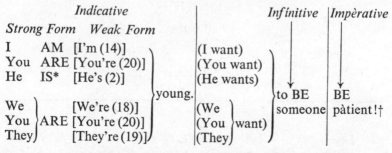

	Indícative		Infínitive	Impèrative
	Strong Form	Weak Form		
I	AM	[I'm (14)]	(I want)	
You	ARE	[You're (20)]	(You want)	
He	IS*	[He's (2)]	(He wants)	
				to BE	BE
We		[We're (18)]	(We	someone	pàtient!†
You	ARE	[You're (20)]	(You want)	
They		[They're (19)]	(They		

young.

* *In all verbs*, he, she *and* it *take the same form.*
† pàtient (13: ti = sh).

TABLE 15

The verb TO HAVE

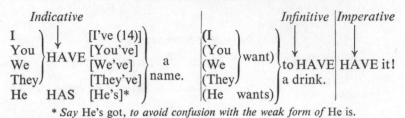

| Indicative | | | | | | Infinitive | Imperative |

I) [I've (14)] (I)
You } HAVE [You've] (You)want) to HAVE   HAVE it!
We) [We've] a (We) a drink.
They) [They've] name. (They)
He   HAS [He's]* (He wants)

*Say He's got, *to avoid confusion with the weak form of* He is.

147. *Learn Tables 14 and 15 by heart.*

TABLE 16

Mòdal (17) Vërbs

I, you, he, we, they { CAN / MUST } be patient!

(No infinitive. No imperative.)

148. *Learn Table 16 by heart.*

TABLE 17

Full verbs

Indicative	Infinitive	Imperative
I, you, we, they SEE	(We want) } TO SEE	SEE for yourself!
He SEES	(He wants)	

149. *Learn Table 17 by heart. USE IT FOR 'FULL' VERBS, i.e. ALL VERBS in English excëpt* be *and* have, *and* can, must, will *and the few other auxiliary and modal verbs which you will study later. Now study Table 18.*

TABLE 18

Plural of Nouns		Verbs	
		Infinitive	3rd Person Singular
			Sound of ending
Soft sounds	trees, pens	play, run	He plays, runs [z]
Hard	hats, books	stop, put, take	He stops, puts, takes [s]
Hissing sounds (piece)	pieces	dance	He dances [iz]
(match)	matches	touch (10)	He touches [iz]
(box)	boxes	wash	He washes [iz]
Consonant/y (city)	cities	try	He tries [z]
Ending in o (hero)	heroes	go	He goes [z]
		do (9)	He does (10) ⎱ excep-
		say (13)	He says (3) ⎰ tions

150. *Say and spell the 3rd Person Singular (e.g.* he plays*) of the following verbs:* eat, drink, win, lose (9 + z), go, stay, laugh (5 + f), cry, hit, miss, join, mix, bring, fetch, dress, brush, enjòy, amùse, còpy, bùry (3). [20]

151. *Learn the following verbs and give the 1st, 2nd and 3rd person singular of each one:*

(*a*) *Mövements* (9) *of the bòdy:*

start	put (8)	bend	throw (17)
stop	take	stretch	catch
go	push (8)	turn	hold
come	pull (8)	twist	drop
hùrry (10)	press	touch (10)	keep (something)
wait	draw	rub	let (something) go
run	give (2)	shake	climb (14: *b silent*)
walk	get	break (13)	slip
jump	send	tear (19)	stand
fall	recèive (1)	bite	sit [40]

(*b*) *Acts of the senses:*

look, listen (*i.e. give your attëntion with eyes, or ears*);
see, hear (*i.e. recëive an imprëssion on the sènses*);
feel, smell, taste (*i.e. either give attention or receive an impression*);
like, love (10), want. [10]

81

(c) *Mental acts:*

know	believe (1)*	remember	mean	hope	agree
think	doubt	forget	understand	wish	prefer
		wonder (10)	[15]		

152. *Fill each gap with a verb from 151. Use as many of the verbs as you can:*

(a) Let's — at the beginning. In the morning, I wake up, — my eyes, — out of bed, — my feet on the cold floor, and — to the window. I — there, — the fresh air on my face, and — my arms.

(b) —. Can you — that music? —. Can you — the new moon? — this coffee: is there soap in it? Can you — gas?

(c) A. This ice is dangerous. You can ëasily — on it. B. I —; you're right. — at my wrist. It's very painful. Don't — it. I — I have broken a bone.

(d) Here is a letter. — it, — to the post-office, — a stamp, stick the stamp on the envelope, and — the letter in the box. —. Here is some money for the stamp. Don't — it. — it in your pocket.

(e) — with me to the post-office. I must — a telegram. Don't —. There's plenty of time. There's no need to —.

(f) A. Who is that, I —. Is it Árthur? B. I — it is, but I'm not sure. A. I — it's Paul (7). Yes, now I'm certain, I — it's Paul.

(g) I can't — this word. What does it —?

(h) What can we do with paper? We can — it. With glass? We can — it. With a piece of rubber? We can — it, — it, and — it. What can we do with chocolate? We can — it. We — clothes, and — water from a well.

(i) A. — me the key of the cupboard. Don't — it: I can't —. Thank you. But I can't open the door. B. You must — the key twice, then — the door, and —.

(j) How high can you —? Can you — a mountain?

(k) I — something to drink. I don't — coffee. I — tea.

(l) — that man! Don't — him go. — him to prison.

(m) That's enough. I — that's all. I — you a Häppy Nëw Yèar. [60]

153. *Study.*

(a) *Some words are both nouns which refër to an actïvity in géneral, and verbs which tell us what the subject dòes; e.g.*

Wörk is a üseful actìvity. Most men work.
Play is a pleasure. Children play.
Slëep is nècessary. We sleep at night.

* *Note the spelling of* believe *and* receive. *The rule of thumb, 'i before e except after c,' applies to a number of words of similar type, e.g.* relieve, deceive.

(*b*) *Some words are both verbs, and nouns which refer to a single act; e.g.*

I walk home in the evening, and go for a walk on Sundays.
Some people have a little sleep after lunch.

(*c*) *Many words are nouns which refer to things, and also verbs; e.g.*

Where there is smoke, there is fire. You smoke too much!
A vegetable is a plant. We plant vegetables in soft soil.
Please lock the door. I can't, there is no lock on it.
One* drinks a lot in hot weather. Have a drink now!

(*d*) *Some words can be both adjectives and verbs; e.g.*

The door is ópen (17), the window is shut.
Shut the door, open the window.
Clean this floor and dry it.
It is neither clean nor dry.

154. *Study. We can always form a kind of noun from verbs by adding
-ing to the infinitive. The form ending in -ing can be called the verbal
noun or gerund: it refers to action or pròcess. Examples:*

Wälking and swïmming are böth göod èxercise.
Too much smoking is bad for your lungs.
Young people like singing† and dancing.†

155. *Learn the examples in paragraphs 153 and 154. Say which words
in those examples are used as (a) nouns, (b) adjectives, (c) verbs, and
(d) verbal nouns.*

156. *Study. Sometimes a noun ends in a hard consonant which is soft
in the corresponding verb: e.g.*

Nouns	Verbs
life (14), breath (3), use,	live (2), breathe (1), use,
excùse, house, advìce,	excùse, house, advìse,
proof (9), belièf	prove (9), belìève

In práctice (4 + 2: *noun*) and pràctise (4 + 2: *verb*) *the final consonant is pronounced the same* (*hard*). *Corresponding to the noun* bath
(*hard*) *there are two verbs:* bath (*hard*) *and* bathe (13, *soft*). *From the
verb* bathe *we can then form a noun,* bathe (*soft*), *e.g.* We bathe in the
sea (or have a bathe) and bathe a wound, but bath a baby. *Note the*

* *We can say* People drink . . . *or* we drink . . . *or* you drink . . . *or* one
drinks . . .

† *Note the spelling of:* swim, swimming; dance, dancing. *This is in accordance
with the rule given in the footnote to 87. Do not pronounce any separate g sound
after the ng sounds in* singing: *compare* 139 (b).

adjective close (*hard s*) *and the verb* close (*soft s*): My house is close (*adj.*) to the sea. I must close (*verb*) the windows when the sea is rough. *Sometimes a noun is accented on the first of two syllables, and the corresponding verb is accented on the second:*

Nouns	Verbs
rècord, ìmport, èxport	recòrd, impòrt, expòrt

157. *Fill each gap by a noun or verb from 156:*

(*a*) We — in an interesting world. — is interesting.
(*b*) Always — through your nose. Take a deep —.
(*c*) A. I'm sorry, — me. B. I accèpt your —.
(*d*) A. I need your —. B. Then I — you to stop smoking.
(*e*) — your verbs. Do half an hour's — every day.
(*f*) I understand the — of the articles, but I can't — many verbs yet.
(*g*) I — you are right. That is my —. But I have no —. I can't — it.
(*h*) We — people in houses. Which is your —?
(*i*) We have a — in the bathroom. We — in the sea, — a wound, and — the baby.
(*j*) It's cold in here. — the door and sit — to the fire.
(*k*) When we — a speech, we put it on —.
(*l*) Traders — certain foods. Those are called —. They — other goods. Those are called —. [30]

158.   **A swìmmer is a përson who swìms.**
              Workers are people who work.
              A cär-driver is a përson who drïves a càr.
              Höuse owners are pëople who öwn hòuses.

Use one of these patterns with each of the words below:

advìser	mèat ëater	shòpkeepers	readers
begìnners*	farmers	killer	recèiver
believer	fighters	lèaders (1)	hòrse rïders
buìlders	finder	learners	ruler
buyers	flier	lìsteners	runners*
callers	fòllower	loser	bòokseller
mòney-chänger	giver	mùsic lover	singers
cleaners	frùit gröwers	shòemakers	smokers
climber	helper	hòuse owner	pìpe smöker
dancers	fòod impörters	teà-plänter	speaker
bùs-drïvers	intèrpreter	tènnis pläyer*	teachers
wàge-ëarner	bèe keeper	piàno pläyer*	thinker

tràveller*	winners*	actor	protèctors
walkers	worker	beggars	sailors
watcher	writers	stàmp-collëctor	vìsitor [60]

159. *Do Exercise 158 again, putting the singular words into the plural, and vice versa (14; 11, 12).*

160. *In a few cases the same word is used for the verb and the noun referring to the person who performs the action;* e.g. cook, guard, guide, judge: a cook cooks, etc. *On the other hand,* a cooker is an apparatus or pot for cooking, a roller is something which rolls a soft substance flat. *Note:* a swimmer is someone who . . . , a roller is something which . . .

161. *Answer:* What is a cook, a guard, a guide, a judge, a heater, a leader, a tìn-öpener, a tàpe-recörder, a cigarètte lïghter, a scrèwdrïver, a tràin drïver, a wïse rùler, a wöoden rùler, a spàce träveller, a bìrd wätcher?

Agreement of Subject and Verb

162. **One of the light bulbs is broken.**
Öxygen (6, 2, 12) and hÿdrogen (14) are gàses (4).
Oxygen, like hydrogen, is a gas.
Our family has its own house.
Our family have their own house.

Put the verb into the singular or plural:

(a) (be) The news (*see 68 g*) — very good today.
(b) (be) Some people — thoughtful, others — thoughtless.
(c) (have) The commïttee — their meeting every Friday.
(d) (be) The full story of these evënts — on rècord.
(e) (want) The gövernment (10) — its own way.
(f) (be, make) 16 and 18 — 34. Blue and yellow — green.
(g) (have) One of those men — a gun.
(h) (have) Each family — — own house.
(i) (have) Everybody — — own likes and dìslikes.
(j) (be) All the milk in these bottles — sour.

* *Note the spelling of* begìn, begìnner; run, runner; wïn, winner: (*see footnote to* 87). *Note* tràvel, tràveller, tràvelling, *although the second syllable in* travel *is not the stressed one. Note also that* we play tennis (a game) *but* play the piano (a musical instrument).

Complëting the Prèdicate

163. (a) *The verb* to be (*also* become *and* seem) *must have a còmplement:*

Sùbject	Verb	Còmplement
My bröther	is	{ an àrchitect. vëry bùsy (2). in the nëxt ròom.
He	sëems (or löoks)	tìred.

(b) *Some verbs must have an òbject; e.g.*

		Object
My üncle	häs	a càr.
He	owns (17)	a hòuse.
Yoü	can transläte	thïs sèntence.

(c) *In some contexts, a verb needs an* **àdverb**, *or adverb phrase* (*answering the question* how, where *or* when) *to complete the sense, e.g.*

	Adverb
You wrïte	clèarly.
Geörge wörks	in an òffice.
He wörks	äll dày.

(d) *Verbs need a subject, and this is sometimes supplied by* **it**; *e.g.* It is early, it's late (light, dark, cold, hot, raining, snowing). It doesn't matter. It seems to me . . .

(e) *Note the example in 60:* There is a pencil in your pocket; *and, on the same pattern,* There is plenty to eat. There are many people in the world.

The Direct Object

164. *See 163* (b). *Verbs which take an object are called* **trànsitive**. *Those that do not, like* come *or* go, *are* **intränsitive**. *Some verbs can be transitive or* **intransitive**, *accòrding to the sense; e.g.*

Birds fly (*intransitive*). Men fly àeroplanes (*transitive*). *Note that* lie (14) *and* rise *are intransitive only:* lay *and* raise *are only transitive. Examples:*

Don't lie on the wet ground.

The sun and the moon rise at different times.

Lay the ïnjured (2, 12) man gently on the ground. Raise his head a little.

165. *The personal pronouns* except *you* (Table 7) *change in form when they are the object of the verb. They are then said to be in the* **objëctive càse.** *When a personal pronoun is the subject of the sentence, it is said to bè in the* **nominative** *(6) case. The personal pronouns, and* who,* *are the only words in English which change their form in this way. See and learn Table 19.*

TABLE 19

Personal Pronouns: Case

Nòminative		*Objèctive*	
WHO (9)	sees	WHOM (9)?	
I	see	YOU	(*2nd person*)
You	see	ME	(*1st, singular*)
We	see	HIM	(*3rd, singular, masculine*)
He	sees	HER	(*3rd, singular, feminine*)
They	see	US	(*1st, plural*)
We	see	THEM	(*3rd, plural*)

(It *is the same in both cases*)

Always use the objective case after prepositions, e.g. to, from, on, in, by, with, of, between, etc. *Examples:* Give that to me. Between you and me.

Reflëxive Prònouns

166. *When the subject and the object of a verb are the same person, we use the* **reflëxive prònouns,** myself, yourself, himself, *etc. for the object. Examples:*

I löse MYSELF in a stränge cìty. (*Stress:* I lòse myself)
Enjòy YOURSELF. Behàve (13) YOURSELF! (singular)
Nöbody can sëe HIMSELF as òthers see him.
A wöman löoks at HERSELF in a mìrror.
A cät wáshes ITSELF, and amùses itself.
We drÿ OURSELVES with a tòwel.
Dön't decèive (1) YOURSELVES. (plural)
Söme people kïll THEMSELVES with wòrry (10).
Note: Twö pëople mèet EACH OTHER. Möre than two people mèet ONE ANOTHER.

* Who *often remains unchanged even when it is the object. Use* whom (*a*) *when you wish to emphasise that you are referring to the object* (e.g. Who beat whom?) *or* (*b*) *after a preposition.*

167. *Use* myself, yourself, *etc. also to give emphasis to the subject, e.g.*

Whö drïves this càr? Ï drïve it. I drïve it mysèlf.
Yoü are a páinter? Höw ìnteresting! Ï am a päinter mysèlf. I päint mysèlf. *i.e.* Ï päint tòo.
He cüts his häir himsèlf. *i.e.* He cuts his own hair.
I thïnk you are wròng mysélf | — thät is mỳ opïnion. Yoü yoursèlf are quïte süre you are rìght.

Direct and Indirect Object

168. *In 163 (b)* a car, a house, *this sentence are* **direct objects.**

(*a*) *The verb* ask *can have two direct objects, e.g.*

I ask $\begin{cases} \text{a question. 'What is the price?' I ask the price.} \\ \text{somebody. I ask the shopkeeper.} \\ \text{somebody a question. I ask the shopkeeper the price.} \end{cases}$

But note: I want a loaf. I ask the baker for a loaf.

(*b*) Call, make, appoint *can have a direct object followed by a noun in apposition to it, e.g.*

We call this material plastic.
We make the right man President.
We appoint him President for four years.

(*c*) *Other verbs take a direct object and an* **indirect object.** *Learn the following patterns:*

Pattern 1.

	Give	WHAT	To WHOM?
a.	„	this lëtter	to the mànager (4).
b.	„	it	to the manager.
c.	„	that letter	to me.
d.	„	it	to me.

Pattern 2.		*Indirect Object*	*Direct Object*
	Give	WHOM	WHAT?
a.	„	the mänager	this lètter.
b.	(Do not use the equivalent to Pattern 1 b.)		
c.	„	me	that letter.
d.	„	me	it.

169. *If you have to choose between Pattern 1 and Pattern 2 in 168:*
(a) *put the emphasis at the end; e.g.*

Gïve this lëtter to the mànager (to nöbody èlse).
Gïve the mänager this lètter (nöt thät bòok).

(b) *put the longer phrase after the shorter one; e.g.*

Gïve   thïs létter | to the Mänager of the Nätional (4) Bànk.
Gïve   the Mánager | thëse thrëe ürgent lètters.

170. (a) **Where is your book? Shòw me.**
     What is your name? Tell me.

The indirect object can stand alone, without a direct object, after
show *and* tell.

(b) **Spëak Ènglish (Tälk sènse, Expläin this sèntence) to me.**
    Expläin to us höw this machïne wòrks. Expläin it.

Use speak, talk *and* explain *with Pattern 1 in 168, but not with
Pattern 2, nor with the pattern in 170 (a).*

171. *Learn the examples in 163–170, and make up other examples on
the same patterns.*

172. *Fill each gap with a suitable pronoun so as to make sense:*

(a) This box is too heavy. I can't lift —. Please help —.
(b) I can't lift it —. Perhaps — and — can lift — together.
(c) It's no use. There are too many books in —. Take some of —
out.
(d) Let — help — now. — can do — together. Let — both try.
(e) Whose books are — ? Yours and mine. — belong to —.
(f) Stop that man! Hold —! Don't let — go!
(g) We know —. — is a thief. — gives — a lot of trouble.
(h) One of our tyres is flat. — can mend —? We can mend — —.
(i) Be careful! — is very muddy. Don't make — dirty.
(j) I like her, and — likes me. In fact, — like — — very much.
(k) We trust them, and — trust —. — trust — — completely.
(l) We want to hear the news. Read — to —. Tell —. Explain —.
(m) I need those papers. Find — and bring — to — at once.
(n) Your friend is not well. — must take care of —.
(o) Some people take too much care of —. — are selfish.
(p) The police are outside. — want to come in. Let — come.
(q) Listen to the news. — is important. The people are worried. —
want to know the truth. [50]

173. Bring, fetch, give, hand, lend, òffer, owe (17), pass, pay, prömise (6, 2), read, sell, send, show, take, teach, tell, throw, wish, write.

Use these verbs and the patterns in paragraph 168 to make up 20 sentences with the words or phrases given below. Use a different verb every time, and supply to *if necessary:*

(a) a cup of coffee, me
(b) the truth, them
(c) it, him
(d) a rope, the man on the quay*
(e) your tïcket, the tìcket-collector
(f) some flowers, your wife
(g) that newspaper article, us
(h) my clothes, the dry-clèaners
(i) your mother, the bread
(j) some money for a hàir-cut, him
(k) a letter of thanks, your host (17)
(l) that piece of string, me
(m) the money, the cashíer (18), not to me
(n) a Häppy Nëw Yèar, you all
(o) English, your students
(p) a shìlling, you
(q) your paper, the exàminer at the back of the hall
(r) something to drink, your visitors
(s) you, an apòlogy (6)
(t) the way to the garage, Mr Bàiley (13, 2) [20]

174. Say *means* 'speak a word or words', *or* 'make a statement'. Tell *means* 'give information, or an account of something, to some-body'. Tell *fits into Patterns 1 and 2 in paragraph 168,* say *only into Pattern 1. Fill each gap with* say *or* tell:

(a) — 'She sells sea-shells.'
(f) Can you — me the time?
(b) — us the latest news.
(g) Don't — that story to me.
(c) — the inspëctor the truth.
(h) Be quiet. Don't — that.
(d) Please — that again.
(i) Why? Because I — so.
(e) — good-night to your parents.
(j) Do what I — you.

175.   **Gët a tïcket for mè. Gët me a tìcket.**

Use the two patterns in 168 (but using for *instead of* to) *with:*

(a) Get, a chair, Mr Rose; (b) Fetch, that new book, me; (c) I'll buy, it, you; (d) Order, a copy, yourself; (e) Can you build, a house, us? (f) No, but I can make, a cake, you; (g) Will you find, a seat, Mary? (h) Yes, and I'll pick some roses, her. (i) I'll choose a few red ones, myself. (j) Save some, me. [10]

* *Pronounce* [kee].

Adverbs

176.　　a. Wïpe the wïndscreen clèan. Këep it clèan.
　　　　b. You must sëe the röad clèarly.
　　　　c. Be careful. Drive slowly and change gear carefully.

Clean, *in a., is an adjective (see 86) saying what condition the windscreen must be in.* Careful, *in c., is also an adjective, saying what your behaviour must be like.* Clearly, slowly *and* carefully *are* **adverbs,** *saying how you must* see, drive, *etc. An* **adverb of manner** *tells how the subject acts. As a general rule, form adverbs of manner by adding* -ly *to an adjective. Note the spelling when the adjective ends—*

in -l: èqual (1), èqually; careful, carefully;
in -le, *preceded by a consonant:* able, ably; gentle, gently;
in -y: happy, happily; gay, gaily; day, daily;
in -ic: scïentìfic, scïentìfically; äutomàtic,* äutomàtically;
in -e: *follow the rule, except with* true, truly; whole, wholly (17).

Exception: adjective, good; *adverb,* well.

177.　**That is a lïkely evënt—it will pröbably (6) hàppen.**
　　　A friendly man acts in a friendly way (or friëndly mànner).

When an adjective already ends in -ly, *e.g.* fatherly, friendly, likely, *use an adverb formed from a word of similar meaning, or use an adverbial phrase. However,* early *can be used as an adverb as well as an adjective:* An early riser rises early.

178.　　　**A läte stärter ïs a përson who stärts làte.**
　　　　　This is härd wòrk. We must trÿ hàrd.
　　　　　A fäst rünner rüns fàst. Aïm hïgh. Lïe lòw.

Late, hard, fast, high, low, far, near *are used both as adjectives and as adverbs. However,* we can speak highly of someone, i.e. praise him; *and* a story can be highly amusing, i.e. amusing to a high degree. Lowly *is an adjective referring to a low position in society.* Hardly *and* nearly *are adverbs of degree (see Table 9); and* lately *means* 'in rëcent (1) times'.

179.　*Adverbs are, as a rule,* 'compared' *like the longer adjectives in Table 12.*

Positive:　　　I write carelessly.
Comparative: You write more quickly.
Superlative:　John writes the most neatly.

* *Pronounce 7, 12, 4, 2.*

Exceptionally, the adverbs late, hard, fast, high, low, near, *also* early *and* soon, *are compared like the shorter adjectives in Table 12.*

I get up early, and work hard.
You get up earlier, and work harder.
John gets up the earliest, and works the hardest.

Special cases: well, better, best; badly, worse, worst; far (*as in Table 12*).

180.   **A fäir jüdge jüdges fàirly.**
          A cäreful cär driver drïves a cär càrefully.

Use one of these patterns with: a more careful driver; a dangerous driver; a hard worker; a cheerful giver; a fast runner; a faster runner; a simple writer; a good writer; a bad writer; a worse writer; the wisest judge; a friendly adviser; an able ruler; true lovers; a harmless weed killer; a clear speaker; the clearest speakers; a patient listener; a scientific explorer; a good football-player; a faithful follower; slow starters; heavy cigarette smokers; a natural actor; late comers; early risers; earlier risers; the gentlest players; the highest bidder; an honest money-changer. [30]

181.   (*a*) *An **adverb of place** tells us where the activity takes place;* e.g. We have our meals *here.* We have them *in the garden.*
        (*b*) *An **adverb of time** tells us when; e.g.* Summer begins *today.*
        (*c*) *An **adverb of quantity** or **extént** (cf. Table 9) tells us to what extent the activity is performed; e.g.*

He eats *enough,* drinks *very little* and sleeps *too much.*
Stop *a little.* I can't do *more.* I can't go any *farther.*

Note that little, a little, much *and* far *are compared as in Table 12.*

(*d*) *An **adverb of degree** tells us how far an act is completed; e.g.*

He *hardly* says a word. In fact, he can *hardly* speak.
I *quite* understand. I *fully* agree.
I can *just* hear you. I can *nearly* reach the ceiling.

(*e*) *An **adverb of fréquency** or **relative time** tells us how often or at what distance of time an act is performed; e.g.* àlways, gènerally, ùsually, òften, sòmetimes, sèldom, ràrely, nèver; soon, rècently (1). *Note:* soon, sooner, soonest; oftener *or* more often.
(*f*) Still, yet, already; *examples:*

At 10 o'clock. Your coat is wet: so is mine.
At 10.15. Yours is already dry. Mine is still wet: it is not yet dry.

182. *An adverb can also modify a numeral, an adjective or another adverb, e.g.*

It is *about* six o'clock. You are *very* kind, *too* good, *äbsolütely* rìght. You do that *very* well, *really most* carefully. In fact, you're *räther* wònderful, but you're not quick *enough*.

183. *Fill each gap with a suitable adverb, so as to make sense of each group of sentences:*

(a) Your writing is not good —. You must do —.

(b) You are — fat. You eat — —. Eat —.

(c) John is — good. He — does his work —, though he is — — slow. He must work —.

(d) George — brushes his teeth properly, and he — forgets to brush them at all.

(e) The tank is — empty. There is — any water in it.

(f) Now it is — empty. It is — dry.

(g) In northern Europe, it gets dark — in summer. It is — light at nine o'clock. But it gets dark — in winter: it is — dark at five. It is three o'clock now. It is not dark —.

(h) Bring the paper a little —. I can — read it. [25]

Position of Adverbs

184. (a) **You spëak Ënglish vëry wèll.**
   Yòur plàce is thère. Thère is your plàce.
   We have a hòliday todäy. Todáy we have a hòliday.

DO NOT PUT ANYTHING BETWEEN THE VERB AND ITS OBJECT. Put all adverbs, except those of degree and frequency, after the verb and after the object. However, adverbs can also be placed at the beginning of the sentence, especially to give emphasis or to provide a setting in place or time for the statement that follows.

   (b) **It öften ràins here, but it's nëver vëry còld.**
   You must älways täke a ràin-cöat with you.

Put adverbs of degree and frequency before the verb if it consists of a single word, but after the verb to be, *and between a modal verb and its infinitive. See also examples in 181 (d) and 181 (f). Often can come at the end of a sentence, for the sake of emphasis; and sometimes can come at the beginning of the sentence as well as at the end. Yet often comes at the end. Examples:* It rains here often. Sometimes you must wear rubber boots. It is not dry yet.

93

(c) **We häve our mëals hère nöw.**
We üsually ëat in the gärden in sùmmer-time.

If an adverb of place and an adverb of time occur in a sentence together, put the adverb of place first.

(d) **You are quïte rìght. I drïve töo quìckly.**

When an adverb modifies an adjective or another adverb, put it before the word it modifies. However, put enough *after an adjective or adverb; e.g.* That is nöt gòod enoügh. You dön't wrïte clèarly enoügh.

185. *In the following sentences, put a suitable adverb of degree or relative time in the normal position:*

(*a*) Aeroplanes land here.   (*b*) They arrive at midnight.
(*c*) They arrive on time.   (*d*) They fall in the sea.
(*e*) We can see Mars.   (*f*) We have a fog in winter.
(*g*) It is time to go home.   (*h*) I agree with you.
(*i*) We must be serious.   (*j*) You take life seriously. [10]

The General Aspect and the Continuous Aspect of the Verb

The Ordinary Present Tense (as in Table 17, first column).

We write with a pen or pencil.

186. *Fill each gap with a suitable verb:*

(*a*) We — on our own feet.   (*b*) We — with our teeth.
(*c*) We — with our tongue.   (*d*) We — air into our lungs.
(*e*) We — on chairs.   (*f*) We — up ladders.
(*g*) We — things with knives.   (*h*) We — photographs with a camera.
(*i*) The sun — in the east.   (*j*) It — in the west. [10]

187. *Repeat the following as a dialogue. Speaker A gives a command, Speaker B obeys, completes the action and speaks at the same time. Then A repeats the command, B obeys it again but without speaking, and C comments on B's action.**

A. Shüt your bòok!   B. I shüt my bòok.   C. He shuts his book.

Continue with: Put it down. Stand up. Open the door. Now shut it. Switch on the light. Switch it off. Sit down. Pick up your book. Open it. Put it on the table. [10]

* See note.

188.   **We üsually gö öut on Sùnday.**

Fill each gap with a suitable word or phrase:

We always — on Monday. We generally — on Tuesday. We occasionally — on Wednesday. We often — on Thursday. We sometimes — on Friday. We never — on Saturday afternoon.

189.   *Use the Ordinary Present Tense of the verb to express the idea of*

(*a*) *the activity in general (186);*

(*b*) *an act completed at the time of speaking (187);*

(*c*) *a whole series of acts repeated regularly, occasionally, often, always, etc., in present time (188).*

Note: this Tense is a 'simple' one, i.e. it is composed of one word only.

The Present Continuous Tense

190.   *Repeat the following as a dialogue. A gives a command, B obeys it and speaks WHILE THE ACTION IS IN PROGRESS, i.e. after the action starts and before it finishes. Then A repeats the command, B obeys it again and C comments while the action is in progress.*

A. Löok öut of the window. B. I AM LÖOKING öut of the window.

C. HE IS LOOKING out of the window.

Continue with: Walk round the room. Touch your chin. Rub your eyes. Do that again. Speak English. Watch my hand. Move your head. Think of a number. Hold this watch to your left ear. Listen to it. Write your name and address. Look at page 24. Read it. Draw a map of Africa. Put in the chief rivers. [15]

191.   *The Present Continuous Tense is a compound one composed of the Present Tense of* be (*called the* **auxiliary**) *plus the form of the verb ending in* -ing. *The* -ing *form is called the* **present pàrticiple** *when it is used in this way. In form it is the same as the gerund (154) and it remains unchanged. See the footnotes to 154 and 158, and spell the present participle of:* run, rub, move, write, rain, hold, put, begín, refér, occúr, prefér, súffer, trável, beliéve, intèrpret.

Note: try, trying; applý, applÿing; die, dying; lie, lying.

192.   **We are bùsy. WE ARE HÄVING a lèsson.**

Use this pattern in the 1st Person Plural with: learn, English; study, for an exäminàtion; do, our best; make, good prògress; get better;

95

impröve (9), all the time; grow, older. *Begin with different introduction instead of* 'We are busy'; e.g. Don't worry (10), *or* We're tired. *Repeat with* you are —, he is —, she is —, they are —.

193. (a) **I üsually gët üp at sèven, | but I AM GETTING UP at six thïs wëek, | to revïse for my exäminàtion.**

Repeat with: we, George, Mary, George and Mary.

(b) **The people next door ARE ALWAYS QUARRELLING.***

Repeat with: that child, playing the piano; old man, asking for money; you, looking at the clock; vïsitors, börrowing my bòoks; I, trying to gët them bàck.

194. *Use the Present Continuous Tense to emphasise the idea of:*

(*a*) *activity in progress (190, 192).*
(*b*) *a temporary habit (193 a).*
(*c*) *a constant, unending habit (193 b).*

Note the idea of incompletion expressed by this tense: in (a), the activitity is still in progress, not complete; in (b), we are not concerned with a regular habit, but with a temporary one—a partial series of acts; in (c), the habit is unending and therefore incomplete.

195. *We can imagine activity in progress more easily with some forms of activity than with others. We can easily imagine it with* look, listen, work, study, play, walk; *less easily with* switch on a light, shut a book, see, hear, know, remember. *You can apply Exercise 190 to* look *and* listen; *but do not apply it to the verbs in 151 (b) when they refer to receiving an impression on the senses, nor to* like, love, want, *nor the verbs in 151 (c). Use these words only in the Simple Present Tense until you can appreciate the subtleties of meaning which are expressed when they are used in the Present Continuous. Note the difference between:* You are having a lesson (*emphasis on activity in progress*) *and* You have brown eyes (*no such emphasis*).

Interrogative and Negative

196. *Learn Table 20. Form 20 questions on each of these patterns, using different words from those in brackets.*

(*a*) *Then form questions to get the following answers:*

Yes, I'm ready. Yes, I can see it. Geòrge is äbsent. At home. No, he's nöt ïll. No, we're not late. The Smïths are. Yes, we must stop

---

* *quárrel* (6), *quàrrelling;* cf. *travel, travelling* (158 b).

TABLE 20

Questions

Auxiliary and Modal Verbs

Statements	Questions to identify the subject	All other Questions Put the verb before the subject.	
I am (sorry).	Whò is (sòrry)? (Ì am.)	ÄM I (làte)?	WHY AM Ì (so tired)?
I am (study)ing.	Whò is (study)ing? (Ì am.)	ÄM I (màking prógress)?	WHÄT AM I (dò)ing?
We are (go)ing.	Whò are (gò)ing? (Wè are.)	ÀRE WE (móv)ing?	Whère ARE WE (gò)ing?
(Dinner) is (ready).	Whàt is (rèady)? (Dìnner is.)	IS (DÌNNER rèady)?	Whèn IS (DÌNNER rèady)?
You can (say that).	Who can (sày that)? (Yoù can.)	CÄN YOU (sày thàt)?	Höw CAN YOU (sày thàt)?
He must (buy it).	Whò must (bùy it)? (Hè must.)	MÜST HE (bùy it)?	What MUST HE (bùy)?

now. No, you can't go yet. John can. Yes, it's most useful. The clòck is bröken. Yes, it's warm inside. Because it's snowing. He must wrïte a repòrt. My name is —. I am very well, thank you. I am twenty-two. The time is half-past six. The date is August 8th. [20]

(b)   **What are you doing? I'm studying.**

Form questions to get the following answers:

He's washing. They're playing tennis. Yes, we're moving fast. She's eating a peach. No, we're working. They're going to a football match. I'm making a radio set. No, I'm making a radio set. Because I want to do it. Because it is a useful language. Because I've no chair. Because this story is so funny. [12]

197. **A. Thëre is your bàg. Ïs your bäg thére? Whÿ is your bäg thère?**
B. There is plënty to dò. Ïs there müch to dó? Whÿ is there plënty to dò?

Use the two question-patterns in (A) or the two in (B), with each of the following:

(a) Thëre is my wàtch. (b) There is some brëad on the tàble. (c) Here is the doctor. (d) Here are the police. (e) There is a policeman at the door. (f) There are some soldiers at the gate. (g) There are the soldiers. (h) There are a lot of people in the street. (i) There are several good plays to see. (j) There are the tickets. [10]

198. *Learn Table 21. Using the patterns in Table 21, form questions to get the following answers:*

Yes, I know the Joneses. Yes, I like them very much. They live next door to me. They both drive their car. Carefully. He wàlks to his öffice. They stay at home, or sometimes go to the theatre. Because they like it. They see actors. The play lasts about two hours. I speak Italian but not Spanish. Yes, I wear glasses for reading. No, I never smoke. Yes, he smokes cigars. He smokes a cigar after dinner. They want clothes. H-U-R-R-Y. It means 'go quickly'. That book costs thirty shilliÿgs. I read ten pages in an hour. [20]

199.   **a. Häve you a péncil?* Dö you häve a péncil?**
b. Dö you häve súgar in your cöffee?

With have, follow either Table 20 or 21 when have means possess. Follow Table 21 only when have is used in other senses. Form questions on pattern (a) or (b) to get the following answers:

Yes, thank you, I have a cup. No, thank you, no sugar. Yes, please

* *Or, informally,* Have you got a pencil?

98

TABLE 21

Questions: 'Full' Verbs

Statements	Questions to identify the subject	All Other Questions Put do or does before the subject, and put the infinitive of the full verb after the subject.	
I play the piano.	Who plays the piano? (I do.)	DO I play well?	What DO I play?
We want Robert.	Who wants Robert? (We do.)	DO we want Richard?	Whom (or who) DO we want?
You speak English.	Who speaks English? (You do.)	DO you speak English?	Why DO you speak it?
They catch fish.	Who catch fish? (They do.)	DO they catch fish? DO fishermen catch fish?	Where DO they catch fish?
He plays.	Who plays? (He does).	DOES he PLAY?	What DOES he play?
It hurts.	What hurts? (That does.)	DOES it HURT? DOES the injection HURT?	Whom (or who) does it HURT?
He tries.	Who tries? (He does.)	DOES he TRY?	How DOES he TRY?
She sings.	Who sings? (She does.)	DOES she SING?	When DOES she SING?

plenty of milk. Yes, I have some writing paper. No, I have no envelopes. Yes, here are the tickets. I have my bath in the morning, not at night. Yes, I have a bad cold.

200.　　**Whïch is bìgger, the sún or the mòon? The sùn ïs.**
Whö can änswer this quèstion? Ì cän.
Whät flöats in wàter? Wòod döes.

Using these patterns form questions and answers to them from the following statements.

(*a*) Charles is away today. (*b*) Doüglas (10, 12) and Rälph are àlso awäy. (*c*) Frank knows where they live. (*d*) Hënry and Dönald (6) lïve nëxt dòor to them. (*e*) We must äll dö our bèst. (*f*) Ëxercise is gòod for us. (*g*) Föod këeps us alìve. (*h*) Yöur car göes fäster than mìne. (*i*) Yöurs has a bëtter èngine. (*j*) Ì have a späre kèy. (*k*) You are right. (*l*) Thìs word is wrong.

Indirect questions

201.	*Direct*	*Indirect*
a.	**Whö ìs it?**	**I dön't knöw whò it ïs.**
b.	**Häve you a máp?**	**I wönder if you have a màp.**
c.	**Äre you rëally enjöying yourself?**	**Äsk him whëther he is rëally enjòying himsëlf.**

In statements in English the subject normally comes before the verb. In the 'other questions' in Table 20, the verb comes before the subject: in other words, we have inversion of the subject and the verb. In the 'other questions' in Table 21, the auxiliary do *precedes the subject. In indirect questions, as in the examples at the beginning of this exercise we return to the normal order, subject and verb. Notice that the question in example (a) does not require the answer* Yes *or* No; *in example (b) the questioner expects a clear answer* Yes (or No); *in example (c) the questioner feels that the answer is in doubt. Form indirect questions beginning with the words in the right-hand column:*

(*a*) Where are we? I have no idea.
(*b*) How are you today? Tell me.
(*c*) Are you better? Everyone is asking.
(*d*) Do you want something to eat? Tell the nurse.
(*e*) How high is that mountain? I wonder.
(*f*) How far is it to the top? Ask the guide.
(*g*) Is there a good view? Who knows.
(*h*) Can we get back before supper? I doubt (it).
(*i*) Whose camera is that? Does anyone know?
(*j*) Does anyone want this old camera? It is hardly worth asking.

TABLE 22

The Negative

Auxiliary and Modal Verbs

Formal or emphatic	Informal either	or	Negative—Interrogative* Informal	Formal or emphatic
I AM NOT...	I'm not...	—	AREN'T I...?	AM I NOT...?
You are not...	You're not...	You aren't...	Aren't you...?	Are you not...?
He is not...	He's not...	He isn't...	Isn't he...?	Is he not...?
We are not...	We're not...	We aren't...	Aren't we...?	Are we not...?
They are not...	They're not...	They aren't...	Aren't they...?	Are they not...?
My brother is not...	My brother's not...	My brother isn't...	Isn't my brother...?	Is my brother not...?
I HAVE NOT...	I've not...	I haven't...	HAVEN'T I...?	HAVE I NOT...?
He has not...	He's not...	He hasn't...	Hasn't he...?	Has he not...?
I CANNOT...	I CAN'T (5)...		CAN'T I...?	CAN I NOT...?
I MUST NOT...	I mustn't (first t silent)...		Mustn't I...?	MUST I NOT...?

Imperative. Formal. Do not be... Do not have...
Informal. Don't be... etc. *Emphatic:* Don't you be... etc. Can *and* must *have no imperative.*

* *Examples of the Negative Interrogative:*
(a) Whý aren't you réady? (i.e. You're not ready. Why?)
(b) Isn't it 8 o'clock yét? (i.e. It isn't 8 o'clock—time is passing slowly.)
(c) Isn't it 8 o'clóck? (I think it is.)
(d) Isn't it hòt today! (It is very hot!)

TABLE 23

The Negative

Full Verbs

I DO NOT (run)	I DON'T (17) (run)	DON'T I (run)?	DO I NOT (run)?
HE DOES NOT (run)	HE DOESN'T (run)	DOESN'T he (run)?	DOES HE NOT (run)?

Imperative: Do not run. Don't run. Don't you run.

---

202. *Put into the negative, then into the negative-interrogative (formal):*

I am the Chairman.* You are a member of the Committee. She is the Secretary. They are all càndidates. This is in order. I can explain. We must speak for ourselves. We know it. He änswers lëtters règularly. The Committee agrees. [10]

(informal: give two forms when possible)

I'm good enough. It's working. You're looking smart. The news is bad. You can tell me. I must look. I believe it. That man drives fast. That man's a fast driver. This engine runs smoothly.

**203.   Ïs he älways ríght? He is nòt älways rïght.
Döes he öften compláin? He does nòt öften compläin.**

Put 185 into the interrogative, and then into the negative, with a suitable adverb of degree or relative time.

Do

**204.   What are you doing? I'm working. I'm mäking a càrd ïndex.
What do you do after supper? Sometimes I play cards.**

Answer the question What are you doing? *(or* What am I doing? *or* What is — doing?) *20 times, when emphasis falls on action in progress (see 194 a). Then answer the question* What do you do? *(or* What do I do? *or* What does — do?) *20 times with the following adverbial expressions to express the idea in 189 (c):*

in the morning, after breakfast, in the afternoon, in the evening, at night, on Sundays, on Mondays, at Christmas, in the holidays, at the office, in a library, in a shop.

* *Use a capital letter for* Chairman, Committee, *etc. when referring to a specific example.*

205.   I wàlk höme (I dön't rùn, | or gö by càr).
        I dò wälk | — you säy I dön't, but I dò.

Use do (*a*) *for emphasis* (I dò wälk), *to make an affirmative statement in contrast to a negative one; and* (*b*) *to avoid repeating another
verb* (You säy I dön't but I dò). *Read and study the following dialogue, filling in the gaps:*

A	B
I play the violin.	Sö do Ì, (i.e. I dö tòo.)
You write exactly like John.	Why, sö I dò! (What a surprìse!)
Your writing's just like his.	Why, sö it ìs! (You're right.)
You must try to write as John does.	But sö I dò. (Thät is whät I dö alrèady.)
You look tired.	— — — (You do too).
It's snowing.	— — — — (What a surprise!)
We wear gloves in winter.	— — — (We do too.)
George wears a scarf.	— — — (John — too.)
John must wear a scarf.	— — — — (That is what he —.)

206.   Ìs Jöhn búsy? I thìnk só. Yës, he ìs.
        Döes Märy spëak Frénch? I dön't thìnk sö. Nö, she dòesn't.
        Häve you äny móney? I hòpe só. Yès, I hàve.
        Cän you mëet me tonìght? I expèct só. Yës, I càn.

*Use one of these patterns with each of the following, using a pronoun
in the answer.*

(*a*) Is Mr. Jones in?   (*b*) Are we late?
(*c*) Are you all right?   (*d*) Do you see what I mean?
(*e*) Can you understand?   (*f*) Is Margaret waiting?
(*g*) Does she want some tea? (*h*) Can you all hear?
(*i*) Is today Wednesday?   (*j*) Does this coat fit me?
(*k*) Do bears like hóney (10)? (*l*) Can you come to tea today?
(*m*) Can you find the way? (*n*) Are these questions difficult?
              (*o*) Must we stop now?

207.   You äre pléased, áren't you? You ären't àngry, àre you?
        You täke sùgar, dòn't you? You dön't smóke, dó you?

Repeat first with a rising intonation (*asking for the answer* yes *or* no),
then with a falling intonation (*suggesting you feel sure your statement
is true*). *Then use one of the patterns* (*and either a falling or rising
intonation according to your meaning*) *with each of the following:*

I am right. He is kind. That isn't cheap. You mean that seriously.
You do trust me. Surely you don't believe it. We can see each other

103

sometimes. He plays beautifully. You aren't looking for this magazine. We must take care of our pàrents (19). [10]

208. **I have nö pèn, I have no ink, I have no books. (Räther fòrmal.)
I häven't a pèn, I haven't any ink, I haven't any books. (Möre införmal*.)**

Use both of these patterns in putting the following into the negative:

I have work to do. We have time to spare. I have a car. I have some oil. That child has a coat. This door has a lock. These flowers have water. There is a spare tyre in the boot. There are tools in the toolbox. I am making a complaint. [10]

209. **A single man is one who is not married.
An orphan is a child who has no father or mother.
A painless operation is one that does not hurt.
Unbreakable glass is glass we cannot break.**

Make up sentences, using a verb in the negative, to explain each of the following:

a läzy (13) màn
a blind beggar
a dëaf and dümb chìld
a false statement
dïfferent wàys
a nön-smòker
a nön-stöp tràin
unëqual (1) sïdes
undrïnkable wàter
an ïncomplëte ànswer

an impössible quèstion
an immövable òbject
irrëgular vèrbs
ëndless troùble (10)
a forgëtful pèrson
thöughtless pèople
tästeless fòod
a hëlpless ìnvalid
a pöwerless gòvernment
defënceless wòmen [20]

Negative Prefixes, etc.

210. **Thïs dësk is üntìdy (i.e. not tidy)**

Use the following in sentences of your own: uncertain, uncommon, unhappy, unhealthy, unnatural, unnecessary, unwise, incomplete, ïmpolïte, impossible, irregular, illegal.

211. *Study these two aspects of the negative:*

(a) He does not obey me; i.e. he does not act as I tell him to act.
He disobeys me; i.e.   he acts as I tell him not to act.

* *More informally still.* I haven't got a pen, I haven't got any ink, etc.

(b) I put up a ladder, and take it down; i.e. I revërse the procèss.
Men build houses, and deströy them later.
We do work, and ündö it àfterwards.
We dress in the morning, and undress at night.
We fasten the door, and unfasten it next day.
The stars appëar, and dìsappear.

Passages for Reading, Study and Dictation

212. Sümmer on a Grëek Ìsland

Èvery däy and àll dáy, | the sün shïnes döwn fïercely from a clöudless skỳ. We begïn wörk èarly, | with the fïrst mörning light, | while it is stïll compäratively còol. By twö o'clóck, | the hëat is sö överpówering | that it is ünwïse to lëave the shäde or dö ánything | excëpt slèep.

To gët to our hŏuse, | we must clïmb a hündred stëep and wïnding (14) stéps | üp from the hàrbour. Our wälls are immënsely thïck and hìgh, | with fëw wïndows, | äll quïte öut of rëach of the gròund. We fästen the dŏor | —ünnëcessarily in thëse dáys— | with hëavy ïron róds | which höok ïnto ïron rïngs in sölid ròck. Insïde, | the wälls of the stäirs are cövered with gúns, swórds* and öther remïnders (14) of wàr.

Yét, | at this móment, | I am sïtting on the térrace, | löoking at the möst péaceful scëne you can imàgine. It is gëtting làte, | and the töwn is alrëady in shàdow (4, 17). I am fïrst wríting, thën löoking at the vïew. To my léft, the läst glöw (17) of sünset is dÿing behïnd the möuntains on the màinland. A cöol brëeze blöws ïn from the sëa and fäns my chèek. Alöng the närrow päth belŏw me, | a strïng of müles is retürning from some dïstant pärt of the ìsland. The squäre whïte-washed höuses, lÿing quïetly on the hìll-sídes, | are türning grèy, | and the grèy is grädually dïsappëaring into the därk bàckground. A lìght appèars; | and anòther. Nöw I can önly sëe päle yëllow stärs on a bläck vëlvet cùrtain. A rèal stär, | päle whíte, | shïnes abòve (10).

I gët üp to türn ön my öwn light, | but stòp. Behïnd the grëat rŏck, | a thöusand fëet hìgh, | on the öther sïde of the tŏwn, | the skỳ is gröwing whïter and whìter. I wàtch, | and súddenly | a whïte fläme bürsts over the skỳ-lïne. Surprïsingly quíckly, | hälf a mŏon, | thrëequàrters of a móon, | the füll möon itsèlf rïses. It rësts for a mòment, | äfter its clìmb, | on the hìll-top; then detáches itsëlf, | flöating like a ballöon in the àir.

* sword (7)—w silent.

The chürch clöck strìkes. Óne, twó—it is strïking èight. I smell frësh fïsh cöoking on chàrcoal, | and fëel hùngry.

213. Tea

Tëa is not sïmply an òrdinary drïnk. It is a mätter of táste and cèremony.* Chöose göod tèa-leaves | —gréen, brówn or bláck, as you lïke— | and këep them in an äir-tight contàiner, | prëferably in a tìn. Pöur (20) püre (y, 21) frësh wáter into a clëan kèttle, | nöt into a säucepan whère you cöok àny kïnd of föod. Mäke süre the tëa-pot is èmpty, | clëan and drỳ. Mäke cërtain that nöne of these utënsils have the hörrible täste of söap or detèrgent.

Püt the kéttle on, | fìrst. Wärm the pòt. Këep it wärm and drỳ. Püt the tèa-leaves ïn. Püt ïn öne téaspoonful | for èvery twö cüps of tèa. Höw füll must the tëaspoons bè? Thät depènds on your tàste, | and on the strëngth of the tèa. Këep the pöt besïde the kèttle. As söon as the wäter is rëally bóiling, | and whïle it is stíll böiling, | pöur a lïttle ön to the tèa-leaves. Püt the lïd on the tëa-pot and waìt a möment. Then ädd möre of the böiling wäter untïl the pöt contäins as múch as you nèed. Wäit föur or fïve mínutes, | but këep the pöt hòt.

Nöw the tëa is rèady. Söme people drïnk it äs it ìs; | söme with lémon, or súgar, or bòth; öthers with mílk, or sùgar, or bòth. In any cäse, there is nöthing lïke a göod cüp of tèa.

TESTS

214. *Fill each gap with a suitable word, counting* don't, *etc. as one word:*

(*a*) I see, you see, he —; they go, she —; I do, he —; you say, he —: they can, she —; I dress, he —; we must, he —; I have, he —; we try, she —, he doesn't —.

(*b*) Where is the door? There — —. And the stairs? There — —. Shut the door; shut — quietly. Climb the stairs; climb — slowly. Listen to the speaker; listen to —; — — very interesting. Listen to the bells; listen to —; — ·— unusually clear this evening.

(*c*) Please — quiet. Move —. — make such a noise. I can — hear myself speak.

(*d*) He speaks very good English. He speaks English — —. He has a careful pronunciation. He — his words —. But he is too quick. He speaks — —.

(*e*) (advice, advise, practice, practise) What must I do? What is

* cèremony: four syllables (3, 2, 12, 2).

your —? What do you —? You must —. Do an hour's — every evening.

(*f*) (lie *or* lay) Don't — on the wet floor. Get up. — your head on this cushion.

(*g*) That picture is not — —. Can you — (rise *or* raise) it?

(*h*) (say *or* tell). — me, how do you — this in English? Can you — me the time?

(*i*) (do *or* make). You — too many mistakes. You must — better than that.

(*j*) (show *or* explain). Please — me how to do this work. — me. Please — this word to me. — it. [50]

215.   **I do not see myself as others see me.**

Repeat this sentence beginning with "you do not see yourself . . . ; *then with* he, she, we, you (*plural*) *and* they.

216.   *Answer each question with a complete sentence:*

(*a*) What are you doing at this moment? (*b*) Are you reading a novel? (*c*) Do you understand what you are reading? (*d*) Where do you come from? (*e*) What are you sitting on? (*f*) Can you tell me the weight of the sun? (*g*) How often do you have an English lesson? (*h*) Are you making good progress? (*i*) Do you always correct your mistakes? (*j*) Are you trying to answer this question correctly? [10]

217.   *Put the following sentences into the interrogative:*

(*a*) You're tired. (*b*) You need a rest. (*c*) You can go to sleep. (*d*) The guests are here already. (*e*) There is no one to receive them. (*f*) You have a bath every day. (*g*) I have a towel. (*h*) The bath's getting cold. (*i*) It holds a lot of water. (*j*) You advise me to wait.

218.   *Form 3 questions for each of the following answers:*

(*a*) George is working in a factory. (*b*) He must earn some money this week. (*c*) John drives a car carefully. (*d*) Jane types her own letters. (*e*) There is too much traffic in the town. (*f*) I can go to the concert tomorrow night. (*g*) Ice melts slowly in winter. (*h*) The days are longer than the nights in summer. (*i*) I have a pain in my back. (*j*) We have an English lesson every day. [30]

219.   *Put the sentences below into the negative:*

(*a*) (*formal*). Please apòlogise! I understand. A worker works for nothing. He can live on air. A vòluntary worker expects payment. He

107

is interested in profit. Does he deserve a reward? You realise the difficulties. There are very many. I have something to say. [10]

(b) (*informal*). Drop that vase! It's raining. I think so. Do you want some cake? I have a plate. We have chicken for dinner every day. We can wait. You must be impatient. You look well. I'm feeling very well. [10]

220. *Arrange the following groups of words so as to form a complete sentence with the proper word-order:*

(a) you, very, well, English, speak.

(b) the moon, can, we, see, very, sometimes, clearly.

(c) I, hardly, that, question, myself, answer, can.

(d) that, sense, sentence, make, not, does, quite.

(e) What, you, in, the holidays, do, do?

(f) in the summer, to the sea, we go, usually.

(g) Who, his friends, sends, good wishes, at Christmas?

(h) You, not, are writing, that, enough, carefully.

(i) We, no, have, often, lessons, on Saturday.

(j) strangers, your private business, do not tell. [10]

5. RELATIONS IN SPACE AND TIME:
POSITION AND DIRECTION

Prëposìtions

221. (a) *PRËPOSÏTIONS*, like to, at, from, *exprëss compärative posïtions in späce and tìme. They often express*

————————→ mövement in óne dirëction

←———————— mövement in the ópposite dirëction

O mövement in nò dirëction, or nö mövement at àll.

We can consider movement in relation to something which we imagine as having no dimension, or unspecified dimension, i.e. a point in space or time; or as something with one dimension, i.e. a line; with two dimensions, i.e. a surface; or with three dimensions, i.e. a space.

(b) *A preposition stands before and 'governs' a noun, noun-group (see 94) or pronoun; and nothing can stand between the preposition and what it governs. 'Governs' in this sense means 'express some relationship with the thing referred to'.*

(c) *Certain verbs express movement from one place to another, e.g.* come, go, walk, run, bring, send, *and such verbs are therefore associated with prepositions which indicate movement. Other verbs suggest no movement from place to place, e.g.* stay, wait, live, stand, sit, lie, *and such verbs are associated with prepositions which do not indicate movement.*

222. *Study Table 24 and refer to it often.*

Relätions (13) in Spàce

Mövement from pläce to pláce, | or nò mövement from pläce to pläce.

223. **Gö to the dòor. Wäit at the dòor.**

Fill each gap with to *or* at:

(a) Come — my room. (b) Run — the gate. (c) Stand — the gate. (d) Sit — the table. (e) I must send this — my lawyer. (f) He is waiting — his office for it. (g) Bring the answer — my house. (h) We buy sugar — the grocer's. (i) The grocer sells sugar — his shop. (j) He sells it — his cùstomers. [10]

TABLE 24

Prepositions

Relations in Space

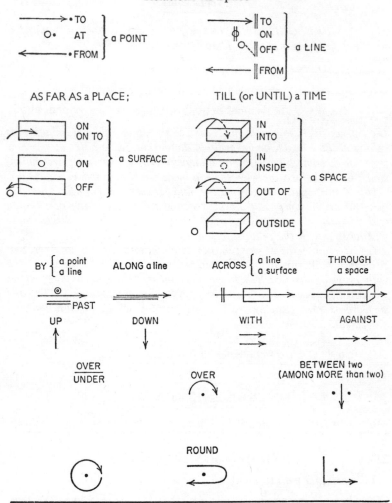

to, at, from

224.   Come to this spot. Go to the window. Gïve thät to mè.
This road leads to the fròntier.

TO *ïndicates mövement approaching a pòint, a place (i.e. a point on a map), a person or thing, or a line. Note:* Go home.

Wait at this spot. Meet me at the airport.

At *ïndicates no mövement in relation to a point or place. Note:* Stay at home.

A river runs from the mountains to the sea.
It flows away from the mountains.

From *indicates movement, the opposite of approaching; or separation. The idea of separation is often strengthened by the use of* away *before* from, *especially when* to *is omitted.*

225. *Supply* to, at *or* from:

(a) You can change your money — any bank. Why not go — the bank now?

(b) Send this parcel — my house. I live — number 30.

(c) My car is — the door. Take it — the garage.

(d) Take that knife away — him and bring it — me.

(e) How far is it — here — the next 'bus stop?

(f) Many visitors come — our town and stay — the Grand Hotel.

(g) This road leads — the coast. It ends — Ashton.

(h) I am sitting — my desk, writing a letter — Cècil.

(i) We escape — danger, or others rescue us — it.

(j) We spend the week-end — home and return — work on Monday. [20]

226. *With* speak, talk, listen, belong, *we are interested in the direction of the action and use* to; *with* arrive, look, aim, shoot, laugh, shout, *we are interested in the final point of the action and use* at. *With* point *and* throw *we can use either* to *or* at *according to where we want to put the emphasis. Supply* to *or* at:

(a) Look — me and listen — what I am saying.

(b) Give that — me. It doesn't belong — you.

(c) A train travels from place — place and arrives — its destination.

(d) Throw the ball — Jane, but don't throw it — her.

(e) A compass needle points — the north. We aim — a target.

(*f*) Don't point — other people. Don't laugh — them, and never shout — them.

(*g*) I walk — work and arrive — my office at nine o'clock. [15]

on, off; in, into, out of, outside

227. **Put your book on the table. Don't run on the flòwer-bëds.**
Sit on the grass, on the side of the road. I am on my way home.

On *indicates movement approaching a surface; or movement or rest when an object has reached a surface or a line, and is supported by it.*

Hëlp me lïft this hëavy bóx | ön to the chàir.

On to *emphasises the idea of movement ending on a surface, or the effort of making that movement.*

Take your feet off the chair.
We're not on the right road—we're a löng wäy òff it.

Off *indicates movement, the opposite of approaching; or separation.*

Now put your book in the drawer. Don't run in school.
Stay in your class-room. *Note:* **Write in English.**

In *indicates movement entering a space; or movement or rest when an object has entered a space and is enclosed by its limits.*

Run into the shelter, then lie flat.

Into *emphasises the idea of movement entering a space.*

Take your book out of the drawer again.

Out of, *movement, the opposite of entering.*

There is a telephone box outside our post-office.
There are also three telephones inside the building,
but you can only use them when the post-office is open.

Öutsìde = not in; **ïnsìde** = not outside.

228. *Supply* on, on to, off, in, into, out of, inside *or* outside:

(*a*) Put this — the floor, — the chair, — your pocket, — your head, — the cupboard, — the kitchen, — the terrace, — the glass, — the wall.

(*b*) Take it — the floor, — the chair (*continue as in* (*a*)).

(*c*) We swim — water; a ship floats — the sea; an aeroplane flies — the air; we ride — horse-back, and ride — a 'bus.

(*d*) You can easily jump — a hole, but you can't jump — it so easily. You can easily fall — a roof, but you can't climb — it so easily.

(*e*) It is freezing — the house. It is much warmer — it. Come — the hall. [30]

229. (*See* 227) *Put* into *or* on to *whenever possible in the following examples; otherwise* in *or* on:

Stand — the platform. Step — the ladder. Dive — the pool. Drive — the town. He is asleep — bed. Slip — bed. Take a seat (i.e. sit down) — the waiting-room. Take these papers — the waiting-room. Help me lift this box — the kitchen, and that one — the roof. [10]

230. *Fill the gap with* at *when you are thinking of a place or a point on the map*, on *when you are thinking specially of a surface*, in *when you are thinking specially of a space or area. Say:* at the beginning, at the end, in the middle.

(*a*) A train arrives — a station. Our friends arrive — the platform. We arrive — the city. A plane arrives — an airport. The plane starts from Páris (4), calls — Beirút (13, 9), and stops — Hongkong.

(*b*) I was born — Wimbledon. I live — Greece. My brother lives — London.

(*c*) There are three buttons — my coat, and a handkerchief — my pocket.

(*d*) — table, we sit — a chair. After lunch Mother rests — an armchair and goes to sleep.

(*e*) — many countries, all children go to school. They stay — school until they are 14 or 15.

(*f*) It is raining hard; we must stay — school today.

(*g*) When we read a book, we start — the beginning. We don't stop — the middle, we finish it — the end. [20]

by, alòng, acròss, through

231. **I pass by your house on my way to work. I go past it. Come and sit by me (*or* besìde me). Let's walk along by the river.**

By *indicates movement passing a person, place or thing; or either movement or no movement at the side of a person or thing.*
Past *emphasises the latter part of the* by *movement and means 'by and farther than' the thing referred to.*
Beside *emphasises the idea of 'at the side of'.*

Imägine a ràilway lïne | rünning alöng the cóast, | göing acröss a ríver, | then acröss a wïde pláin, | throügh a dëep fórest | and throügh a löng tùnnel.

Alòng, *movement following a line;*
Acròss, *movement from one side of a line or surface to the other, at the same level;*
Through, *movement into and then out of a space.*

232. *Fill the gap with* by, past, along, across *or* through:

On my way home, I walk a hundred yards — the street, go — a wide ávenue (3), — the muséum,* into the park, right — the park, — the gate at the other side, — the bank of the river and — the river to the other side. I pass — some old trees, walk — a narrow path — the railway line, and then take a train. [10]

---

up, down; with, without, against; between, among, etc.

233. **Up, down,** *e.g.* We climb up a hill. If we are not careful, we slide down a slippery slope.

With *indicates movement in the same direction as something else, accòmpanying* (10) *it; e.g.*

Please come with me, I don't want to go alone.
The alphabet starts with A and ends with Z.
Join forces with us.

But note: fight with, quarrel with, argue with.

Withòut *indicates that one thing is not accompanied by another; e.g.*
I don't want to go without you.

Agàinst *indicates movement in opposite directions, so that two forces meet in öpposìtion; e.g.*

I can't swim against the current. Don't lean against the glass.

* y + 8, 1.

Òver, *movement or no movement; e.g.*

We have a roof over our heads to cover us.
A horse can jump over a fence.

Ünder, ündernèath: *movement or no movement; e.g.*

It's raining—but I am shëltering ünder my umbrèlla; *i.e.* my umbrella covers me. It's raining hard—get right underneath the umbrella.

Round (or **aròund**), *e.g.*

I wear a belt round my waist, and a collar round my neck.
My house is just round the corner.

About, *movement or no movement, suggests* 'on all sides', 'in different places'; *e.g.*

The world about us.

Betwèen (two), *movement or no movement; e.g.*

My desk is between the door and the window.
Choose between life and death. Divïde this möney betwèen you
(*two*).

Amòng (10) (more than two). Share it among you (*more than two*).

234. Other relationships in space

For *indicates the öbject or pùrpose of the* to *movement; e.g.*

This train is going to Istanbul: it is the train for Istanbul.
I am giving this present to you: it is for you. I'm sorry for you.
We ask (call, care, hope, long, look, send, wait) for something.
Note: What are you doing that for? *i.e.* Why are you doing it?
For what purpose? What is this thing for?

Towàrds (7) *indicates movement in the direction of a point; e.g.*

Be careful—there is a car coming straight towards us.

As far as *emphasises the extent of a movement; e.g.*

Walk with me as far as the end of this road.

In front of; behìnd (14); *e.g.*

There is a small garden in front of our house, and a larger one behind it.

Òpposite; *e.g.*

I am on this side of the table, you are on the opposite side. You are opposite me.

115

Near, *i.e. at a short distance from a place; e.g.*

Our house is near the sea. Yours is nearer the town.

Next to, *i.e. nearest to, the nearest thing to; e.g.*

I don't like rough wool next to my skin.

Beyònd, *to or at a farther point.*

Don't go too far: don't go beyond your limits.

Abòve (10), *i.e. at a higher lèvel* (3); *e.g.*

Keep your head above the water.

Belòw (17), *i.e. at a lower level; e.g.*

It is very cold—ten degrees belöw frèezing pöint.

235. *Fill each gap with one of the prepositions from 233 or 234.* (*A 'preposition' may consist of two or three words*):

(*a*) My brother and I work well togèther. He works well — me, and I can't work — him. (*b*) He and I divide the work — us, though sometimes we divide it — several people. (*c*) In these days, people often travel — the world. (*d*) We can fly from London to Tokyo — the North Pole. (*e*) In stormy weather, aeroplanes fly — the clouds. (*f*) It is a long way to Rome. We cannot walk — Rome; but we can go some way — it. (*g*) There is a train leaving — Rome soon. (*h*) The train goes farther than Rome. It goes — it. (*i*) When we read, we hold the book — us. (*j*) The back of the chair is — us, and the floor is — our feet. (*k*) The chair and the floor provïde us — support. (*l*) Ask — what you want, and hope — the best. (*m*) I can't find my purse. I am still looking — it. (*n*) In football, two teams play — each other. The rëferëe (3, 12, 1) warns them — foul play. [20]

Relations in time

236. *Study Table 25 and note the following examples:*

to, till (or until)

The lïbrary (14) is open from 9 to 5 (or from 9 till 5). It is open till 5. *Use* till *when* from *is omitted. The librärian (19) stays till 6. The activity continues through a period ending at that time.*

from, since

The library is open from 9 daily. *Use* from *although* to *is omitted.* It has been open daily since 1946. *Use* since *to mean 'through a period starting at that time in the past'.*

TABLE 25

Prepositions: Relationships in Time

T = a point or period of time

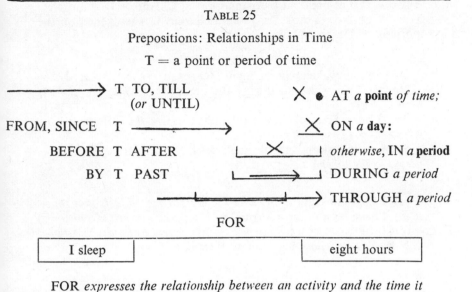

FOR *expresses the relationship between an activity and the time it lasts.*

before, by, till

We cannot start our journey before 5 (*i.e.* earlier than 5). It's too dark before then.

But we must be on our way by 6 (*i.e. in the progress of time ending not later than then*).

We shall not arrive till 7 this evening. (*Our journey will end then.*)

Certainly, we shall not be there by 6. (*We shall arrive after 6.*)

after, past

If we arrive after 8 (*i.e. if our arrival takes place later than* 8) all the hotels will be full.

It is now half-past 11, past my usual bedtime (*i.e. time, in its progress, has gone beyond 11, etc.*).

at, on, in

The library opens at 9 on every day of the year, except on Sunday.*

It is open in the day-time, in the morning, in the afternoon, in the evening, in spring, in summer, in autumn, in winter; in January, in February, etc. It was opened to the public in 1946, on March 14th.

* On *is frequently omitted*, e.g. the library is open every day except Sunday.

117

It is closed at night, at Christmas (*or* on Christmas Day), at New Year (*or* on New Year's Day) and at Easter. It was opened on the morning of March 14th.

in, during, through

Do you ever wake up in the night? (*i.e. at some point in that period*)
Do you ever wake up during the night? (*i.e. while the night is progressing*)
Yes, I often lie awake during the night. (*Here the activity of lying awake is also progressing.*)
Some people sleep right through the night. (*From one end of the period to the other.*)

for

(*a*) I sleep for eight hours every night. (*My sleep lasts that time.*)
(*b*) I have been ill for a fortnight. (*My illness has lasted that time.*)
(*c*) I will be away for three weeks. (*My absence will last that time.*)
N.B. *You may omit* for *in these examples.*

for, before

We shall not arrive before 6 o'clock.
It is now 4 and we shall not arrive for two hours. (*Do not omit* for *in this case.*)

for, in, within

My father walks for half an hour every morning. (*His walking lasts that time.*)
He walks to his office in twenty minutes. (*His walk to the office is completed by the end of that period.*)
I can walk that distance within twenty minutes easily (*i.e. inside the limits of that period*).
John will be home in five minutes (*i.e. at the end of a period lasting 5 minutes from now*).

237.   *Fill each gap with one of the prepositions from 236:*

(*a*) I was born — five o'clock — the morning, — February 3rd. I have lived here — 1956.
(*b*) I was born — the morning of February 3rd, — winter.
(*c*) The sun shines — the day-time, the stars shine — night.
(*d*) Tuesday comes — Monday and — Wednesday.
(*e*) I go to bed — ten, sleep — six, or half — six. I never wake up — the night, but sleep right — it.
(*f*) We start work — eight — the morning — the summer, and finish — one, except — Saturday, when we work — half — twelve.

(g) I study — three hours every day — October — April. So I study — the autumn and all — the winter.

(h) Go on working — lunch-time. Finish this exercise — then. If you finish it — then, start the next. In any case, work quietly — the next hour.

(i) Mr. Taylor is out. He will be back — a quarter of an hour.

(j) Can you keep your head under water — two minutes?

(k) I want to buy some food. The shop closes — 6. So I must get there — 6. I cannot get there — 5.30 but that gives me enough time.

(l) We started learning English — 1966. It is now 1968. We have been learning it — 1966, — two years.

(m) We shall go on studying it — a long time yet. [40]

Relationships of a more abstract kind

238. **Of** *.
We get coal from the earth. Bricks are made of earth or clay.

(a) *While* from *expresses the idea of physical movement or separation,* of *expresses a relationship of a more general or abstract kind.*

(b) Of *expresses the relationship between a part and the whole, a member and the whole body, a quality and the thing possessing it; e.g.* A quarter of an hour, the cause (7) of the accident, the effèct of it; a member of a socìety (12, 22, 2), the heat of the sun.

(c) Of *indicates* **rëference** *to something in thought or speech; e.g.* Think of a number. We are thinking of you (*i.e.* you are in our thoughts). We were speaking of George (*i.e.* refèrring to him). What do you think of Kàtherine? (*i.e.* What is your opinion of her?) Everyone speaks well of her.

About *indicates general treatment of the subject-matter of thought, e.g.* A book about bees. Think about your work, don't talk about it. We know (speak, ask, write, agree, worry, dream, care) about something.

On *indicates a more exact treatment of the subject-matter; e.g.* A book (a lecture) on the phÿsical effècts of spàce trävel. Can we now agree on a dëfinite propósal (17)?

By *indicates the agent or means by which something is done or produced; e.g.* A book by a fämous (13) aùthor. Made by hand. Travel by train. Häppen by chànce.

* *Pronounce of as* [ov].

119

With *indicates the instrument or mànner; e.g.*
Write with a pen, with care. (*See also 233.*)

For *indicates exchànge; e.g.*
How much do you pay for a new pair of shoes? Thank you for
your kind attention.

Like *indicates comparison; e.g.*
Open the window. This room is like an oven. It is more like a Tur-
kish bath. A noise like thunder. He runs like lightning.

As (*i.e. in the capacity of*); *e.g.* He acts as a father to me.

Excèpt; *e.g.* Everyone is ready except you.

Instèad (3) **of;** *e.g.* I don't want to go to the concert. You go instèad
of me.

239. *Fill each gap with one of the prepositions from 238:*

(*a*) Today, we can travel — road, — rail, — sea, — air. We can
still go on foot or on horseback. A train works — steam, — elec-
trìcity, or — dìesel (1) ëngine. Evënts öften häppen — àccident.

(*b*) Workmen work — tools. Döctors perförm öperätions — ìn-
struments. In these days, people no longer fight — bows and arrows,
but they still fight — one another.

(*c*) I know a little — wild flowers, but I want a good book — the
subject — a real expert. Can I change this book — another one? In
other words, can I have another — this one?

(*d*) Scïentists discüss their sübject with öne anòther. They ärgue —
it, and sömetimes agrèe — it, but they sëldom agrëe — a fïnal (14)
ànswer.

(*e*) I often think — (*i.e.* remember) your family. Tell me — them.
Do you get letters — them? What do they think — your discòvery?
Will you get any reward — it?

(*f*) Give me three gallons — petrol, please, — the red pump.

(*g*) What are these chairs made — ? A special wood that comes —
South America. Each set — chairs is made — one tree. They are all
made — hand.

(*h*) There is a good view — the town — the hill, and a good view —
the hill — my window.

(*i*) I dön't emplöy a làwyer. My bròther äcts — my läwyer. How-
èver, he doesn't write — a lawyer: he doesn't use long words.

(*j*) John travels half rate, — a student. He doesn't always look —
a student: he is too tidy. [40]

Some special cases

240. (a) *Prepositions after verbs:*

We *accüse* pëople *of* döing wròng.
We *appröve* (9) *of* whät is right.
We *belïeve in* the pëople we trùst. We häve *fàith in* them.
We often *blame* others *for* our own faults (7).
We *call on* people when we visit them.
The police *charge* wrongdoers *with* their crimes.
We *compare* one thing *with* (*or to*) another.
I *congrätulate* you *on* your succèss.
Cover these things *with* a cloth. They are *covered with* dust.
Lët us first *decïde on* whät we wànt. Thät *depënds on* whät there ìs.
Fill this bottle *with* water. It is now *full of* water.
Forgïve me *for* interrùpting. I don't want to *ïnterfëre with* you—I
mean *interfere in* your discussion: but may I *join ìn* it?

(b) —*after adjectives:*

We are *afräid of* the dárk, *ashämed of* our wéakness, nöt älways
cërtain *of* the trúth, *fönd of* pléasure, *füll of* stränge idëas and ím-
pulses, *guïlty of* mäny érrors, *jëalous* (3) *of* öther pëople's succèss and
nöt älways *süre of* succèss oursèlves. We can get *rid of* some of these
faults, but not all of them. Each one of us is *different from* his neighbour, and each is *interested in* himself. We wänt to be *fämous for*
sòmething. Are you *tired of* this? Then let us go on with the next
subject.

(c) —*after nouns:*

Trÿ to änswer these quèstions: mäke an *attèmpt at* them.
Whät is the *effëct of* a bräke *on* a machine?
Whät *ïnfluence* dòes a göod fäther häve *on* his chìldren?
Höw can he këep *contròl over* them?
Dòes he täke *cáre of* them?
Whät is your *opïnion on* (*or* about) cäpital pùnishment?
Häve you äny *ínterest in* this mätter, or any doúbt aboüt it?

241.   **Whëre are you gòing to? Tö a mèeting.**

*Fill each gap with a suitable preposition. Then answer the question
with a phrase beginning with the same preposition, as in the model.*

(a) Where do you come —?   (b) What are you sitting —?
(c) What are you looking —?   (d) Who is this book —?
    (*this book*)   (*author*)
(e) What is it —? (*subject*)   (f) What language is it —?

(g) What are the words printed —?

(h) What are you talking —?

(i) Who are you talking —?

(j) What do you write —? (*pen*)

(k) What is your pen full —?

(l) Who does it belong —?

(m) What is bread made —?

(n) Where do we get flour —?

(o) What do we use bread —?

(p) What do we cut bread —?

(q) What are you afraid —?

(r) What are you laughing —?

(s) What are you waiting —?

(t) What are you listening —?

(u) Who is the present —? (*sender*)

(v) Who is it —? (*receiver*)

(w) Which room do you work —?

(x) Which desk do you sit —?

(y) What condition is your book —?

(z) What letter does the alphabet end —?

Test using various prepositions

242. *Fill each gap with a suitable preposition. (A 'preposition' may consist of more than one word.)*

(a) I must call — the Mayor,* then get my ticket — the trável ägency (13), and then go — the bank. My appöintment — the Mayor is — ten minutes. Can you call — a taxi?

(b) There is no need — a taxi. The Mayor's office is only — the corner. The travel agency is — this side — it, the bank is — the other. The Mayor's office is — the travel agency and the bank. — other words, the bank is just — his office.

(c) — the bank, we can go straight — the street — the library. The library is therefore — bank. It is open — four hours — the morning, — nine — one, every day — Sunday. — the afternoon it is open — six, but not — Saturday.

(d) Now walk — me — the university. Or is that too far? Then come — the next cross-roads.

(e) I have a better idea. — that, let's have a drink — this cafe. We'll sit — this table. Tell me — your family. How much do I owe — two cups of coffee?

(f) Thank you — the drink. There's nothing — a good cup — coffee.

(g) John, you've done very well. I congrätulate you — süch a succëssful resùlt. I'm very proud — you. But you haven't much influence — your brother.

(h) George, I must be hònest — you. I am not happy — your work.

* *Pronounce as* [mare].

It is full — mistàkes. You dön't täke enoügh ìnterest — it. I höpe you're ashàmed — yoursëlf.

(i) Jane, there's no doubt — it. You have mèasles. You're covered — spots. You must stay — bed and we'll send — the doctor. Take care — yourself.

(j) People need a roof — their heads, and firm ground — their feet. A swimmer must keep his head — the surface — the water: a diver must not go too far — it. How can a diver stay — the water — air? And how can he get — his suit?

(k) Where is the nearest hòspital, please? You see that garage, two hundred yards — here? Drive — it, but twenty yards — this side — it, turn right. The hospital is then a hundred yards — the road — your left. It's on a hill. Drive — the gate and — the slope.

(l) I don't want to quarrel — George. I'm very fond — him. I can't blame him — being what he is. I am, after all, respònsible — him. But we can't always combïne büsiness — plèasure. It depёnds —cìrcumstances.

(m) Shakespeare was born — Stratford, — 1564, — Saint George's Day. He livcd — 52 years, — 1616.

(n) — many parts — the world, people still draw water — wells. — big cities, they gct it — pipes which bring it — the ground — rèservoirs.* Draw a bucket — water — this well. What is the depth — the well?

(o) My opinion — this subjcct is different — yours. I am afraid I cannot agree — you. Apart — that, I have the greatest respect — your theories, but I think you are mistaking one thing — another. We must think — it again. In any case, can we decide — the date — our next meeting? Good-bye, then, — next Tuesday.

(p) Think — English — your English lesson. — it, remember what you have learnt. [100]

Ädvёrbiai Pàrticles

243. *Words like* on, off, in, up, down, across, through, *etc. can be used either (a) as prepositions which govern a noun, or pronoun, or (b) as adverbs telling us how or in what direction or position an action takes place. Examples:*

Preposition + *Noun or Pronoun*	*Adverbial Particles*
Come into my office.	Cöme ìn.
Stay in your room.	Stäy ìn.
Keep inside the house.	Kёep insìde.

* *Pronounce—voir (French) as* [vwar].

123

Don't go outside it.   Dön't gö outside.
Don't run across the street.   Wàlk acröss.
I pass by your house.   Every day, I päss bỳ.
Imagine you are walking along the road.   You are wälking alòng.
Step on the 'bus.   Stëp ön quìckly.
Jump off it.   Jümp òff agäin.

You may use the following words as prepositions, or as adverbial particles to indicate direction or position: on, off; in, inside, outside; up, down, across, through; over, under; by, along, past. *Do not use* to, at, from, *and* with *as adverbial particles.*

Note these special cases:

Preposition	Adverbial Particle
Go out of the room.	Gö òut.
Stand in front of the class.	Ständ in frònt.
Come away from the fire.	Cöme awày.

And note these adverbial particles:

Keep still: dön't rün abòut (i.e. in any or every direction).
Türn ròund: face the other way.
Türn òver: make the movement in Table 24.
Dön't gö awày: plëase cöme bàck.

And these uses of adverbial particles:

Is Mr. Smith in? I am sörry, he is òut.
Whät tïme do you gët ùp?
Are you still in bed, or äre you ùp?
There goes the bell—the lësson is òver (finished).
There is no more bread—there isn't any òver (remaining).
Upward(s), downward(s), forward(s), backward(s), *emphasise movement to a higher level, to a lower level, to the front, to the back; e.g.*

This arrow is pointing upwards ⟶ , this is

pointing downwards ⟶ , this is pointing

forwards ⟶, and this backwards ⟵ .

Use after *as a preposition,* afterwards (*i.e.* later) *as an adverb;* before *as both. Examples:* Do you read your newspaper before breakfast or after it? I have seen this before. I will see it again afterwards.

Üpstäirs *and* dòwnstäirs* *are adverbial expressions used only with the meaning* 'up, or down, the stairs in a building; on a higher or lower floor'.

244.   ÈNTER   = CÖME (or GO) ÌN
              ÈNTRANCE = WÄY ÌN

Enter *means* come (or go) in, *and* an entrance is a way in. *The choice is a question of style. Come* in *and* way in *are not only less formal but also more emphatic. In any case, the pattern of simple verb (or noun)* + *particle is very common in English. We often feel that the simple verb needs completion by an adverbial particle. Thus we wake up, pick something up, throw something away.*

245.   *Fill each gap with a suitable adverb from 243 and 244:*

(*a*) EXIT means 'way —'. 'Return' means 'go —'.   (*b*) The path to the sümmit is the way —.   (*c*) We go up the hill and — again. (*d*) We're on the wrong side of the river. How can we get —?   (*e*) A fence. How can we get —? A hole in the wall. How can we get —? (*f*) Don't come in here. Stay —. I don't want that. Take it —. (*g*) Let me see the back of your coat. Turn —.   (*h*) I can't walk any farther. I must go — now, and lie —.   (*i*) Why are you walking — all the time. Sit — and relàx.   (*j*) You're sitting on my hat. Get —. (*k*) When prisoners escape, they run —. The police hope to bring them —.   (*l*) There is an interesting article in that paper. I want to cut it —. Don't throw it —.   (*m*) When you see someone lying badly hurt in the street, do you stop or simply walk —? Do you try to pick him —?   (*n*) We are not getting — (*i.e.* making progress). In other words, we're not moving —. On the contrary, we're going —. (*o*) Old Mrs. Jones is in bed. Her room is above us. In other words, she is —, but she is not —.   (*p*) There is no food —, so the meal is —. (*q*) Show that to me after the lesson. I want to see it —.   (*r*) In which direction is the second arrow pointing in 243? —.

246. **Come to my office. My öffice is üpstàirs. Cöme üp to my òffice.**

We often emphasise the direction or position of an action by using this pattern. In the example given, up *is an adverbial particle,* to *is a preposition.*

Fill the gaps in (*a*) *and* (*b*), *then continue in the same way with the rest of the exercise:*

(*a*) Go to the basement. We are now upstairs. Go — — the basement. (*b*) Go to the post-office. It is on the other side of the street.

* *In isolation, pronounce* üpstàirs; dòwnstàirs.

Go — — the post office. (*c*) Then go to the bank. It is farther along the street. (*d*) Then go to the baker's. That is round the corner. (*e*) Go to the post-office again. It is bäck thère. (*f*) Put this on the roof. (*g*) Lay it on the floor. (*h*) Here is a wall. Jump to the other side. (*i*) Here is a hole. Crawl to the other side. (*j*) There is somebody hurt in the road. Don't pass on the other side.

Other uses of adverbial particles

247. **On** *can mean* 'fòrward' (——→); *e.g.* Gö òn (contìnue).

Up *can indicate a stop, e.g.* höld ùp (delay), gïve ùp (surrènder); *or it can indicate ar òusal, or the accëleràtion or complëtion of an action, e.g.* Hùrry üp, pläy ùp, ëat ùp.

In *can indicate collapse, e.g.* Give in.

Off *can indicate* 'off or away from a starting line'; *e.g.* Stärt òff (*or* sët òff) on a journey. We are off, *i.e.* we have started.

Out *can suggest a sudden or wide opening; e.g.* Bürst öut làughing. Sprëad òut; *or taking or digging something out of a mass of other things; e.g.* Hëlp me wörk öut the ànswer. Plëase pöint öut my mistàkes. Fïnd öut yöur òwn mistäkes; *or it can suggest disappearance: e.g.* Blöw öut the càndle. The fïre is òut.

248. *Fill each gap with one of the little words from 247:*

(*a*) Don't stop. Go —. You're holding everyone —.

(*b*) What is the answer? Don't give —. Work it — for yourself.

(*c*) Wake —. Hurry — and get — with your breakfast. Eat it —.

(*d*) I can't talk about it now, I'm just going — to a meeting.

(*e*) Please point — what we are doing wrong. We can't find —.

(*f*) You are all too close together. Spread —.

(*g*) In many countries, maläria (19) is now dying —; and scientists are thinking — höw to prevënt òther disëases.

(*h*) I can't hear you. Speak —. [15]

249.   **Wälk up the hìll. Pïck üp your hàt.**

Pattern A   Wälk up the hìll.

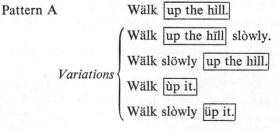

Variations {

Wälk up the hïll slòwly.

Wälk slòwly up the hìll.

Wälk ùp it.

Wälk slòwly üp it.

Pattern B   (i) Pĭck ŭp your hàt. (ii) Pĭck your hàt ŭp.

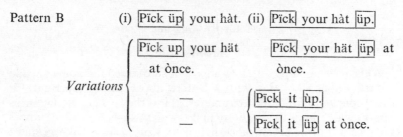

Variations

Pĭck up your hät at ònce.

Pĭck your hät ŭp at ònce.

—

Pĭck it ŭp.

—

Pĭck it ŭp at ònce.

In Pattern A, the verb walk *is intransitive and has no object;* up *is a preposition governing* the hill. *Notice that the preposition is not separated from the noun it governs, and that the adverb,* slowly, *comes either after the verb or after the prepositional phrase. In Pattern B, the verb* pick *is transitive and has an object,* your hat. Up *is a particle indicating the direction in which the action is performed. We might say that the verb is really* pick up. *But notice that the direct object can come either after* pick *or after* pick up. *If the object comes after* pick, *then* up *must come immediately after the object. Notice the position of the adverb* at once. *Notice, also, that if the object is a pronoun,* it, *then* pick it up *is the only possible arrangement.*

250. *Say whether the sentences below follow Pattern A or Pattern B in 249, or the pattern in 246. If a sentence follows Pattern B* (Pick up your hat) *then give its alternative form* (Pick your hat up):

(*a*) Put on your coat.
(*b*) Take off your hat.
(*c*) Sit on the cushion.
(*d*) Look at the pictures.
(*e*) Work out the answer.
(*f*) Walk out of the room.
(*g*) Walk up the road.
(*h*) Wake up the children.
(*i*) Drink up your tea.
(*j*) Go up into the gallery.
(*k*) Call for the doctor.
(*l*) Call up the doctor (*i.e.* telephone him).
(*m*) Set off on a journey.
(*n*) Put on the kettle.
(*o*) Call on the doctor.
(*p*) Look up the chimney.
(*q*) Look up this word.
(*r*) Give me back my wallet.
(*s*) Take away this rubbish.
(*t*) Take out your books.
(*u*) Write to Margaret.
(*v*) Bring along your friends.
(*w*) Run along the path.
(*x*) Swim across the stream.
(*y*) Throw over a rope. [25]

251. *In 249, there are 4 variations on Pattern A, and 5 on Pattern B. Provide similar variations for the examples in 250. Supply suitable adverbs: you need not choose a different adverb every time.*

Passages for Reading and Study.

252.   A Japanese Inn

At last the taxi turns up into a narrow side street and stops outside a dark wooden building with a lantern above the entrance into[1] a small courtyard full of shrubs and ferns; it is the *ryokan*, the Japanese inn, in which I am to spend my first few days in Tokyo. Glass doors slide back on to[2] an entrance hall a foot or so above the ground; women wearing kimonos kneel above the step, bowing their foreheads to the ground in salutation. We remove our shoes and step up on to the polished wooden floor and slip our feet into slippers which have neither heels nor backs, and one of the women leads us up steep bare wooden stairs into a corridor of similarly polished bare boards. There are sliding screens all down[3] one side and outside some are slippers. At the end she slides back a screen into[4] a tiny entrance hall, then slides yet another screen into[4] a room empty of everything except a low table in the middle. The floor is covered with what looks like finely woven straw matting. We discard our slippers and step into the room, on to the *tatami*. We sit on flat cushions on the floor, round the table.

Pick out all the prepositions and adverbial particles in this passage and study the meaning of them in the context. Note the following cases, marked by numbers in the text:

1. into: through the entrance, we go *into* a small courtyard.

2. back on to: the doors slide *back*, and are then open; this allows us to step up *on to* an entrance hall.

3. all down: as we go *down* the corridor, *i.e.* away from our starting point, we see that all of one side consists of sliding screens.

4. into: a screen covers an entrance through which we go *into* an entrance hall: and another screen covers an entrance through which we step into a room.

253.   As Others See Us

An African chief, whom I had often met in his native land, came to England for the first time when he was past sixty. He had never before left his own country—in which he held a high and responsible post—and he flew over to London in a few hours, from the home he knew so well, to a strange and over-crowded city. A friend of mine went to call on him the morning after his arrival. My friend asked the chief how he was and whether he was enjoying himself. The visitor said that he was feeling well, but that he had had a frightening ex-

128

perience that morning. He had gone, he said, for a walk round the streets and had found himself at Victoria Station. He said 'Naturally, I went in to see your trains. I stood near some iron railings, by an iron gate, to watch a train come in. It was there that I saw this frightening thing.' As the train came nearer and nearer to where I was standing, all the doors at one moment swung outward, and while the train was still moving, a great many men jumped out, quite silently, and began to run towards me. They carried umbrellas like spears, and their faces were set and unsmiling. I thought something terrible was about to happen, so I ran away.'

Well, there it is. There is your business train, the 8.50 or the 9.15 arriving at a London station. And there we are, as this elderly African sees us, on his first day among us.

Pick out all the prepositions and adverbial particles in this passage. Then answer the following questions, beginning each answer with a preposition or a particle, as in the example.

Example: **Where did the chief go to? To England.**

(*a*) Where had the speaker met him before? (*b*) How old was he? (*c*) Where did he fly? (*d*) Where did he fly from? (*e*) Who did the speaker's friend go to call on? (*f*) Where had the chief gone earlier that morning? (*g*) When had he gone for a walk? (*h*) Where did he find himself? (*i*) Where did he go then? (*j*) Where did he stand? (*k*) In which direction did the doors swing? (*l*) In which direction did the men jump? (*m*) In which direction did they begin to run? (*n*) How did they carry their umbrellas? (*o*) On which day did this happen?

6. ACTIVITY SEEN FROM VARIOUS ASPECTS OF TIME

The Ordinary Past Tense

254.   **I waited all last week for your letter
and only received it yesterday.**

I waited *and* I received *are in the* **Ordinary Past Tense.** *Use this
Tense when your point of view is a moment or period in the past separated from the present. An adverb like* yesterday, *or* last week, *shows
that the speaker's point of view is in the past.*

The Pre-present Tense

255.   **We have clïmbed a löng wày. We're nearly there.
I have clïmbed Füji ònce—I don't want to do it again.**

We have climbed, I have climbed *are in the* **Pre-present** (*or* **Present
Perfect**) **Tense.** *Use this tense when your point of view is the present
moment* (*e.g. the time when you say* 'We're nearly there, I don't
want') *but when you are looking back to action performed until or
before now* (*e.g.* We have climbed). *Our point of view is not at a
particular time in the past separated from the present: it is now.*

256.   *The Past is a 'simple' Tense. It consists of one word, i.e. a certain
form of the verb. The Pre-present is a compound tense, consisting of an
auxiliary* (*e.g.* have) *plus a form of the verb called the* **Päst Pàrticiple.**
*The Past Tense and the Past Participle of regular verbs have the same
form; and this form is the same for every person, singular and plural.
In the Pre-present, only the auxiliary changes, as in Table 15.*

Example:

Past Tense	Pre-present
I (you, he, we, they) climbed	**I (you, we, they) have climbed** **he has climbed**

257.   (*See Table 26*)   **I play**   (*1st Person singular, Present Tense*)
              he plays   (*3rd ,,   ,,   ,,   ,,*)
              he played (*3rd ,,   ,,   Past   ,,*)

Say and spell these three parts of the following regular verbs:

act, advïse, applÿ, attënd, close, clothe, bathe, beg, breathe, brush,
call, change, dance, fit, föllow, help, lïsten, own, paint, pass, refër,
smoke, süffer, trävel, use, vïsit, walk, wash, watch, wrap. [30]

TABLE 26
Scheme for Forming
the Past Tense and Past Participle
of Regular Verbs

Infinitive ending in	*e.g.*	*Past Tense and Past Participle*	*Note*
Soft sounds (*except*) d	play, call, raise, judge	played, called, raised, judged	*same number of syllables; ending in sound* d
Hard sounds (*except* t)	stop, work, dress, wash, touch, fix	stopped, worked, dressed, washed, touched, fixed	*same number of syllables; ending in sound* t
d *or* t *sound*	mend, want, fade, taste	mended, wanted, faded, tasted	*extra syllable, i.e. id*

Compare this with Table 18

Note: stop, stopped; prefer, preferred; try, tried; raise, raised. (See footnote to 87.)

Exceptions (*in spelling only*): lay, laid (*see* 164); pay, paid.

Irrëgular Vèrbs

258. *Irregular verbs in common use* (*to which Table 26 does not apply*) *are given in the lists below. Learn their* **principal parts** *in the tradïtional òrder—Infinitive, Past Tense, Past Participle:*

I. *Past Tense and Past Participle ending in* d

Infinitive	*Past Tense*	*Past Participle*
have (4)	had	had
hear (18)	heard (11)	heard (11)
make	made	made
say (13)	said (13)	said (3)
sell	sold	sold
spread (3)	spread (3)	spread (3)
tell	told	told

II. *Past Tense and Past Participle ending in* t

(*a*)	burst	burst	burst

(*like* burst: cost, cut, hit, hurt, let, put, set, shut, split)

(*b*)	bend	bent	bent

(*like* bend: lend, send, spend, build)

131

	Infinitive	*Past Tense*	*Past Participle*
(c)	burn	burnt	burnt

(*like* burn: learn, smell (smelt), spell (spelt), spill (spilt), spoil. *These six verbs have regular forms also*.)

(d)	(1)	(3)	(3)
	creep	crept	crept
	feel	felt	felt
	keep	kept	kept
	meet	met	met
	sleep	slept	slept
	sweep	swept	swept
	deal	dealt	dealt
	dream	dreamt	dreamt
	leave	left	left
	mean	meant	meant

(e)		(6)	(6)
	get	got	got
	lose (9)	lost	lost
	shoot (9)	shot	shot

(f)		(7)	(7)
	bring	brought	brought
	buy	bought	bought
	fight	fought	fought
	think	thought	thought
	catch	caught	caught
	teach	taught	taught

III. *Past Participle ending in* n

(a)	(17)	(9)	(17)
	blow	blew	blown
	grow	grew	grown
	know	knew	known
	throw	threw	thrown
also	fly (14)	flew	flown

(show, sow, sew—*see footnote*)

(b)	(7)	(9)	(7)
	draw	drew	drawn

show, sow and sew—*all three pronounced with vowel* 17—*have regular forms but the old past participles* shown, sown, *and* sewn (*all vowel* 17) *are still used*.

Infinitive	*Past Tense*	*Past Participle*
(c) (19)	(7)	(7)
bear	bore	borne
swear	swore	sworn
tear	tore	torn
wear	wore	worn

Mixed

(d) be	was* (6) were* (11)	been
do	did	done (10)
go	went	gone (6), (*or* been, *see* 265)
lie (*see* 164)	lay	lain

(lie, *meaning* 'tell an untruth', *is regular*)

see	saw	seen
shine	shone (6)	shone (6)

IV. *Past Participle with an extra syllable, ending in* n

(a)	(17)	(17)
freeze	froze	frozen
speak	spoke	spoken
steal	stole	stolen
break (13)	broke	broken
wake	woke	woken†
choose (9)	chose	chosen
(b)	(8)	(13)
shake	shook	shaken
take	took	taken
(c)	(17)	(2)
drive	drove	driven
ride	rode	ridden
rise	rose	risen
write	wrote	written

Mixed

(d) beat	beat	beaten
bite	bit	bitten
eat	ate	eaten
fall	fell	fallen
forgët	forgöt	forgòtten
give (2)	gave	given (2)
hide	hid	hidden
tread (3)	trod	trodden

* I was, he was; you, we, they were.   † Regular forms are also used.

V. *Vowel change only, without an added* d, t *or* n.

Infinitive	Past Tense	Past Participle
(a)	(3)	(3)
bleed	bled	bled
feed	fed	fed
hold	held	held
lead (1)	led	led
read (1)	read (3)	read (3)
(b)	(4)	(10)
begïn	begän	begùn
drink	drank	drunk
ring	rang	rung
sing	sang	sung
sink	sank	sunk
spring	sprang	sprung
swim	swam	swum
run	ran	run
(c)	(10)	(10)
dig	dug	dug
hang	hung*	hung*
stick	stuck	stuck
sting	stung	stung
strike	struck	struck
swing	swung	swung
win	won	won
(d) (14)	(16)	(16)
bind	bound	bound
find	found	found
grind	ground	ground
wind	wound	wound†
(e)		
come (10)	came	come (*see* 265)
sit	sat	sat
stand	stood (8)	stood (8)

259. *Learn the irregular verbs, a group or two at a time. However, you will remember them best by using them in exercises, noticing them in reading, and using them again in conversation and written composition.*

* *However, we say* 'Criminals used to be hanged'.
† *Do not confuse this with the regular verbs* wind (2) *and* wound (9).

Interrogative and Negative of Past and Pre-present Tenses

TABLE 27
Past Tense
Interrogative and Negative

I was, you were	Was I? Were you?	I was not.* You were not.*
I had	Had I?	I had not.*
I played	DID I play?	I DID NOT* play.

* *Contracted forms:* I wasn't, you weren't, I hadn't, I didn't play.

260. **He lòoked. Dïd he lóok? Yès, he lòoked. Nò, he dìdn't löok.**
He saw. Did he see? Yes, he saw. No, he didn't see.

Repeat with:

watch	remember	draw	bite	ring
notice	forget	paint	swear	knock
listen	fight	try	arrive	learn
hear	think	succèed	leave	teach
talk	sleep	know [25]	write	buy
speak	climb	understand	telephone	sell
go	fall	dive	ask	steal
come	wake	swim	answer	hide
win	walk	drive	sing	begin
lose	run	ride	drink	end [50]

261. **You älways sàid so. Dïd you ever sáy so? Nö, I nèver säid so.**

Repeat with the first 25 words in Exercise 260, using various adverbs of frequency and adding something suitable, in place of so, to complete the sentence.

TABLE 28
Pre-present Tense
Interrogative and Negative

I have bèen	Háve I bëen?	I have nòt* bëen
I have had	Have I had?	I have not had
I have played	Have I played?	I have not played

* *Contracted form :* I hàven't or I've nòt.

262. I have been (in many places). Have I been (everywhere)?
No, I haven't been (everywhere).

Repeat with first 25 words in Exercise 260, adding something suitable to complete the sentence.

263. We have älways bëen (sòmewhere). Häve we ëver bëen (hëre befóre)?
Nó, | we have nèver bëen (hëre beföre).

Repeat with the second 25 words in Exercise 260, using various adverbs of frequency, and adding something to complete the sentence.

Choice between Pre-present and Ordinary Past

264. A. I am writing a pòem (17 + 2). Have yoú ever written a pöem?
B. Yës, I hàve. I hàve written a pöem.
(*or* Nö, I hàven't. I've nèver written a pöem.)
A. When did you write one? B. I wrote one last week.

Make up similar sequences, beginning with the sentences below. Use different expressions of time in place of last week, e.g.

last month, last year, last spring, last summer, last autumn, last winter, the year before last, yesterday, the day before yesterday, two days ago, when I was a child (at school, on holiday).

(*a*) I am rëading a nòvel (6).
(*b*) I am making a cake.
(*c*) doing an expèriment (3).
(*d*) drawing a map of Japàn.
(*e*) teaching a class.
(*f*) building a wall.
(*g*) painting a picture.
(*h*) catching cold.
(*i*) eating a mèlon (3).
(*j*) wearing dark glasses.
(*k*) very angry with George.
(*l*) John drives a car.
(*m*) George rides a bìcycle (14).
(*n*) He swims in the river before breakfast.
(*o*) John runs a mile in five minutes.
(*p*) He speaks on the radio.
(*q*) Mary is using a typewriter.
(*r*) She wants a typewriter of her own.
(*s*) She has found a purse.
(*t*) Oh, I trod on a snake.
(*u*) I've bitten my tongue.
(*v*) I've torn my finger-nail.
(*w*) I fëll döwnstàirs yësterday.
(*y*) I've forgotten my mother's birthday.
(*z*) I've left my book at home.

A. (You are here now).
   Where have you been?

   Have you ever been $\begin{cases} \text{to Peking?} \\ \text{here before?} \end{cases}$

   Yes, I have. I've been $\begin{cases} \text{there once.} \\ \text{here before.} \end{cases}$

   When did you $\begin{cases} \text{go there?} \\ \text{come here?} \end{cases}$

   I $\begin{cases} \text{went there} \\ \text{came here} \end{cases}$ twenty years ago.

B. George has gone to Mexico.
   He has been to Spain.
   He went there first.
   Now he is in Mexico (or on his way there).

Use been *as the past participle of* go *when the goer has visited a place but is no longer there. Use* been *as the past participle of* come *when referring to a previous visit. Use the two sequences above, A and B, with other subjects (instead of* you *and* George*), other places and other expressions of time.*

266. a. Öpen the dòor, plëase. I've òpened it. (*Say this after the action is finished.*)

   b. Wäsh your hànds. $\begin{cases} \text{But I've wäshed them alrèady.} \\ \text{I've alrëady wàshed them.} \end{cases}$

   c. Häve you sëen the néwspaper? Yes, I've jüst sèen it.
   d. Has Chárles sëen it yët? No, he hàsn't sëen it yët.
   e. Höw löng have yoü bëen hère? (*i.e. until now*).
      I arrived at twelve o'clock. It is now three.

      I have been here $\begin{cases} \text{since twelve o'clock.} \\ \text{for three hours.} \end{cases}$

      (Since *marks the beginning of the pre-present period. Use* for *when you state the length of the period.*)
   f. Have you ëver döne this ëxercise beföre?
      Yès, | we've döne it ònce (twice, three times, etc.) beföre.
      No, | we've nèver döne it beföre.

Learn these models by heart and repeat them as a dialogue. Then give a suitable response to each of the following commands or questions, basing your answer on one of the models above:

(a) Shut the window.
(b) Put your elbows on the table.
(c) Take them off again.
(d) Shut the window.
(e) Go to the door and then go back to your place.
(f) Open the book at page 16.
(g) Find the 8th line from the bottom.

(*h*) Have you read this page be- (*i*) Turn to the next page.
fore?

(*j*) Read the first line. (*k*) Start reading page 17.

(*l*) Have you finished page 17? (*m*) Have you read the first line?

(*n*) (You're very slow) Haven't you finished page 17 yet?

(*o*) (You're very quick) Have you finished it already?

(*p*) Have you been to the dentist? (*q*) How long have you had this
book?

(*r*) Since when have you been able to read English?

(*s*) Think of a number and write (*t*) Here are five cards: choose
it down. one.

(*u*) Have we finished this exercise? [20]

267. (*a*) *Supply the missing verbs in a suitable tense:*

I did Exercise 266 yesterday, and performed certain actions. First
I — the window, then I — my elbows on the table and — them off
again. I — not — the window again, because it — shut already. But
I — to the door and then — back to my place. I — my book at page
16 and — the 8th line from the bottom. Then I — to the next page.
[10]

(*b*) *In the following passage, change* every day *to* this morning *(i.e.
earlier in the day, in time which you consider past) and make the necessary changes in the verbs:*

Every day, I wake up at about seven. I lie in bed and read for five
minutes. Then I get up, wash, get dressed, and have breakfast. I leave
my house at eight o'clock, walk down the road and buy a newspaper.
Then I catch a 'bus. I pay my fare, and the conductor gives me a
ticket. The 'bus takes a very long time, but fortunately I am not late.
[15]

(*c*) *Replace* today *by* yesterday, *and make other necessary changes:*

Today, I am not very well. Are you? And how is Thomas? And
how are the boys? It is rather cold outside, isn't it? This is an excellent tea. (*Change* this *to* that). These are delicious cakes, aren't they?
(*Change* these . . .)

(*d*) *Supply the missing verbs in a suitable tense:*

It — very wet yesterday, so I — indoors.

I — to you last week. — you — my letter?

— you — the latest news? Then listen.

— you — that shot (a moment ago)?

I — my leg last Thursday and — not — able to walk since.

Gandhi — born in 1869 and — in 1948.

— we — Exercise 264? Yes, we — it last week. [12]

Used to

268. **A father tells his children stories.** (*In the present*)
My father often told us stories when we were children. (*A past habit*)
Does your father tell you stories? (*In the present*)
He used* to tell us stories, but he doesn't now. (*Past habit: contrast with present*)

Use the Past Tense for repeated or habitual action in the past. Used to *emphasises the idea of habitual action in the past in contrast with present habit. Make up sequences, as in the examples above, beginning from the situations below. In the second line, supply a clause or phrase like* when we were children, fifty years ago, *etc.*

(*a*) Some mothers make their own children's clothes. My mother made our clothes herself . . .

(*b*) Some boys go to school by bus. I always went . . . Do you . . . ?

(*c*) Some people spend their holidays by the sea. We sometimes . . .

(*d*) Some people get up late. My parents usually . . . Do your parents . . . ?

(*e*) Some people keep money in a stocking. My grandmother . . .

(*f*) Some girls are shy. Jane . . . Is Ruth . . . ?

(*g*) One can wear a hat. Men always . . . Do they now?

(*h*) One can buy vegetables at the market. We generally . . . Does your wife . . . ?

(*i*) Choose your own ties. My husband . . . Does your husband . . . ?

(*j*) We find English very difficult. I . . . Do you . . . ?

269. **The Pre-present Continuous and Past Continuous**

Every day, I study from 8 o'clock till 12. It is now 9 o'clock.
I am busy. I am studying. I have been studying for one hour.
What have I been doing? (*Answer*)
Suppose it is now 10 o'clock. I am tired. Why?
Because I have been working hard.
Yesterday, at 9 o'clock I was studying.
At 9.15, I was still studying.
What was I doing at 9.30? (*Answer*)

* *In* use (*verb*) *and* used, *the* s *is soft; but in* used to, *the* s *becomes hard under the influence of the* t.

In present time, we use the Present Continuous Tense to emphasise the idea of action in progress, or uncompleted action, or the process rather than the act. In the Pre-present and the Past, we can use continuous tenses to make the same kind of emphasis. Repeat the sequence given at the beginning of the exercise, using rest, *then read* then *play the piano, and making other changes according to the sense. Then repeat the whole exercise, including the models, beginning:* Every day, you study . . . , *then* Henry studies . . . Ann studies . . . we study . . . the students study . . .

270. **It's 10 o'clock. It's raining. We can't go out.**
   It's 11 o'clock. The rain has stopped. But the streets are wet.
   Why? Because it has been raining.
   Why didn't we go out earlier? Because it was raining.

Learn the models. Then complete the following, using the words in parentheses in a suitable tense and answering all the questions:

(*a*) Why is the wall so hot? (sun, shine on it)

(*b*) Why are you out of breath? (run up and down stairs)

(*c*) Is your father very ill? (Yes: work, too hard)

(*d*) Mary plays that piece very well. (No wonder; practise, six months)

(*e*) What was Mary doing three weeks ago?

(*f*) What was your father doing before he fell ill?

(*g*) You are learning English. Suppose you started learning two years ago. How long (learn English) till now?

(*h*) We are waiting for the doctor. We got here half an hour ago, so (we wait) for half an hour. What (we do) ten minutes ago?

(*i*) What are you doing? What (you do) this time yesterday?

(*j*) It is time to stop. What (you do) for the last ten minutes? [10]

The Pre-past

271. *Just as you use the* **Pre-present Tense** *when you look back on time preceding the present moment and are interested in some event* **before or until now,** *so you can use the* **Pre-past Tense** *when you look back from some moment in the past and are interested in an event* **before or until then.** *For example:*

(a) **I saw Michael* on Sunday for the first time this year.**
   He had been ill: that is why I had not seen him for so long.

He had been (*contracted form:* he'd been) *and* I had not seen (*contracted form:* I hadn't seen) *are in the Pre-past Tense. Use that*

* *Michael:* pronounce [mike-l].

*tense to make it clear that Michael's illness and my not seeing him occurred **before** the meeting on Sunday. If you said* he was ill, *that might mean that Michael was ill on Sunday. Now notice this example:*

(b) **Michael was still resting: he had not gone back to work yet.**

Yet *means **either** before or until now, **or** before or until then, **and** is therefore associated with the Pre-present or Pre-past Tense. Here it means* until then, *and is therefore associated with the Pre-past. In the following example:*

(c)   **Did you pass your examination? No, I failed.**
         Yoü fáiled?* But you had wòrked sö hárd!

*I am chiefly interested in the fact that you failed, **then,** and that your hard work had come **before then.** I could also say* you worked so hard *in that context: in that case my interest moves back to the time when you worked. In example (c) the Pre-past Tense gives a certain emphasis but the meaning would be basically the same if we used the Ordinary Past in that context.*

272.   *Use the Pre-past Tense, therefore, when this tense is necessary for the kind of meaning in 271 (a) and (b), or when you wish to emphasise the idea of one past event being the **prelude** to another. It is not necessary to use the Pre-past Tense simply when events happen one after another. For example, we say:*

      Caesar came, he saw, he conquered.

In that case, our point of interest moves forward with each new event.

273.   (a) **We looked for him all day. Then we gave up the search.**
        We gave up the search. We had looked for him all day.
        Had we looked everywhere? No, we hadn't looked everywhere.
    (b) **We often went to the sea. Last year we went there again.**
        We went to the sea last year. We had often been there before.
        Had we always been to the sea? No, we hadn't always been to the sea.

Use one of these sequences with:

(*a*) We invited a lot of people. Then we gave a party.
(*b*) We ordered plenty of food. There was enough to eat.
(*c*) We usually rented a cottage. Last year we stayed in a hotel.
(*d*) My father was never ill till last year. Last year, he caught pneumonia (see 20).

      * *Notice this way of asking a question.*

141

274. *Put the verbs in brackets in the Past or Pre-past Tense:*
(*a*) We (arrive) at the station ten minutes late. The train (leave already).
(*b*) We (arrive) without our luggage. We (leave) it all behind.
(*c*) I (meet) the new President last night. I (not, meet) him before.
(*d*) I (never see) him before, but I (rëcognise) him at once.
(*e*) John (know) him already: he (meet) him several years before*.
(*f*) We (find) our guide at the foot of the cliff. He (fall) from the top.
(*g*) He (lay) there for several hours, and (be) nearly frozen.
(*h*) When we (have) a good sleep, we (feel) much better.
(*i*) When they (reach) the end of their journey, they (travel) four thousand miles, and (climb) mountains that no one (ever, explore).
[20]

Pre-past Continuous

275. **At 10 o'clock it was raining. We could† not go out.**
By 11 o'clock the rain had stopped. But the streets were wet.
Why? Because it had been raining.
Why hadn't we gone out earlier? Because it had been raining.

Look at 270 and put the model for it into the Past or Pre-past Tense, as above. Then do the same with all of 270. Begin (g) with: 'This time last year'. *Begin (h) with:* 'This time yesterday'. *Begin (i) with:* 'This time yesterday' *and continue* 'the same time the day before'.

The Ordinary Future Tense

276. **Today is Monday. Tomorrow will be Tuesday. It will not be Wednesday. Will it be Thursday? No, it won't be.**

*Form the **Ordinary Future Tense** with **will plus the infinitive**. Contracted forms:* I'll, you'll, he'll, she'll, we'll, they'll. *Interrogative:* will I? *etc. Negative:* will I not *plus infinitive; contracted form* won't (17) I, *etc. Use* will *and* won't *for all persons, singular and plural. The Future can also be formed with **shall** plus the infinitive, **in the first person singular and plural**, e.g.* I shall see you on Thursday: we shall see each other then. *However,* will *is widely used for all persons and it is not a 'mistake' to use it with* I *and* we.

---

* *Say* ago *to mean* back from now; *but* before *to mean* back from then.
† Can *in past narrative becomes* could (8: 1 *silent*). *Negative,* could not: *contracted form* couldn't. Can *has no infinitive or past participle.*

277.   **A. Answer the telephone.   B. I'll answer the phone.**

Repeat, as a dialogue, with:

Write down this message. Take it to the captain. Tell him it's urgent. Don't make any mistake. Please come at once. Don't go. Carry this parcel for me. Find me a seat. Bring me a glass of water. Don't leave me. Be here again tomorrow. Write to me. Don't forget. Don't be angry. Do your best.

Future Continuous

278.   **What are you doing now? I am studying.**
          What will you be doing this time tomorrow?
          I will still be studying.

The Future has a continuous form, like the other tenses, with the same kind of emphasis. Fill the gaps below:

Every day, I study from 8 o'clock till 12.
It is now 9 o'clock. I am busy. I am studying.
I — — — for three more hours.
What — — — doing for the next three hours? (Answer.)
I am sorry, I can't go out before 12. Why? (Answer.)

Repeat with rest, read, play the piano, *as in 269.*

The Pre-future

279.   **What is that book like?**
     I will tell you next week. I will have finished it by then.

*Use the **Pre-future Tense**, formed by **will have** + **the past participle**, when you imagine yourself looking back from some moment in the future and when you are interested in some action performed **before or until then**. Use the sequence at the head of this exercise 5 times, beginning with the following questions:*

What do you think of the ëxhibìtion? (tomorrow)
How do you like Peter's new song? (on Thursday)
Whät is yöur imprëssion of the nëw mànager? (this evening)
How much space will you need for your àrticle? (tonight)
Whät do you advïse me to dò about this cäse? (think about it)

143

The Future in the Past

280.   **Today I say, 'I will write: I promise.'**
Yesterday I promised I would* write.

Use the **Future in the Past** (*formed by* **would** + *the infinitive*) *when you imagine yourself looking forward from a point of view in the past. You will only need to use this tense† after the Past Tense of words like* say, tell someone, know, think, expect, promise. *Put the following into the Future in the Past, beginning with* I said, I told you, *or something similar:*

It will rain. It will be a busy day. It will be a long way. George will be late. He will bring us a bottle of wine. We will forgive him. I will tell you the answer.

We are going to leave, we are leaving, we leave, in the future.

281.   (a) **We are going to finish this chapter** ⎫
           It is going to rain   ⎬ **tomorrow.**
    (b) **The President is arriving**   ⎪
    (c) **He arrives at half-past four**   ⎭

Use pattern (*a*) *to emphasise present indications of what the future will bring. 'Present indications' may be intentions or preparations* (We are going to finish this) *or they may be signs telling us what will happen* (It is going to rain—I feel it in my bones, I see the clouds, the baròmeter). *These indications point to some future event, i.e.* we will finish, it will rain.

Use pattern (*b*) *to express the idea that plans or arrangements for some future action have been made, so that the action has, in a sense, begun. Do not use it instead of* It is going to rain: *that is not a matter of plans or arrangements.*

Use pattern (*c*) *when a programme has been made and when you feel so certain an event will happen that you imagine it as completed.*

If you do not want to make any of these kinds of emphasis, use will *for the future, as in 276.*

282. *Study the following examples:*

(*a*) Tomorrow will be Tuesday. (*A simple statement of the future; or emphasis on the future event, not on any preparations for it.*)

(*b*) (*The telephone rings.*) I'll answer it. (*The question of intention or of preparations does not arise.*)

    * Would *rhymes with* could.   † See note on 280.

(c) I have read your letter. I am going to study it carefully and answer it in a day or two. (*Here the question of a process of intention and preparation does arise, and I wish to emphasise it.*)

(d) I will (or shall) study your letter carefully. (*This is a statement of the future, without the emphasis made by example (c).*)

(e) I am going to sneeze. (*I feel it, I know the symptoms and I know what the result will be.*)

(f) We are discussing your case at our meeting next Friday. The ship is sailing at three. (*Arrangements have been made.*)

(g) We discuss your case next Friday. The ship sails at three. (*The discussion is on the agenda. The sailing is on the time-table. You can assume they will take place.*)

(h) We will (or shall) discuss it on Friday. The ship will sail at three. (*See note to example (d).*)

283. *The sentences below (not the sentences in parentheses) refer to future action. Use the* **words** *in parentheses to fill the gap. Choose the most suitable of the four ways of expressing the future given in 276 and 281 and give reasons for your choice.*

(a) (we, have) (Mother is busy in the kitchen.) What . . . for dinner?

(b) (come) (She has laid an extra place at the table.) Who . . . for lunch?

(c) (you, break) (You are sitting on a chair, leaning back.) Be careful . . . that chair.

(d) (sell) I . . . my car. Oh, what made you decide to do that?

(e) (collapse) (There is a fire.) Stand back. The roof . . .

(f) (carry) (I meet my old aunt unexpectedly. She is carrying a parcel.) Let me take that. I . . . it for you.

(g) (I, open) It's hot in here. . . . the window, if you like.

(h) (we, have) It is hot. I think . . . a thunderstorm.

(i) (be) How old are you? Twenty-four. I . . . twenty-five next month.

(j) (you, do). You're always engaged. What . . . this evening, for example?

(k) (leave, arrive) (What is your time-table for tomorrow?) I . . . here at eight and . . . in London at six in the evening.

(l) (have) In that case you . . . a tiring journey.

(m) (take place) Our meeting . . . on June 1st.

(n) (not, be: go) Mr. Williams . . . present. He (go) abroad.

(o) (see) Have you seen the doctor yet? Not yet. I . . . him this morning. I have an appointment at twelve.

145

It's time we went. I wish it was. I wish I were.

284. (a) You haven't gone yet. It's tïme you lèft.
I'm not rich. I wïsh I wàs. I wïsh I wère.
(b) I didn't go. I haven't gone yet. I wïsh I hàd (gone).
(c) I haven't gone yet, but I will go. I wïsh you wòuld (go).

*In (a) the action **has not taken place**; we **imagine** it happening in the present but use the form of the Past Tense (left, was). When we think of the fulfilment as highly improbable, we can say I were, he (she or it) were, after if and wish. In (b) the action did not take place, or has not taken place: we imagine it happening in the past and use the form of the Pre-past (had gone). In (c) the action has not taken place, but we imagine it happening in the future and use the form of the Future in the Past. Use the form of the Past, Pre-past or Future in the Past to fill the following gaps:*

(*a*) It's very late. It's time we — home.
(*b*) George is still asleep. It's time he — up.
(*c*) Waiter! We ordered coffee half an hour ago. It's time you — it.
(*d*) I don't like this place. I wish I — far away from it.
(*e*) I can never be President. Sometimes I wish I — .
(*f*) George often behaves as if he — President.
(*g*) I hear John's story was very funny. I wish I — it.
(*h*) I'll ask him to tell it again. Oh, I wish you — him.
(*i*) I saw John but forgot to ask him. Oh, I wish you — him.
(*j*) Where is today's newspaper? I've burnt it. Oh, I wish you —.
I haven't read it yet. [10]

Sequence of Tenses

285. (a) I assure you. We have had a wonderful time and will come again.
(b) I assured him we had had a wonderful time and would go again.

Choice of tenses depends on the speaker's point of view and the particular meaning he wishes to express. But, as in the examples above, we often find the following combinations of Tenses:

(*a*) Present, Pre-present, Future.
(*b*) Past, Pre-past, Future in the Past.

286. *In the following sentences, put the first verb into the Past Tense and make any other changes that are then necessary:*

(*a*) I cannot understand him. Does he think we do not know how to beháve (13)?
(*b*) I promise I will not forget. I hope you will believe me.

TABLE 29

The English Tenses

Tense	Speaker's point of view	Direction of speaker's attention	Ordinary Tense	Continuous Tense
Present	Now	Now	I walk	I am walking
Pre-present	Now	Time before now	I have walked	I have been walking
Past	Then (past)	Then	I walked	I was walking
Pre-past	Then	Time before then	I had walked	I had been walking
Future	Then (future)	Then	I will walk	I will be walking
Pre-future	Then	Time before then	I will have walked	I will have been walking
Future in the Past	Then (past)	Time after then	I would walk	I would be walking

Notes. 1. *Past habit, contrasted with the present*—I used to walk.
2. *Other ways of expressing the future:*

(a) *Emphasis on present indications pointing to a future event, e.g.:*

It is going to rain. You are going to break that chair.

(b) *Emphasis on present (human) arrangements which are the beginning of an activity, e.g.:*

George is coming to dinner tomorrow.

(c) *Emphasis on a firm plan or time-table, e.g.:*

His train arrives at eleven tomorrow morning.

(c) Night is falling. It has been a perfect day,
(d) but who can tell what tomorrow* will bring?
(e) We are sunburnt. The sun has been shining in our faces all day.
(f) Our leader is pleased. I think he really feels we have done our best.

* tomorrow *means* 'the day after today'. *In the past or future, say* 'the next day'.

147

(g) The wind is getting stronger. I am sure there will be a storm. Several boats have already returned to the harbour, and people are fastening heavy shutters against their windows.

(h) The damage is very serious. Twenty houses have been destroyed, and it will take days to clear the streets. [25]

TABLE 30

The Continuous Forms

I am studying every day for an examination. (*Emphasis on the idea that I am in the process of my studies.*)

I study every day from 8 to 12. (*No such emphasis; or emphasis on the whole operation, the regular series of acts.*)

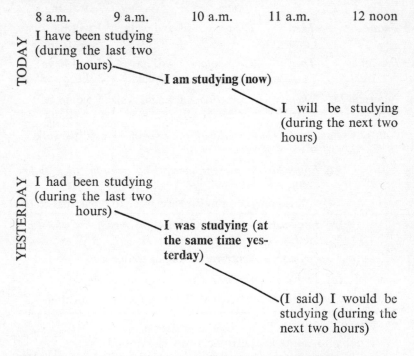

| 8 a.m. | 9 a.m. | 10 a.m. | 11 a.m. | 12 noon |

TODAY
I have been studying (during the last two hours)—
I am studying (now)
I will be studying (during the next two hours)

YESTERDAY
I had been studying (during the last two hours)—
I was studying (at the same time yesterday)
(I said) I would be studying (during the next two hours)

Note the use of during. *In saying* 'I have been studying' *we are interested in action in progress at any time* **during** *the two hours, or* **for** *the whole period.*

Miscellaneous Exercises in the Tenses and Irregular Verbs

287. *Put the verb in brackets into the most suitable tense. Where there is no verb given, think of a suitable one and put it in the appropriate tense.*

(*a*) In this chapter, we (deal) with irregular verbs. I — you (not, forget) them.

(*b*) 'Where (you, get) that bruise on your forehead (6, h *silent*)?' my wife — me this morning. I — up my hand and — a lump. Then I (remember). 'In the middle of the night', I — her. 'I — up and (think) I — a noise downstairs. You — fast asleep. I (creep) to the door, — it carefully, and —. Then I — the noise again. I (begin) to creep downstairs. Suddenly I (catch) my foot on a stick which someone (leave) on the stairs, and I —. I (wonder) you (not, hear) me. When I (pick myself up), I (find myself) at the bottom of the stairs. The front door — open and a man (stand) outside. He (shine) a light at me. Then I — he a policeman. He — "— you all right, sir? (you hurt) yourself? I only (come) to tell you your door — open. I — you — to fasten it properly last night." I — him, — the door, — back to bed, and (sleep) soundly until you (wake) me up.' 'What (you do) with the stick?' my wife asked. 'Nothing', I —. 'I — not find it. It — probably still on the stairs and somebody (fall) over it again.'

(*c*) We (do) an exercise on the verbs. We (not, do) any more today: we (do) enough. (You get) them all right?

More Exercises in the Irregular Verbs

288.   I don't want to hear your story. I've heard it already.

For each of the 50 sentences below, make up another as in the model. Use the verb in italics and put it in a suitable tense. Use pronouns in the second sentence when you can.

1. I can't *bear* this muddle. (long enough already)
2. I wanted to *beat* John at tennis. (But he . . .)
3. When did term *begin*? (last month)
4. How did you *bend* this iron rod? (with my own hands)
5. That dog doesn't *bite*. (Don't you believe it! . . . just . . .)
6. Did the wind *blow* very hard last night? (Yes, roof off)
7. I *broke* the window. (How . . . ?)
8. Did you *bring* a message? (Yes)
9. Tell George not to *burn* it. (already)
10. Where did you *buy* that hat? (at a sale)
11. Did you *choose* it yourself? (No, Mary . . . for me)
12. How much did it *cost*? (a lot of money)

13. How did you *cut* your chin? (with a razor)
14. Why did the workmen *dig* this hole? (. . . to lay a drainpipe)
15. Can you *draw* a picture? (yesterday)
16. What do you *dream* about? (not, for a long time)
17. *Drink* up your coffee. (already)
18. Can you *drive* a car? (for years; and still do)
19. Will you have some more to *eat*? Thank you, but . . . a huge meal.
20. How long did the first men take to *fly* across the Atlantic? (in sixteen hours)
21. *Give* the conductor your ticket. (already)
22. How did you *grow* this lovely flower? (in a hot-house)
23. Why did you *hang* my picture there? (so that I can always see it)
24. Did George *hide* the other picture? (Yes, in the cellar)
25. Where did you *hold* the meeting. (in the public square)
26. When did you *know* the results? (late last night)
27. Where did the police *lay* the body? (at the side of the road)
28. Did the dead man's family *lead* the procession? (Yes)
29. Did anyone *lend* them a car? (Yes)
30. *Let* the cat out. (an hour ago)
31. Did you find anywhere to *lie* down? (Yes, on the deck)
32. Where did you *lose* your wallet? (in the street)
33. What did you *mean* when you said no? (exactly what I said)
34. Did you *put* the kettle on? (Yes, ten minutes ago)
35. *Ring* the door-bell. (Twice, but no one has come)
36. How did you get here so quickly? Did you *run*? (Yes, all the way)
37. How much did you *sell* your car for?
38. When did the travellers *set* out? (at day-break)
39. Did you *shake* the bottle? (yes, hard)
40. What did you *shoot* the lion with? (a rifle)
41. Where did the 'Titanic' *sink*? (in the Atlantic)
42. Don't *spend* all my money! (I'm sorry, already)
43. Don't *spoil* my picture! (Don't worry, not)
44. Where did you *spread* out your wet clothes? (in the boiler room)
45. Did the lion *spring* out at you? (Yes . . . as I was about to shoot)
46. Why did you *steal* my purse? (Nobody . . . still in your pocket)
47. It's dark in here. *Strike* a match. (two already, but they're wet)
48. What did you *tell* the driver? (to drive like mad)
49. Did Leander or Byron *swim* across the Hellespont? (Both)
50. I can't *wear* this shirt any longer. (for a week already)

Question Tags

289.   I gàve you the mòney, dìdn't I? (I'm sure I did)
I dïdn't forgét, díd I? (I'm not sure now)
Thère, I dìdn't forgët, dìd I? (You have the money)
I was right after all, wasn't I?

Add similar question tags to the following and read it as a dialogue with either a falling intonation or a rising one (see 207) according to the sense:

	A says:		*B says:*
(*a*)	It is terrible weather.	(*b*)	It was worse yesterday.
(*c*)	It wasn't worse than this.	(*d*)	You remember. It didn't stop once.
(*e*)	But you weren't out in it.	(*f*)	Yes, but I had a raincoat.
(*g*)	It will be better tomorrow.	(*h*)	It can't go on like this.
(*i*)	John and George are brothers.	(*j*)	They aren't alike.
(*k*)	They went to the races on Saturday.	(*l*)	They had never been before.
(*m*)	They had often wanted to go.	(*n*)	Well, they have been now.

Passages for Reading and Study

290.   *Study the passage in 253. Make a list of all the verbs, and give the subject and tense of each, thus:*

Subject + Verb	Tense
I had met	Pre-past
An African chief came	Ordinary Past

291.   *Answer the following questions on 253, using a complete sentence for each answer, as in the example.*

Example: When did the African chief come to England? He came to England when he was past sixty.

(*a*) Where had the speaker met him?   (*b*) How old was the chief?
(*c*) Had he ever left his own country before?   (*d*) What kind of post did he hold?   (*e*) Where did he fly to?   (*f*) Did he know his own country well?   (*g*) When did the speaker's friend go to call on him?
(*h*) What did the friend ask him first?   (*i*) What were the exact words of the friend's first question? ('How — —?')   (*j*) What did the friend ask him next?   (*k*) What were the exact words of the second question?   (*l*) What did the visitor say in reply?   (*m*) When had he had

151

a frightening experience? (*n*) Where had he gone? (*o*) What were the exact words used by the chief at the beginning of his story? (*p*) What did the chief do at Victoria Station? (*q*) Where did he stand? (*r*) What did he see come in? (*s*) When did the doors swing outward? (*t*) To what point did the train come nearer and nearer? (*u*) When did the men jump out? (*v*) Then what did they do? (*w*) How did they carry their umbrellas? (*x*) What were their faces like? (*y*) What did the chief think? (*z*) So what did he do?

292. *Write down the answers to the questions in 291. Then close your text-books, and form questions which will produce the answers you have written.*

MISCELLANEOUS TESTS

293. *Arrange the following words in rhyming pairs, as in 42:*

any, aren't, believe, bowl, build, can't, caught, city, climb, coast, comb, cost, crowd, daughter, drawn, dressed, dried, eye, field, fight, fonder, form, grey, guest, guide, her, home, key, killed, lose, loud, most, occur, owe, penny, pretty, quite, receive, refer, said, sealed, shoes, show, spread, they, their, thought, thunder, time, torn, tossed, tree, try, wander, warm, water, wear, were, whole, wonder. [60]

294. *Arrange the following in pairs so that each member of a pair has the same rhythm as the other. Example:* a hündred stèps, an ängry màn.

(*a*) Write the number of the exercise. (*b*) I'm surprised to hear it. (*c*) And what's the matter now? (*d*) Tomorrow will be Tuesday. (*e*) Thère are some bröken rècords. (*f*) Put the letter in the envelope. (*g*) Don't think of it. (*h*) Hëre is a new machine. (*i*) A sharp pen-knife. (*j*) A healthy condition. (*k*) There are too many mistakes. (*l*) Margaret can't forget. (*m*) In a most reasonable way. (*n*) A steel cupboard. (*o*) Expensive tea. (*p*) He's arriving Monday. (*q*) Drive carefully. (*r*) Give me a glass of water. (*s*) A perfect day. (*t*) Across the Atlantic. (*u*) It's almost empty. (*v*) I wonder if it's raining. (*w*) A most important thing. (*x*) I never heard it. [12 pairs]

295. (*a*) *Spell the 3rd person singular of the Present (e.g.* breaks), *the Present Participle (e.g.* breaking), *the Ordinary Past (e.g.* broke) *and the Past Participle (e.g.* broken) *of:* arrive, begin, carry, choose, die, do, forget, go, lay, lie, lose, occupy, occur, offer, pay, quarrel, refer, rain, run, suffer, travel, try, wake, win, write. [25]

(*b*) *Say and spell the plural of:* city, country, detective story, duty, enemy, excuse, handkerchief, hero, history, holiday, house, lady, lens, loaf, match-box, mouse, mouth, path, potato, picture-gallery, radio, society, son-in-law, wife, woman. [25]

296. (a) *Fill each gap with one of the following:* boys, boy's, boys', buy, by, he's, his, its, it's, their, there, they're, to, too, two, your, you're, were, we're, where.

— are six — in this room. — — ten a moment ago. — are the others? We think they've gone home: — not sure. In any case, now — not here. I don't know these —: what are — names? This — name is Harold. And what is — age? — eighteen. — just had — eighteenth birthday. What are the other — ages? Tell them not to go. — — early — leave yet. Will you be going — the post-office on — way home? If you are, please — me some stamps. If — not, don't worry. Look at that dog: — limping. Poor thing, — broken — leg. [25]

Write out the above sentences, filling the gaps, but replacing all contracted forms by full forms (e.g. we've = we have).

(b) *Supply the missing letters:*

(i) You must pract— your English every day. D—ly pract— is nec—ary. Bel—ve me. Don't dec—ve yourself.

(ii) Mr. Foster is going to Buenos Aires on import— b—ness. He is starting on his j—ney im—diately. He has a wide know— and exp—nce of for—n countries.

(iii) Our next door n—bour is a g—v—ment off—al. He takes his work very s—iously.

(iv) Who knows w—ther the w—ther will be fine or not tomorrow? There is no s—n, either way. But people can find these things out s—entific—ly.

(v) Who was to blame? Whose f—lt was it? I must rec—ve all the blame: I was who—ly respons—le. [25]

297. *Revise the reading passages. Then answer the following questions on them, giving the answer first in a phrase, then in a complete sentence, as in the example:*

Example: (*From 101*) Whät is there in frönt of our hòuse? A smäll gàrden. There is a smäll gàrden in frönt of our höuse.

(*From 101*) (a) What do we grow in the back garden? (b) What can I see from my bedroom window? (*From 102*) (c) What kind of buildings are there in our town? (d) What kind of car does my brother drive? (*From 103*) (e) Who is Dr Freeman? (f) What is Mary like? (*From 104*) (g) What is a compass? (*From 105*) (h) What is a typewriter? (i) What is there at the back of a typewriter?

(*j*) What do we put behind the roller? (*k*) What does the hammer hit? (*From 142*) (*l*) Where is John spending his holiday? (*m*) Where is his room? (*n*) Where does he usually walk? (*From 143*) (*o*) What is Mr. Morris ordering? (*p*) What is he *not* ordering? (*From 212*) (*q*) What do we fasten the door with? (*r*) Which rock is a thousand feet high? (*From 213*) (*s*) What must one keep tea-leaves in? (*t*) What do some people put in their tea? (*From 252*) (*u*) Where does the taxi stop? (*v*) Where does one of the women lead us first? (*From 253*) (*w*) What kind of post did the chief hold? (*x*) Where did he walk to on his first day in London? (*y*) Who jumped out of the train? [25] *Write out the answers. Then, without looking at the book, make up sentences to produce those answers.*

298. *Fill each gap with a preposition or adverb, including a word like still, yet, etc. Note that a preposition, etc., may consist of more than one word. Put the verbs in brackets in a suitable tense. The whole exercise must make complete and connected sense.*

(*a*) The distance — X — Z is 40 miles. I (drive) that distance — one hour. The road — the two places (pass) — Y. Y is — the road, three-quarters of the way to Z. Y is therefore — this side of Z, and Z is — Y.

(*b*) It is now 9.55 a.m. I (leave) — Z — 5 minutes. I (not start) —, but my car is — the door, and I (wait) to start. I (start) — 10 o'clock. I (know) I (arrive) — Z — exactly 60 minutes. It is 9.59: it is time I (start) the engine. It is 10: now I am —.

(*c*) It is 10.10. I (drive). I (leave) X 10 minutes —, and now I (go) — X, and my car (travel) — Y. It (move) — the road at 50 miles an hour. It cannot go faster than that today because there are other cars —.

(*d*) There are — cars — the road: that is to say there are no pedestrians. People are not allowed to walk — the road: they must cross — the road by a foot-bridge. Cars go — the bridge. I (see) two people who (ride) bicycles — the track — me. I (drive) — them and soon they are — me.

(*e*) Now 10.30. I (drive) — 10, i.e. — 30 minutes. I (— complete) 20 miles. I (drive) — 30 minutes more, i.e. — 11. If I drive dangerously, I can arrive — five — 11.

(*f*) 10.50 (I arrive) — Z —? No, not —. 11.02. Now I (arrive). I (arrive) 2 minutes —. I (travel) 40 miles and (drive) — one hour.

(*g*) 11.30. I (leave) X — 10 and (pass) — Y on my way. — 10.30, I (drive), and five minutes later, I (— travel), — hundreds of other cars. I (leave) X 35 minutes —.

(*h*) 11.10. When I (be) — X, I (know) I (arrive) — one hour.

When I (be) at Y, I (travel) 30 miles, and (drive) three-quarters of an hour. — 9.55, I (not start) —, but I (wait) to start.

(i) When I (come) to Z, I (see) two people who (ride) bicycles. I soon (pass) them.

(j) I (drive) — Z alone, — a passenger. You (not come) — me. I wish you (come). [100]

299. *Say the following in a different but acceptable way, as in 145:*

(a) George is not up yet. (b) He woke up two hours ago. (c) Mary is still asleep. (d) You don't eat a great amount. (e) Some people overeat. (f) This boat is overcrowded. (g) That is what I firmly believe. (h) Take a deep breath. (i) He's a hard worker. (j) She makes her clothes herself. (k) I'm asking you what his name is. (l) The name of this material is nylon. (m) Get a chair for your guest. (n) You do not do enough practice. (o) This tea is undrinkable. (p) George always does what I tell him not to do. (q) A building made of wood. (r) The train that takes you to your business. (s) Take away these things. (t) Let's come away from this place. (u) I say to you, 'Is this the right road?' (v) Your room is above mine but not right over it. (w) I saw John when I was on my way home. (x) Please explain the meaning of this sentence to us. (y) It's late: we must stop now. [25]

300. *Arrange the words in the groups below so that each group makes complete sense. Put in suitable punctuation marks.*

(a) go, on, usually, the, Sundays, into, we, country.

(b) the, this, both, blue, old, my, Persian, room, rugs, are, in, uncle's.

(c) all, those, who, the, tomato, yesterday, dug, in, up, garden, plants.

(d) the, these, they, enough, wall, pictures, not, have, put, on, up, carefully.

(e) you, the, they, they, did, were, weren't, see, last, wonderful, night, fireworks.

(f) A, white, professor, was, was, were, talking, listening, walking, to, with, about, and, but, all, students, his, him, nobody, hair.

(g) we, him, Hudson, had, came, heard, never, anything, before, about, James, here.

(h) we, she, you, that, problem, have, not, asked, answered, worked, already, yet, out.

(i) she, we, it, us, had, worked, asked, if, properly, out.

(j) there, is, the, door, anybody, said, knocking, his, guide, on, there, with, the, stick.

155

NOTES AND ANSWERS

NOTES FOR TEACHERS AND ANSWERS
TO SOME OF THE EXERCISES

N.B. Other answers may be correct (see page 9). If in any doubt, adopt the answers given below.

Part One

Proficiency in English—perhaps more than in any major language—depends very much on a firm grasp of the vowel system, of the main principles of stress, rhythm and pitch, and of certain general rules of spelling. The chief purpose of Part One is to form correct habits of pronunciation and spelling which students can apply right through the course, and afterwards. Students who are the most eager to begin reading and expressing themselves freely are often those most likely to be held back by bad habits of pronunciation and spelling later.

Every student will want to know the meaning of the words and phrases he practises on, and you should give the meaning of words and phrases in Part One before you start exercising them. But remember that the best way to learn the meaning of words is to use them in a suitable context. Whenever, therefore, you can make natural use of the words and phrases given as examples, do so. For instance, the numbers are given as examples in Ex. 2 and are meant to be used immediately in English, in answering the questions in the rest of the exercise.

Table 1. This gives the English vowel sounds illustrated by words in frequent use. The first sound is the vowel sound in *see*; and so on. Teach sounds 1–12 as pure vowels, i.e. made with the tongue and lips in one fixed position. Make 1–4 with the front of the tongue raised; 5–9 with the back raised; 10–12 with the middle. These anatomical details are largely for the teacher's guidance. However, **keep Table 1 in your own and your pupils' minds right through the course.** Why not make a chart of it?

In practising the 'pure' vowels, start with 12, the vowel sound of the unstressed syllable in *better*. Make it with the tongue relaxed, in a neutral position; and make it short, i.e. take a comparatively short time over producing it.

Prolong No. 12 to get 11. Do not put any *r* sound in 11. There is no need for beginners to be aware of the possibility of an *r* sound in it at this stage.

Make 10 with a sudden opening of the mouth. Keep it short. Think of the sound and meaning of *sudden*.

Start with 12 again to get 2 and 8, which are also short and relaxed, and sound rather like 12. In fact, if your pupils confuse *live* with *leave*, tell them to pronounce *live* with 12 when speaking quickly and when it comes in the middle of a sentence. 2 is a small sound, as in *pin*.

Now go to No. 1. Feel the tongue move forwards and upwards and get more tense as you move from 2 to 1. Keep No. 1 long.

159

Open the mouth a little more widely as you move from 2 to 3, and again from 3 to 4. Make 3 short. Keep the jaw fixed for 4. Practise *pin, pen, hand, arm.*

Make 5 long, like an arm. Put no *r* sound in it.

6, short. Practise saying *hot* quickly, as if you have picked up something hot and drop it at once.

7, long, like the sound of a horn. No *r* sound, but a slightly smaller mouth opening than 6.

9, long, with a slightly smaller opening than 8.

Teach 13–19 as diphthongs, in which the tongue and lips move from the position required for one pure vowel to the position required for another. Make all the diphthongs long sounds, but give the first element more stress and length than the second. Let each diphthong glide towards the short relaxed sounds 12, 2 or 8, thus:

Number	Starting point	Gliding towards
13	Between 3 and 4	
14	Between 4 and 5	2
15	7	
16	Between 4 and 5	
17	12	8
18	2	
19	3	12

(Note: When 18 is unaccented, as in *Austrália,* make both elements short, with equal stress.)

Exercises 1–14 should be used, at first, only for practice in hearing and reproducing English sounds—not for identifying written symbols.

Exercise 1. Students should be able both to recognise and to reproduce these sounds correctly, to use both the numbers and the key words in identifying the vowel sounds in new words. Thus, *want*—vowel No. 6, as in *hot.* The most important thing is to hear and make the distinction between words likely to be confused.

2. Students should be very familiar with the words in heavy type in the instructions, e.g. **vowel.** Teach the numbers, up to 20, in English, and make the pupils answer in English. Then proceed thus: *one*—vowel number ten. Pronounce *four* with sound No. 7 in this exercise. Pronounce *seven* with one vowel, also *Table* and *Listen* (see note Ex. 11). Pronounce *eleven* as two syllables, *elèven* (2, 3), explaining that it is one word with two vowel sounds. Pronounce *vowel* as two syllables (16, 12). Give unaccented syllables a natural but clear pronunciation (see notes to Ex. 14). Be careful of *are* (5), *was* (6), *were* (11), *wòman* (8, 12), *wòmen* (2, 2), *child* (14), *children* (2, 12), *key* (1), *word* (11), *one* (10), *not* (6) and *nought* (7). If in doubt about a pronunciation, work through this course thoroughly on your own; or consult a good pronouncing dictionary.

3. Be careful of *walk* (7), *work* (11), *law* (7), *wars* (7), *màny* (3, 2), *ònly* (17, 2). Count *ankle* (4) and *uncle* (10) as one vowel; and pronounce *more*

as 7 at this stage. Use this exercise as a test, and count the 'score' (maximum 100). Repeat the test and try to improve the result.

Table 1a. Four, more, door, etc. can be either 7 or 20.

$$
\left.
\begin{array}{l}
\text{No. } 20 = \ \ 7 \\
\quad\ \ 21 = \ \ 8 \\
\quad\ \ 22 = 14 \\
\quad\ \ 23 = 16
\end{array}
\right\} \text{ gliding towards 12}
$$

4. Pronounce *poor* as 21, though both 20 and 7 are common.
6. Make up exercises as necessary. However, do not spend too much time trying to achieve perfection. Go on with the course, let the students get accustomed to hearing the language, and drill difficult pairs as you come to them.

Table 2. In the column headed Sound, pronounce *b* like the second syllable of *rubber*; *p* like the first syllable of *perhaps; m* like the second syllable of *summer*, etc. Give *l* two pronunciations—one at the beginning of a word, as in *leave*, the other as in the second syllable of *table*. There is no letter of the alphabet for the middle consonant in *measure*, and the phonetic symbol [ʒ] is used for this sound in the Table. The sound [ʒ] does not usually occur at the beginning of English words; nor does the sound *ng*.

The 'soft' sounds are voiced, i.e. the vocal chords are open when these sounds are made. The 'hard' sounds are unvoiced or voiceless—the vocal chords are closed. The importance of this difference will be seen later. Note voiced *b* corresponds with unvoiced *p*; *v* with *f*; soft *th* with hard *th*; *d* with *t*; *z* with *s*; [ʒ] with *sh*; *g* with *k*. In the middle or at the end of a word, voiced consonants tend to be longer than unvoiced.

Consonants are made when the breath meets some obstruction as it passes through the vocal organs. With *b, p, m, w*, the obstruction is caused by the lips. English *p* at the beginning of a stressed syllable is accompanied by a sharp puff of breath, or aspiration. The sound *m* is nasal, i.e. the breath passes through the nose. Make *w* by putting the lips together, pushing them slightly forward and then drawing them quickly back: keep the tongue flat.

Pronounce *v* and *f* by placing the lower lip firmly against the upper teeth; *th*, by placing the tip of the tongue between the teeth.

Pronounce *d, t*, and *n* with the tip of the tongue against the upper teeth or teeth-ridge. Note that *t* is aspirated, like *p;* and *n* is nasal. To pronounce *l*, press the tip of the tongue against the teeth-ridge so that the middle of the mouth is closed and breath passes out at the side. To pronounce *r*, let the tip of the tongue lightly touch the teeth-ridge once, keeping the rest of the tongue low and contracted.

For *s* and *z*, raise the blade of the tongue to the teeth-ridge leaving a very narrow passage through which the air can pass: keep the teeth close together. For *sh*, raise the tongue as for *s*, but leave a wider passage at the front and a narrower one farther back. Push the lips forward and let the breath escape with a sharp hiss. [ʒ] is the voiced equivalent of *sh*.

For the consonant sound *y*, place the tongue as for vowel No. 2, then quickly pull it away and pronounce the vowel that follows.

161

Make *g, k* with the back of the tongue against the soft palate. Similarly with *ng*, letting the air pass through the nose. Note that *k* is aspirated, like *p* and *t*.

Practise *h* by forcing breath through the glottis. At the beginning of a word or syllable *h* must be pronounced (but see exceptions in Ex. 20). But do not pronounce it at the end of a word or syllable, e.g. *Oh!*

8. Pronounce *what, where, when*, etc. simply with the sound *w*. Do not worry about the voiceless *w* which is sometimes heard in these words. Pronounce *who, whose* with the sound *h*. Pronounce *pà/per, lès/son, to/mòr/row, nùm/ber, fìn/ger* (see 9), *vìl/lage, wèa/ther, sù/gar*, dividing the syllables as indicated by the oblique stroke. See note to 14.

9. Take care when a word ends in a consonant. Place the vocal organs in the position required for the consonant but release them softly without adding the sound of vowel No. 12. Say *rub this out* by placing the lips as for *b* and then placing the tongue as for *th*, without an intervening vowel sound. Pronounce *rùb/ber, stòp/per, sùm/mer, rùn/ner* as indicated, but with only one medial consonant sound. Pronounce *lò/ver, bà/ther* (13), *rì/der, wrì/ter, gà/rage, stù/dy, stù/dent*.

Note that *p* is less aspirated in the middle and end of a word than at the beginning. The same applies to *t* and *k*.

lived, stopped are words of one syllable; *en/ded* has two (see Table 26).

In *stronger, longer* (adjectives), *English, finger, single*, pronounce a *g* sound after the *ng* sound, and pronounce as *strong/ger*, etc. But do not do this with *singing, longing* (verbs) and *singer:* pronounce *sing/ing*, etc.

11. The accents and the numbers in brackets, e.g. *pèople* (1), will be explained later. They are given now for guidance during revision. *Table, people, little*, etc. have two syllables. Let the second consist simply of *b* (or *p*, or *t*, etc.) plus the 'dark' *l* sound (like the last sound of *pull*), without a vowel. Pronounce *table* as follows: sound *t*, vowel 13; then sound *b* followed by sound *l* as at the end of *pull*. If necessary, practise by saying *tày bull*. Similarly, pronounce *listen* as *l*, vowel 2; then *s*, followed by sound *n*, as in *sun*.

Table 3. In compounds (*j, ch, dr* and *tr*) two consonants come together so quickly that the first is not finished before the other begins. The two elements in *j* are *d* and [ʒ]; in *ch, t* and *sh;* in *dr, d* and *r;* and in *tr, t* and *r*. In the clusters (the rest of the combinations in Table 3) pronounce two consonants in one articulation without a gap or vowel between, and be careful not to put a vowel *before* the clusters.

12. Do not allow a vowel between *John* and *George*, etc. Where there is no comma, as in *bright blue*, place the tongue etc. in position for *t*, keep it there for a second and then pronounce *blue* without completing the release of the *t*. Pronounce *jumped, packs, clothes* as one syllable. If *clothes* is too difficult at first, pronounce it like the verb *close*, which is what many people actually say in fluent conversation: but this applies only to the noun. Pronounce the verb, as in *He clothes us*, with the ending soft *th* + *z*.

13. Note the consonant sound *y* at the beginning of the pronunciation of the letter *u*, and of the words *useful, united, university*, etc. Note also that *y*

often precedes vowel No. 9 as in the words in 13 (b). This is indicated thus: *view* (y + 9). Do not insist on the *y* sound after *d* or *t* if the student has already learnt a different acceptable pronunciation.

14. A mark like \, ·· or / (see 28–39), indicates that the syllable containing the vowel sound whose symbol is thus marked is accented. Be careful to accent the right syllable and always pronounce the vowel in the accented syllable fully and accurately. When teaching a new word or speaking deliberately, as in dictation, pronounce the unaccented syllables clearly, too. However, in many unaccented syllables, the vowel becomes simply No. 12 in fluent speech, e.g. in *cònsonant, photògrapher*. In others, it becomes No. 2, e.g. in *pràctise, explàin, knòwledge*. Long vowels and diphthongs in unaccented syllables tend to keep their full value, e.g. *rècord* (3, 7), *tomòrrow* (8, 6, 17), though even in such cases No. 12 in the unaccented syllables may be acceptable, as in *tomörrow mòrning*. Pronounce *thirteen, fourteen*, etc. with the stress on both syllables to avoid confusion with *thirty, forty*, etc. However, in the series, 13, 14, 15, etc. the syllable -*teen* generally loses its stress though it keeps the quality of its vowel sound (No. 1). This loss of stress commonly occurs on the repetition of a syllable or word.

In this exercise, words of more than one syllable are divided *in print* according to their etymology. This division is traditionally observed on paper when it is necessary to put part of a word on one line and part on another. Students should be advised not to try dividing words in writing until they are sufficiently advanced to understand the principles involved. Modern pronunciation does not always coincide with etymology in this respect. Thus, the first sound of the accented syllable in *explanation* is *n*. This is indicated by the sign ‿. Thus the second syllable of *English* begins with the sound *g*.

Note: rècord, òbject (nouns); recòrd, objèct (verbs).

Do Ex. 14 first deliberately, then more fluently. The key is given for the teacher's guidance only. The pronunciation in brackets indicates more fluent speech:

(*a*) 2 + 2; 10 + 12; 4 + 2; 2 + n; 3 + 12 + 14.

(*b*) 9 + 2 + 8; 9 + 2; 8 + 13 (12 + 13); 8 + 6 + 17 (12 + 6 + 17); 3 + 12 + 13 (3 + 12 + 2).

(*c*) 7 + 2; 5 + 12 + 9; 1 + 2 (eve = 1 syllable); 10 + 13 (10 + 2); 9 + 13 (9 + 2).

(*d*) 3 + 13 (3 + 2) (pronounce *Wednes-* as *wenz*); 11 + 13 (11 + 2); 14 + 13 (14 + 2); 4 + 12 + 13 (4 + 12 + 2); 10 + 13 (10 + 2).

(*e*) 11 + 1; 11 + 2; 7 + 1; 7 + 2; 2 + 1; 2 + 2.

(*f*) 17 + 12 + 5 (or 4); 12 + 6 + 12 + 12; 17 + 12 + 4 + 2; 4 + 12 + 13 + 12.

(*g*) 3 + 13 (2 + 13); 3 + 4 + 13 + 12 (3 + 12 + 13 + 12); 17 + 16 (12 + 16); 6 + 10 + 2 + 13 + 12 (12 + 10 + 2 + 13 + 12).

(*h*) 17; 6 + 3 (6 + 2); 4 + 2 + 12; 4 + 2 + 3 + 12 + 2 (in fluent speech, the 4th syllable may be omitted).

(*i*) 10 + 12 + 12 + 1 (in fluent speech, the 2nd vowel sound may be omitted); 5 + 19; 13 + 2 + 17; 3 + 2 + 2 + 12.

(*j*) 3 + 7; 3 + 7 (2 + 7); 6 + 3 (6 + 2); 6 + 3 (12 + 3); 2 + 7 + 12; 3 + 3 + 3 + 2 (3 + 12 + 12 + 2).

The Alphabet. Students should be able to spell in English, and to put lists in alphabetical order.

Table 5. Many English words follow this scheme, and native speakers of English frequently use it when reading new words or when spelling phonetically. In this book, use it as a key to pronunciation, unless a number in brackets after the word indicates something different. (It may be necessary to explain that English spelling has remained largely unchanged for centuries, while the pronunciation, of vowels particularly, has changed considerably.)

Pronounce *-ook* as 8, otherwise *-oo* as 9, though see exceptions in 18. Note *pin* (2), *pine* (14); *not* (6), *note* (17); *hat* (4), *hate* (13); *get* (3), *scene* (1); *car* (5), *care* (19); *her* (11), *here* (18); *fir* (11), *fire* (22); *pay* (13), *pain* (13); *boy* (15), *boil* (15). This gives a useful guide to the pronunciation of a good many monosyllables.

18. Note that *after, half, branch, can't, dance*, etc. are also pronounced with No. 4. Do not insist on 5 if the student has already been taught 4. Words like *translate* may be pronounced 4 + 13 or 5 + 13 by the same speaker. Pronounce *wear* and *where* exactly the same (see note to 8). *Tear* (18) is a drop of liquid coming from the eye; *tear* (19) is an action. *Room* can be 8 or 9. *Bow* has different meanings according to its pronunciation.

19. *Talking:* the inflexion (e.g. *-ing*) at the end of a word is unaccented. *English* (2), *student* (y + 9), *study* (10): in this book one number in brackets immediately after a word indicates the pronunciation of the vowel in the stressed syllable. If the word has only one syllable, that one is, of course, the stressed one. More than one number, e.g. Good-bye (8 + 14), indicates the pronunciation of the separate vowels in the order in which they occur.

20. Use Table 2 and Ex. 20 as guides to the pronunciation of consonants, unless something different is indicated. Pronounce *pneumonia* (*new* + *mòan* + unstressed 18). Pronounce *psychology* (*sigh-còllogy*).

Notes of the pronunciation of *r*. Pronounce *r* whenever it begins a word or syllable, or when it comes before a suffix or word beginning with a vowel. It is not necessary (though it is usual in some important forms of English) to pronounce it in *car, care, near, her, here, fir, fire, for, more*, etc. Pronounce it in *nearest, here is, there are, far away, take care of it*.

The *s* of the plural of nouns and the 3rd person singular, Present Tense, of verbs, is pronounced *z* after a vowel or voiced consonant, and pronounced *s* after a voiceless consonant. Otherwise, final *s* is sometimes pronounced soft (as in *is, has, please*), sometimes hard (as in *house, us*).

Do not pronounce *w* at the end of a word, as in *law, saw, throw away*.

21. Read this to your students and explain what it means before they read it themselves. Do the same with 22.

22. The stress and intonation marks (see 28–39) are at first for the teacher's guidance. The student should follow them when he revises this exercise after finishing all of Part One.

23. Use dictation as an exercise in listening carefully, in reproducing something that makes sense, and in spelling.

25. **Stress.** Certain words in a sentence are pronounced with stress. They are the words which the speaker feels should be emphasised in the circumstances in which he is speaking. While syllable-stress is more or less fixed, word-stress within a sentence can vary according to where the speaker wants to put the emphasis. Some little words are so often unstressed that they develop a weak pronunciation, like the weakened syllables within a word. The pronunciation of these weak forms is indicated in the third column of Ex. 25 and by italics in the examples. Note that the strong form is used in deliberate speech, or in hesitation, or when the word receives emphasis, or stands in an exposed position, e.g. at the end of the sentence. However, the weak forms for *us* and *them* can be used even at the end of a sentence, when those words are unstressed. Use *a* before a consonant sound, including the first sound in words like *university*. Use *an* before a vowel sound, including words beginning with a silent *h*. Do not try to abbreviate *is* after a hissing sound (*s, z, sh, ch*). Weak *is* becomes *z* after a vowel or voiced consonant, *s* after a voiceless consonant. The vowel in weak *the* is 12 before a consonant sound, 2 before a vowel. Weak *to* has 12 before a consonant, 8 before a vowel. *For*, even when weak, has an *r* sound before a vowel. Weak *it is* is written *it's*—not to be confused with *its* (see 112 a).

26. Let the pupils make up as many examples as they can in a given time, so long as the examples make sense. However, make sure that in using the articles (*a, the*) they follow a common pattern of usage: see, for example, 54 and 78.

27. **Rhythm** makes language more enjoyable to speak and more attractive to listen to. It compels attention, helps us to remember, and is an important factor in many fixed expressions and common patterns of speech. In English it depends on a regular beat of stressed syllables, and on an equal interval of time between each stress. Notice how the spacing of the stresses, combined with the use of long or short vowels, or with an easy or difficult movement of the tongue from one position to another, affects the tempo of the line. For example, line *j* begins with six rapid notes, followed by a long one. See note on 29.

28–39. **Pitch and Intonation** are important factors in English. Intonation is the tune produced by changes of pitch as the voice moves during, away from, or towards a stressed syllable, or from one stress to another. It expresses a good deal of meaning. There are many varieties and subtleties of intonation which are not indicated in this book. The learner can best acquire them by hearing and imitating people who speak English naturally and well, or by studying them for himself later.

The large sign ◗ indicates a fall in pitch during the pronunciation of a stressed syllable; ◗ rise in pitch. ● indicates that an accented syllable is followed by an unaccented syllable at a lower pitch; ◗ rise in pitch,

165

starting on a stressed syllable and still continuing on the following un-stressed syllable.

Difference in 'meaning' between falling and rising intonation. Assume that the falling tone is (a) normal, or (b) an indication of finality; while the rising tone indicates that there is something more to be said, either because there is more to follow, or because the speaker is expressing doubt or sur-prise or wants more information, or perhaps because he wants to let his audience feel that he has not said the last word. Note that a question can have either intonation. *Whät is thìs?* suggests *Thät is äll I wänt to knòw.* But *Is this trúe?* suggests *I wänt to knöw mòre: I am not certain whether the answer is 'Yes' or 'No'.* Normally, use a falling intonation with questions, unless they require the answer 'Yes' or 'No'.

29. Note that while *water, garden,* etc. have a similar pattern of stress and pitch, the length of the syllables varies. In *garden,* the first vowel is long; in *city* it is short. Length is also affected by the nature and combination of consonant sounds. See notes on Table 1 and 2 regarding length of sounds.

30. When more than one stress occurs in a sentence, start the first stress at a relatively high pitch, drop down on the next stress, and so on until the 'nucleus' is reached, when the ❝ pattern or the ⌣ pattern occurs. Pro-nounce unstressed words at the beginning of a sentence on a low pitch before jumping up to the first stress point in the intonation pattern. After ❝ pronounce any remaining syllables on the same low note: after ⌣, on the same high note, rising at the end.

Strong emphasis or emotion can be expressed by special stress, accom-panied by a sharp fall or rise in pitch, e.g.

Stop!   What?   Go away

Simplified Method of Marking Stress and Intonation

The following system is used in this book whenever guidance has been thought to be necessary or helpful.

(i) Stressed syllables are marked with \, /, or ¨ over the vowel. Although the stressed syllable usually begins with a consonant, the vowel has been chosen to bear the stress-mark partly because that method raises no problem in printing, as it does not require special type. It also has the ad-vantage of drawing attention to the stressed vowel which the student must be particularly careful to pronounce correctly: see note on 14.

(ii) The sign \ indicates falling intonation, starting on a stressed syllable; the sign / indicates rising intonation on a stressed syllable. The sign ⌣ indi-cates an intonation beginning with a fall and ending with a rise: see 39. The rise or fall is the nucleus of the intonation pattern. Sometimes a rise occurs after the nucleus as a sign that we wish to modify what has gone before.

The sign ¨ indicates a stressed syllable occurring before or after the nucleus. When stresses come *before* the nucleus, begin the first on a relatively high pitch, then drop down a little on each stress, finally falling or rising on the nucleus. *After* the nucleus, pronounce each stress on the same pitch, low or high, as was reached by the fall or rise.

(iii) When a word has more than one stress, e.g. *ünderstànd, äfternòon,* follow the same intonation pattern as in (ii) and give prominence to the final stress. However, in many compound words, e.g. *pòst-öffice,* the first element is given prominence.

(iv) The sign | indicates the end of an intonation pattern before the end of a sentence. After | begin the pattern again, as in (ii).

N.B. Students are expected to read and repeat the examples in this book with the stress and intonation indicated; but they are not expected to assume that these indications are the only possible ones, except with regard to *syllable stress within a word.* With that exception, therefore, students need not *learn* how the indications are given.

31. Follow the instructions in the notes of Ex. 30, including the note on special stress.

32. Say the additions on the same final low pitch, with an extra little drop at the end.

34. Note the loss of stress on repetition of a syllable or word in examples c, j and k.

37. Say the additions on the same final high pitch, with an extra rise at the end.

38. Use a rising tone also at a break in the middle of a long sentence when the descent in intonation might otherwise be too long, e.g.

A bìrd in the hánd | is worth twö in the bùsh.

39. In expressions which are meant to be polite, a falling tone can sound final, abrupt and dictatorial. A rising tone after the initial fall softens this effect.

42. (a) Examples: *are, car; bed, head; break, make;* etc.

(d) to (m): give as *unseen* dictation. Test ability to distinguish sounds and to give an appropriate spelling for the sound dictated. Vary the order or insert different words, in case students have prepared the test beforehand. But be sure you dictate the sounds you intend, and keep a note of the order in which you dictate them.

Part Two

Exercises 43–52. A mass-word refers to a thing in general, or a sample of it, not divided into separate units; e.g. a solid substance, or liquid, activity (such as *work, play*), thought or feeling. Abstractions such as *beauty* or *truth* come into this category, so long as we imagine them as something undivided and not as separate units.

43. *earth,* i.e. the substance in general, not the planet. Similarly *bone, hair* in general; *glass,* the substance, not the drinking vessel, etc. Do not

merely translate these words. Let your pupils see or imagine examples of the things the words refer to, so that a direct association is made between the thing and the English word. The words can be learnt through thoughtful use in the exercises that follow, or better still, in a natural context.

44. From now on, a model is given in heavy type, at the head of many of the exercises. The model should be properly understood, and then practised orally with correct pronunciation and intonation (see Part One). It should be learnt, and then imitated. In 44–47 inclusive, the mass-word refers to the thing in general. *Answer* 44 with words from 43, e.g. *Meat is flesh. Mud is earth. Music is sound. Science is knowledge. Leather is skin.*

47. A few verbs are introduced here simply to give additional practice with nouns.

In 48–51 inclusive, the mass-word refers to a sample of the thing, not the thing in general.

48. Distinguish between *this* (near the speaker) and *that* (away from the speaker). *It* refers to the thing mentioned.

49. Note *fresh air (water, meat, bread); stale bread; strong* or *weak tea (coffee)*.

52. *Some* gives the idea of a small quantity of the mass (see 127, where *some* will be given special treatment). Compare *Give me some water* with *This is water* (48): in 48 emphasis is on the thing itself, the class of thing, without reference to quantity.

Exercises 53–64. These deal with words referring to things seen or imagined as separate whole units, many having definite shape (see 56) or being measurable.

53. Again do not merely translate, but make a direct association between thing and English word whenever you can. A drawing or picture will often help to establish this association.

Exercises 54–59. In these exercises, *a line*, etc. refers to one example of that class of thing, with emphasis on the *class*. In Exercises 60–64, *a pencil*, etc. refers to one example, with emphasis on quantity as well as class. Notice what happens when these ideas are expressed in the plural, Ex. 70, 71 and 72. Thus the plural of *a line* (54) is *lines*, but the plural of *a stamp* (64) is *some stamps* (72). Notice the use of *one* instead of *a* in 64 to emphasise the idea of 'one, not two or more', or of 'one as distinct from another'.

55. *Answer:* An ant is an insect, etc.

56. A *ball (watch, clock*, etc.) is also round. The students should have a clear idea of the shape of objects and the shape indicated by certain adjectives.

59. Prepositions (*to, at, in*, etc.) will receive special treatment later. Answer to (i): *We work at a table or desk* (or *at a shop or office*).

60. Dialogue between A and B. Note the shift of emphasis in *Thère is a pëncil* (emphasis on the *place indicated*), *Mínd! There's a neèdle* (emphasis on the *thing mentioned*), *There's a pëncil in your pòcket* (emphasis on the existence of the thing mentioned in the place mentioned, and disappearance of emphasis on the place *indicated*). Note also: *There is some water (some sugar, milk, ink, paper*).

64. Dialogue between A and B.

65, 66. The general principle is that the noun takes no article when it refers to the thing in general, and takes an article when it refers to an isolated, whole example of the thing. However, this principle cannot be applied equally to all nouns. Thus, *a paper, a glass, an iron,* refer to certain classes of objects only; and some words, e.g. *money, music, furniture, information, advice, progress* are not normally used with the *in*definite article at all. These details can best be learnt by observation of actual usage and by experience of the language through reading and conversation. In Exercises 65 and 66, the teacher should work through the examples himself with beginners before letting them attempt the exercises on their own. *Answers:* 65. (*a*) light, a light; (*b*) a fire, fire; (*c*) time, a time (or *time*), a time (or *time*); (*d*) space, a space; (*e*) pleasure, pain, a pain; (*f*) an (interesting) life, life; (*g*) fuel, a fuel (or *fuel*), a fuel (or *fuel*), a food (or *food*); (*h*) a pleasure.

66. (*a*) piece of paper, paper, some paper, a paper; (*b*) glass, piece of glass, a glass; (*c*) piece of iron, an iron; (*d*) cloth, piece of cloth, a cloth; (*e*) some money, Money; (*f*) a game, job, work, play; (*g*) some information, piece of information; (*h*) some advice, piece of advice; (*i*) some furniture (or *furniture* alone), piece of furniture; (*j*) progress.

70. *Birds fly,* i.e. things of that class, in general: emphasis on class. Possible answer to (*k*): *Men wear suits and shirts. Women wear dresses.*

71. *Lines.* Here we are not referring to things of that class *in general,* but to more than one example of a thing of that class, with emphasis on class. Be careful to distinguish in pronunciation between *this* and *these* and in meaning between *these* (near the speaker) and *those* (away from the speaker). *They:* the things mentioned.

72. *Some stamps:* i.e. a small quantity of things of that class. For pronunciation of *some,* see Ex. 25 and notes.

73. In this exercise, *the* serves as a signal that we are specifying one particular example of a class of thing, as distinct from another, and that we assume our audience knows which example we mean. Note the stress pattern.

74. Here, *the* serves as a signal that we are specifying a thing of one class as distinct from something of another class. Note the stress pattern.

75. Here, *the* serves as a signal that we are specifying something already introduced. We know from the context what key is meant.

77. Here, *the* serves as a signal that we are referring to an object which is normally considered the unique example of its class. There can be other suns, but this is the one we usually mean.

78. Here, *the* serves as a signal that we are referring to some marked and known part of the map of our experience. There can be other ceilings, but we have only one in mind when we say *the ceiling.*

80, 81. 80 (*a*) is like 73, but in the plural; 80 (*b*) like 74 plural; 80 (*c*) like 75; 80 (*d*) like 76; 81 like 78. A plural example of 77 would be *the stars.*

82. In *to school, by bus,* etc. we are not primarily concerned with a specific school or bus, but with activity communally associated with those things.

THE NEW ENGLISH GRAMMAR

Expressions like *go to school* are accepted conventions: you are not free to invent them for yourself.

83. *The water:* here we are specially concerned with a particular sample of water—this sample as distinct from the rest.

85. The subject of the sentence is *water* (singular) and the verb must therefore be *is* (see 162).

86. The sign / indicates contrast. *Pretty* and *beautiful* can both be contrasted with *ugly*.

90, 91. Note the stress and pitch: *stöne wàll, bëdroom wìndow*. Do not use *golden* or *silken* except in recognised metaphorical or poetic expressions.

Answers to 91: a drawing-room carpet; my office desk; your garden gate; a village doctor; the station clock; our school hall; the city walls; a university examination; a government official; a mountain road; a winter evening; an October morning.

92. Note the stress and pitch: *spàce shìp, tòoth-brush*, etc. However, though the second element is on a lower pitch than the first, it usually retains some stress and the full vowel value of the separate word. In Ex. 92 pronounce the second element, in every case, with the full vowel value of the separate word, e.g. *flower* (23) *shop* (6). Point out that in some old compounds, e.g. *penknife*, a meaning is produced which is now different from that of both elements separately. The use of hyphens is very difficult to describe systematically. Generally speaking, a new combination, e.g. *space ship*, has no hyphen; the hyphen tends to be used as the combination becomes more familiar; then a new compound is formed, e.g. *penknife*. In this matter, the student can only observe usage and consult a good dictionary. Note that *oil, powder, paste* are mass-words, therefore say *it's hair-oil, it's face-powder, it's tooth-paste*. Note: *note-book, tooth-brush*.

93. *Answers:* sunny weather, sun-glasses; rainy weather, rain-coat; a windy day, wind instrument; a soap factory, soapy water; sandy soil, stony ground; beautiful girls, beauty competition; music lessons, musical; danger sign, dangerous corner; science teachers, scientific; poisonous, poison bottle.

94. *Answers:* This is soft yellow sand; some fresh white bread; the deep blue sea; that warm water in the basin; my black sun-glasses; etc.

95. *Answers:* (a) etc. This story is interesting. (b) This story is about war. (d) This cupboard is for china. (f) This juice is from grapes. (l) This bottle is for beer. (j) This official is in the government.

96. Use *healthy* attributively to refer to a permanent condition. Except in traditional, fixed expressions (e.g. *It's an ill wind that blows nobody any good*—meaning a very bad wind) do not use *ill* attributively; and it is advisable to avoid using *dear* attributively when referring to price.

97. Avoid *a ripe, some ripe*, etc. without a following noun. Note the special use of *the living*, etc. referring to people of that class in general, as in 70. Do not use this construction in any other sense.

98. You can invent compounds on this model, e.g. *a roomful, a houseful, a tankful*, etc.

170

100 (*d*). See *English as a Foreign Language* for *London University, the London Library*. Note which of these forms happens to be used when you come across them.

103. Note *the Freemans*, following the scheme in 67.

106. Answer with words or constructions occurring in 44 onwards. Beware of alternative possibilities. *A corn* can be right; it depends what you have in mind. If you mean '*corn*' (i.e. grain) in general, then *a corn* is wrong. *A fruit* is right, if you mean a kind of fruit. We can say *rain*, in general; or *the rain*, i.e. the rain that is now falling, or *the rain* as distinct from *the wind*. *Stone*, substance; *a stone*, object. *The world* (the one we all know) or *a world*. An answer is 'right' if it expresses exactly what the speaker has in mind.

108. Tell the students not to use *the* unless they are referring to a specified thing. *Answers:* (*a*) water, a bath, matches, a box, beer, barrels. (*b*) Fire, ash. The smoke, fire. (*c*) the ash, a cigarette, an ash-tray. (*d*) Sheets, cotton, blankets, wool. (*e*) A car, a machine, A carpet, an article, furniture. (*f*) A loaf, bread, some milk, some biscuits. (*g*) the post-office, some stamps. (*h*) a new hat, a good one. (*i*) hats, the brown one. (*j*) a hot day, the food, ice-box. (*k*) school, bus, home, foot. (*l*) school, science, mathematics. (*m*) Students, law, medicine, (a, the, or no article) university. (*n*) some ink, some ink, the bottle. (*o*) a letter, the date, the top, the paper. (*p*) wonderful weather, a cloud, the sky. (*q*) room, the light, the switch. (*r*) the capital, the Philippine Islands. (*s*) The river Ganges, the Himalayas, the Bay of Bengal. (*t*) heat, light, sound. (*u*) a good knowledge, English, progress. [70]

109. *Answers:* Cities are big towns; villages are small places. On summer evenings, we have meals in the open air. Book-shelves are long boards or sheets of metal. Knives are instruments with sharp blades. Put these matches and these leaves in those boxes. Write answers to the following questions. In the pictures, we see men, women and children. Mothers-in-law are the mothers of husbands or wives. There are some ladies and gentlemen outside. There are some sheep in the fields and (some) wolves in the forest.

113 (*c*). Note the use of *some* in this kind of affirmative sentence, and *any* in this kind of interrogative and negative sentence. But do not insist that *some* must always be used in the affirmative, and *any* always in the negative and interrogative. See 127.

116. *James's* has two syllables (*James-iz*). Pronounce *Church's* like *churches*. Avoid *s's* after non-English names or long names. Say, for example, *Söphocles' plàys* or *the pläys of Sòphocles*.

117 (*b*). *Answers:* It's Napoleon's hat, Shakespeare's theatre, the President's birthday, Dante's birthplace, a play about Caesar's death.

117 (*c*). i.e. my brother's home, the baker's shop, etc.

121. All the answers can follow the pattern of stress and intonation in *ròad-sìde*, but *sëa-sìde* and *wëek-ènd* are very common.

122. Use 116, 120 and 121 as guides in doing this exercise.

123 (*c*). 16, 18, is 23, is 41, is 16.

128. *Answers:* All earth is solid, but not all earth is hard. All the earth in this garden is soft, etc.

Table 9 *and* 131. In common usages, as in 131 (*b*), we tend to avoid using *little* and *few* without a modifying adverb.

132. Note: When there are only 5 gallons in it (rising intonation), the tank is half empty (fall). The tank is half empty (rise), when there are only 5 gallons in it (fall).

134. *Much or little: How much?* Note that in the question we normally use the word which indicates the higher degree. Similarly, *how old,* etc.

135. Note that in this kind of situation we avoid using *much, many, far, long,* by themselves in affirmative sentence. These words can, however, be used in affirmative sentences of greater length or in more formal style.

136. *Answers:* a piece of meat weighing 3 kilos. The piece is 2½ kilos. It is not heavy enough, etc.

143. Notice the stress patterns in *Öxford Ròad,* but *Nòrth Street.*

144. *Answers:* (*a*)What, someone (somebody), the; (*b*)Who, It's. (*c*)are some; is also a. (*d*) Which, more, the. (*e*) all, are important, some, this, very (or most) important, it, an (or any). (*f*) no, the (or your), Whose. (*g*) Charles's, who. (*h*) He, of mine, best (or any other suitable adjective), He, one of the, this (or that). Which. (*i*) The, the, what, next (or second, or last, etc.). (*j*) his, my letters, any. (*k*) something, else. (*l*) anything, some, ice.

145. *Answers:* 1. What letter is that? 2. Who is that? 3. Whose is this towel? 4. That towel is hers. 5. Your father's name. 6. Your parents' address. 7. An elephant's trunk. 8. The road-side. 9. An evening's work. 10. I have no idea. 11. Everyone (or everybody) is happy. 12. Anyone (or anybody) can tell you. 13. Ask someone (somebody) else. 14. There is very little time. 15. There are very few plates. 16. But there is plenty (a good deal) of bread. 17. The basket is empty. 18. The box is nearly (almost) full. 19. This is a different box. 20. But is it the same size? 21. Answer the next question. 22. It is cooler today. 23. Tin is lighter than lead. 24. (3 + 4) is twice as much as (2 + 3). 25. This is as long as that. 26. I am as old as you. 27. What size is this room? 28. Give me another one. 29. Where are the others? 30. Both my sisters are married. 31. My brothers-in-law are doctors. 32. A doctor's life is a busy one. 33. His day is too short. 34. This chair is not high enough. 35. It is not so low as the next one. 36. Harold is younger than Peter. 37. Peter is Harold's elder brother. 38. Your work is better than mine. 39. Mine is better than his (His is not so good as mine). 40. Yours is the tidiest. 41. I can't understand all of this. 42. The room is half empty. 43. Here is another (one more) example. 44. This is private property. 45. This belongs to me, to nobody else. 46. I don't like such weak tea. 47. I don't like coffee as strong as this. 48. Mr Porter is a music teacher. 49. Ralph is a student of his. 50. I can't sleep on a bed as hard as this.

152. *Suggestions:* (*a*) start, rub, get, put, go, stand, feel, stretch. (*b*) Listen, hear, look, see, taste, smell. (*c*) slip, agree, Look, touch, think

(believe). (*d*) take, go, get, put, Wait, drop, keep. (*e*) Come, send, hurry, run. (*f*) wonder, think (believe), know. (*g*) understand, mean. (*h*) tear, break, bend, stretch, twist, bite, press, draw. (*i*) give, throw, catch, turn, shake, pull. (*j*) jump, climb. (*k*) want, like, prefer. (*l*) stop, let, take (send). (*m*) hope, wish. [60]

162.   A group of people (*committee, government*, etc). may either be considered as a *body* (singular) or as a body of *persons* (plural). Either say '*A family has its* . . .' or '*A family have their* . . .'; and do not make the same noun singular in one sentence and plural in the next. *The police* are generally plural. Regard *each* and *every* as singular. However, a sentence like 'Everyone wants their own way' is now very common.

166.   Do not stress *myself*, etc. in 166, but do so in 167.

172.   (*a*) it, me. (*b*) myself, you, I, it. (*c*) it, them. (*d*) me, you, We, it, us. (*e*) they, they, us. (*f*) him, him. (*g*) him, he, he, us. (*h*) Who, it, it, ourselves. (*i*) it, yourself. (*j*) she, we, each other. (*k*) they, us, We, one another. (*l*) it, us, us, it. (*m*) them, them, me. (*n*) he, himself. (*o*) themselves, They. (*p*) They, them. (*q*) It. They. [50]

174.   (*a*) Say. (*b*) Tell. (*c*) Tell. (*d*) say. (*e*) Say. (*f*) tell. (*g*) tell. (*h*) say. (*i*) say. (*j*) tell.

183.   (*a*) enough, better. (*b*) too, too much, less. (*c*) very, always, well, sometimes, rather, faster. (*d*) never, sometimes. (*e*) nearly (almost), hardly. (*f*) quite, nearly (almost, quite). (*g*) late, still, early, already, yet. (*h*) nearer, hardly. [25]

186–188.   Use the Ordinary Present Tense in these exercises.

187.   The purpose of this exercise will perhaps be clearer if speaker A begins by saying to B 'I will tell you to do something. You do it, and at the same time tell me what you do'. Then A says to C 'I will tell B to do that again. As he does it, you tell me what he does'.

194.   Use the Present Continuous to give one of the kinds of emphasis specified in 194. Note that the author has avoided exercises which require the student to decide whether the Ordinary Present or the Present Continuous should be used. That choice depends very much on context and exactly what the speaker has in mind.

197.   See note 60. *Answers* In (*a*), use pattern A. In (*b*), use pattern B. In (*c*) A; (*d*) A; (*e*) B; (*f*) B; (*g*) A; (*h*) B; (*i*) B; (*j*) A.

198.   Do not use pronouns in the questions unless your audience knows who the pronouns refer to.

Suggestions for answers: Do you know the Joneses? Do you like them? Where do they live? Who drives their car? How do they drive? How does he go to his office? What do they do in the evening? Why do they go to the theatre? Who do they see there? How long does the play last? Do you speak Italian? Do you wear glasses? Do you smoke? Does your father smoke? When does he smoke a cigar? What do those people want? How do you spell 'hurry'? What does 'hurry' mean? How much does this book cost? How many pages do you read in an hour?

201.   Either *if* or *whether* could be used in *c, d, g, h* and *j*, but *if* is more likely in *c, d,* and *g,* and *whether* expresses the uncertainty in *h* and *j*.

212. This is an extract from a diary, not something especially written as a grammatical exercise. Note the alteration of Ordinary Present and Present Continuous Tense, the former giving a snap-shot or general view, the latter taking a motion picture and emphasising action in progress.

214. (*a*) he sees, she goes, he does, he says, etc.   (*b*) There it is, there they are, shut it, etc.   (*c*) be quiet. Move quietly. Don't make . . . I can hardly hear . . .   (*d*) very well; pronounces, carefully; too quickly.   (*e*) advice, advise, practise, practice.   (*f*) lie, lay.   (*g*) high enough, raise.   (*h*) tell say, tell.   (*i*) make, do.   (*j*) show, show, explain, explain.

215. Be careful of *himself, themselves*.

216. Use the Present Continuous in *a*, *b*, the second part of *c*, in *e*, *h*, *j*; and the Ordinary Present in the first part of *c*, in *d*, *f*, *g* and *i*.

218. *Who is working in a factory? What is George doing? Where is he working?* etc. Note that stress and intonation in the answer would vary with the question.

220. (*a*) You speak English very well.   (*b*) We can sometimes see the moon very clearly (or sometimes we can see . . .).   (*c*) I can hardly answer that question myself.   (*d*) That sentence does not quite make sense.   (*e*) What do you do in the holidays?   (*f*) We usually go to the sea in the summer (*or*, In the summer, we usually go).   (*g*) Who sends his friends good wishes at Christmas?   (*h*) You are not writing that carefully enough.   (*i*) We often have no lessons on Saturday (*or*, On Saturday, we often have . . . *or*, Often, we have . . .).   (*j*) Do not tell strangers your private business.

223. to, to, at, at, to, at, to, at, at, to. [10]

225. (*a*) at, to.   (*b*) to, at.   (*c*) at, to.   (*d*) from, to.   (*e*) from, to.   (*f*) to, at.   (*g*) to, at.   (*h*) at, to.   (*i*) from, from.   (*j*) at, to. [20]

226. (*a*) at, to.   (*b*) to, to.   (*c*) to, at.   (*d*) to, at.   (*e*) to, at.   (*f*) at, at, at.   (*g*) to, at. [15]

228. (*a*) on, on, in, on, in (*or* on, *or* on top of), in, on, in, on.   (*b*) off, off, out of, off, out of (*or* off), out of, off, out of, off.   (*c*) in, on, in, on, in (*or* on).   (*d*) into, out of, off, on to.   (*e*) outside, inside, into (*or* inside). [30]

229. on, on to, into, into, in, into, in, into, into, on to. [10]

230. (*a*) at, on, in, at, at, at.   (*b*) at, in, in.   (*c*) on, in.   (*d*) at, on, in. (*e*) in, at.   (*f*) in.   (*g*) at, in, at. [20]

232. along, across, by (or past), through, through, along, across, by, along, by. [10] Note *through the park* is better in this context, following into, which suggests a space; but *across* the park is also possible. Avoid *pass past*, because of the repetition of sound.

235. (*a*) with, without.   (*b*) between, among.   (*c*) round.   (*d*) over. (*e*) above.   (*f*) as far as, towards.   (*g*) for.   (*h*) beyond.   (*i*) in front of. (*j*) behind, under.   (*k*) with.   (*l*) for, for.   (*m*) for.   (*n*) against, against. [20]

237. (*a*) at, in, on, since.   (*b*) on, in.   (*c*) in (or during), at.   (*d*) after, before.   (*e*) at, till, past, in (or during), through.   (*f*) at, in, in (*or* during), at, on, till, past.   (*g*) for, from, to (*or* till), during, through.   (*h*) till, by, before, for.   (*i*) in.   (*j*) for.   (*k*) at, before, till.   (*l*) in, since, for.   (*m*) for [40]

239. (*a*) by (*in every case*).   (*b*) with (*in every case*).   (*c*) about, on, by,

for, instead of. (*d*) about, about, on. (*e*) of, about, from, of (*or* about), for. (*f*) of, from. (*g*) of, from, of, from, by. (*h*) of, from, of, from. (*i*) as, like. (*j*) as, like. [40]

241.

(*a*) from.	(*b*) on.	(*c*) at.	(*d*) by.	(*e*) about.
(*f*) in.	(*g*) on.	(*h*) about.	(*i*) to	(*j*) with.
(*k*) of.	(*l*) to.	(*m*) of.	(*n*) from.	(*o*) for.
(*p*) with.	(*q*) of.	(*r*) at.	(*s*) for.	(*t*) to.
(*u*) from.	(*v*) for.	(*w*) in.	(*x*) at. (*y*) in.	(*z*) with.

242. (*a*) on, at, to, with, in, for. (*b*) for, round, on, of, on, between, in, past (*or* beyond). (*c*) from, across, to, opposite, for, in, from, to (*or* till), except, in, till, on. (*d*) with, to (*or* as far as), as far as. (*e*) Instead of, at, at, about, for. (*f*) for, like, of. (*g*) on, of, on. (*h*) with, about, of, in, of. (*i*) about, with, in, for, of. (*j*) over, under, above, of, below, in (*or* under *or* below), without, out of. (*k*) from, towards, on, of, along, on, through, up. (*l*) with, of, for, for, with, on. (*m*) at, in, on, for, till. (*n*) In, of, from, In, from, under, from, of, from, of. (*o*) on, from, with, from, for, for, about, on, of, till. (*p*) in, during, after. [100]
245. (*a*) out, back. (*b*) up. (*c*) down. (*d*) across. (*e*) over, through. (*f*) outside, away. (*g*) round. (*h*) back, down. (*i*) about, down. (*j*) off (*or* up). (*k*) away, back. (*l*) out, away. (*m*) by, up. (*n*) on, forwards, backwards. (*o*) up, upstairs. (*p*) over, over. (*q*) afterwards. (*r*) downwards. [30]
246. (*a*) down to. (*b*) across to. (*c*) along to. (*d*) round to. (*e*) back to. (*f*) up on. (*g*) down on. (*h*) over to the other side. (*i*) through to the other side. (*j*) by on the other side. [10]
248. (*a*) on, up. (*b*) up (*or* in), out. (*c*) up, up, on, up. (*d*) off (*or* out). (*e*) out, out. (*f*) out. (*g*) out, out. (*h*) up. [15]

250.

(*a*) B.	(*b*) B.	(*c*) A.	(*d*) A.	(*e*) B.
(*f*) A.	(*g*) A.	(*h*) B.	(*i*) B.	(*j*) 246.
(*k*) A.	(*l*) B.	(*m*) 246.	(*n*) B.	(*o*) A.
(*p*) A.	(*q*) B.	(*r*) B.	(*s*) B.	(*t*) B.
(*u*) A.	(*v*) B.	(*w*) A.	(*x*) A.	(*y*) B.

257. In the 3rd person, verbs ending in d or t, e.g. *attend, visit,* have an extra syllable in the past, not in the present; verbs ending in a hissing sound, e.g. *advise, brush, change, dance, use, watch,* have an extra syllable in the present, not in the past. Note the spelling of: *applied, begged, fitted, referred, suffered, travelled, visited, wrapped.*
267. *Answers:* (*a*) shut, put, took, did not shut, was, went, came, opened, found, turned. (*b*) woke up, lay, read, got up, washed, got dressed, had breakfast, left, walked, bought, caught, paid, gave, took, was. (*c*) was not, were you? how was, how were, was, wasn't it? That was. Those were, weren't they? (*d*) was, stayed; wrote, did you get (*or* receive); have you heard? Did you hear? hurt, have not been able; was, died; Have we done (finished)? did (*or* finished).

268. *Proceed as follows:* (*a*) Does your mother make your clothes herself? She used to make our clothes herself, but she doesn't now. (*b*) I always went to school by bus. Do you always go, etc. I used to go, etc., but I don't now, etc.

269. *Specimen answer:* Every day, I rest . . . It is now 9 o'clock. I am not busy. I am resting. I have been resting for one hour. What have I been doing? (Answer) Suppose it is now 10. I am not tired, etc.

270. *Answers:* (*a*) Because the sun has been shining on it. (*b*) Because I have been running up and down stairs. (*c*) He has been working too hard. (*d*) No wonder: she has been practising it for six months. (*e*) She was practising a piece of music. (*f*) He was working too hard. (*g*) How long have you been learning English? I have been learning it for . . . (*h*) We have been waiting. What were we doing? We were waiting. (*i*) I am doing an exercise (answering a question). What were you doing? I was . . . (*j*) What have you been doing? I have been doing this exercise (answering these questions).

273. (*a*) We gave a party. · We had invited a lot of people. Had we invited everybody? No, we hadn't . . . (*b*) There was enough to eat. We had ordered plenty of food. Had we ordered everything? No, we hadn't . . . (*c*) Last year we stayed . . . We had usually rented a cottage before. Had we always rented (or stayed) . . . ? etc. (*d*) Last year, my father caught . . . He had never been ill before. Had he ever been ill (had he always been well) before? No, he had never been ill (he had always been well) before.

274. (*a*) arrived, had left already (*or* had already left). (*b*) arrived, had left. (*c*) met, had not met. (*d*) had never seen, I recognised. (*e*) knew, had met. (*f*) found, had fallen. (*g*) had lain, was. (*h*) had had, felt. (*i*) reached, had travelled, had climbed, had ever explored. [20]

275. The model for 275 is the past of the model for 270. Proceed as follows: (*a*) Why was the wall so hot? Because the sun had been shining on it. (*b*) Why were you . . . ? Because I had been running . . . (*c*) Was your father . . . Yes, he had been working . . . (*d*) Mary played . . . she had been practising . . . (*e*) What had M. been doing three weeks before? She had been . . . (*f*) What had your father been doing? He had been . . . (*g*) We were learning . . . Suppose you had started two years before. How long had you been learning till then? (*h*) We were waiting . . . We had got here (*or* there) half an hour before, so we had been waiting . . . What had we been doing half an hour before? (*i*) What were you doing? What had you been (or were you) doing? (*j*) It was time . . . What had you been doing for the last ten minutes?

278. *Answers:* I will be studying for three more hours. What will you be doing? etc.

279. *Answer:* (I'll tell you tomorrow) I will have seen it, heard it, met him, written it, thought about it, by then.

280. There are, however, other uses of *would*. These will be dealt with later.

283. (*a*) *What are we having?* (something is already started). '*What are we going to have*' is possible (present indications), but not necessary. 'What

will we have' and 'What do we have' are also possible, but do not fit so well into the context.

(*b*) *Who is coming?* (something is obviously planned).

(*c*) *You are going to break.* (The 'present indications' are clear.) '*You will break*', emphasising the future event, is equally possible. '*You are breaking*', as a reference of future action, would be wrong; no one has arranged it.

(*d*) *I am going to sell* (my present intentions tell me what will happen). '*I am selling*' is also possible, though it might be taken as an example of 190 or 192.

(*e*) *The roof is going to collapse.* (Present indications are clear.) '*The roof is collapsing*' as a reference to *future* action would be wrong, as in (*c*).

(*f*) *I'll carry.* (The question of intentions, arrangements, etc. does not arise. There is no time for it anyway.)

(*g*) *I'll open.* (There are no present indications of what the future will bring, since I don't know what you want.)

(*h*) *we're going to have* (emphasis on 'present indications').

(*i*) *I'll be.* ('*I'm going to be*' is also possible, but unnecessary.)

(*j*) *What are you doing?* (emphasis on plans) '*What are you going to do*' is also possible (emphasis on present intentions).

(*k*) *leave, arrive* (according to programme).

(*l*) *You're going to have* (judging from the present indications). *You'll have* (emphasis on future) is also possible.

(*m*) '*will take place*' or '*takes place*'; but '*is taking place*'; '*is going to . . .*' are both also possible, though unnecessary: the plain statement of future or of programme is more business-like.

(*n*) '*will not be*' (plain business-like statement). '*He is not going to be*' is also possible, but unnecessary and would result in undesirable repetition in view of the second sentence, which should be '*He is going abroad*' (He has arranged it: that is why he will not be there).

(*o*) *I am seeing him.* (I have arranged an appointment.) '*I am going to see*,' or '*I'll see*', are also possible.

284. (*a*) went. (*b*) got. (*c*) brought. (*d*) was (*or* were). (*e*) were. (*f*) was (*or* were). (*g*) had heard. (*h*) would ask. (*i*) had asked. (*j*) hadn't.

286. (*a*) could not, did he think, we did not know. (*b*) I promised I would not forget. I hoped you would believe me. (*c*) was, It had been. (*d*) Who could tell what the next day would bring? (*e*) were, had been shining. (*f*) was, I thought . . . he felt . . . we had done. (*g*) was getting. I was sure there would be . . . had already returned . . . were fastening. (*h*) was, had been destroyed, it would take. [25]

287. (*a*) have been dealing, I hope you have not forgotten (or will not forget). (*b*) did you get, asked, put, felt, remembered, told, woke, thought, heard, were, crept, opened, listened, heard, began, caught, someone had left, fell, I wonder, did not hear, picked myself up, found myself, was, a man was standing (*or* stood). He shone, saw, was, asked (*or* said), Are, Did you hurt (Have you hurt), came, was, think, forgot, thanked, shut,

177

came (*or* went), slept, woke. What did you do . . . , I said (answered), could not find, is, will fall over it.

(*c*) are doing, (*or* have been doing). We will not do (won't do), we have done. Have you got (*or* Did you get).

288. 1. I have borne it . . . 2. But he beat me. 3. It began . . . 4. I bent it . . . 5. It has just bitten (me). 6. It blew the roof off. 7. How did you break it? 8. Yes, I brought one. 9. He has burnt it already. 10. I bought it . . . 11. Mary chose it . . . 12. It cost . . . 13. I cut it . . . 14 They dug it . . . 15. Yes, I drew one . . . 16. I haven't dreamt . . . 17. I have drunk it up already. 18. I have driven one for years . . . 19. I have eaten . . . 20. They flew across in . . . 21. I have already given it to him (given it to him already). 22. I grew it . . . 23. I hung it . . . 24. he hid it. 25. We held it . . . 26. We knew them . . . 27. They laid it . . . 28. Yes, they led it. 29. Somebody lent them one. 30. I let it out . . . 31. I lay down on the deck. 32. I lost it . . . 33. I meant exactly . . . 34. I put it on . . . 35. I have rung it twice . . . 36. I ran . . . 37. I sold it for . . . 38. They set out at day-break. 39. Yes, I shook it hard. 40. I shot it with a rifle. 41. It sank . . . 42. I've spent it all . . . 43. I haven't spoilt it (*or* I won't). 44. I spread them out in the . . . 45. it sprang out . . . 46. Nobody stole it (*or* has stolen it): it is still in your pocket. 47. I have struck two . . . 48. I told him to drive . . . 49. Both swam across it. 50. I've worn it . . .

291. *Answers* to (*a*), (*b*), and other questions can easily be found in the text. Note: (*c*) No, he had never left his own country before. (*f*) Yes, he knew it very well. (*h*) The friend asked him how he was. (*i*) 'How are you?' (*j*) The friend next asked him whether he was enjoying himself. (*k*) 'Are you enjoying yourself?' (*l*) The visitor said he was feeling well. (*n*) He had gone for a walk round the streets. (*o*) 'I went for a walk round the streets and found myself at Victoria Station.' (*r*) He saw a train come in. (*s*) The doors swung outward as the train came nearer and nearer. (*t*) The train came nearer and nearer to where he was standing. (*u*) They jumped out while the train was still moving.

294. *Answers.* Put (*a*) and (*f*) together; (*b*) and (*p*); (*c*) and (*w*); (*d*) and (*v*); (*e*) and (*r*); (*g*) and (*q*); (*h*) and (*l*); (*i*) and (*n*); (*j*) and (*t*); (*k*) and (*m*); (*o*) and (*s*); (*u*) and (*x*).

298. (*a*) from, to, drive, in, between, passes, through, on, on, beyond. (*b*) am leaving (or *leave*, or *will leave*, or *am going to leave*), for, in, have not started, yet, at, am waiting, am starting (or *start*, or *will start*, or *am going to start*), at, know, will arrive, at, in, started, off. (*c*) am driving, left, ago, am going, away from, is travelling, towards, is moving, along, in front. (*d*) only, on, across, over, under, see, are riding, along, beside, drive, past, behind. (*e*) have been driving, since, for, have already completed, will drive (or *will be driving*), for, till (*or* until), by, to. (*f*) Have I arrived at Z yet? No, not yet, have arrived, arrived, ago, have travelled, have been driving, for. (*g*) left, at, passed, through, at, was driving, was still travelling, with, had left, before. (*h*) was, at, knew, would arrive, in, was, had travelled, had been driving, at, had not started, yet, was waiting. (*i*) was

coming, saw, were riding, passed. (*j*) I drove, to, without, did not come, with, had come.

299. *Possible answers:* (*a*) George is still in bed. (*b*) He has been awake for two hours. (*c*) Mary is not awake yet. (*d*) You don't eat very much (or *a lot*). (*e*) Some people eat too much. (*f*) There are too many people in (or *on*) this boat. (*g*) That is my firm belief. (*h*) Breathe deeply. (*i*) He works hard. (*j*) She makes her own clothes. (*k*) I'm asking you his name. (*l*) This material is called nylon. (*m*) Get your guest a chair. (*n*) You do not practise enough. (*o*) I (or *we* or *you*) cannot drink this tea. (*p*) George always disobeys me. (*q*) A wooden building. (*r*) Your business train. (*s*) Take these things away. (*t*) Let's leave this place. (*u*) I ask you whether (or *if*) this is the right road. (*v*) My room is below yours but not right under (or *underneath*) it. (*w*) I saw John when I was coming (or *going*) home. (*x*) Please explain to us the meaning of this sentence. (*y*) It's late: it's time we stopped.

300. *Answers:* (*a*) We usually go into the country on Sundays. (*or* On Sundays, we usually go into the country). (*b*) Both the old blue Persian rugs in this room are my uncle's. (*c*) Who dug up all those tomato plants in the garden yesterday? (*d*) They have not put these pictures up on the wall carefully enough. (*e*) Did you see the fireworks last night? They were wonderful, weren't they? (*f*) A professor with white hair was talking but his students were all walking about and nobody was listening to him. (*g*) Before James Hudson came here, we had never heard anything about him. (*h*) 'Have you worked out that problem already?' she asked. 'Not yet,' we answered. (*or* 'Have you worked that problem out . . .) (*i*) She asked us if we had worked it out properly. (*j*) 'Is there anybody there?' said the guide, knocking on the door with his stick.

INDEX

List of Tables

INDEX

Subjects and words treated.

Numbers refer to paragraphs and exercises (or, when stated, to tables)

The New English Grammar

The New English Grammar

MORE LESSONS IN ENGLISH AS A FOREIGN LANGUAGE

By R. A. CLOSE

PARTS THREE AND FOUR

How to Use the Verb

London
GEORGE ALLEN & UNWIN LTD
RUSKIN HOUSE   MUSEUM STREET

PRINTED IN GREAT BRITAIN
by Photolithography
BY JOHN DICKENS AND CO LTD
NORTHAMPTON

In memory of

GEORGE TRYPANIS

*teacher of English from 1950 to 1967 at the
British Council's Institute in Athens
and President of the Greek Association of Teachers of English
who so often insisted that the verb
is the crucial problem in English grammar*

PREFACE

This second volume (Parts Three and Four) of *The New English Grammar* concludes the practical exercises on the problems discussed in *English as a Foreign Language*. It concentrates on what is perhaps the greatest difficulty in English grammatical usage, namely the verb and the various constructions in which the verb is the main part.

While each of the two volumes is independent of the other, students working through the second are assumed to have covered the groundwork in the first; and both together make up a complete course. This does not mean they contain all the English grammar possible. That would fill many pages, take up far too much of the learner's time, and delay his progress in the free use of the language unnecessarily. As the preface to the first book said, the learner will soon reach a point where progress can be made not by doing more and more grammar, but by hearing, reading and using the language in real and interesting contexts. He will then, incidentally, extend his knowledge of grammar and strengthen his command of it.

What the author does claim is that these two volumes provide practice in overcoming certain difficulties that constantly recur in the use of English as a foreign tongue. Such practice is necessary, for school pupils, university students, teachers in training, and others requiring a sure command of English for public and professional purposes.

But the best aids to good English are, always, a good dictionary and the example of those writers who are acknowledged to be masters of their craft. Partly to lead the student to such writers, though primarily to present models of the kind of English that survives, I have made considerable use of well-known quotations, limiting my borrowings to language that is still current today. I have also included many proverbs and common sayings. As well as providing good examples of grammatical structure, of typical rhythms, and of other lasting features of the language such as alliteration and assonance, English proverbs are evocative and memorable in a way that much of the language commonly used in English lessons today is not.

The book is intended for practice, study, and reference. Exercises should normally be done orally, though many of them should also be accurately written out. Answers to certain of the exercises are given at the back of the book. For present and future reference, there is a list of useful verbs with a key to the patterns in which they commonly occur.

I have referred constantly to *The Oxford Dictionary of English*

Proverbs (W. G. Smith and Janet Haseltine; second edition revised by Sir Paul Harvey); to *The Penguin Dictionary of Quotations* (J. M. and M. J. Cohen: Penguin Books) from which I have taken a number of examples; to *A Guide to Patterns and Usage* (A. S. Hornby: Oxford University Press) and *A General Service List of English Words* (compiled by Dr. Michael West: Longmans Green), to make sure that I have dealt with a complete range of useful words and structures.

For further reading, teachers and students with linguistic training are referred to *A Linguistic Study of the English Verb* by Professor F. R. Palmer, Longmans Green, 1965.

ACKNOWLEDGEMENTS

I am indebted to Mr Andrew Bonar and Mr Brian Richards for reading the typescript of this book and for suggesting corrections and improvements; and to Mr J. Y. K. Kerr for further suggestions at the proof stage.

R.A.C.

Athens, 1967

CONTENTS

PART THREE

THE VERB

BASIC INFORMATION

The information in this section of the book is essential for anybody hoping to use the English verb fully and correctly. Grammatical terms are used for reference only: it is not necessary to learn them.

1   i. There are 10 verbs in English, called **Modal verbs**, that are treated differently from all other verbs. They are:

will   shall   can   may   must
would should could might ought

ii. *Would, should* and *could* are sometimes used as past forms of *will, shall* and *can*; and, less often, *might* is used as a past form of *may*. (*Would, should, could* and *might* serve other purposes also.) Otherwise the 10 modal verbs have one form only. They do not add *s* to the 3rd Person Singular; they have no continuous forms, no perfect tenses, and none of the other forms taken by the full verbs (see 2).

iii. The interrogative of modal verbs is formed by placing the verb before the subject: *Must I?*

iv. The negative is formed by adding *not*: *must not*. Exceptionally, the negative of *can* is usually written as one word, *cannot*.

v. A modal verb can only be used when another verb is added to it, or is understood: *I can understand. We all can* (understand).

vi. Modal verbs will be studied further in Section Ten of this book.

2   All other words serving as verbs in English can be used as **Full Verbs**. *Need* and *dare* are used sometimes as modal verbs, sometimes as full verbs: see Section Ten. A full verb can be the only verb in a sentence; and all full verbs can fit into the scheme in Table 1.

TABLE 1

FULL VERBS

A. Finite Forms

Tense	Ordinary Form	Continuous Form
Present:	I eat/he eats	I am eating
Pre-present:	I have eaten	I have been eating
Past:	{ I ate / I used to eat	I was eating
Pre-past:	I had eaten	I had been eating
Future:	I will eat	I will be eating
Pre-Future:	I will have eaten	I will have been eating
Future-in-the-Past:	I would eat	I would be eating

Imperative: eat

B. Non-finite Forms

Infinitive: (to) eat   *Perfect Infinitive:* (to) have eaten
Present Participle and
   Gerund: eating   *Past Participle:* eaten
      Perfect Participle: having eaten

---

3   *Notes on Table 1:*

i. The part of the verb that you look for in the dictionary, e.g. *eat*, is called the *stem*.

ii. The *Ordinary Present Tense* of all full verbs has the same form as the stem, except that the 3rd Person Singular always adds the ending *s* or *es* to the spelling (*see Footnote*).

Exceptions: The 3rd Person Singular of *have* is *has*; and the Ordinary Present of *be* is as follows:

I am; you (we, they) are; he (she, it) is

iii. The *Ordinary Past* of most verbs in English, including all verbs recently added to the language (like *telephone*), has the ending *ed* or *d* added to the spelling of the stem (*see Footnote*). The Past of a closed class of old verbs is irregular: see 11 below. The *Past* of *be* is *was* for the 1st and 3rd persons singular, and

Note: 3 ii and iii. For the different pronunciations and spellings of the 3rd Person Singular, Present Tense, and of the Past Tense and Past Participle, see *The New English Grammar*, Part Two, Tables 18 and 26.

were for *you* and all persons plural. The Past of all other verbs has the same form for all persons, singular and plural.

iv. *Used to* plus the stem emphasizes past habit. It has no present form in modern English. To express the idea of present habit, use an adverb, e.g. *I usually eat.*

v. The *Ordinary Future* is formed by *will* plus the stem. *Shall* is often used instead of *will* for the 1st Person Singular and Plural: see Section Ten.

vi. The *Future-in-the-Past* is formed with *would* plus the stem. *Should* is often used instead of *would* for the 1st Person Singular and Plural. The Future-in-the-Past has the same form as the *Conditional*: see 82.

4 The verbs *be* and *have* are used both as full verbs and as **auxiliary verbs** helping to form certain of the tenses. *Used to* is an auxiliary only. *Will, would, shall* and *should* are used both as auxiliary verbs helping to form tenses, and as modal verbs expressing a 'mood' or attitude towards an action or state, as explained in Section Ten.

5 To form the **interrogative** of full verbs:

i. Begin with the auxiliary (or the first auxiliary, if there is more than one); then put the subject; then the rest of the verb:

Have you eaten? Have you been eating?

ii. Avoid the interrogative and negative of *used to* + stem (*see Footnote*).

iii. When there is no auxiliary, as in the Ordinary Present and Ordinary Past, supply the auxiliary *do* in the Present (3rd Person Singular, *does*) and *did* (Past). Form the interrogative by putting the auxiliary first, then the subject, then the *stem*:

Do I eat? Does he eat? Did we eat?

iv. *Exceptions*: *Be*, in the interrogative Present and Past, follows the pattern of the modal verbs (1, iii): *Am I? Were you? Have*, in the Present (and, less often, in the Past), when it means 'hold' or 'possess', may follow the modal verb pattern, as well as the full verb pattern. Thus *Have you a match?* and *Do you have a match?*

Note: 5 ii. *Used you to go?* and *I used not to go* are traditionally taught as 'correct', though they may sound unnatural; while *Did you use to go?* and *I didn't use to go*, though widely used, are still classed as 'incorrect'. You can avoid this uncertainty by saying *Did you (usually) go?* and *(Usually) I did not go.*

15

are both correct. When *have* has some other meaning, use the full verb pattern only:

Do you have breakfast in bed?

6 To form the **negative** of full verbs:

i. Put *not* after the (first) auxiliary, then add the rest of the verb. Where there is no auxiliary (as in the Ordinary Present and Past) supply the auxiliary *do* (*does*, *did*); put *not* after it, then add the stem:

I have not eaten.   He does not eat.   They did not eat.

ii. Avoid the negative form of *used to* + stem (*see Note to* 5, ii).

iii. *Exceptions*: *Be*, in the Present and Past, follows the pattern of the modal verbs (1, iv): *I am not. They were not.*
Have, in the Present (and, less often, in the Past) may follow the pattern of the modal verbs, as well as the pattern of the full verb, when it means 'hold' or 'possess'; with a different meaning, it follows the full verb pattern only: Thus,

I haven't any money or *I don't have any money*; but *I don't have breakfast in bed.*

iv. Note: Are we late? I don't think so (*or* I think not).

But say only: I hope not *in that situation.*

Shall we meet again? I don't suppose so (*or* I suppose not).

But say only: I fear not *in that situation.*

7 To form the **negative-interrogative**, put *not* immediately after the subject in the interrogative construction: *Do I not eat?* However, in spoken English, and even in written English too, the **contracted** form of the negative-interrogative is generally used (see 12, column 5), and the full form is avoided except in very formal language.

8 To **emphasize** the affirmative in contrast with the negative, the verb *be*, the (first) auxiliary or the modal verb is strongly stressed in speech and often underlined in writing. In the Ordinary Present and Ordinary Past of other full verbs, supply the auxiliary *do* (*does* or *did*) for emphasis, and then add the *stem*:

You say I'm not working, but I *am* working.
You say I can't do this, but I *can* do it.

You say he doesn't know you, but he *does* know you.
You say I didn't eat anything—I *did* eat something.

9 i. The **imperative** can have three emphatic forms:

    a. *Eat*, don't talk (emphasizing the verb).
    b. *Do* eat something (emphasizing the affirmative).
    c. *You* eat your breakfast (emphasizing the person addressed).

You, the subject of the verb, is absent except in c.
ii. The negative is:
Do not drink that   (Don't drink that). Don't you drink it.
But note the survival of an old form in *Waste not, want not* (common saying).
iii. To form the indirect imperative, say:
I told you to eat something. I told you not to drink that.

10 By convention, a sentence should contain a verb in one of its **finite** forms (see 2). A non-finite form is not sufficient by itself to act as the **Predicate** of what is generally called a sentence (*see Footnote*).

Irregular Verbs

11 The verbs listed below are irregular in either the Past Tense or the Past Participle, or both. A number against a verb refers to the notes at the end of the list. Be careful of the pronunciation of forms marked by an asterisk: see Part Two, 258.

Stem	Past	Past Participle	Stem	Past	Past Participle
arise	arose	arisen*	blow*	blew	blown*
be[1]	was*/		break*	broke	broken
	were*	been	breed	bred	bred
bear*	bore	borne[2]	bring	brought*	brought*
beat	beat	beaten	build*	built*	built*
become*	became	become*	burn[3]	burnt	burnt
begin	began	begun	burst	burst	burst
bend	bent	bent	buy*	bought*	bought*
bid	bid	bid	cast	cast	cast
bind*	bound	bound	catch	caught*	caught*
bite	bit	bitten	choose	chose	chosen
bleed	bled	bled	cling	clung	clung

Note: 10. See Part Two, Table 13.

Stem	Past	Past Participle	Stem	Past	Past Participle
come*	came	come*	lead	led	led
cost	cost	cost	lean[3]	leant*	leant*
creep	crept	crept	leap[3]	leapt*	leapt*
cut	cut	cut	learn[3]	learnt*	learnt*
deal	dealt*	dealt*	leave	left	left
dig	dug	dug	lend	lent	lent
do*	did	done*	let	let	let
draw	drew	drawn	lie[6]*	lay	lain
dream[3]	dreamt*	dreamt*	light[3]	lit	lit
drink	drank	drunk	lose*	lost	lost
drive	drove	driven*	make	made	made
eat	ate	eaten	mean	meant*	meant*
fall*	fell	fallen*	meet	met	met
feed	fed	fed	pay	paid	paid
feel	felt	felt	put*	put*	put*
fight	fought*	fought*	read	read*	read*
find*	found	found	ride	rode	ridden
flee	fled	fled	ring	rang	rung
fling	flung	flung	rise	rose	risen*
fly	flew	flown*	run	ran	run
forbid	forbade	forbidden	say	said*	said*
forget	forgot	forgotten	see	saw	seen
forgive*	forgave	forgiven*	seek	sought*	sought*
forsake	forsook	forsaken	sell	sold	sold
freeze	froze	frozen	send	sent	sent
get	got	got	set	set	set
give*	gave	given*	shake	shook	shaken
go	went	gone[4]*	shed	shed	shed
grind*	ground	ground	shine	shone*	shone*
grow*	grew	grown*	shoot	shot	shot
hang	hung	hung[5]	show*	showed	shown*
have*	had	had	shrink	shrank	shrunk
hear	heard*	heard*	shut	shut	shut
hide	hid	hidden	sing	sang	sung
hit	hit	hit	sink	sank	sunk
hold	held	held	sit	sat	sat
hurt	hurt	hurt	sleep	slept	slept
keep	kept	kept	slide	slid	slid
kneel[3]	knelt	knelt	sling	slung	slung
know*	knew	known*	slit	slit	slit
lay	laid	laid	smell[3]	smelt	smelt

Stem	Past	Past Participle	Stem	Past	Past Participle
sow*	sowed	sown*	sweep	swept	swept
speak	spoke	spoken	swim	swam	swum
speed	sped	sped	swing	swung	swung
spell[3]	spelt	spelt	take[9]	took	taken
spend	spent	spent	teach	taught*	taught*
spill[3]	spilt	spilt	tear*	tore	torn
spin	spun	spun	tell	told	told
spit	spat	spat	think	thought*	thought*
split	split	split	throw*	threw	thrown*
spoil[3]	spoilt	spoilt	thrust	thrust	thrust
spread*	spread*	spread*	tread*	trod	trodden
spring	sprang	sprung	wake	woke	woken
stand[7]	stood	stood	wear*	wore	worn
steal	stole	stolen	weave	wove	woven
stick	stuck	stuck	weep	wept	wept
sting	stung	stung	win	won*	won*
stink	stank	stunk	wind*	wound[10]	wound
stride	strode	stridden[8]	wring	wrung	wrung
strike	struck	struck	write	wrote	written
swear*	swore	sworn			

Notes:
1. See paragraph 3, ii and iii.
2. But 'I was born in 1930'.
3. These verbs also have regular forms.
4. But 'I went to Paris last year'. I am not there now. Therefore I can say 'I have been to Paris'. (See Part Two, 265.)
5. But criminals used to be *hanged*.
6. *lie* meaning 'to tell a lie' is regular.
7. Similarly, *understand*, *understood*, etc.; *withstand*, etc.
8. Past participle rarely used.
9. Similarly, *mistake*, *mistook*, *mistaken*; *undertake*, etc.
10. *wound**, i.e. to cause injury to, is regular.

PRACTISE *the irregular verbs by using them correctly in meaningful sentences. You have plenty of opportunities of using them in this book.*

12 Contracted Forms

Be and *have*, both as full verbs and as auxiliaries, *do* as an auxiliary, and most of the modal verbs have a weak pronunciation in fluent speech and contracted spellings in informal written English, as in Table 2. Check the pronunciation of forms marked with an asterisk.

Regard the examples in this book which contain contracted forms as being examples of informal English. Use the full forms in formal written composition.

TABLE 2

1	2	3	4	5
Full form	*Contracted*	*Contracted Negative: Use either 3, or 4*		*Negative-Interrogative*
I am	I'm	I'm not	—	Aren't I?
You are*	You're	You're not	You aren't	Aren't you?
He is (she is)	He's (she's)	He's not	He isn't	Isn't he?
It is	It's[1]	It's not	It isn't	Isn't it?
We are	We're	We're not	We aren't	Aren't we?
They are	They're	They're not	They aren't	Aren't they?
I was*	*(No contracted spellings in this position, but* was *and* were *pronounced weak in fluent speech.)*		I wasn't	Wasn't I?
You were*			You weren't	Weren't you?
I have*	I've	I've not	I haven't	Haven't I?
He has	He's[2]	He's not	He hasn't	Hasn't he?
I had	I'd	I'd not	I hadn't	Hadn't I?
I do*	*(No contracted spellings in this position, but* do *and* does *pronounced weak in fluent speech.)*		I don't*	Don't I?
He does*			He doesn't	Doesn't he?
I did			I didn't	Didn't I?
I will	I'll	I'll not	I won't*	Won't I?
I would*	I'd[3]	—	I wouldn't	Wouldn't I?
I shall	I'll	I'll not	I shan't	Shan't I?
I should*	I'd	—	I shouldn't	Shouldn't I?
I can	*(No contracted spellings in this position, but* can *and* could *pronounced weak in fluent speech.)*		I can't	Can't I?
I could*			I couldn't	Couldn't I?
I may	—	—	*(Avoid contractions here.)*	
I might	—	—	I mightn't	Mightn't I?
I ought* to	—	—	I oughtn't to	Oughtn't I to?
Let us	Let's	Let's not	*or* Don't let's	

Notes:

1. Distinguish the contraction for *it is* from the possessive *its*, as in *What's its name?*
2. The contractions for *he is* and *he has* are the same (*he's*). But it is usually better not to contract the *full* verb *has*.
3. The contractions for *I had* and *I would* are the same. We can usually tell by the pattern which one is meant. Thus *I'd worked* must be the Pre-past, *I had worked*; and *I'd work* must stand for *I would work. I'd put* may be either: why?
4. Do not use the contractions in column 2 ('m, 're, 's, etc.)
   i. as the final word of a sentence or clause. We say, '*You're good, I'm not*' but must say '*You're better than I am*' or '*I'm still in charge, and while I am, you must do what I tell you*';
   ii. when the verb is strongly stressed: *It is hot in here.*
5. The contraction '*s* can be used with *there, what, that* and with nouns: *There's been an accident. That man's badly hurt.* The contractions '*ve*, '*ll* and '*d* may also be used with *there.*

13   DRILL. *Read the following as a dialogue between A and B:*

A. Wash your hands.   B. I've washed them already.
A. When did you wash them?   B. I washed them —.

a. *Supply a suitable adverbial, e.g.* two minutes ago, yesterday, etc. *to fill the gap. Then make up a similar dialogue beginning with the sentences below:*

1. Bring a map.	12. Mend this fuse.
2. Buy some new shoes.	13. Pick up a stone (*Footnote*)
3. Choose a good book.	14. Put your pens down.
4. Clean your shoes.	(*Footnote*)
5. Cut me some bread.	15. Read this article.
6. Do this exercise.	16. Ring the bell.
7. Drink some milk.	17. Show me your passport.
8. Find the place.	18. Shut the window.
9. Go to the bank.	19. Throw that rubbish
(*See 11, Note 4.*)	away. (*Footnote*)
10. Learn these verbs.	20. Write the date.
11. Meet Mr. Middleton.	

b. *Put the following first into the negative, then into the interrogative, then the negative-interrogative, giving first the full form, then the contracted form:*

Note: 13 (19). For the position of the particle, e.g. *up, down, away,* see Part Two, 249.

21

21. You're ready.
22. You understand.
23. He believes us.
24. John has a coat.
25. George is coming.
26. You heard the news.
27. You can see it.
28. We've done this before
29. We did it last year.
30. You've had breakfast.

31. It's raining.
32. It's been raining.
33. The door's shut.
34. He went early.
35. He'd stayed long enough.
36. You'd like that house.
37. You'll be here tomorrow.
38. I'm coming with you.
39. They know the way.
40. We ought to stop.

Now repeat 21–40, stating the affirmative emphatically.

c. *Find the subject; then choose the right form of the verb:*

41. Here (is/are) a series of exercises on agreement of subject and verb.
42. The pages of that book (is/are) torn at the edges.
43. Everyone in the club (want/wants) their own way.
44. The crowd (was/were) getting out of control, and the police (was/were) standing by.
45. (Do/Does) people always believe what you say?
46. One of my false teeth (has/have) just fallen out.
47. Every morning, a blackbird and a robin (come/comes) and (sit/sits) on my window-sill.
48. In the fields, the cattle (was/were) feeding peacefully.
49. Physics, as well as chemistry, (is/are) an essential part of modern education.
50. The employment of children under a certain age, in most countries, (is/are) now forbidden.

14 EXERCISE *Pick out all the* **Finite** *verbs in the passages below, and give the subject, tense and stem of each one, thus:*

Subject	Verb	Tense	Stem
I	looked	Ordinary Past	look

a. I went on, cutting steps in the snow. I had been doing this continuously for two hours and felt very tired. My companion, too, was now moving very slowly. I wondered how long we could continue. Then I looked up to see a narrow ridge running up to a snowy summit. I gave a few more blows with the ice-axe in the firm snow, and at last we stood on top. (Adapted from *The Ascent of Everest* by Lord Hunt.)

b. At one and the same moment, the drivers all gave their horses the whip and shook the reins. The horses set off across the plain and quickly left the ships behind. The dust rose from underneath their chests and hung in the air like a fog. At one moment the chariots were in contact with the earth, and at the next they were bounding high in the air. The heart of each driver, as he stood in his car and struggled to be first, was beating hard. The drivers yelled. The manes of their horses flew back in the wind. (Adapted from Homer's *Iliad*, translated by E. V. Rieu.)

c. Penelope told the maid, 'Bring the bed outside this room, and put blankets on it.' Ulysses was very angry and said, 'Who has been taking my bed from the place where I left it? I made it with my own hands, building it round the stump of an olive tree.'

When Penelope heard this, she broke down and wept. She flung her arms round his neck, crying, 'I only wanted to be sure you were indeed Ulysses. Now I know you are. Do not be angry with me. We have suffered, both of us, for twenty long years, ever since you left for Troy. Oh, I hope we shall never be separated again.' (Adapted from Homer's *Odyssey*, translated by Samuel Butler.)

HOW TO USE THE TENSES

Ordinary Present

15 Use the *Ordinary Present Tense*

i. in referring to all time, or when no distinction is made between present and past, or present and future:
   a. The earth *revolves* round the sun. *Does* it ever *stop?*

ii. in referring to the present moment:
   b. *Do* you *understand?* Yes, now I *understand* perfectly.

iii. in referring to the present period, to a series of acts in the present, or to present habit:
   c. You used to come at ten o'clock. Now you *come* at noon.
   (*from a nursery rhyme*)

iv. in newspaper headlines referring to 'news' (but not in articles beneath the headlines) reporting past events:
   d. PRESIDENT *RESIGNS*. (President Taylor submitted his resignation to Parliament yesterday.)

v. in the middle of narration of past action, for dramatic effect:
   e. Tom *stands* up on the coach and *looks* back at his father's figure as long as he *can* see it. (from *Tom Brown's Schooldays*)

16 Remember the ending of the 3rd Person Singular.

EXERCISE. *Supply a suitable verb to fill each of the gaps in well-known proverbs, choosing one of the following:* alter, begin, bite, can, catch, come, dig, do, eat, excuse, flock, have, know, like, live, make, may, must, ought, quarrel, suck, wait, want.

1. A bad workman — with his tools.
2. Barking dogs seldom —.
3. Where the bee — honey, the spider — poison.
4. Each bird — to hear himself sing.
5. Birds of a feather — together.
6. Charity — at home.
7. Circumstances — cases.
8. The darkest hour — before the dawn.
9. People who — too much — their graves with their teeth.
10. One — draw the line somewhere.
11. The early bird — the worm.

24

12. If you — to eat the kernel, you — crack the nut.
13. Empty vessels — the greatest sound.
14. Everything — to him who —.
15. A fishing rod — a fool at one end and sometimes a fish at the other.
16. What the fool — in the end, the wise man — at the beginning.
17. One half of the world — not — how the other half —.
18. Ignorance of the law — no man.
19. No man — to be judge in his own cause.
20. You — lead a horse to water but you—not make him drink.

17 DRILL. *Pronounce and spell the 3rd Person Singular of the following (see Note to 3, ii)*
ask, apply, arrange, be, brush, carry, choose, copy, count, cry, dance, do, dress, echo, enjoy, exist, fancy, finish, fix, fly, go, guess, hurry, influence, joke, judge, lay, lie, marry, may, miss, mix, must, notice, obey, pinch, pity, play, please, raise, recognize, reply, rise, say, seem, stretch, study, teach, try, vary. (50)

Present Continuous

18 Use the *Present Continuous* to express one of the following ideas:
i. that action is in progress, has begun but is not completed:
    a. *You are reading* these words: *you are doing* that now.
Note the use of the Present Continuous when the speaker immediately recalls a particular action, as in the following conversation:
    b. *George:* Oh John, your car. I forgot to put the brakes on, and it rolled into the river.
    John: What *are* you saying? Are you telling the truth?
Contrast this with: What do you say (as a general rule) when other people are in the wrong? Do you tell them the truth?
ii. that a series of actions has been started and is in progress, although the doer may not be performing the action itself at the time of speaking:
    c. John is six. He is already going to school (though at this moment he happens to be in bed).
Contrast this with: He goes to school by bus (as a general rule).
iii. that a series of actions is being performed temporarily:
    d. I *am getting up* at six every day this week (normally I get up at seven).
iv. that a series of actions goes on and on, and never ends:
    e. Sorry, I'*m always making* that mistake.

Note 1. **If you are not expressing one of these ideas, use the Ordinary Present** (but see 28).

2. **Apply similar instructions in using the continuous form of all the other tenses.**

19 Take care how you use the continuous form with the following:

i. *be:* say *you are being* (*patient*), *he is being* (*silly*) to mean 'you are acting (as in 18, i) in a patient manner,' 'he is acting in a silly way'. Use the continuous form with *be* in that way only, and only in the Present and Past.

ii. *have:* say *I am having* (*my breakfast*), *we are having* (*an English lesson*) to mean 'I am in the process of eating my breakfast', 'we are busy with an English lesson'; and other examples of that kind. Avoid the continuous form with *have* when *have* means 'hold' or 'possess'.

iii. *see, hear; like, love, want; know, believe, remember, forget, mean, understand, agree, prefer, realize.* With these, and similar verbs describing a state of the senses or of the mind, normally avoid using the continuous form: but see Footnote.

iv. *smell, taste.* Avoid using the continuous form with these verbs unless they are used in the sense of 18, i. *This food smells good* (i.e. has a good smell). *That milk tastes sour* (i.e. has a sour taste). But note: *Why are you smelling that egg? Do you think it's bad?*, where *smell* is used in the sense of 18, i.

v. *think.* Avoid using the continuous form of this verb when it means 'hold the opinion'; e.g. *I think you are right.* But note: *Be quiet. I am thinking: I am using my brain.*

20 SPELLING TEST. *Write down the Present Participle of the following* (*see Footnote*)*:* begin, bite, buy, carry, cover, cut, die, dig, drop, dye, eat, enter, escape, fail, fly, forbid, forget, hesitate, hinder, hit, join, kidnap, kneel, lay, lose, meet, occur, offer, omit, panic, plan, prefer, quarrel, rain, raise, refer, regret, rub, serve, signal, sleep, slip, split, stop, strike, tie, trap, travel, try, visit (50)

Which form of the Present to use?

21 EXERCISE. *Put the verbs, in brackets, into the ordinary form of*

Note: 19 iii. The verbs in 19 iii *can* be used in the continuous forms, as explained in *English as a Foreign Language*, 146–152. But this is best avoided until the student knows the language very well.

Note: 20. For the spelling of the Present Participle, see Part Two, footnotes to 87 and 154.

the Present Tense, or the continuous. Say in what circumstances you imagine these sentences would be used:

1. Thank you very much for your invitation for dinner on the 1st. I (accept) with pleasure.
2. Send reinforcements immediately. The enemy (advance) rapidly and (attack) all along the line.
3. Stop making that fuss. You (behave) very badly. You (be) childish. You usually (behave) so well.
4. Don't say any more. I (believe) you. I (know) you (tell) the truth. You (be) one of those people who always (tell) the truth.
5. Many people nowadays (buy) their own houses, but (borrow) the money from a building society.
6. Please, that's enough. I (can) not carry anything else. I (carry) too much already.
7. You (have) no coat. You (shiver). I (think) you (catch) cold.
8. My hairdresser (charge) me two dollars to do my hair. What (yours, charge)?
9. I (not know) if this bill is correct yet. I (still check) it.
10. Ordinary milk (contain) a good deal of fat. This milk (have) only 1%.
11. Some of the patients (bear) pain quietly and never (complain).
12. Old Mrs. Pike (always complain) of some ache or other.
13. Don't shoot the pianist. He (do) his best. He (only try) to entertain you.
14. *Fred:* What (you do) at week-ends? *Frieda:* It (depend) on the weather.
15. I (be) so happy this evening. I (have) a wonderful time and I (enjoy) myself immensely.
16. Iron (expand) as the temperature (rise). It (rust) in a damp atmosphere.
17. *Smith:* How is business? *Jones:* It's excellent. Trade (expand), and everyone (make) a lot of money.
18. How (you explain) the use of the articles in English? I (not remember).
19. The Andes range (extend) for more than 4,000 miles.
20. A sickness insurance (provide) income when you cannot work.
21. The Yang-tse-kiang (flow) into the Yellow Sea.
22. Grapes (not grow) in northern climates, unless one (keep) them in a hot-house.

23. *Wife:* What (happen)? Why (you, slow) down? *Husband:* We (run) out of petrol, so I (look) for a garage.
24. What (happen) if you (put) sodium in water?
25. PLANE (CRASH) INTO TREE. PASSENGERS (JUMP) TO SAFETY.

Pre-present

22 i. Use the *Pre-present Tense* in referring to
either time beginning in the past and continuing till now:

    a. 'In my long life I *have seen* many changes.' wrote Somerset Maugham at the age of eighty.

    b. We *have lived* here since 1965 (and, incidentally, live here still).

or time before now, but not specified (by an adverb of time), nor fixed by the context:

    c. I *have been* to Paris twice (I don't say when).

ii. Use the *Pre-present Continuous* to emphasize the same ideas as those in 18 but applied to time beginning in the past and continuing till now, or to unspecified time before now. Note that when the emphasis is on action that is not completed, the action—because it *is* uncompleted—may or may not continue into the present:

    d. We *have been learning* English for four years (and are still learning it).

    e. Father's very ill. He *has been working* too hard. (He is not working now: he is ill in bed.)

Note the special use of the Pre-present Continuous when the speaker is accusing someone of a wrong action:

    f. Who has been taking my bed from the place where I left it? (14, c).

Note: *Since*, meaning from (then) until now, marks the beginning of the Pre-present period:

    g. I have lived (*or* have been living) here since 1965.

Past

23 i. Use the *Past Tense* in referring to time before now which is specified, or understood in the context:

    a. A tornado *struck* the city of Topeka, Kansas, last night (*newspaper report*).

    b. 'When I was eighteen, I *became* a medical student', Somerset Maugham continued.

    c. When he was a student, he *had* only a glass of milk for lunch.

    d. Homer *was* a great poet (at the time when he was alive).

ii. The ordinary Past Tense can be used to refer to an act

performed once (see a.), repeatedly or habitually (see c.). We also refer to past habit by the construction *used to* plus the stem:
e. You're late. You *used to come* at ten o'clock and now you come at noon. (*For interrogative and negative of* used to, *see Note on 5*, ii.)
iii. Use the *Past Continuous* to emphasize the same ideas as in 18 but applied to time before now, specified or understood:
f. I said, 'How are you? Are you enjoying yourself?'
I asked him if he *was enjoying* himself.
g. While the train *was* still *moving*, a great many men jumped out.

24 QUICK DRILL. *Pronounce and spell the Past (and the Past Participle) of the following regular verbs (see Note on 3*, iii).
accept, accuse, add, advance, aid, answer, apply, arrest, attack, boast, brush, bury, carry, cry, demand, die, drag, drop, elect, enjoy, gas, hurry, include, invite, limit, marry, multiply, occupy, occur, offer, omit, pass, permit, play, prefer, profit, qualify, quarrel, reach, recommend, refer, reply, rob, satisfy, signal, tap, tape, travel, unite, wonder. (50)

Pre-past

25 Use the *Pre-past Tense* in referring to time previous to a time for which you have used the Past:
a. I passed my English examination last year. I *had studied* hard for it (in time previous to the time when I passed it).
b. I felt very cold—I *had left* my warm coat behind.
c. Father was very ill in the winter. He *had been working* too hard (before he fell ill).

Notes: 1. It is only necessary to use the Pre-past when precise meaning or emphasis requires it. Meaning requires it in b. and c. above; and emphasis requires it in a. In the example:
d. The train left before we arrived at the station
it is already stated that the train left before we arrived: in that case it is not necessary, though not wrong, to say 'the train had left'.
2. *Since* (see 22g) can also mark the beginning of the Pre-past period.

Which past tense to use?

26 EXERCISE *Put the verbs in brackets into a suitable form of the Pre-present, Past or Pre-past:*

1. *Invitation to a party*
John: (you have) an invitation to the Freemans' party?

Jill: Yes, one (arrive) yesterday evening, but I (not answer) it yet. And you?

Mary: I also (receive) an invitation yesterday, and I (accept) it at once. I want to go very much: I (not see) the Freemans for a long time.

John: (later, as he is leaving the party) Thank you very much, Mrs. Freeman. I (have) a wonderful time. You (arrange) everything beautifully. I'm so glad I (come).

2. *Fishing*

Tom: Let's watch that man fishing. Do you think he (catch) anything yet?

Tim: I (watch) him for the last hour. He (catch) a few little ones, but he (throw) them back into the water at once.

Tom: (you ever try) to catch a fish?

Tim: I (try) it once, but I (have) no luck at all.

3. *Who was it?*

Shopkeeper: Somebody (steal) some money from the cash-box this morning. Who (go) into my office while I (be) out?

Assistant: I (not see) anyone.

Shopkeeper: (*later*) I still don't know who (take) that money. I (already speak) to everybody about it. When I (speak) to Philip, he (admit) he (be) in the office but (swear) he (not touch) the cash-box. I (believe) he (tell) the truth then, but I'm not sure now.

4. *A street accident*

Passenger: Stop! There (be) an accident. Somebody's hurt. (*To pedestrian*) (anyone send) for the ambulance or (call) the police? What (happen)?

Pedestrian: That blue car (come) out of the side street too quickly. The driver of the other car (not notice) it soon enough, and (crash) into it.

Someone else: The blue car (be) brand new. The poor man (only just, buy) it and (drive) it for the first time. And it (not be) insured.

A busybody: What about the other driver? (he look) where (he go)? (he not, exceed) the speed limit? When he (stagger) out of his car, I (think) he (drink).

Her husband: No, I'm sure he (not drink), my dear. I know him: he (never touch) alcohol in his life.

5. *At a meeting*

Chairman: Ladies and Gentlemen. At our last meeting we (discuss) the plans for our new building, and (decide) that

several changes (be) necessary. Will the Architect please tell us what he (do) since we last (meet)?
Architect: Yes, Mr. Chairman, I (draw up) new plans and (make) all the necessary changes.
Chairman: Thank you. Last time we also (deal) with applications for membership, and we (elect) four new members. (the Secretary write) to them?
Secretary: Yes, Mr. Chairman, and they (all pay) their first subscription.
Chairman: Now the accounts. Can the Treasurer explain why we (spend) so much on printing last year?
Treasurer: Certainly. I (point out) to the Committee six months ago that we (spend) far too much on our monthly bulletin. Last year, it (cost) us over £400. In January, we (cut) down the size of it. Since then, we (save) £200 on the bulletin alone.

6. *Beginning of a story*
One night, a little girl named Margaret (stay) with her aunt in a village on the coast of Scotland. While she (sleep), a fierce wind (arise). Next morning, when they (wake) up, they (look) out of the window and (see) that the sea (become) very rough. Great waves (break) against the cliffs. Not far from the shore, a tall sailing-ship (drift) helplessly nearer and nearer the rocks. It (lose) its rudder and most of its sails, and the captain (can) do nothing to save it.

7. *Short biographies*
Italy (give) many great artists to the world. One of the greatest of them (be) Michelangelo. He (be) born in 1475 and (die) in 1504.

8. When (be) *you* born; and where (you live) when you (be) a child?

9. Alfred Nobel (be) a Swedish chemist. He (invent) dynamite. By the time he (die) in 1896, he (make) a huge fortune.

10. Amundsen (plant) the Norwegian flag at the South Pole on December 14th, 1911. Scott (reach) the Pole on January 18th, 1912, and (find) a letter from Amundsen who (arrive) just over a month before.

27   2000 DIE IN EARTHQUAKE

1. *Report of events till now: early morning.*
   a. At least 2000 people *have lost* their lives as a result of yesterday's earthquake at Tourville.

b. Rescue workers *have been searching* the ruins for survivors all night.

2. *Report of events in the past.*

c. The earthquake (*the one that happened yesterday*) *was* the most violent for many years. It *began* at 5.38 p.m.,

d. when half the population *were returning* from work.

e. Fires *broke out* immediately, and quickly *spread.*

f. Many *were* still *blazing* at midnight.

3. *Report of events previous to 5.38 p.m.*

g. It *had been* very hot during the day (*in a period before the earthquake*),

h. and experts *had been expecting* a major catastrophe.

EXERCISE. *Learn this story of the Tourville earthquake by heart. Make up a similar sequence of tenses under the following headings:*

1. BERTRAND BREAKS WORLD RECORD. *Use the following skeleton:*

a. do it at last;

b. train hard for six months;

c. set new record yesterday afternoon;

d. half-way, run second;

e. finish five metres in front;

f. last man just beginning the final lap;

g. spectators take their seats two hours before;

h. crowd waiting hopefully.

2. CROWDS WATCH THRILLING RESCUE.

3. ASTRONAUT WALKS ON MARS.

Future

28 Four ways of referring to the future:

Present Time		Future Time	
A. He is going		to leave	
It is going		to rain	
B.	He is leaving		
C.		He sails	tomorrow
D.		He will leave	
		It will rain	

Use:

Pattern A when emphasis is on present indications (human

decisions, preparations, signs, etc.) which point to a future result. This pattern is very often used in spoken English.

Pattern B (which is the same in form as the Present Continuous) when human decisions have started an action—or have made preparations for an action—which is expected to be completed in the future. This construction can be used instead of *We are going to leave* (as a result of human decisions) but not of *It is going to rain*, or *I am going to sneeze*, where human decisions play no part.

Pattern C when a future event has been decided and included in a time-table, programme or instruction.

Pattern D to make a plain statement about the future when there is none of the emphasis of A, B or C, or when there is a positive emphasis on the future event.

Shall, instead of *will*, can be used for the 1st person singular and plural: see 3, v.

Pre-future

29 The *Pre-future* refers to time previous to future time, just as the Pre-past refers to time previous to past time:

John will be out at 9 o'clock. He *will have left* the house by then.

Future-in-the-past

30 Note what happens when the examples of the future in 28 are reported in the past:

John told us
{
A. he was going to leave / it was going to rain
B. he was leaving
C. he sailed
D. he would leave / it would rain
}
tomorrow (or the next day: *see Footnote*)

In D, *should* can be used for the 1st Person singular and plural instead of *would*: see 3, vi.

31 EXERCISE. *Put the verbs in brackets into a suitable form of the Future or the Future-in-the-past. Say whether you are using Pattern A, B, C or D (28, 30).*
1. We (not be able) to finish this exercise this morning.
2. I told you we (not be able) to finish it.

Note: 30. 'Tomorrow' means 'the day after today'. *He told us he would leave tomorrow* is possible but only if the 'tomorrow' referred to has not yet come.

3. I (not be) here in the summer. I (go) abroad.
4. Don't make that mistake again. I (be) very angry if you do.
5. Thank you for your offer. I (accept) it with pleasure.
6. Didn't I tell you I (accept) your offer?
7. You're shivering. You (catch) cold.
8. Look at those heavy clouds. We (have) snow soon.
9. There. I was sure it (snow).
10. A. You must return that book to my library. When (you do) it?
11. B. I (not take) it back this afternoon. I (play) in a football match.
12. Why didn't B. take that book back to the library? (*Answer*)
13. Hurry up! Your plane (leave) in just over an hour.
14. Goodbye. I (give) your love to Mary. I (see) her on Friday.
15. A. This house is too big for us. We (move) to a smaller one. B. What (you do) with your present one? A. Oh, we (sell) it.
16. What did A (in 15) say he (do) with his house?

Sequence of Tenses

32 The choice of tenses in a passage of English depends on the situation, the context, the speaker's point of view in time, for each separate verb. Notice how this applies in the exercise below.

EXERCISE. *Complete the following so that the whole sequence makes sense:*

Humphrey takes life far too seriously. He follows the same strict routine every day. He gets up at 7, goes for a run, and runs hard for half an hour. Then he has a cold shower, and has a little breakfast. He reads from 8 sharp till exactly 12; though at 10.30 he leaves his desk for a few minutes and drinks a glass of milk.
1. Here he is, at 7.15. He . . . . . . out of bed and now . . . . . In a quarter of an hour . . . . . .
2. See him at 7.30. He . . . . . . for his run. He is breathing deeply because . . . . . . so hard. . . . . . . his breakfast yet.
3. Look at him now. It's 8 o'clock. Punctual as usual, he . . . . . . down at his desk and . . . . . . to work. He . . . . . . steadily for two and a half hours.
4. 8.30. For the last half hour, ... He . . . . . . twenty pages since 8 o'clock. At that rate, by tomorrow lunch-time . . . . . . the whole book.
5. 10.28. What . . . . . . in two minutes' time? Why? Because . . . . . . since 8 and . . . . . . thirsty.

34

6. 11.55. He ...... to stop work soon. He ...... a headache. No wonder: ...... far too hard.

7. 12.10. He ...... his breakfast over four hours ago, and ...... anything since. So ...... his lunch soon—if he is not too tired to eat.

8. At 10 o'clock yesterday morning, Humphrey ..... He ...... for a run, ... his breakfast and ...... for two hours without a break.

9. At 10.30 yesterday morning, he ...... feeling thirsty. Why? Because ...... in a warm room and ...... anything to drink since breakfast.

10. At 10.35 yesterday, he ...... at his desk again. By 11.35, ... forty more pages. He ...... determined he ...... the whole book in two days.

11. Tomorrow, he ...... at 7 as usual. At 7.15, he ...... again. At 8 o'clock, once more he ...... start studying; and by lunch-time ...... that book.

12. Humphrey hasn't always been like this. A few years ago, ... stay in bed as long as he could. Then ...... spend every morning looking at the television. He ...... be quite gay. ...... much more serious since then.

33 In many sentences and paragraphs, Present Tenses tend to combine with Pre-present and Future; and Past Tenses with Pre-past and Future in the Past, thus:

Present	—	Pre-present	—	Future
Past	—	Pre-past	—	Future-in-the-Past

EXERCISE. *Put each verb in brackets into a suitable tense:*

1. One June morning, when I was nineteen, I (pack) all I (have) on to my back, (leave) my native village, and (walk) up to London.

2. I am now living in London. I (be) here for the last fifteen years, and (probably stay) here for the rest of my life.

3. Since 1851 till now, we (live) through the greatest revolution in history: we (still, live) in it.

4. It is now sixty years since I (go up) to Cambridge. The world sixty years ago (be) a much quieter place than it (be) now.

5. It was then sixty years since I (go up) to Cambridge. Sixty years before, the world (be) a much quieter place than it later (become).

6. One Christmas Eve, after he (lie) sick for many days, the

35

young man (fall) into a feverish sleep. He (dream) that he (sail) away to a distant land and (never, see) his own home again.

7. *Visitor*: Is Mr. Pendlebury in, please? *Secretary:* I (be) afraid not. He (go) out and no one (know) when he (be) back.

8. The visitor asked if Mr. Pendlebury (be) in. The secretary (explain) that he (go) out and no one (know) when he (be) back.

9. On October 8th, 1754, Henry Fielding (die) at Lisbon where he (go) in a last attempt to recover his health. When he (leave) London, he (hope) he (return) but later he (realize) that (be) impossible.

10. Imagine you (fly) to Australia. The journey (take) forty-eight hours and you are now half-way. You (travel) for the last twenty-four hours and (travel) for twenty-four hours more.

Tenses in reported speech

34 i. The combination of tenses mentioned at the beginning of 33 affects reported speech, thus:

Direct Speech	*Indirect Speech*
a. 'It's raining.'	I tell you it's raining.
	I said it was raining.
b. 'No, it's stopped.'	Do you think it's stopped?
	You told me it had stopped.
c. 'He'll be there.'	I'm sure he'll be there.
	I was sure he'd be there.

In indirect speech, note the combination of Present with Pre-present and Future, and Past with Pre-past and Future-in-the-past.

ii. However, what was said at the beginning of 32 is more important: the choice of tense depends first of all on the speaker's point of view. In the four following examples, I am speaking on Monday:

d. I say, today (Monday), that Bill will be there tomorrow (Tuesday).

e. I said last Friday that he would be absent the next day (Saturday).

f. I said yesterday (Sunday) that he would be there tomorrow (Tuesday).

or g. I said yesterday (Sunday) that he will be there tomorrow (Tuesday).

Note that g. as well as f. is possible, in spite of what is said at the beginning of 33: for a speaker, speaking on Monday, Tuesday *will be* tomorrow.

iii. If you remember the advice at the beginning of 32, you should have no difficulty with the tenses in the following examples:

h. *Direct speech:* 'I made it with my own hands.'

i. Ulysses said he had made it with his own hands.

In example i., the Pre-past tense (*he had made*) refers to time previous to the time for which we have used the Past (*said*), as in 25.

35 EXERCISE. *Re-form the following sentences as reported speech, beginning with the phrase in brackets:*

1. 'We have had breakfast and are ready to start.' (Hillary reported that they . . .)

2. 'Tensing seems very fit and is going well.' (He noted that Tensing . . .)

3. 'They will reach the summit by midday.' (Lord Hunt thought that . . .)

4. 'We have been climbing continuously for two hours.' (Hillary recorded that . . .)

5. 'Bring the bed outside the room.' (Penelope told the maid . . .)

6. 'I built my bed round the stump of an olive tree.' (Ulysses said that . . .)

7. 'Do not be angry with me.' (She begged him . . .)

8. 'I only wanted to be sure.' (She explained that . . .)

9. 'We have both suffered very much.' (She reminded him that . . .)

10. 'We shall never be separated again.' (She hoped that . . .)

11. 'I tried to fish once, but had no luck at all.' (Tim said that . . .)

12. 'I still don't know who took that money.' (The shopkeeper told me that . . .)

13. 'At our last meeting, we discussed the plans for our new building and decided that several changes would be made.' (The Chairman began by saying that . . .)

14. 'We are spending too much on our monthly bulletin and will have to cut down the size of it.' (The Treasurer explained that . . .)

15. 'At least 2000 people have lost their lives in the earthquake, and rescue workers have been searching the ruins for survivors all night.' (The radio reported that . . .)

HOW TO ASK QUESTIONS

36 In the understanding and use of English, questions play an important part. You must be able not only to answer questions accurately, but also to ask them in the right way. Study the following types of question:

A. *Questions asking for the subject of the verb:*

These begin with an interrogative word, *what, which, who* or *whose,* that can be replaced by the answer required. Examples:

    a. What floats on water? —*Wood* floats on water
                                Wood does.
    b. Who wants coffee?   —*We all* want coffee.
                                We all do.

Note that this type of question does not require the interrogative form of the verb described in 5 and in 1, iii.

B. *Questions requiring the answer Yes or No:*

These begin with the interrogative form of the verb described in 5 or in 1, iii, so that the first word of the question is a part of the verb *be* or *have,* an auxiliary, or a modal verb:

    c. Are you ready?   d. Have you finished?
    e. Do you smoke?   f. Can you hear me?

C. *All other questions:*

These begin with

i. *What, which, who* (or *whom*), *whose* in questions asking for the *object* of a verb or of a preposition:

    g. What can you see? — I can see a ship.
    h. What are you looking for? — My glasses.
    i. What language do you speak? — English.
    j. Which of the two books did you choose?
    k. Whose coat have you taken?
    l. Who do you wish to speak to? (*Footnote*)

Note: 36 C,l. In C, *who* or *whom* can ask for the object. In A, *who,* not *whom,* asks for the subject. Use *whom* when asking for the object (person) in very formal English, or to emphasize the fact that it is the object you are asking for. Use *whom,* not *who,* immediately after a preposition.

ii. *How, When, Where, Why:*

   m. How are you? How do you do?
   n. When did he arrive?
   o. Where are you going to?
   p. Why are we waiting?

iii. *How many, how much, how big (far, high, long, old, wide, etc.), how often:*

   q. How many people are there in this room?
   r. How much does this cost?
   s. How long must we wait?

iv. *An interrogative phrase consisting of a preposition followed by what, which, whom, whose or when:*

   t. In what month was Shakespeare born?
   u. Since when have you been at this school?

Notes: 1. All type C questions begin with an interrogative word or phrase, followed by the interrogative form of the verb as described in 5 or in 1, iii.

2. In spoken English, questions ending with prepositions (examples h, l, o) are very common, especially when the preposition is closely associated with the verb, as in *What are you looking for?* Example 1. could be phrased *To whom do you wish to speak?*, but that is very formal. Example t. could be phrased, informally, *What month were you born in?* But put *since* at the beginning of the question only.

3. Intonation is important. Normally pronounce type B questions with a *rising* intonation at the end. A falling intonation in type B questions may sound abrupt or impolite. Normally pronounce both the other types of question with a *falling* intonation at the end. A rising intonation in types A and C may suggest doubt, uncertainty, a request for the answer to be repeated, or something else like that.

Indirect questions

37 Indirect questions are preceded by *ask, wish to know, don't know, wonder,* or a similar introductory word or phrase. Form indirect questions as follows:

Type A questions. Simply put the introductory word or phrase before the question:

   Ask who wants coffee.

Type B questions. After the introductory word or phrase, put *if* or *whether*. *Whether* suggests doubt; the answer may be Yes or may be No. After *if*, or *whether*, return to the normal word order of subject plus verb:

The driver wants to know if you are ready yet.
The waiter is asking if you have finished.
I have forgotten whether you smoke or not.
I wonder if you can all hear me.

TABLE 3

QUESTIONS

DIRECT

Type	Interrogative word	Be, auxiliary or modal	Subject	Main verb	
A	Who			spoke?	
	What			happens	in Hamlet?
B		Are	you		ready?
		Have	you	finished?	
		Can	you	hear	me?
		Do	you	speak	English?
C	What	is	a space rocket		like?
	What	have	you	done	with my keys?
	When	can	you	come?	
	How	do	you	feel?	
	Why	did	you	say	that?

INDIRECT

Type	Introduction	Connecting word	Subject	Be, etc.	Main verb
A	I asked	who			spoke.
B	I want to know	if	you	are	ready.
C	Tell me	why	you		said that.

Type C questions. After the introduction, repeat the interrogative word or phrase, then return to the normal word order of subject plus verb:

Please tell me what you are looking for.
I have no idea when he arrived.
Guess how many people there are in this room.
Write down in what month Shakespeare was born.

38 DRILL. *Turn the following statements into questions requiring the answer Yes or No; then form questions to which the words in italics would be the answers:*

1. You speak *English.*
2. Mary sings *well.*
3. *Joan* sang badly.
4. You heard her *last night.*
5. I saw you *at the concert.*
6. I sent her *some flowers.*
7. I bought *twenty* roses.
8. They cost *a lot.*
9. We come *twice a week.*
10. We've been here *six months.*
11. Tom told me *the truth.*
12. Anne wore a *blue* dress.
13. She chose it *herself.*
14. You have *a pen* in your hand.
15. We have a lesson *every day.*
16. There were *ten* people present.
17. I fetched it *because you asked for it.*
18. *We have been working.*
19. *Charles* will have gone by tomorrow.
20. *He will have gone.*

39 EXERCISE. *On each of the sentences below form a question to which the word or words in italics, or in brackets, would be an* **exact** *answer.*

1. There are *thirty* days in the month of June.
2. The table in front of us is *two metres* long.
3. The minute hand of a clock goes round *24 times* a day.
4. We have been learning English for *four years.*
5. We started learning it *four years ago.*
6. Martin left his native village in the month of *May.*
7. He packed all his belongings *on his back.*
8. He was looking for *gold and glory.*
9. Our modern scientific ideas first came from *Greece.*
10. Scientific knowledge made no advance in the Middle Ages (*No, none*).
11. Europe knew less about science in 1500 than Archimedes (*No, less*)
12. A scientist is interested in *natural phenomena.*
13. A good scientist works *methodically.*

41

14. An airliner takes *five hours* to cross the Atlantic.
15. Japan is *a beautiful country, with many mountains.*
16. We still don't know the cause of cancer. (*Not yet*)
17. Nigeria covers an area of *372,674 square miles.*
18. That is about *four* times the size of Britain.
19. The Aswan Dam was built *to store the waters of the Nile.*
20. A space rocket can travel at *18,000 miles an hour.*
21. Stephen Hales heated saltpetre and *obtained oxygen.*
22. He *heated* the saltpetre to obtain oxygen.
23. *Joseph Priestley* also made experiments to get oxygen.
24. Rutherford went to Manchester in *1908.*
25. At Montreal, *he had discovered three important radioactive rays.*
26. This is *the room where we have all our meetings.*
27. *I have put them back in your bookcase.*
28. *He fell downstairs and broke his leg.*
29. *I'm sorry, I couldn't find the brake and it crashed into the wall.*
30. *I was just putting it in the garage.*

40 EXERCISE. *Form questions, on the three passages in Exercise 14, to which the following would be exact answers:*

a. 1. steps   2. in the snow   3. for two hours   4. very tired
5. because he was moving so slowly   6. how long they could continue   7. snowy   8. an ice-axe   9. firm   10. both of them
b. 1. a chariot race   2. horses   3. a plain by the sea   4. dusty
5. like a fog   6. with a whip   7. No, they were standing   8. hard   9. because they were so excited   10. the long hair on a horse's neck
c. 1. to bring the bed outside   2. she wanted to see if the man was really Ulysses   3. No, he was very angry   4. He had made it himself   5. the stump of an olive tree   6. She broke down
7. Not to be angry with her   8. twenty years before   9. for twenty years   10. Yes, both of them had

CONTRACTED FORMS AND SHORT ANSWERS

41 All the verbs in 12 can be used
i. as the verbal element in a short response:
a. It's very hot today. — Yes, it is.
b. We're not making much progress. — No, we're not.
c. Can you all hear me? — Well, I can.
ii. in question tags, with a falling intonation, which expect agreement with an affirmative or a negative statement immediately preceding:
d. It's very hot, isn't it? (*Typical response:* It certainly is.)
e. You aren't angry, are you? (*Typical response:* Of course not.)
iii. in question tags, with a rising intonation, which ask for confirmation or denial of an affirmative or negative statement:
f. You were away yesterday, weren't you? (Yes, I was *or* No I wasn't.)
g. We haven't finished yet, have we? (No, not yet *or* Yes, we have.)
iv. in question tags, with a rising intonation, which turn an affirmative statement into a question, expecting the answer Yes or No:
h. There's enough to eat, is there? (Yes, there is *or* No, there isn't.)
v. For the present and past of full verbs, use *do, does* or *did* in question tags and in short responses:
i. You agree with me, don't you?
j. I hope you enjoyed yourselves? Yes, we all did.
Note: the full forms, e.g., *is it not? are we not? It is not,* etc. also occur in question tags and short responses; but only use these forms in very formal speech or for emphasis.
vi. Note the difference between:
k. John speaks well. — So do you (=you do too).
John doesn't hesitate. — Nor (*or* neither) do you (=you don't either). and
l. Dr. Watkins has a wig! — So he has! (=You're right)

42 a. QUICK DRILL. *Fill the gaps.*

Speaker A	B's Responses
1. Can you understand me?	Yes, I —.
2. I understand it all.	So — I.
3. That food smells good.	It — indeed.
4. I'm hungry as a hunter.	So — I.
5. I haven't eaten anything since breakfast.	— you? Nor — I.
6. I only have toast for breakfast anyway.	— you?
7. John's a very good boy, — he?	Yes, he —.
8. He's grown a lot lately, — he?	Yes, so he —.
9. Bill's broken his leg.	— he?
10. He fell all the way downstairs.	— he really?
11. We must go and see him, — we?	Yes, we —.
12. There's a concert this evening, — —?	Yes, there —.
13. It's the last one of the season, I believe.	Yes, it —.
14. There are no tickets left, — —?	I'm afraid there —.
15. Why, who wants a ticket?	I think Fred —.
16. We went for a long walk yesterday.	— you?
17. It rained very hard, — —?	I believe it —.
18. We'd no rain-coats, — —?	Why — you?
19. I told you you'd get wet, — —?	Yes, you said we —.
20. Everybody wants security, — they?	Of course they —.
21. What dissolves in water?	Salt —.
22. Who cut down the cherry tree?	I —, father.
23. You'll be in for supper, — —?	Yes, we all —.
24. You've made an appointment for me, — —?	Yes, I —.
25. You made an appointment for me, — —?	Yes, I —.
26. There's nothing to pay, — —?	No, I'm sure — —.
27. Nobody telephoned, — they?	Yes, somebody —.
28. You'd never believe it, — —?	No, I don't think — —.
29. There were no letters, — —?	Yes, — —.
30. We ought to stop now, — —?	Yes, — — to.

b. EXERCISE. *Fill the gaps in the following cross examination:*

1. A Now then, Mrs. Ferguson, let's go over your statement again. Are you listening?
2. B Yes, I —.

3. A You went to Woolley's at five yesterday afternoon?
4. B Yes, I —.
5. A Woolley's sell furs, — they?
6. B Yes, they —.
7. A And you've wanted a fur coat for a long time, — —?
8. B Yes, I —.
9. A But your husband won't buy you one, — —?
10. B No, he —.
11. A He says they're too expensive.
12. B I know he —.
13. A And *are* they expensive?
14. B Of course — —.
15. A You chose a fur, put it on, walked out into the street and then walked away.
16. B No, I —. I wanted to see what it looked like in the light.
17. A But the shop assistant wouldn't believe it, — she?
18. B I know she —. As a matter of fact, I saw a friend of mine on the other side of the road. I wanted to speak to her.
19. A You can't expect me to believe that.
20. B Yes, I —, and I —.
21. A Now, Mrs. Ferguson, there's something else I have to point out to you.
22. B — —?
23. A Yes. Last year you tried to walk off with a television set from Mark's. I suppose you were trying to see how it looked in the light then?
24. B No, I —. The manager said it was a portable set, so light that you could carry it for miles without feeling the strain.
25. A And — you?
26. B I don't know. I'd only gone as far as the door when the policeman stopped me.

SECTION FIVE

'HAVE A LOOK AT THIS'

43 A verb can refer to an activity in general, to a single act or to repeated acts. To refer to one single act, we often use a single verb like *give, have, make, take*, etc. plus a noun. Thus we:

give (someone) some advice, an answer, a blow, an explanation, some help, a kick, a kiss, a pinch, a promise, a push, a reply, a welcome; or *give* (something) a brush, a polish, a trial, a wash.
go for a drive, a run, a swim, a walk.
have an argument, a bath, a bathe, a dance, a drink, a fight, a game, a look, a rest, a sleep, a talk, a swim, a wash.
make an arrangement, an attack on someone, an attempt at something, a bargain, a choice, a complaint, a copy, an enquiry, an excuse, an improvement, a mark, a mistake, a move, a noise, a note (of), progress, a report, a request, a suggestion.
offer somebody an apology, one's congratulations.
pay attention to, a call on, a visit to, someone.
put a question (to somebody), put something on record.
take a breath, care (of), hold (of), note (of), notice (of), a photograph (of), pity (on).

EXERCISE. *Replace the verb in italics by a verb like* give, *etc. plus a noun, and make other changes where necessary:*

1. *Breathe* deeply. *Hold* my arm.
2. May I *look* at your book? I want to *note* the publisher.
3. Will someone please *wash* my car, while I *bathe*?
4. Wait for me, I'll just *polish* my shoes and *wash*.
5. Every evening, I *walk* in the park, or *drive* down to the sea.
6. Would you like to *play* tennis, or *swim*?
7. We haven't *improved* much. In fact, we've *progressed* very little.
8. I have a problem. Can you *advise* me, or *suggest* something?
9. They didn't *welcome* us very warmly, but we mustn't *complain*.
10. You have *chosen* very well. May I *congratulate* you?
11. Ours is the best soap you will ever find. Why not *try* it?
12. I want to *enquire* about hotels. And please can someone *help* me with my heavy luggage?

13. You must *call* on the Minister or he won't *attend* to your application.
14. May I *ask* something? I would like to *photograph* your beautiful garden.
15. Now you *ask* and I'll *answer*.

VERBS USED TRANSITIVELY, INTRANSITIVELY

44 A verb is transitive when it has a direct object. Otherwise it is intransitive. Examples:

Transitive	*Intransitive*
a. Lay your head down	Lie down on the sofa
Raise your head again	The sun rises in the east
b. Don't make a noise	—
—	Go away. Don't fall.
c. We boil water in a kettle	Water boils at 100 degrees
The thief hid the money	The thief hid in the cupboard

Note that, as in *a*, different words are sometimes used according to whether the verb has an object or not; as in *b*, some verbs are used only transitively, others only intransitively; and, as in *c*, some are used in either way.

Note in the right hand column of c. *the water boils* (it is not we who boil); *but the thief hides.*

45 EXERCISE. *Supply suitable subjects to fill the gaps below:*

1. I bathe my eyes in cold water: — never bathe in dirty water.
2. I often break my glasses: — often break.
3. We burn sticks, not stones: — burn, — don't burn.
4. Fast drivers burst their tyres: — burst at high speed.
5. Shopkeepers here close their shops at six: — close at six.
6. I have just dropped my pen: — dropped out of my hand.
7. Farmers feed their cattle: — feed on grass.
8. Men fly aeroplanes, pigs don't: — can fly, — can't fly.
9. Shepherds gather their sheep together: — gather together to keep warm.
10. We keep eggs in a refrigerator: — do not keep in warm air.
11. We hang our pictures on walls: — hang from little hooks.
12. The dentist didn't hurt my tooth: — didn't hurt.
13. One can melt ice in hot water: — melts in hot water.
14. You can't mix oil and water: — don't mix.
15. Dancers move their limbs gracefully: — move gracefully.
16. Every visitor to our house rings the bell: — rings loudly.

17. Wood cutters roll tree-trunks down to a river: — roll downhill.

18. Students sell second-hand books: — sell easily if they are clean.

19. Doctors set broken limbs: — do not set quickly.

20. Somebody is shaking the table: — is shaking.

21. We can smell these fish a mile away: — smell rotten.

22. Drivers stop their cars at a red light: — stop if they are too hot.

23. We can't turn these screws: — won't turn.

24. Jack wrote this letter with his new pen: — writes beautifully.

25. John has worn that suit for seven years: — has worn well.

VERBS TAKING DIRECT OR INDIRECT OBJECTS

46 Verbs, when they are transitive, have an object, which may be a noun, a phrase, a clause, or a pronoun. Here are examples in three proverbs:

    a. The sea has *fish* for every man. (noun)
    b. He's like the cow that gives *a good pint of milk* (phrase). and then kicks *it* over (pronoun).
    c. The English never know *when they are beaten* (clause).

EXERCISE. *Pick out the objects in the following proverbs or common sayings:*

1. One can't make bricks without straw.
2. He looks like a dog that has lost its tail.
3. If you want to eat the kernel, you must crack the nut.
4. You've hit the nail on the head.
5. A small leak may sink a great ship.
6. Much money makes a country poor, for it sets a dearer price on everything.
7. Never mind what people say.
8. Putting oil on the fire is not the way to quench it.
9. Respect a man and he will do the more.
10. Don't blow your own trumpet.

47 Some verbs can take a double object:

    a. We call this tree an oak. We call it an oak.
    b. They made the young man King. They made him King.

Some verbs can take a single object or a double one:

    c. They named the child. They named the child David.
    d. We envy our neighbours. We envy our neighbours their possessions.

With other verbs, two objects can be stated separately or together:

    e. They appointed a President. They appointed Lee. They appointed Lee President.
    f. (Use *elect* and *nominate* in the same way as *appoint*.)
    g. I must charge you for the damage. I must charge 5 dollars.

I must charge you five dollars.

h. I want to ask the way. I'll ask that man. I'll ask that man the way.

(Use *ask* in this way when it refers to a request for knowledge; not when it refers to a desire to have something, as in *The police asked me for my identity card.*)

48   Direct and Indirect Objects

		Direct Object	*Indirect Object*
A.	I showed	my ticket	to the man on duty at the gate
B.	„ „	my ticket	to him
C.	„ „	it	to the man on duty at the gate
D.	„ „	it	to him

These examples answer the questions: 'To whom did I show my ticket?' or 'Who did I show it to?'
Other examples of A:

Do a good turn to somebody every day.

Say, 'Good morning' to your colleagues.

You may use the above patterns with all the following words:

Group 1 ('tell' group)

bring, cause, do, give, grant, hand, leave, lend, offer, owe, pass (*as in* pass the salt, please), pay, promise, read, recommend, refuse, render, return (i.e. give back), sell, send, show, take, teach, tell, wish, write; *also* advance (money), deal (cards), drop (a line, i.e. a letter).

Group 2 ('say' group)

announce, confess, describe, entrust (something valuable), explain, introduce (someone or something), propose, say, suggest.

The difference between these two groups will appear in 49 and 50.

EXERCISE. *Make up four sentences in the Past Tense, using models A, B, C, D above, for each of the verbs in Groups 1 and 2. Examples of direct objects for Group 2:*

announce a decision, or results; confess one's sins; entrust all my money; explain a meaning, or a sentence; introduce a person, or a subject; propose or suggest an answer, a solution, a course of action.

	Indirect Object	Direct Object
49 A.	They gave the traveller	{ a good meal / their best room
B.	They gave him	{ a good meal / their best room
C.	They gave the traveller	{ one / —
D.	They gave him	{ one / it

Examples A and B answer the questions: What did they give (to) the traveller?

i. Use these patterns with the 'tell' group (in 48); also with *allow, accord, cost*; but **not** with the 'say' group.

ii. Use pattern C with *one* and *some*, but not with *it* or *them*.

iii. Instead of *'gave him it'*, we may say *'gave it him'*; but do not use this alternative with *one* or *some*.

EXERCISE. *Use patterns A, B, C, D in sentences of your own with each of the verbs in the 'tell' group:*

50 Will you explain { to my wife / to her } how this washing machine works?

EXERCISE. *Use this construction with each of the words in the 'say' group, and with a phrase or clause as direct object.*

51	1		2	
A. I bought	{ a present / that watch	for Mary	I bought Mary	{ a present / that watch
B. ,, ,,	{ a present / that watch	for her	,, ,, her	{ a present / that watch
C. ,, ,,	{ one / it	for Mary	,, ,, Mary	{ one / —
D. ,, ,,	{ one / it	for her	,, ,, her	{ one / it

These examples answer the question:

'For whom did I buy a present?' *or* 'Who did I buy a present for?'

These examples answer the question:

'What did I buy for Mary?'

52

Instructions: Use these patterns with the verbs in italics in the Exercise below. Use C, 2 with *one* or *some*, but not with *it* and *them*.

EXERCISE. *Apply patterns A, B, C and D, both 1 and 2 (but see instructions above) to the following, providing a subject, and a verb in the Past Tense:*

1. *Bring* some coffee for the guests.
2. *Build* this house for my children.
3. *Call* a taxi for this gentleman.
4. *Catch* a fish for us.
5. *Change* a traveller's cheque for the visitor.
6. *Choose* a dress for the bride.
7. *Cut* a piece of cake for your friend.
8. *Draw* a diagram for the students.
9. *Fetch* that file for the manager.
10. *Find* a place for my sister.
11. *Get* a newspaper for me.
12. *Keep* that seat for the Chairman.
13. *Leave* the bones for the dog.
14. *Light* a cigarette for me.
15. *Make* a new suit for my son.
16. *Order* some flowers for your wife.
17. *Paint* a picture of this view for Elizabeth.
18. *Save* some of these fish for the others.
19. *Spare* some of our tea for the old widow.
20. *Write* a report for me.

52 EXERCISE. *Put the following together in a suitable order, inserting* to *or* for *if necessary (see 48-51, and Verb List on page 149):*

1. The guide explained / us / everything / very clearly.
2. You must tell / the truth / the inspector.
3. We said / anybody / nothing.
4. He said / me / , 'Can you tell / me / the time?'
5. I lend / money / my friends, but not to strangers.
6. Please advance / me / a hundred dollars.
7. Can you suggest / us / a better way of solving the problem?
8. I am going to buy / some ice-cream / the children.
9. I bought / that ice-cream / them, not for you.
10. I would like to introduce / you / my Uncle James.
11. Ask / at least one question / every person in the room.
12. Please describe / me / exactly what happened.
13. I shall announce / the results / candidates / tomorrow.
14. The old man left / all his money / his housekeeper—none to his greedy neighbours.

15. They offered / us / a room overlooking the park.
16. Will you do / a favour / me?
17. I can't promise / you / anything / yet.
18. Kindly return / the completed form / the officer named in the top left hand corner.
19. A gentleman tries not to cause / trouble / other people.
20. It is good for us to confess / someone / our faults.

VERBS FOLLOWED BY A PREPOSITION

53 i. Some verbs are followed immediately by a direct object:

 a. *Obey* your leader. *Obey* the rules.
 b. Don't *discuss* politics or religion with strangers.

 ii. Some verbs require a preposition before the object:

 c. *Listen to* what your parents tell you.
 d. *Talk about* those things somewhere else.

 iii. Some verbs are followed by an object or by a preposition according to the sense:

 e. *Write* an essay. *Write about* space travel.

 iv. Some verbs are followed by an object and are then associated with a particular preposition:

 f. I *congratulate* you. I *congratulate* you *on* your success,

If you are uncertain whether a verb requires a preposition or not, or which preposition to use, refer to the Verb List on page 149.

EXERCISE. *Replace the oblique stroke by a suitable preposition or by nothing at all.*

1. Jim believes / every word you say. He agrees / you entirely.
2. Then I can't understand why he accused / me / telling a lie.
3. Please excuse / me. I apologise / you / that remark.
4. Forget / it. Don't let's argue / one another / it again, for goodness' sake.
5. Your son does attend / my classes, Mrs. Smithers, but I'm afraid he never attends / anything I tell him.
6. It's no use complaining / me / your room. If you don't like it, why don't you change / it / another one.
7. May I come and discuss / a private matter / you when you have a moment?
8. I'll never forgive / you / making such a fool of me.
9. We shall inform / you / the result of your application later.

55

10. I've never met / Buster, so I don't know / him. But I know / him, of course.

11. Listen / a moment. I want you to listen / this bit.

12. May I refer / you / my letter of March 21st?

13. Thank you / reminding / me / Jack's party tomorrow. I'd completely forgotten / it.

14. Well, really! How can that woman expect / anyone to respect / her / saying a thing like that?

15. Jane always talks good sense. That's why everyone sympathises / her.

16. A pleasant surprise awaited / us. There was Uncle Jim, waiting / us on the doorstep.

17. If you can provide / us / a truck, we can supply / the rest.

18. Your diet consists / nothing but sugar and starch. You should not eat / anything that contains / either of these things, for at least a month.

19. We all admire / you / your courage and congratulate / you / your success.

20. People who care / a lot / their health don't care / staying up late.

Phrasal verbs (or verbal phrases)

54   i. Simple verbs expressing physical action, like *bring, come, fall, get, give, go, hold, keep, let, make, pull, put, send, take, throw, turn,* are often used with a preposition or adverbial particle, in the following way:

     a. *Go up* the stairs. *Come into* my office.

     b. Please *go up*. Do *come in*.

In such examples *go up* and *come in* are far more generally used, and are much less formal, than 'ascend' and 'enter'. Note that in a phrase like *go up, come in,* each word is used in its basic literal sense.

ii. Some verbs combine with a preposition or an adverb particle to form a phrase with *a special idiomatic meaning*. Examples:

A. Verb + preposition

call on somebody (=visit him)   *look after* the children
come across something (=find it)   *look on* me as a friend
deal with a matter (=treat it)   '+' *stands for* 'plus'

N.B. In these phrases, place the preposition immediately before the noun, noun-group or pronoun that the preposition governs. The monosyllabic preposition is unstressed.

B. **Verb + particle,** forming an **intransitive** verbal group:

go on (=continue)   keep on (=don't stop)
break down (=collapse)   look out (=beware)
grow up (=become adult) turn round (=face the other way)

N.B. In these phrases, place the particle immediately after the verb. The particle is stressed.

C. **Verb + particle,** forming a **transitive** group:

$$\begin{cases} call\ up \text{ a friend (=telephone him)} \\ call \text{ a friend } up,\ call \text{ him } up \end{cases} \begin{cases} give\ back \text{ that book} \\ give \text{ that book } back, \\ give \text{ it } back \end{cases}$$

$$\begin{cases} find\ out \text{ the answer} \\ find \text{ the answer } out,\ find \text{ it } out \end{cases} \begin{cases} give\ away \text{ your money} \\ give \text{ your money } away, \\ give \text{ it } away \end{cases}$$

N.B. In these phrases, the particle can come immediately after the verb, or immediately after the direct object. However, there are a few phrases on this pattern in which the particle usually comes after the object only: e.g. Don't answer your parents back; see Verb List on page 149. If the direct object is a pronoun, however, the particle must always come immediately after it. Stress the particle when it follows the object.

D. **Verb + particle + preposition**

get on with your work   stand up to your enemies
set out on a journey   put up with difficulties
stand up for your friends I've run out of ink

N.B. In these phrases, keep the particle with the verb, and keep the preposition with the noun it governs.
If in doubt whether a verbal group (or phrasal verb) belongs to category A, B, C, or D above, check with the Verb List on page 149.

EXERCISE. *Use all the phrasal verbs in A, B, C, and D above in original sentences, giving alternative positions when possible for the particle in C and adding a suitable adverb of manner (e.g. properly) or of time (e.g. tomorrow) or of place (e.g. at home).*

PASSIVE AND PAST PARTICIPLE

Great things are done
When men and mountains meet (William Blake)

55 i. The verb-forms reviewed in Section 1 are those of the *active voice*, i.e. those used when the person or thing to which the subject of the verb refers performs the action referred to by the verb itself. In the example *Some men do great things*, *men* is the subject, *great things* the object, and *do* a transitive verb in the active voice. In *Great things are done* the object of the previous example becomes the subject, and *are done* is a verb in the *passive voice*. Only a transitive verb is used in the passive voice, but not all transitive verbs are used in the passive; we can turn *The Consul married George and Mary* into the passive, but not *George married Mary*.

ii. The passive is formed with the verb *be* plus the past participle. It is found in the following finite and non-finite forms. The tenses are used in the same way as in the active voice:

	Finite Forms	
Tense	*Ordinary*	*Continuous*
Present	am/is/are asked	am/is/are being asked
Pre-present	have/has been asked	—
Past	was/were asked	was/were being asked
Pre-past	had been asked	—
Future	will/shall be asked	—
Pre-future	will/shall have been asked	—
Future-in-the-past	would/should have been asked	—

	Non-Finite Forms
Infinitive:	(to) be asked, e.g. you ought to be asked.
Perfect Infinitive:	(to) have been asked, e.g. you ought to have been asked.
Present Participle (and Gerund):	being asked — see 126 and 131.
Perfect Participle:	having been asked — see 139.

Notes: 1. Where there are gaps in the third column above, avoid using the passive, though the passive *can* be used in these positions.

2. In the Future, the forms given in 28A and B can be put into the passive, thus:

You're going to be examined tomorrow.
Your case is being discussed next Friday.

Use of the passive

56 Use the passive:

i. to draw attention to the person or thing that suffers the action:
a. Quick! Mary! *She's been bitten* by a snake!
b. Thousands of people *are killed* in traffic accidents every year.
ii. when the agent or the doer of the action is unimportant in the context, or is unknown:
c. Don't count your chickens before they *are hatched*.

This use of the passive is common in scientific writing, when we are chiefly concerned with what happens to things rather than with what people do:

d. When the substance *was weighed* again, *it was found* to be three times heavier.

iii. when the speaker wishes, for reasons of tact for example, not to name the doer of the action:
e. Weren't you expecting me? *I was invited* to call here at 10 o'clock. (Actually you invited me yourself.)
iv. when the form of the sentence makes the passive more suitable than the active:
f. Little birds that can sing but won't sing *should be made* to sing (Popular saying.)
(*Try writing that sentence without using the passive.*)
v. when the passive, not the active, is used in conventional expressions and constructions; e.g.
g. This book was first published in 1968.

WARNING. The exercises that follow require the student to turn an active construction into a passive one. This is a convenient way of developing the habit of using the passive *when it is appropriate to do so*. The student must not be allowed to suppose that every construction with an active transitive verb can appropriately be made passive. Use the passive in the kind of circumstances described above, not otherwise.

By the agent

57 Note that in 56 the agent or doer of the action is mentioned only in example a. In that example, one must say 'by a snake' in order to give all the important information. Sometimes the agent must be mentioned in order to complete the sense, as in:
'War and Peace' was written by Leo Tolstoy.

EXERCISE. *Re-phrase the sentences below using the passive whenever possible, and adding* 'by (*the agent*)' *when necessary. Note that in the quotations, proverbs, etc. the passive was used originally.*

1. God (or Nature) formed man for society. (*Sir William Blackstone*, in '*The Laws of England*')
2. People always suspect, and usually oppose, new opinions. (*John Locke*)
3. People often tell the cruellest lies in silence. (*R. L. Stevenson*)
4. Builders made London Bridge for wise men to go over and fools to go under. (*Proverb*)
5. Many things grow in the garden that no one ever sowed there. (*Proverb*)
6. One does not snare an old fox easily. (*Proverb*)
7. Sir Alexander Fleming discovered penicillin.
8. Someone stole jewels worth 100,000 dollars from a room in the Grand Hotel last night.
9. Did anyone catch the thief? Yes, the police arrested a man and charged him.
10. A large and enthusiastic audience applauded the speech.
11. People did not build Rome in a day. (*Proverb*)
12. A strange-looking man with a long beard attracted my attention.
13. We shall hold our annual general meeting next Friday.
14. Advances in medical sciences have caused a great increase in world population.
15. We need more water for agriculture, yet we are now wasting hundreds of tons of water a day.
16. In a nuclear power station they use a nuclear reactor to provide heat.
17. There is danger that in the fight against starvation we shall exhaust the land.
18. The ancient Greeks could boast that their culture had reached and penetrated every contemporary civilisation.
19. A change in man's beliefs precedes every change in society. (*Noel Arran* on *J. S. Mill*)

20. Doctors do not mean people to live on medicine. (*Proverb*)
21. A hundred years ago we would have written all our letters by hand.
22. Man is ruining his environment by his own carelessness. (*Julian Huxley*)
23. Nature forms the earth's land surface by what we call sedimentary rocks.
24. Every government seems to have recognized the importance of compulsory education.

58 People say that he lived to be 120. **It is said** that he lived to be 120.

EXERCISE. *Re-phrase the following, beginning each sentence with* It *and a verb in the passive, as in the model above:*
1. We agreed that we should take no action till Monday.
2. Everyone in the capital assumes there will be elections very soon.
3. The Committee has decided that work on the new building should begin at once.
4. The newspapers generally expect that prices will fall in the spring.
5. One hopes that the harvest this year will be better than last.
6. Scientists have proved that smoking has some relation to lung cancer.
7. An official spokesman announced that 150 people had lost their lives in the disaster.
8. We took it for granted that we should be allowed to leave early.
9. Experts think that the world population has increased by 1,000 million since 1900.
10. You will all understand that no one can leave the building till the police have finished their enquiries.
11. Science has shown that we can overcome hunger and disease.
12. The authorities have found it necessary to close all the schools.

59 We can wash this. This **can be washed.**
We ought to have stopped that. That **ought to have been stopped.**

EXERCISE. *In the following sentences, use a modal verb plus the passive infinitive, as in the examples above:*
1. We must hold our position to the last man. (*Earl Haig*)

2. Never put off till tomorrow what you can do today. (*Popular saying*)

3. The designer ought to take these plans back and do them again.

4. You ought to have made this clearer.

5. We regret we cannot admit children without their parents.

6. You must show your tickets to the inspector.

7. Over-eating may shorten a man's life.

8. You needn't tell me what my duty is.

9. People must have known this for thousands of years.

10. Man might apply atomic physics to destroy half the world.

11. We can never catch the bird of truth but perhaps we can find some of its feathers. (*Noel Arran* on *J. S. Mill*)

12. A little more care might have prevented this terrible accident.

60 a. We soon dealt with the matter. The matter was soon **dealt with.**

b. They drew up an agreement. An agreement was **drawn up.**

In example a., *with* is a preposition and is unstressed; in b., *up* is an adverb participle, stressed (see 54 and Verb List on page 149).

EXERCISE. *Re-phrase, using the passive:*

1. Has someone accounted for all the breakages?

2. I think the clerk has added up my bill incorrectly.

3. You must clear all those things away before tomorrow.

4. A dentist ought to see to your teeth.

5. My father brought me up to believe that honesty is the best policy.

6. What do astronomers use a radio telescope for?

7. What have you spent all my money on?

8. We mustn't let our enthusiasm carry us away.

9. The exploration of space opens up new possibilities of research.

10. We may think of the prolongation of life as a feat of endurance.

61 He aimed a gun at the target.

a. **The gun was aimed.** b. **The target was aimed at.**

Pattern a. can be used with a transitive verb, but not with an intransitive verb such as *arrive*; but pattern b. can be used with an intransitive verb plus preposition such as *arrive at*, e.g.

c. We arrived at that point. That point was arrived at.

EXERCISE. *Re-phrase, using the passive:*

1. What a pity no one ever looks at these beautiful pictures!
2. People looked on him as one of the greatest men of his time.
3. You haven't looked after this machine properly.
4. We have gone over this ground twenty times already.
5. Jones is a man whom people will always listen to.
6. This chair will collapse as soon as anyone sits on it.
7. One of your employees spoke to me very rudely when I came in.
8. Have they come to any decision yet?
9. John is a man whom you can always rely on.
10. Mr. Bolster did not come home last night; at least he has not slept in his bed.

62 We shall paint our house white.
Our house will be **painted white**:

EXERCISE. *Use the passive where possible.*

1. You must keep the patient very quiet.
2. Some people are always right. You can never prove them wrong.
3. 'When I am King, I shall set all prisoners free,' said the young Prince.
4. They found him working in the garden.
5. You can't keep the manager waiting.

63 a. They appointed a President. A President was appointed.
(*See 47.*)

b. They appointed Jackson. Jackson was appointed.

c. They appointed Jackson President. **Jackson was appointed President.**

Note that in c. only the first object (Jackson) can become the subject of the passive verb.

EXERCISE. *Re-phrase, using the passive:*

1. We call this tree a plane.
2. People will ask a lot of questions.
3. People will ask you a lot of questions.
4. What else will they ask us for?
5. Always ask what the price is, or they may charge you too much.
6. People pay good translators five dollars a page.

7. The editors will pay 500 dollars for the best short story.
8. You are the wisest: we shall make you our spokesman.
9. When will they nominate a new President?
10. They elected Professor Hill President of the Association.

64 I shall offer a prize to the best speaker.
I shall offer the best speaker a prize. (see 48)

    a. **A prize will be offered** to the best speaker.
    b. **The best speaker will be offered** a prize.

EXERCISE. *Re-phrase, on both models, a. and b.*

1. The teacher gave every student a new book.
2. The newsagent has sent us the wrong newspaper.
3. An uncle of his left him two thousand dollars.
4. The guide showed us everything in the museum.
5. Someone will hand you your passport as you leave the ship.
6. Nothing costs so much as what someone gives us. (*Proverb*)
7. Did they tell everybody the same story?
8. You have caused a great deal of trouble to innocent people.
9. We recommend this drug to all our patients.
10. She wrote all her helpers a personal letter of thanks.

65 I don't like people criticizing me.
I don't like **being criticized.**

EXERCISE. *Re-phrase, using the passive:*

1. I am tired of people telling me to come back tomorrow.
2. I hope you don't mind my asking you so many questions.
3. I am not accustomed to people speaking to me in that way.
4. Can you tell me how to avoid petty officials holding us up?
5. Don't be afraid of anyone laughing at you.

66 They say that thousands of people are suffering from influenza.
    a. Thousands of people **are said to be suffering** from influenza.
They say many people died (or have died) from the after-effects.
    b. Many people **are said to have died** from the after-effects.
(In b., *to have died* can replace both *died* and *have died*.)

EXERCISE. *Re-phrase, on model a. or b.*

1. We know that half the inhabitants of some countries are undernourished.
2. They know that Roberts left home yesterday morning.
3. Journalists report that all northern Italy is covered with snow.

4. Doctors think that this drug has a very bad effect on the heart.
5. Caesar's friends believe he has crossed the Rubicon already.
6. The author assumes that students working through the second book have covered the groundwork in the first.

Active used instead of passive

67 a. I have worn this suit for years. It has worn well.
b. Do booksellers sell many of your books? Do they sell well?
c. Nobody blames you. You are not to blame.
d. 'House to Let' (Advertisement)
e. There's a lot $\begin{cases} \text{to do.} \\ \text{to be done.} \end{cases}$
f. There's a great deal $\begin{cases} \text{to settle.} \\ \text{to be settled.} \end{cases}$

Note that in a. the suit, in fact, has *been worn*; in b. the books *are sold*. In such cases, an active verb is used with a passive meaning. In c. you are really not *to be blamed*; in d. the house is *to be let*. In such cases the active infinitive is used with a passive meaning. In e. and f. we can use either active or passive, the former emphasizing personal activity, the latter drawing attention to work that has to be dealt with.

The Past Participle

68 i. The past participle can either be 'active', i.e. part of a verb in the active voice, or 'passive', i.e. part of a verb in the passive.
ii. It can sometimes be used as an adjective referring to a condition:

a. He was married (i.e. a married man) when I knew him.
Or the same word can be part of the passive voice:
b. He was married (i.e. he got married) last June.

Similarly:

c. I felt thoroughly discouraged. (*condition*)
d. I was discouraged by everybody. (*passive*)

69 a. All **articles found** (i.e. that have been found) in trains—
b. are taken to the '**Lost Property**' Office.
A passive past participle can be freely used in pattern a. Other examples include:

c. There is no bread left.
d. All the staff concerned should attend the meeting tomorrow.

Pattern b. is normally found only in certain expressions which have become adopted through frequent use, e.g.:

e. It's no good crying over spilt milk. (*Proverb*)

When a past participle is used in this way, it may be a part of an intransitive verb (active voice) e.g.:

a faded rose = a rose that has faded;

but it is more likely to be in the passive voice, e.g.:

an injured man = a man who has been injured
unwanted children = children who are not wanted

Note that the prefix *un-* can be added to a large number of past participles, e.g. unbeaten, unbroken, unchanged, undamaged, etc.

EXERCISE. *Define:* a broken window, a changed character, damaged goods, an exaggerated claim, a fallen tree, a felled tree, a forgotten work, ground coffee, a heated room, an interested spectator, a knotted cord, a limited amount, a married man, a numbered seat, an organised attempt, a painted screen, a qualified engineer, a recorded talk, a sheltered harbour, a trained athlete, an unbroken line, unheated rooms, an unknown writer, unused copies, unused equipment, a written report.

70 a. A few past participles are used not only in pattern 69, b, but also as adjectives, which can be preceded by *very* and *too*, and can be compared, e.g.:

very tired, more tired; very interested, more interested; very distinguished, more distinguished.

But most past participles that are used before nouns are not treated in this way; they cannot be compared, and *very* and *too* are avoided before them. Instead of *very*, one can use a different adverb, e.g.:

much, or very much, admired; badly damaged; greatly, or highly, exaggerated; completely forgotten; keenly interested; strictly limited; much married; well organised; well, or highly, qualified; well, or highly, trained. Instead of *too*, one can say, 'too badly damaged', etc.

b. A few old past participles survive as adjectives, side by side with normal forms, but occur only in certain expressions or types of usage:

I appeal to you, on *bended* knees.
A *drunken* sailor is one who has drunk too much.

When we have lit a candle, we see a *lighted* candle before us.
Rotten wood is wood that has rotted.
A man who has just shaved is *clean-shaven.*

Note that in *blessed* as an adjective (e.g. the Blessed Virgin; there's that blessed cat again) the *-ed* is pronounced as a separate syllable: the past participle *blessed* in *I have blessed* is regular: see note on 3, iii. The *-ed* is also pronounced as a separate syllable in the adjectives *aged, crooked, naked, ragged, wicked* and *wretched.*

71 Ask someone
You need someone } to clean your shoes.

Have (or get)
You need } **your shoes cleaned**

EXERCISE. *Re-phrase, using a past participle after the direct object:*

1. Why don't you get the barber to cut your hair?
2. I must get the dentist to take this tooth out.
3. Do you need someone to dig your garden?
4. A politician tries to make other people feel his presence.
5. Can we ask the cleaner to sweep up this rubbish?
6. You must ask your secretary to write that letter at once.
7. Please have the lawyers (=tell the lawyers to) draw up a new agreement by tomorrow.
8. Do you want someone to wring your neck?
9. Tell the truth, or you will find that everyone will ignore you.
10. Drive carefully, or the police will take your licence away.

72 a. When Paul was asked to reply, he could not say a word.
   When it is used as a modal verb, *need* is not followed by *to.*
   b. **Asked to reply,** Paul could not say a word.
   When **used** as a modal verb, *need* is not followed by *to.*

Use the past participle as in b. only when it is part of a passive construction, or when it is an accepted adjective, and when there is no ambiguity as to whom or to what the past participle refers. See also 139.

EXERCISE. *Use pattern b. when possible:*

1. By the time we arrived at the house we were drenched to the skin.
2. As we were tired out, we were glad to find shelter.

3. When we had taken off our shoes, we went straight upstairs.

4. He was invited to speak first, and held the floor for half an hour.

5. When we had been given a meal, our host showed us to our rooms.

6. When it was placed in water, the substance burst into flame.

7. After the water had been allowed to cool, we examined it again.

8. The house was severely damaged by the earthquake and had to be pulled down.

9. The walls had been painted blue and looked hideous.

10. The ceiling had been painted pink and we couldn't bear to look at it.

MODAL VERBS

Will

73 *Will* is used both as an auxiliary to form the Future Tense (as in 28, D) and as a modal verb expressing an attitude towards a possible future event. Here are examples of *will* as a modal verb, expressing an attitude:

i. The speaker is certain that the event will take place:

a. You will do what I tell you. (*This is a command. The speaker is confident it will be obeyed.*)
b. I promise you, you will have the money tomorrow.

ii. The speaker refers to his own, or someone else's, willingness:

c. *Eric:* Isn't anyone going to get me a drink?
Dick: All right. I will (I am willing to)
d. *Dick:* Can I get you one too?
Frank: Yes, if you will.

iii. The speaker refers to his own, or someone else's, determination or refusal. This attitude can also be imagined in an inanimate object, as in g.:

e. A. Don't do that.   B. I will.
   A. Listen to me.   B. I won't. (*see also 77, iii*)
f. Mules are obstinate. They won't move if they don't want to.
g. What's the matter with this light; it won't stay on.

iv. The speaker refers to his own or someone else's deliberate or persistent habit. In this kind of example, *will* has a strong stress and is not contracted:

h. Do shut the door. You *will* leave it open.
i. I can never use a typewriter properly. I *will* hit the keys in the wrong order.
j. If you *will* smoke (=if you insist), please go outside.

Compare example j. with k.:

k. If you want to smoke (*emphasis simply on the idea of wanting*), please go outside. *Do not use* will *simply to mean* want.

v. The speaker foretells the future from his knowledge of what has happened before:

l. When the cat's away, the mice will play. (*Proverb*)
m. Uncle Tom will sit here for hours, just gazing at the sea.

74 *Will* occurs in questions, as follows:

i. The speaker asks a question about the wishes of somebody else, and at the same time issues an invitation:

a. Will you have a cup of tea? (*Possible answers:* Yes, please *or* No, thank you.)
b. Who will have another slice of cake? (*Possible answer:* I will, *which echoes a word in the question.*)
c. Will you come in for a minute? (*Answer:* Thank you.)
d. Won't you sit down? (*Answer:* Thank you.)

ii. The speaker asks a question which expresses his own wishes in a request or command:

e. Will you come in for a minute? (*Answer:* Yes, certainly.)
f. Won't you sit down? (*Possible answer: silent agreement.*)

In e. and f., which contain the same words as c. and d., the speaker is making a request. The difference between c./d. and e./f. is made by tone of voice or is understood in the context.

g. Will you turn that radio off for a minute? (*request: rising intonation*).
h. Will you turn that radio off at once! (*command: falling intonation*).
i. Sit down, will you? (*invitation, request or command, according to the speaker's tone of voice*).

75 Note the use of (*that*) *will be* to mean 'I assume it is':

a. Let me see, that will be the Jackson's house, the one with the green shutters.

The speaker is not able to make a definite statement of fact, but he believes his assumption will prove to be true.

Shall

76 Use *shall*, as an auxiliary, as an alternative to *will*, to form the Future Tense, but only when the subject of the verb is *I* or *we*. This alternative is optional: consider both *will* and *shall* as correct after *I* or *we* in the Ordinary Future. With the first person singular or plural, prefer *shall* to *will* in the following circumstances:

i. to seem modest about your own future or to avoid sounding too positive about it:

a. (*Extract from a letter*) I shall send you a full report at the end of the week.

ii. to avoid a repetition of words or similar sounds:

b. We shall wait for Walter.

Prefer *will* to *shall*

iii. even after *I* or *we*, to emphasize the idea of certainty (see 73, i):

c. We will find a cure for cancer.

iv. if *we* is replaced by a phrase:

e. You and I will . . .   John and I will . . .   Both (or all) of us will . . .

77   Use *shall*, also as a modal verb, to express:

i. deference to (or respect for) the wishes or opinions of someone else:

a. I promise you, you shall have your money tomorrow if you need it.

(Emphasis on the speaker's deference to someone else: compare this with 73, b., where the emphasis is on the certainty of the result.)

b. Shall I pour you out another cup of tea? (Do you want me to?)

c. Let's pack up and go home, shall we? (Do you agree?)

ii. decision, determination or defiance on the part of the speaker with regard to the future of someone (or something) else:

d. Government of the people, by the people and for the people shall not perish from the land. (*Abraham Lincoln*)

e. The Committee agrees that the Secretary shall receive a salary of £1,500 a year (*emphasis on the decision*).

f. You shall do what I tell you. You shan't escape. (*emphasis on the speaker's determination with regard to someone else's actions.*)

g. That man is a traitor. He shall die. (*emphasis on a decision or resolution concerning the man's fate.*)

h. They (the enemy) shall not land on our shores. (*We are determined not to let them.*)

i. That shall be the Jackson's house. (*The speaker decides to allot that house to them.*)

iii. Determination on the part of the first person (I or we) with regard to his own actions can be expressed by *will* (as in 73, e.) or by *shall*:

j. A. Don't do that. B. I shall. A. Listen to me. B. I shan't.

78 EXERCISE. *Fill each of the following gaps with* will *or* shall, won't *or* shan't. *If only one word will fill the gap in the context, say so. If both will fill the gap, say so; and explain what difference, if any, there will be in the meaning if one word is used instead of the other:*

1. It — be Saturday tomorrow, and we — work only in the morning.
2. You — have a holiday tomorrow.
3. There's someone at the door. It — be the postman, I expect.
4. Don't lean on the glass. It — break. — you do as I tell you?
5. — you look after my watch for me? I'm afraid I — break it.
6. The doctor — come at once. He says he — come straight here.
7. If you heat iron, it — expand, — it?
8. Go away, — you? If you touch me, I — scream.
9. If you help us, we — finish the job by Friday.
10. If you — only agree, we — be able to make some progress.
11. — I 'phone for a taxi? I'll ask for a big one, — I?
12. A. — I put the car in the garage? B. Yes, if you —.
13. A. — we see the new laboratory? B. Yes, if there's time.
14. A. — John and I go on foot? B. Yes, please do.
15. A. — John and I go by train? B. Yes, that is the plan.

Will/shall be doing

79 Use the Future Continuous Tense:

i. as a future equivalent of the Present Continuous:

a. We are studying now. In an hour's time, we shall be eating our lunch.

i.e. We are engaged in this activity now. We shall be engaged in another (or the same) activity later.

ii. as a variation of the pattern *I am leaving tomorrow:*

b. I am at home now, and say, '*I'm not leaving the house this morning, but I shall be going to town this afternoon. Can I get anything for you then?* Both patterns, *I'm leaving* and *I shall be going* refer to future action that has been arranged: use the first to emphasize the present arrangement, the second to emphasize action at a future time.

iii. to state the 'pure future', avoiding an ambiguity that can arise because of the various meanings of *will* or *shall*:

c. A. Is there a seat reserved for me for the meeting?
B. Yes, you will be sitting on the Chairman's left.

In that example, *you will be sitting* makes a plain statement about the future: *you will sit* sounds too positive and might be understood as a command (see 73, a).

d. Will you be having any more? If not, I'll put the tea things in the kitchen.

This, again, refers to the 'pure future', while *Will you have . . .?* might be understood as an invitation, as in 74, a.

Will/shall have done

80 Use the Pre-Future Tense:

i. when the speaker is looking back from a point in future time:

a. I will tell you what I think of this book tomorrow. I shall have finished reading it by then.

b. By next June, we shall have been learning English for six years.

ii. to make an assumption about the pre-present or past:

c. You will have heard the news (I assume you have heard it).

d. I assume you all saw the play last night. You will all have seen it.

81 EXERCISE. *Re-phrase the following sentences, replacing the phrase or word in brackets with a construction containing* will *or* shall, *affirmative, negative or interrogative:*

1. My plane (arrive) at 11.55. I hope you (be) there to meet me. If I do not see you at the airport, I (go) to the airway terminal.
2. If you see John, (please ask) him to telephone me.
3. If you (are willing to answer) my question, I (be able) to help you.
4. We are working hard now. This time tomorrow we (enjoy) a well-earned rest.
5. I (know) the result of my experiment by eight o'clock this evening. I (finish) all the practical work by seven.
6. This (I expect is) Mary. (Please introduce) me.
7. Why are you standing? (Please sit down).
8. You (have met, I assume) Elizabeth already.

9. (Please allow) me to call you by your first name.

10. You (all heard, no doubt) this story last night, so I (not repeat) it now.

11. Some people are terrible bores. They (tell) you the same story over and over again.

12. All officers (must carry out) the following instructions.

13. This writing is disgraceful. You (do) it all again.

14. I'm glad you like this work. You (do) it again tomorrow.

15. (I'm determined not to let you) escape.

16. If you read too long in that light, you (have) a headache.

17. If you come first in your class, you (have) a watch.

18. If you don't give these plants plenty of water, they (die).

19. That man has betrayed our allies, and they are very angry because of it. We swear that they (be) satisfied. If we capture the villain, he (die), and then our allies (be) content.

20. (I want you to) turn on the central heating.

21. (Do you want me to) turn it on for you?

22. I can never make this thing work. I (always) press the wrong buttons.

23. When I am away, my dog (always lies) by my chair all day, waiting for me to come back.

24. It is easy to declare that all men (live) in peace, but we know that they (continue) to quarrel.

25. (Do you want Miss Johnson to) go, or (do you want her to) wait?

26. If you (insist on having) the radio on, I (be) obliged if you (kindly keep) the windows shut.

27. What are you doing this evening? (You stay) out late?

28. The Committee has resolved that you (leave) the club at once.

29. I refuse to accept that decision. I (stay) where I am.

30. Give us the tools and we (finish) the job (*Winston Churchill*).

would

82 Use *would*:

i. as an auxiliary to form the Future-in-the-Past:

   a. She asked who would be in for supper this evening.
   b. I said I would.

ii. to form the **Conditional Mood**:

Present Tense	*Future*
a. If I smoke, (I am a smoker, or it is possible that I will become one) . . .	I will smoke a pipe.

Past Tense Form	**Conditional**
b. If I smoked, (I do not smoke, or am not smoking now, but suppose I *did* smoke) . . .	I would smoke cigars.

83   Use *would*, also, to express past attitudes similar to those expressed by *will*:

a. I promised you would have your money tomorrow (*positive Future-in-the-Past: see 73, b*).

b. I asked if you would have a cup of tea (i.e. if you wanted one: *see 74, a*).

c. I asked you if you would turn the radio off (*request or command: see 74, g or h*).

d. Uncle Tom would sit there for hours. (He often sat there: *see 73, m*. Would, *in this sense, is commonly used in past narrative*).

e. The mules were obstinate. They wouldn't move. (They refused: *see 73, f*).

f. I could never use a typewriter properly. I would (*strong stress*) hit the keys in the wrong order (*see 73, i*).

84   Use *would* to express less positive present attitudes than those expressed by *will*:

a. That would be the Jacksons' house. (i.e. I assume, less positively than in 75, that it is).

b. Would you come in for a minute? (*invitation, less definite than* will).

c. Would you turn that radio off for a minute? (*request, less definite than* will).

d. Would you turn that radio off at once! (*command, weaker than* will).

e. Can I carry that for you? Yes please, if you would.

Note that only *would*, not *will*, is used in the form of polite request beginning *Would you mind . . .?*

f. Would you mind explaining this to me? (*meaning* Please explain it to me).

The less positive *would*, not *will*, is also used in sentences expressing wishes, as follows:

g. I wish you would stop that noise (*see 172, Table 6*).

h. If only the sun would come out!

and in the construction *would like*, which refers to future action:

i. I would like a short rest. Then I would like to go for a drive.

j. Would you like an ice-cream? Would you like to dance?

Note the use of *would* in:

k. You've left your keys behind. You would (*strong stress*) do a thing like that! (*meaning* That is typical of your habits. It is the kind of thing you often do. (*See 73, h.* You will leave your keys behind *makes a more direct statement about your habits.*)

should

85 Use *should* as an alternative to *would* (but only when the subject of the verb is *I* or *we*) to form the Future-in-the-Past and the Conditional Mood. As in 76, this alternative is optional, and there is no difference in meaning. With the 1st person singular or plural, prefer *should* to *would* or *would* to *should* in similar circumstances to those in 76.

86 Use *should*, also, to express past attitudes similar to those expressed by *shall*:

a. I promised you that you should have your money to-morrow (*see 77, a*).

b. I asked you if I should pour you out another cup of tea. (Did you want me to? *see 77, b*).

c. The Committee agreed that the Secretary should receive a salary of £1,500 a year (*77, e*).

d. They were determined the enemy should not land on their shores (*77, h*).

In the last three examples, do not contract *should* to '*d*.

87 Use *should* to express less positive present attitudes than those expressed by *shall*:

i. **obligation,** indicating what is right or due rather than what will happen: *You shall have your money now* expresses my decision or promise in this matter, and also suggests that you will *get* your money. But note:

a. I think you should have your money now. *This means* You have earned it, or you are due for it, but I do not say that you will actually get it. *Similarly,*

b. We agree that the Secretary should receive £1,500 a year. She earns it. It is a fair salary. But that does not mean she will get it; we may not have enough money to pay her.

c. Your work is inaccurate. You should be more careful.

Do not contract the *should* of obligation to *'d*.

ii. Still less positive statement than that expressed by *will* (75) or *would* (84, a):

d. That should be the Jacksons' house, the one over there. (It looks like it, it answers to a description of it, though I'm not saying that it is).

e. That should be the north, there. (According to the stars, or other evidence, the north is in that direction.)

f. It should be a fine day tomorrow, judging by the signs (but perhaps it won't be).

Would and should in conditional clauses

88 In 82, ii, the part of the sentence beginning with *if* is called a *conditional clause*: the rest is the main clause. *Would* and *should* can be used in both clauses:

a. If each person would (=were willing to) sweep before his own house, we should have a clean street. (*Proverb*)

b. I should be grateful if you would reply by cable (i.e. if you were willing, and kindly replied). *This is less positive than* I should be grateful if you replied; *and still less than* I shall be grateful if you reply, *which sounds very curt.*

c. If you would be interested (*hypothetical; less positive than* if you are interested), I will tell you the whole story.

d. If you should be interested, etc. (*more hypothetical still*).

e. If you should (*strong stress*) be interested, etc. (*meaning* I do not suggest that you are, but suppose your reaction is positive). *On the other hand*, if you were (*strong stress*) interested, etc. *suggests that your reaction is already negative.*

f. Should you be interested, etc. *has a similar meaning to* If you should be interested, etc., *but use only* should, *not* would, *in this construction.*

Ambiguities in the use of would and should

89 Because *would* and *should* both have various meanings and uses, ambiguities arise, as with *will* and *shall*. For example:

a. In *We said we should find a cure for cancer*, the word *should* could express pure Future-in-the-Past, or it could express obligation.

b. In *We said we would find a cure for cancer if we had the necessary facilities for research*, *would* could express either positive Future-in-the-Past, or the Conditional Mood. To make the meaning of positive Future-in-the-Past clear, therefore, we must say something like *We said a cure for cancer was certain, or was assured, if etc.*

c. *That should be the Jacksons' house* could mean *We assume hesitantly, that it is* (87, d) or *We think that is a suitable house for them* (example of 87, a). We can avoid this ambiguity by using a different expression, e.g. *That looks like the Jacksons' house* or *That is the house they ought to have.* (see 93)

Would/should be doing

90 Use this construction for the past equivalent of all the examples given in 79 and for the Conditional:

a. If it was warmer (now), we should all be sitting outside (now).

Would/should have done

91 i. Use this construction for the past equivalent of all the examples given in 80, and for the Past Conditional:

a. If it had been warmer (then, in the past), we should all have been sitting outside.

ii. Use *should have done* to indicate pre-present or past obligation or expectation not fulfilled; or action fulfilled in spite of obligation to the contrary:

b. Our guests have not arrived. They were due to arrive at 6. It is 6 now. They should have arrived by now.

c. I did not tell you this news yesterday. It was my duty to tell you then. I should have told you it yesterday.

d. You did not see George's comic act. It was a pity you did not. You should have seen it.

e. Why did you kick that poor dog? You shouldn't have done that.

f. What were you doing at the club last night? You should have been studying. You certainly shouldn't have been dancing till two o'clock in the morning.

iii. Use *would have liked* as the past, unfulfilled, of *would like*, as in 84, i and j.

92 EXERCISE. *Re-write the following sentences, replacing the phrase or word in brackets by a construction containing* would *or* should *or by* would *or* should *alone*:

1. The journalists wanted to know if the deputy (proposed to) resign.

2. The deputy was guilty but refused to admit it. Everyone thought he (resign), but they knew (he was determined to) keep his seat as long as possible.

3. My neighbour asked me (to lend)* him my tape-recorder. I said I (lend) him anything he needed. He promised I (have) it back in a few days. If I borrowed anything from him, I hope I (remember) to return it promptly.

4. I couldn't work the tape-recorder myself. I (always pressed) the wrong switch. Or if I did press the right one, the machine (failed to) start.

5. Grandmother enjoyed the television. She (often sat) looking at it all day. We sometimes asked her if (she wanted us to) take her for a drive, but she (refused to) move.

6. According to the map, this (be) our road. If it is, we (go) south-west.

7. I wish you (not discuss) our private affairs with other people. (Please) keep them to yourself.

8. You have done wonderfully. I think you (are due for) a prize. You (were due for) one last year, but you were unlucky.

9. I am afraid I was very rude. I know I (apologise).

10. If you (allow) me to speak, I (be) able to explain everything.

11. Surely you knew that if you poured petrol on the fire it (explode)!

12. If a fire broke out, I know what (it is my duty to do), but I'm not sure what I (do).

13. The water was cut off last night. If a fire had broken out, we (be) helpless.

14. We decided that our next meeting (take place) on June 15.

15. You've been driving with the hand-brake on. That is the kind of silly thing you (do), and the kind of thing you (never do).

16. A. Look at these curtains. You told me you were certain the colours (not fade). B. I'm extremely sorry. Something has gone wrong. They (not fade) like that.

17. If it (be) convenient to you, I (like) to call on you some time next week. (it be) possible for you to see me on Monday, (your secretary kindly give) me a ring?

18. If you filled a thermos flask full of ice and shook it, the ice (expand) and break the flask. You (never put) too much ice in it, therefore, unless you want the flask broken.

19. A. I put a kettle of water on the stove. (Kindly see) if it is boiling? B. No, it isn't. A. But I put it on ten minutes ago.

* say *if I — lend*

79

It (be) boiling by now.   B. No doubt it (be) boiling if you had turned the electricity on.

20. A. It was a pity you didn't reach the summit. You (have) a marvellous view. You (try) again one day.   B. I (like) to try it again, if only someone (cut) me some steps. That last slope is very dangerous. Amateurs like me (not be) allowed to attempt it.

21. If each (sweep) before his own house, we (have) a clean street.

Should, ought to

93   *Should* (as in 87) is used to express obligation, but obligation which we are free to avoid if we wish. It is also used (87, d) to make an assumption about which we do not feel very certain and which may prove to be false. *Ought* is used in the same ways two. It can be used as an alternative to *should*; but it often makes the feeling of obligation stronger, and it can avoid the kind of ambiguity discussed in 89.

Examples:

i. *Obligation*

    a. I think you ought to have your money now.

    b. The Secretary ought to receive £1,500 a year.

    c. You ought to be more careful.

In these three examples, *ought* expresses the idea of what is right or due more strongly than *should* in 87, a., b. and c.

ii. *Assumption*

    d. That ought to be the Jacksons' house.

This makes the same kind of assumption as 87, d. It is also ambiguous: it could mean that is the house the Jacksons ought to have, the right house for them.

Notice the negative and interrogative of *ought*:

    a. The patient is sleeping. We ought not to disturb him.

    b. He's breathing very fast. Ought we to call a doctor?

    c. Oughtn't we at least to call the nurse?

Ought to have done, ought not to have done

94   Use *ought to have done, ought not to have done*, as in 91, ii, to indicate pre-present or past obligation not fulfilled, or action fulfilled in spite of obligation to the contrary:

    a. We have done (*or* we did) what we ought not to have done; we have left undone (*or* we did not do) what we ought to have done.

b. Why were you playing? You ought to have been working. You certainly ought not to have been playing cards.

Must

95 *Must* expresses obligation, necessity or compulsion, which we are not free to avoid; or makes an assumption which, we feel, cannot prove to be false.

i. *Unavoidable obligation, necessity or compulsion*

a. You must have your money now. (I, or anyone else, cannot refuse to give it to you; and you cannot refuse to take it.)

b. If you must fly, fly well (*Proverb*).

In b., *must*, strongly stressed = 'are determined to', so determined that you cannot act otherwise.

For the negative and opposite of *must* in this sense, see 101 and 102.

ii. *Safe assumption.*

c. You must be exhausted after your journey. (It is not possible that you can be otherwise.)

For the negative of *must* in this sense, see 105, k.

Must have been

96 *Must have been* is the pre-present or past equivalent of *must* in the sense of 95, ii, but not of 95, i.

a. You must have been exhausted when you arrived last night (i.e., I'm sure you were exhausted). But you look rested now. You must have had a very good sleep (i.e. I'm sure you have had).

Have to

97 *Must* in the sense of 95, i, not as in 95, ii, can be replaced by *have to* (or, in spoken English, *have got to*), when the obligation is the result of a prescription, a plan, an instruction, an arrangement that has been made, etc. *Have to* tends to put more emphasis on the prescription and less on the compulsion, and therefore often sounds less compelling than *must*. Examples:

a. A. I have to take these pills three times a day. The doctor prescribed them and told me to take them. But they make me feel giddy so I'm going to stop taking them for a day or two. B. But you *have* (strong stress) to take them. The doctor told you to.

Interrogative
Present: Have I to take? (*rather formal*) *or* Do I have to take? (*less formal*) *or* Have I got to take? (*common in spoken English*)
Past: Had I to take? (*formal, now rare*); *or* Did I have to take? (*normal*).
Negative
Present: I do not have to take (*normal*) *or* I haven't got to take (*common in spoken English*).
Past: I did not have to take.

98 *Must* is used only in certain tenses; for the remaining tenses, parts of '*have to*' are used: see 102. In past reported speech and in the future, *must* can still be used. But for the past, other than in reported speech, use *had to*; and when emphasis is on obligation in the future, use *will have to*. Examples:

   a. We must consider this matter carefully (*Present*)
   b. We agreed we must consider it carefully (*Past reported speech. Call this the weak Past of* must).
   c. We must re-consider it at our next meeting. (*Future, indicated by next meeting. Call this the weak Future*).
   d. We had to examine the whole question. (*Past. Had to is necessary here to express the past. Call this the strong Past.*)
   e. We shall have to re-consider the matter. (*The strong Future. Must is also possible in this sentence, but shall have to emphasises the idea of an obligation in the future.*)

Am to

99 *I am to do something* means that someone expects me to do it, because of instructions, plans, a time-table, etc., emphasis being still more on the plan, instruction, etc., than it is in *I have to*. Examples:

   a. I must finish my essay by Friday (*emphasis entirely on obligation or compulsion*).
   b. I have to finish it by Friday (I am obliged to do it because someone has told me to, or because I have made plans accordingly).
   c. I am to finish it by Friday (those are my instructions).
   d. What are we to do now? (What are our orders?)

Note the past:

   e. I gave you your instructions clearly. You were to go first to the factory, then to the warehouse. Is that what you did?
   f. I was to have gone to the factory first, but as the ware-

house was on my way, I went there first instead. (Those were the plans but I did not carry them out.)

For the negative and opposite of 'am to', see 101 and 102.

Need

100 Use *need*

i. as a full verb (*He needs. He doesn't need. Does he need? He needed*), followed by a direct object or by *to* plus the infinitive of a verb, to indicate what is necessary for the subject person:

a. George needs some money. (It is necessary for him. He will have to pay for various things.)

b. He needs to go to the hairdresser's. His hair is almost as long as a girl's.

ii. as a modal verb (*Need he? He need not*), followed by an infinitive without *to*. The modal *need* usually occurs in the interrogative or negative, to question or deny obligation or necessity. To state necessity affirmatively, use the ordinary verb, as in b.

c. Need we learn this? (Do we have to?)

d. Keep calm. You needn't worry. There's nothing to worry about.

In c. and d., the ordinary verb *need* can also be used (*Do we need to learn that? You don't need to worry*) with no real difference in meaning. But there are some fixed expressions in which only the modal *need* is used; and some examples where both forms can be used but with a difference in meaning:

e. We need never know (*no alternative form*).

f. I need hardly tell you (*no alternative form*).

g. Need anyone know what really happened? (Does it matter if everyone remains in ignorance?)

h. Does anyone need to know? (Is there anyone for whom this knowledge is necessary?)

iii. *Past and future of* need

Like *must*, the modal *need* is also used as a weak past form in past reported speech, and in the future. For the strong past form, the Past Tense of the ordinary verb is used. The strong future is *will need to:*

i. We asked if we need take rain-coats. He said we needn't (yesterday) and we needn't tomorrow either.

j. They won't need to tomorrow (*emphasis on future absence of necessity*).

83

Didn't need

k. Did they need to take rain-coats? No, they didn't need to take them: there wasn't a sign of rain anywhere. (*This tells us that it was not necessary to rake rain-coats. Perhaps they took them, perhaps not.*)

Needn't have denies obligation *after* the event:

l. A few of them took rain-coats; but they needn't have done: it proved to be unnecessary.

You needn't. You mustn't. You're not to

101 a. *Must I wait?* queries compulsion. *Have I* (or *do I have*) *to wait?* queries obligation based on a prescription. *Am I to wait?* asks for confirmation about an instruction. Note the answers:

Must I wait? — Yes, you must; you have to; you are to.
— No, **you needn't**; you don't have to.

b. *Need I wait?* queries obligation and often expects a negative answer. Note the answers:

Need I wait? — Yes, you must; you have to.
— No, you needn't; you don't have to.

c. *I mustn't go* is a negative answer to the question:

Am I allowed to go? — Yes, you may.
— No, **you mustn't**; you are not to.

Note that *I am not obliged to go* is expressed by *I need not go*; and *I am obliged not to go* is expressed by *I must not go*. Note also that while *I have to go* and *I am to go* express a similar meaning, *I don't have to go* expresses absence of obligation, leaving me free to go or not as I please, but *I am not to go* expresses prohibition, compelling me to stay.

Must, have to, am to in the various tenses

102 TABLE 4

		Affirmative Obligation	Negative (No obligation)	Opposite (Prohibition)
PRESENT	I	I am obliged to (go)	am not obliged to (go)	am not allowed to (go)
	II	I must (go)	need not (go)	must not (go)
	III	I have to (go)	do not have to (go)	—
	IV	I am to (go)	—	am not to (go)

84

		Affirmative Obligation	Negative (No obligation)	Opposite (Prohibition)
PRE-PRESENT	I	have been obliged to	have not been obliged to	have not been allowed to
	II	—	—	—
	III	have had to	have not had to	—
	IV	—	—	—
PAST	I	was obliged to	was not obliged to	was not allowed to
	II	must (*weak*)	{ need not (*weak*) / did not need to (*strong*)	must not (*weak*)
	III	had to (*strong*)	did not have to (*strong*)	—
	IV	was to	—	was not to
PRE-PAST	I	had been obliged to	had not been obliged to	had not been allowed to
	II	—	—	—
	III	had had to	had not had to	—
	IV	was to have (gone, but did not go)	—	was not to have (gone but went)
FUTURE	I	will be obliged to	will not be obliged to	will not be allowed to
	II	must (*weak*)	{ need not (*weak*) / will not need to (*strong*)	must not
	III	will have to (*strong*)	will not have to	—
	IV	am to	—	am not to
PRES. COND.	I	would be obliged to	would not be obliged to	would not be allowed to
	II	—	would not need to	—
	III	would have to	would not have to	—
	IV	—	—	—
PAST COND.	I	would have been obliged to	would not have been obliged to	would not have been allowed to
	II	—	would not have needed to	—
	III	would have had to	would not have had to	—
	IV	—	—	—

Notes: 1. Where there is a blank, use an existing form in the same column and tense.

2. In past reported speech, and in the future, use the weak forms when the idea of obligation, or lack of it, is not emphasized. Use only the strong forms in the past other than in reported speech.

3. For the infinitive, use *to have to, to be obliged to, not to be allowed to*, etc.:

My grandfather used to have to walk five miles to school.

He was glad not to have to do it any more.

4. *I must (have to, ought to) be going.* Here the idea of the continuous action is emphasized. I *must be going* = I must be on my way.

103 EXERCISE. *Fill each gap with* ought to, must, need, need to *or* have to, *in the appropriate person and tense, affirmative, negative or interrogative.*

(At a party. Four characters are speaking.)

1. *Margaret:* How much longer should we stay? When do you think we — leave?

2. *Robert:* — we to go before the guest of honour? I'm sure we —.

3. *Geoffrey:* I agree we —, but I'm afraid I — leave in five minutes. I — catch a train: it's the last one tonight.

4. *Robert:* When you go, you — slip out quietly, and I — stay. I'm not allowed to leave till 12.30. I — go before then.

5. *Later. Margaret:* The guest of honour's gone now. We — wait any longer. What's the time?

6. *Robert:* My watch has stopped, but it — be 12.30. Geoffrey — left at half past eleven. But we — go yet, it's still quite early.

7. *Hostess:* Where's Geoffrey? I haven't had a chance to speak to him. I — give all my attention so far to the guest of honour.

8. *Robert:* He was very sorry, he — slip away. He — catch a train. We — catch a train, so we stayed on.

9. *Hostess:* He — left so early. Somebody would surely have given him a lift.

10. *Margaret:* And we — go soon. You — be very tired.

11. *Hostess:* Oh no, you — go yet. I'll be very angry if you do. Oh, and Robert, thank you so much for the flowers. But you — sent such a lot.

12. *Later. Margaret:* We really — go now. If we miss the last 'bus, we — walk home.

13. *Robert:* Why do we — walk? Can't we take a taxi?

14. *Margaret:* All the taxis are taken. My mother warned me that if we left too late, we — walk home.
15. *Robert:* We — do that. Bernard is offering us a lift. Thank you, Bernard. If you had not come along, we — walk all the way home.

104 EXERCISE. *Re-phrase the following sentences (not those in italics) using* ought, must, need to, have to *or* am to *wherever possible, in the appropriate person and tense, affirmative, negative or interrogative.*

1. (*There has been a robbery.*) It is your duty to inform the police. It is your duty not to delay.
2. (*The Captain is sound asleep.*) Is it right that we should disturb him? Isn't it better to let him sleep?
3. It was your duty to wake me at once. You were wrong to let me go on sleeping.
4. (*The chief is very angry with his subordinate.*) *You haven't finished your report yet.* Why weren't you writing it all this morning, and why were you doing your own private business instead?
5. *If you are in deep water,* you are compelled to sink or to swim. *If you cannot swim and somebody dives in to rescue you,* don't struggle — keep still, *and let him swim with you to safety.*
6. (*A boy fell into the river.*) I was obliged to jump in with all my clothes on and pull him out. (*Then a girl fell in, and I dived into the river again.*) But it was unnecessary, *because she was a very good swimmer.*
7. (*What terrible news!*) Don't tell his mother. It is essential that she never knows. It is not necessary for his father to know; but, *if he hears about it later,* it will be essential for him to keep it a secret.
8. (*We have bought a new house.*) It has been necessary to borrow some of the money, but it hasn't been necessary to borrow very much.
9. (*Doctor to patient.*) Take one of these pills three times a day. It is not necessary for you to stay in bed, but you are not allowed to stay up late at night.
10. *Put 9 into reported speech, beginning* The doctor said . . .
11. I was obliged to take an enormous pill three times a day. It wasn't necessary to stay in bed, but I wasn't allowed to stay up late at night.
12. (*These are your instructions, Captain Smith.*) Report to Colonel Bogey at 19.00 hours. Then remain under his orders

until further notice. Do not reveal your identity to anyone else. It is not necessary for you to wear a false moustache.

13. Captain Smith wore a false moustache, but it wasn't necessary. (*It made him look so much like a secret agent that the police arrested him on his way to Colonel Bogey.*) His orders had been to report at 19.00.

can

105 Use *can* to express freedom to act or to happen. Freedom can be the result of ability, opportunity, permission, etc. Examples:

i. *Ability: I can* in this sense = *I am able to, because I have the power.*

    a. Some people can write as well with their left hand as they can with their right.

Note the frequent use of *can* before *see, hear, feel, taste, understand, remember,* and similar verbs, e.g.:

    b. I can see Mars; can hear a nightingale; can feel the springs in this chair; can taste paraffin in this butter; can understand everything you say but can't remember it all.

ii. *Opportunity: I can* in this sense = *I am able to, because I have the opportunity.*

    c. Thanks to long-playing records, we can hear a complete symphony in comfort in our own home.

iii. *Availability: I can* in this sense = *I am free to, because I am not otherwise engaged.*

    d. Tell Mr. Brown I can't see him today. I can see him tomorrow at 10.30.

iv. *Permission: I can* in this sense = *am free to, because no one has any objection* (emphasis on freedom to act).

    e. We needn't wait any longer (*see 101, a*). We can go.
    f. *To policeman:* Can I leave my car here for half an hour? *Policeman:* I'm sorry, sir, you can't. It isn't allowed.

v. *Willingness: Can you . . .?* in this sense = *Are you willing to?*

    g. Can you lend me your dictionary?

vi. *Chance: I can* in this sense = *I am quite likely to.*

    h. Keep away from jellyfish. They can give you a nasty sting if you touch them. (That is quite likely to happen.)

Note the use of *can* in this sense in the example:

i. George can be very amusing. He can also be very annoying (i.e. he is quite likely to be, because he often is).

vii. *Definite possibility: can* in this sense = it is possible for someone or something to (do something).

j. You can lead a horse to water but you can't make it drink (*Note*).

Note the idea of possibility in:

k. Can that be Mount Olympus in the distance? Is it possible? No, it can't be: it isn't possible.

And note that the affirmative of *it can't be* in that sense is *it must be* (*see 95, c*).

may

106 Use *may* to emphasize the idea of permission, of possibility (less definite than *can*), or of probability combined with a sense of uncertainty as to which course the future will take. Examples:

i. *Permission: I may* emphasizes the idea that I am allowed to.

a. You need not wait any longer. You may go.

Use *may* in this sense to make a contrast with *can* in the sense of *am able to*:

b. May I speak to Mary for a moment? (*emphasis on asking permission*).

c. I know you *can* use my typewriter, but that doesn't mean you *may* use it whenever you like.

ii. *Possibility with an element of uncertainty:*

d. You may lead a horse to water (I admit it is possible, but . . .), but you cannot make it drink.

May in that sense is often used in the affirmative; but do not use it in that sense in the negative or interrogative. Similarly:

e. That may be Olympus (perhaps it is, but I'm not sure). Compare this with *Can it be? No, it can't be* (105, k).

Note the element of uncertainty or hesitation in:

f. My mother instilled into me such virtues as I may possess. (I do not positively state that I possess any at all):

or the contrast between the less definite *may* and something more positive, as in:

Note: 105 j. In this proverb, one can say 'You can lead' or 'You may lead'.

89

g. George may be amusing (perhaps he is, I concede that), but he can also be very annoying (that is what I want to state more definitely).

iii. *Probability, plus uncertainty, with regard to the future: I may* in this sense = *perhaps I will, perhaps I will not.*

h. I don't think these jellyfish are poisonous. They may sting, or they may not.

i. I may be late home tonight, I can't say yet. Anyway, don't wait up for me. Note the contrast, as in (g).

j. Television may reduce cinema audiences (perhaps it will) but it will never stop people reading (that is more certain).

may/can be going; may/can have gone

107 i. *We may be going* may mean either *perhaps we are going now* or *perhaps we shall be going* (see 79, ii and iii). Examples:

a. Let's look at the map and make sure we're on the right road. We may be going miles out of our way (= perhaps we are).

b. We haven't met our new neighbours yet, but they may be calling on us this evening.

ii. *They may have gone* means *perhaps they have gone* or *perhaps they went* or *perhaps they will have gone:*

c. You may have noticed a few examples of this usage already (perhaps you have).

d. When you were in London, you may have noticed how gloomy some of the buildings looked (perhaps you did).

e. By the end of this century the world population may have doubled itself (perhaps it will have doubled itself).

iii. *Can be doing:*

f. (We are waiting for the teacher.) While we're waiting, we can be preparing the next lesson.

iv. *Can have gone:*

g. Where's Robert? Where can he have gone? He can't have gone far. Oh yes, he can have gone anywhere.

could

108 Use *could*

i. as the past equivalent of *can*:

a. I can speak English fluently now, but I could speak it even more fluently two years ago.

In reported speech:

b. I thought I could taste paraffin (see 105, b).

c. The policeman told me I couldn't leave my car there.

and in the conditional:

d. Can you climb that tree? I could if I tried.

ii. as a less positive or more polite version of *can* (present or future) when asking permission or making a request, or when referring to availability, chance or possibility:

e. Could I park my car here?

f. Could you lend me your dictionary?

g. I could see Mr. Brown at 10.30 tomorrow.

h. Jellyfish could give you quite a nasty sting.

i. George can be annoying (positive). He could also be very amusing (less positive).

j. Could that be Mount Olympus? No, it couldn't be.

k. There's a remedy for everything, if only we could find it (*proverb*).

could, was able to, managed to

109 *Could*, like all the modal verbs, expresses an attitude to an act: it does not refer to the positive achievement of the act itself. Note these examples:

a. A. I could climb Mount Olympus when I was much younger (I had the strength or ability for it). B. Yes, but did you ever get to the top? Did you actually do it?

b. A. I was able to (*or* I managed to) get to the top (*or* I succeeded in getting to the top) once.

c. B. I tried, but couldn't climb it. (I hadn't the strength or ability, consequently I didn't reach the summit.)

might

110 Use *might*

i. as a past equivalent of *may*, but only in reported speech:

a. I asked if I might speak to Mary for a moment.

ii. in the Conditional (see 82):

b. Be careful. If you slipped here, you might kill yourself.

iii. to indicate or ask permission, or express possibility or probability even less certainly than *may*, in the present or future:

c. Might I speak to Mary now? (*polite request for permission*)

d. You might be able to manage this horse, but I very much doubt it.

e. That (the thing we can see now) might be Mount Olympus, but I think it's a cloud.

f. I might be home late this evening, but I'll try not to be.

g. Let's look at the map. We might be going miles out of our way (now).

h. Our new neighbours might be calling on us this evening (future).

Note, also, this special use:

i. You might tell me what he said (I wish you would tell me—you are unkind, or annoying, not to tell me).

could have gone, might have gone

111 Use *could have gone, might have gone*

i. as a past equivalent of *can have, may have:*

a. We wondered where Robert could have gone (see 107, g).

b. I thought (then) you might have noticed other examples of this usage (see 107, c).

ii. *as* a less definite equivalent of *can have*, etc.

c. I wonder (now) where he could have gone.

d. Speaking now, I say 'You might have noticed other examples'.

iii. to indicate that ability, opportunity, etc. were present, but not used; or that a course of action was open, but not taken:

e. I could have passed my examination easily, but I made too many stupid mistakes (so I failed).

f. We could have reached the summit in another two hours, if we had only found the right path.

g. It was a good thing you didn't go any further. You might have been killed.

h. It was so quiet, you might have heard a pin drop (*common saying*).

Note the past equivalent of 110, i:

i. You never told me what he said. You were unkind. You might have told me (I wish you had done so).

can and may in the various tenses

112 Notice how the missing parts of *can* are supplied by *am able to*:

TABLE 5

		Ability	Permission	Possibility
Present	i.	I am able to (go)	I am allowed to (go)	Perhaps I (go)
	ii.	I can (go)	I can *or* may (go)	I may (go)
Pre-present	i.	I have been able to	I have been allowed to	Perhaps I have (gone)
	ii.	—	—	I may have (gone)
Past	i.	I was able to	I was allowed to	Perhaps I (went)
	ii.	I could (go) (*see 109*) *or* I could have (gone) (111, iii)	I could *or* might (go)	I may have (gone)
Pre-past	i.	I had been able to	I had been allowed to	Perhaps I had (gone)
	ii.	—	—	I may have (gone)
Future	i.	I will be able to	I will be allowed to	Perhaps I will (go)
	ii.	I can (go)	I can *or* may (go)	I may (go)
Conditional	i.	I would be able (to)	I would be allowed	Perhaps I would (go)
	ii.	I could (go)	I could *or* might (go)	I might (go)
Past Conditional	i.	I would have been able to	I would have been allowed to	Perhaps I would have (gone)
	ii.	I could have (gone)	I could *or* might have (gone)	I might have (gone)

For the infinitive of *can*, use *be able to*; of *may*, use *be allowed to*. Examples:

Before you can write English, you must be able to speak it.
Before you can swim, you must be allowed to practise.

113 EXERCISE. *Re-phrase the following sentences, whenever possible using* can, may, could *or* might, *or a construction using one of those words, instead of the phrases in brackets:*

a. (Are animals able to) feel pain? (Perhaps they feel it) acutely, but, as only man (has the power to) describe his experiences, we (are not yet in a position to) answer that question in more precise terms. The fact that the forebrain is greater in humans than in animals (is, probably, I hesitatingly suggest) of some interest.

b. Any of you (will perhaps) one day find someone unconscious and (will perhaps) have to give artificial respiration. (Perhaps you will) know the latest methods. In any case, you must do what (lies in your power) to save the patient. (I agree that some of you do not like) the mouth-to-mouth method and (feel unable to) use it. In that case you (are allowed to) use a hand-bellows. But if you hesitate, the patient (will probably soon be) dead. The other day, two children fell into a canal near here. A passer-by dived in and rescued them both. Fortunately he (had experience in giving) artificial respiration and (was able to) save one of the children. But he was (unable to save) the other: he (would have been able to do so), if someone else had been there to help him.

c. By the end of this century (it is possible that the world population will have been doubled). To feed this population, we must use all the facilities that science (is able to) offer. Piecemeal improvements (are, up to a point) useful, but they (are not useful enough to) solve the problem as a whole. We (shall no doubt) have to find a global solution quickly.

dare

114 Use *dare*

i. as a full verb (*He dares, he does not dare, he dared, etc.*) followed either by an infinitive (with or without *to*) or be a direct object plus infinitive with *to*, e.g.

    a. Do I dare eat (*or* dare to eat) an oyster?

    b. The waiter dares you to eat three dozen!

ii. as a modal verb, usually in the negative and interrogative, and only followed directly by an infinitive:

    c. Dare I eat one now?

    d. Oysters once made me very ill. I dare not eat them now.

    e. My father dare not eat them either.

Note the frequent use of *dare say*:

    f. I dare say you're right (=Perhaps you are).

SECTION ELEVEN

INFINITIVE AND -ING

We frequently have to choose between the infinitive and the gerund, i.e. the form of the verb ending in -*ing*.

The infinitive

115 Use only the infinitive, without *to*:

i. after all the modal verbs except *ought*, which takes the infinitive with *to*. Note that *need* and *dare* take an infinitive without *to* when used as modal verbs, as in 114.

ii. after *better* (but see 118, ii), *had better, would rather, would sooner*:

Better wait and see. We'd better go now.
I'd rather wait. We'd sooner die.

Note the negative:

You'd better not say anything. I'd rather not hear it.

iii. after *let, make* and *have*:

Let go of my arm. Let me go.
You can't make me wait here all day.
I'll have you know you can't do that here.

But note the passive:

You'll be allowed to go later.
Meanwhile, you'll be made to wait here.

iv. in examples like:

Why wait? Why not go quietly?
Die, my dear doctor, that's the last thing I shall do (*Lord Palmerston, on his death-bed*).

Note the absence of the infinitive when it is understood:

Can you all see?—Yes, we can.
We'd better stop now.—Yes, we'd better.
I'll make you apologise—You can't make me.
Let me do that for you: please let me.

116 Use the infinitive, with *to*, after the following verbs, in one of these patterns:

95

We expect to go. We don't expect to be left behind.

(can) afford	desire	long	offer	(be) sup-
be allowed	endeavour	manage	pretend	posed
appear	expect	(be) made	prepare	threaten
arrange	fail	mean	promise	undertake
ask	happen	(=intend)	refuse	venture
attempt	hesitate	need (*full*	seek	want (*but see*
(don't) care	hope	*verb*)	seem	*134*)
choose	learn	(be) obliged	wish	

Notes: 1. *In the* pattern *I expect to go. Do you want to cut your hair?*, the same person expects and goes, or wants and cuts.

2. Notice the difference between *he can't afford to buy a new coat* and *he can afford not to worry about expense*.

EXERCISE. *Use the 35 verbs listed above, before an infinitive. Vary the tenses, give some examples in the negative, some in the interrogative, and some with the passive infinitive.*

117 i. Use only the infinitive, with *to*, after the following verbs, plus a direct object in the pattern **I advise you to be careful.**

advise	cause	force	order	recommend	tempt
allow	compel	get	permit	remind	trust
appoint	enable	instruct	persuade	request	urge
ask	encourage	invite	prefer	require	warn
beg	expect	oblige	press	tell	wish

Notes: 1. In this pattern, I advise, but *you* must be careful. *Promise* fits into this pattern but with a different meaning: *I promise you to go = I promise you that I will go.*

2. Notice the difference between *I didn't ask you to do that* and *I asked you not to do it.*

3. All the verbs listed above, except *get, prefer* and *wish*, can be used in the passive, thus: *You are advised to stop.* In that case, the person who is advised is the same as the one who has to stop.

4. Another passive construction using some of these verbs is the following:

Active		Passive	
I allowed	⎫	I allowed	⎫
I asked	⎬ someone to	I asked for	⎬ that
I expected	⎰ do that	I expected	⎰ to be done
I advised	⎭	I advised	⎭

EXERCISE. *Use the verbs in i., above, with a direct object plus the infinitive. Vary the tenses; give some examples in the interrogative, some in the negative, using both forms of the negative. Then use the same verbs, except* get, prefer *and* wish, *with a passive construction.*

ii. Use only the infinitive, with *to*, in the pattern **I am longing for this lesson to stop**, after *arrange, ask, long, prepare.* Note the difference between *I ask you to come* and *I ask someone else for you to come.*

118 Use only the infinitive, with *to*

i. after the following adjectives, in the pattern **I was able to go**

unable	apt	eager	happy	sorry
anxious	bound (obliged)	glad	likely	willing

ii. after *better, essential, important, impossible, necessary, possible, unnecessary,* in the following patterns:

a. It is necessary to examine all the evidence (I, you, or anyone else should examine it).
b. It isn't necessary for you to work so hard. (*You* are working too hard—it isn't necessary.)
c. It is better not (*or* never) to begin than not (*or* never) to make an end (*Proverb*).

EXERCISE. *Use all the adjectives in 118 with an infinitive.*

119 Use only the infinitive, with *to*, after most nouns associated with verbs and adjectives in 116, 117 and 118:

a wish to succeed   a refusal to give up

Note the following exceptions:

no hope of succeeding   a preference for walking
The Importance of Being Earnest   no possibility of failing
There is no likelihood of that happening.

EXERCISE. *Use an infinitive, or a gerund, after the following nouns:*

97

desire, failure, hope, obligation, promise, encouragement, importance, invitation, request, anxiety, ability, necessity, likelihood.

120 Use only the infinitive, with *to*, in the following constructions:

a. Our aim is to know English thoroughly.

b. We don't know what to believe (i.e. what we can, or should, believe).

c. I want something to read (i.e. *I* will read it).

d. Here is something for you to read (*You* will read it).

e. I want something to look at.

f. Here is something for you to look at.

g. That story is too good to be true.

h. The ground is not good enough for her to walk on.

i. He got up to go (=he got up for that purpose).

j. He got up in order (*or* so as) to go (*same meaning as example* i, *but emphasis on the purpose*).

Note the difference between:

k. He left us to pay the bill. (We had to pay it) and

l. He left us in order (*or* so as) to pay the bill. (He went to pay it.)

EXERCISE. *Make up original sentences on the above patterns replacing:*

1. aim, *in* a., *by* ambition, duty, idea, intention, object;

2. what, *in* b., *by* how, when, where, whether or not, which, whom;

3. something, *in* c. *and* d., *by ten different nouns plus an infinitive*;

4. something, *in* e. *and* f., *by ten different nouns plus an infinitive followed by a preposition*;

5. good, *in* g. *and* h., *by six different adjectives*;

6. got up, *in* i. *and* j., *by six different verbs*.

121 Use only the infinitive, with *to*, in the following constructions:

a. He grew up to be one of the most famous men of his day (i.e. he grew up and became one . . .).

b. We arrived only to find the train had left (i.e. we arrived and then found . . .).

c. To tell the truth,
   To speak frankly,   } I cannot give you an answer.
   To cut a long story short,

d. I hope we shall come (*or* get) to know each other better (i.e. I hope we shall eventually know . . .).

e. The year was 1452. Constantinople was to fall within twelve months. (We know it fell in 1453.)
f. It's time to go.
g. Which is the way to go?
h. It pays to tell the truth.
i. It's kind of you to say so.
j. George is often to be seen in the bar. But he's nowhere to be found now. (i.e. one can often see him there, one cannot find him now.)
k. The doctor is often more to be feared than the disease. (*Proverb*, meaning one must fear him more.)

EXERCISE. *Find, or make up, other examples of the above constructions.*

Infinitive either with to or without to

122 Use the infinitive either with *to* or without *to* after:

a. *help*; e.g. *Help me translate this.* Or, in a more complicated sentence: *We must help younger members of the staff to realise that they have their responsibilities too.*
b. *dare* as a full verb; e.g. *Do I dare eat a peach?* or *Do I dare to eat a peach?*

To go, to be going

123 The infinitive can have an ordinary form, e.g. *to go*, as in *We ought to go now*, or a continuous form, e.g. *to be going*, as in *We ought to be going*, i.e. we ought to be on our way. There is an emphasis in the continuous form similar to that explained in 18. To give that emphasis after the verbs etc. listed in 116, use the continuous form of the infinitive, e.g.:

I am writing—*I happen to be writing.*
We're stopping—at least *we appear to be stopping.*

To have gone

124 Observe the difference between the present infinitive and the perfect infinitive:

Present Infinitive

I am glad (now) to see you are so much better (now).
I would like (now) to meet Elizabeth Taylor (now, or future).
I was glad (then) to see you were so much better (then).
I would have liked (then: *see 91, iii*) to meet Elizabeth Taylor (then).

Perfect Infinitive

I am glad (now) to have seen him (before now).
I was glad (then) to have seen him (before then).
I would like (now) to have met Elizabeth Taylor (before now).
I would have liked (then) to have met her (before then).

Note the negative:

I am sorry not (*or* never) to have met you before.

DRILL. *Replace the sentences below with* seem *or* seemed *plus an infinitive, as in the following examples:*

You're getting better.—You seem to be getting better.
You were feeling very ill.—You seemed to be feeling very ill.
It's been raining.—It seems to have been raining.
You looked as if you had been hit on the head.—You seemed to have been hit on the head.

1. It's snowing in the mountains.
2. It was snowing when I was out.
3. It's been snowing heavily.
4. I've broken a bone in my foot.
5. I've been mistaken for somebody else.
6. We're slowing down.
7. We've run out of oil.
8. All the oil has been drained out.
9. The weather is improving.
10. It's got a lot warmer.
11. You're limping.
12. This cheque has been altered.
13. The figures have been changed.
14. You were feeling nervous.
15. You've been overdoing it (*Note*).
16. This window was forced open.
17. George has not come home.
18. His bed has not been slept in.
19. By 8 o'clock we had finished.
20. By then, all the work had been done.

The -ing form

125 i. Generally speaking, the *-ing* form emphasises continuous action, the process, the duration, as in 18:

    a. (You are working too hard) I don't like to see you working so hard.

Note: overdoing it = doing too much (work).

b. (It is cold. We are breathing with difficulty.) The cold air makes breathing difficult.

ii. The *-ing* form sometimes recalls an action that has ended:

c. I posted your letter. I clearly remember posting it.
d. You posted it. Thank you for doing that.
e. How much should I pay that man for washing my car? He has done it very well.

iii. In contrast to both i. and ii., the infinitive frequently directs attention to a new act imagined as completed:

e. Try to do better next time.
f. Stop to think what you're doing.
g. The cold air makes it difficult to breathe.
h. I remembered to post your letter. (I remembered my promise. Then I posted your letter.)
i. You have not kept quiet. I'll thank you to keep quiet now.
j. How much should I pay that man to wash my car? I'll ask him to do it if it isn't too expensive.

In e. and f., in fact, we often say, 'try and do', 'stop and think'; in that case 'do' and 'think' are clearly seen as new acts in the course of events.

This difference between the meaning of the infinitive and the meaning of the *-ing* form is often seen, both in constructions where either the *-ing* form or the infinitive must be used, e.g. *We kept on trying* (continued action) and *We managed to get to the top* (new act), and in constructions where both can be used, e.g. *We saw the car moving towards us* (continued action) and *We saw it crash into the wall* (new completed act).

Present Participle

126 The *-ing* form can occur as a **present participle**, a non-finite form acting partly as a verb, partly as an *adjective*:

i. The present participle may tell us what someone or something is doing or how someone is engaged:

a. Looking at this again, I wonder if it is right (*I* am looking at it).
b. Sleeping on the floor, we had a very uncomfortable night (*We* slept on the floor).
c. We found George sleeping on the floor (*George* was sleeping on the floor).
d. Being pressed for time, we had better leave this exercise out.

Avoid 'unattached participles', as in:

e. Looking at this again, it doesn't seem right.

Or participles which could be linked with the wrong word:

f. Standing in the refrigerator all night, we found the liquid had turned bright blue.

However, a few participles, e.g. *supposing, considering* are often 'unattached', as in:

g. Considering the weather, the meeting will have to be postponed.

h. Supposing you see a house on fire, what is the first thing you would do?

ii. The present participle can also be used in reporting a series of actions:

i. Jumping into his car, he drove away before anyone could stop him.

This means 'He jumped into his car and then drove away'. Compare this with:

j. Jumping into his car, he tore his coat on the door, *or*
k. He tore his coat jumping into his car

where the two actions are simultaneous. Note that in j. and k., the phrase beginning with the participle can begin or end the sentence. In i., *jumping* must come first as that action is performed before he drove away.

EXERCISE. *Re-phrase the following forming one sentence in each case with a present participle used correctly:*

1. We arrived at the station and found the train had left. (*Compare your answer with 121, b. which means the same thing.*)
2. We watched the train as it disappeared into the distance.
3. If you stand up here, you can just see our house.
4. You can just see our house. It stands between those trees.
5. Grazing on the hills, we saw herds of splendid cattle. (*Re-phrase this correctly.*)
6. If one wears rubber gloves, the wire can be handled quite safely.
7. She tore up his letter and said, 'I'll never speak to him again'.
8. When one considers how hot it is outside, this room is surprisingly cool.
9. Hundreds of monkeys were hanging from the branches by their tails. The explorers were astonished to see them.

10. We turned on the light and a swarm of mosquitoes immediately attacked us.

Present Participles used as adjectives

127 i. A few present participles can act as full adjectives, attributive or predicative; they can be used with *very* and *too*, and can be compared; e.g. **This is an interesting story** or **This story is interesting.** It is **very interesting.** It is **the most interesting story** I've ever heard.

DRILL. *Use the following on the pattern of the sentences above:*

amusing	comforting	encouraging	frightening
astonishing	disappointing	entertaining	insulting
charming	disgusting	exciting	surprising

Note: *An interesting story* is a story that interests us. But *boiling water* is water that is in the process of boiling.

ii. Other present participles can be used as adjectives attributively, but not with *very* and *too*, and they cannot be compared:

A dancing bear (=a bear that dances).
The boy stood on the burning deck (=the deck that was burning).

(*Burning*, however, can be used as in i., when it is a metaphor: That is a very burning question.)

iii. Note that when the present participle is used before a noun, as in i. and ii., stress falls on both the participle and the noun.

iv. Unless you know, from examples of actual good usage, that a present participle is used as in i. or ii., avoid using it in that way. Thus you may not find an example of *speaking* used as in i. or ii., but you will find present participles freely used in examples like:

The man speaking to the judge is a journalist.

Gerund

128 i. The *-ing* form also serves as a **gerund**, which acts partly as a *noun*, either as the subject of a verb, or as the object of a verb or preposition:

a. Smoking is bad for me (*subject*).
b. I must give up smoking (*object*).
c. I am interested in dancing but not in playing cards (*object of a preposition*).

Playing, in c., is the object of a preposition, and at the same time it has its own object, *cards*.

d. We can learn a good deal of English simply by (i.e. a result of) listening.

ii. The gerund can also act as an adjunct to a noun, as in the examples:

a dancing floor	i.e. a floor for dancing on
a swimming pool	i.e. a pool for swimming in
a writing desk	i.e. a desk for writing at

iii. Note that in ii., the stress falls only on the gerund (*see 127, iii*).

129 DRILL. *Pronounce and define:*

an astonishing report	the existing regulations
a bathing costume	a fishing village
a biting wind	a hearing aid
boiling water	increasing influence
camping equipment	living creatures
cleaning materials	a milking stool
comforting words	an operating table
a confusing explanation	a running stream
a dining table	running shoes
disappointing results	changing circumstances
a dressing table	a changing room
an exciting story	exploding stars

Participle or gerund

130 The question sometimes arises: should the *-ing* form act as a participle, or as a gerund (i.e. a kind of noun), as in the examples:

a. I can't understand him behaving like that (*participle referring to him*).

b. I can't understand his behaving like that (*gerund, or kind of noun, preceded by 'his'*).

In a., the strict meaning is: I can't understand him, when he behaves like that. In b., the meaning is: I can't understand his behaviour.

The -ing form or the infinitive?

131 Use only the *-ing* form, not the infinitive:

i. after the following verbs, in the patterns:

I enjoy dancing. I dislike being laughed at.

avoid	dislike	give up	mind (=object to)	recollect
carry on	enjoy	include	miss	risk
delay	fancy	keep (on)	postpone	suggest
deny	finish	leave off	practise	

Also cannot help (=cannot prevent myself from).

Note that some of the above verbs, e.g. *carry on, keep on,* refer to continued action; others, e.g. *finish, give up, leave off,* look back on action coming to an end (*see 125, ii*).

ii. after the adjectives *tired* and *fond*:

I'm tired of waiting for you.

iii. after *It's worth . . . It's no good . . . It's no use . . .*:

It's no use crying over spilt milk (*Proverb*).

iv. in the constructions *the difficulty of deciding, the honour of entertaining you, the mistake of talking too much, the pleasure of knowing you.* But see 133.

v. after *the*, or a possessive adjective:

The proof of the pudding is in the eating (*Proverb*).
Excuse my interrupting.

vi. after any preposition except the *to* of the infinitive:

Talk about fishing. Rest after eating a heavy meal.
Wash before eating. Live by hunting.
Thank you for telling me. The pleasure of knowing you.
Help, instead of criticizing. I don't object to standing.
I can't advise you without knowing all the facts.

Note: Do you enjoy swimming?—Yes, I enjoy it.
I'm tired of doing these exercises. I'm tired of it.

132 **Either** the infinitive **or** the **-ing** form can be used, with no substantial difference in meaning after:

i. see watch hear feel listen notice

These verbs follow either of the patterns:

I saw him go I saw him going

However, there is a difference in *emphasis*, as in:

a. We saw the car crash into a tree (impact completed).
b. We watched the bulldozer digging into the bank of earth (impact continued or repeated).

Know is used similarly in the past and perfect tenses, e.g.:

I never knew (have never known) him behave (*or* behaving) like that before.

ii. (can) bear cease hate like omit propose
begin continue intend love prefer start

These verbs follow either of the patterns:

They began to scream They began screaming

For *Would you like to dance?* See note (v) below.

iii. *hate like love want* plus a direct object, as in the pattern:

I don't want you to stand there, or **I don't want you standing there.**

But use only the infinitive in the construction:

I don't want (I would hate) there to be any trouble.

iv. a (*or* the) attempt an (*or* the) opportunity a reason
a (*or* the) chance determined content

Say—an attempt to go, *or* at going
a chance to go, *or* of going
a reason to go, *or* for going; *but only say* the reason for going
decide to go, *or* on going
(be) determined to go, *or* on going
(be) content to go, *or* with going

v. Use only the infinitive after *would like, would love, would hate, would prefer*, to refer to a single specific act, e.g.:

c. Would you like to dance?—Yes, I'd love to. *but*
d. I think I would like dancing if I were taller.

133 Either the infinitive or the *-ing* form can be used in the following constructions:

a. To speak
   or Speaking } in public isn't easy.

b. It isn't easy { to speak
   or speaking } in public.

However, while there are certain fixed sayings like *To err is human*, when the infinitive only is used, the *-ing* form is probably commoner in pattern a., and the infinitive commoner in pattern b. In any case, in pattern b. *speaking* may suggest that we speak but it isn't easy, while *to speak* may suggest that it isn't easy,

so we don't try. Other words which can be substituted for *easy*
in pattern b. are *better, difficult, foolish, hard, lovely, nice, right,
wrong, a pleasure, an honour, a mistake.*

134 Note the substantial difference in meaning with:

afraid: I'm afraid to ski (so I don't do it).
I'm afraid of breaking my leg (it might happen).
ashamed: She was ashamed to appear in public (so she didn't
appear).
She was ashamed of behaving so badly (she did behave badly
and then felt ashamed).
certain, sure: You're certain (*or* sure) to see me there (I will be
there and you will not fail to see me).
Are you certain (*or* sure) of passing your examinations? (Are
you confident that you will pass them?)
deserve: You deserve to win. You deserve to be promoted.
He deserves shooting (*or* to be shot).
forget: You forgot to ask them to dinner (you didn't ask them).
We've come to dinner. Did you forget asking us? (You *did*
ask us).
go on: We went on (=continued) working.
The speaker went on to tell us a very funny story (=he continued speaking and told us . . .).
need, (*see* want).
propose: I propose to stop now (I will stop now).
I propose stopping now (I or others will stop).
remember: I remembered to post your letter.
I remember posting it (*see 125*).
stand: I can't stand (=bear) listening to her voice.
We stand to lose (=risk losing) a lot of money.
stop: He stopped speaking (and was then silent).
Walking along the road, he stopped to speak to an old woman
(=he stopped and spoke).
sure, (*see* certain).
thank: Thank you for keeping quiet (you kept quiet).
I'll thank you to keep quiet (you've said too much already).
think: I never thought (=expected) to see him.
I never thought of asking him (i.e. I forgot).
try: Try to do better next time. (Make the attempt).
Try writing with your other hand. (Make the experiment.)
want, need: Tom wants to play, but needs to work.
He needs watching, i.e. needs to be watched.
N.B. He wants watching = he *needs* to be watched.

Infinitive or -ing after certain verbs

135 **Look at the Verb List on page 149. Refer to this whenever you are in doubt about whether a certain verb is followed by the infinitive or the gerund.**

136 DRILL. *Supply the* -ing *form, or the infinitive with or without* to. *Then repeat the sentences in one of the following ways:*

Shall we ask him to speak? Shall we ask him to?
Let him come. Let him.
I like swimming. I like it.
I like to be appreciated. I like to be.
I don't like being kissed. I don't like it.

1. Shall we ask him (speak)?
2. Yes, let him (speak).
3. Why not (let) him?
4. Do make him (sit down).
5. He'll be made (sit down).
6. Please tell him (write).
7. Will you help me (get up)?
8. I couldn't help (laugh).
9. Oh, do stop (laugh).
10. Don't fail (reply).
11. Do you enjoy (climb)?
12. (Walk) is good for you.
13. But I dislike (walk).
14. Don't run. It's better (not run).
15. Avoid (over-eat).
16. Do you want (lose weight)?
17. I refuse (answer).
18. I refuse (be hurried).
19. I dislike (be hurried).
20. Will you remind them (write)?
21. He was quite unable (bend down).
22. You must give up (smoke)
23. Do you like (drive)?
24. Would you like (drive)?
25. Stop. You're sure (crash).
26. Your hair needs (cut) badly.
27. Don't be afraid (say).
28. We'll be very sorry (leave).
29. I'm not used (work so hard).
30. I won't allow you (do that).
31. Who suggested (put it there)?
32. Do you believe in (diet)?
33. We'd be delighted (come).
34. Don't forget (clean your teeth).
35. We look forward to (see you).
36. Sorry, I didn't mean (say that).
37. You ought (be sorry).
38. You were told (wait).
39. I object to (be pushed around).
40. I would like (be consulted).

137 EXERCISE. *Supply the* -ing *form, or the infinitive with or without* to:

Proverbs

1. You cannot (make) an omelette without (break) eggs.
2. (Pour) oil on the fire is not the way (quench) it.
3. It is hard (please) all parties.
4. It is easier (pull down) than (build).
5. It's a mistake (quarrel) with one's bread and butter.
6. Sailors go round the world without (go) into it.
7. (Say) is one thing but (do) another.
8. There is a time (speak) and a time (be silent).
9. What is worth (do) at all is worth (do) well.
10. You must (lose) a fly (catch) a trout.
11. It's better (never begin) than (never make) an end.
12. The proof of the pudding is in the (eat).

Quotations

13. It's love that makes the world (go round) (*translation from a French song*).
14. (Read) is sometimes a device for (avoid) thought (*Sir Arthur Helps*).
15. It is impossible (enjoy) (be) idle.
16. Jack and Jill went up the hill (fetch) a pail of water (*Nursery rhyme*).
17. Human life ceases (be) free the moment it is founded on (borrow) (*Ibsen*).
18. I have promises (keep) and miles (go) before I sleep (*Robert Frost*).
19. Education has produced a population able (read) but unable (distinguish) what is worth (read) (*G. M. Trevelyan*).
20. Power tends (corrupt) and absolute power corrupts absolutely (*Lord Acton*).

Other examples:

21. I advise you (give up) the idea of (try) (study) two languages at once. There would be no harm in (learn) one after the other.
22. If you went to a British or American university, you would have (be able) (follow) all your lectures in English. The university may therefore insist on your (take) a test in English.
23. There is a lot of difference between (study) for an hour or two in the evening and (work) for a university degree.
24. You cannot (avoid) (promise) (take) them out to dinner.

Avoiding repetition and ambiguity

138 EXERCISE a. *Reduce the number of times* to *is used in the following sentence:*

1. We had to decide to act quickly and to begin to make plans without delay.

b. *Remove the ambiguity in the following:*

2. They decided to make another attempt to cross the river and to abandon all their equipment.

3. The great civilisations of the world have relied on their ability to control important sea routes, to increase their wealth.

Having gone, having been invited

139 The form *having* plus the past participle can be used either as a participle or as a gerund:

a. (*Participle*). Having travelled round the world fifty times, the old captain was content to settle down.

b. (*Gerund*). Imagine having mastered these wretched verbs at last!

Compare these two examples with:

c. Travelling round the world, one can see many countries without really knowing any of them.

d. Imagine trying to sit still on your heels all day long.

In c., *travelling* and *seeing* take place at the same time. In d., *trying* refers to present or future. In a., b., *having travelled* and *having mastered* refer to time *previous* to the time when the captain was content or when we use our imagination. We could replace *having mastered* by the Pre-present, and *having travelled* by the Pre-past, thus:

e. He had travelled round the world and was now content to settle down.

f. We have mastered these wretched verbs at last. Imagine it!

Note the passive:

g. Having been invited, I intend to stay and enjoy myself, i.e. I have been invited, and intend . . .

And note the negative:

h. I regret not (*or* never) having told you earlier.

140 DRILL. *Re-phrase the following sentences using* having + *the past participle:*

1. I have not seen the newspapers for days and have no idea of what has happened.

2. You have made a fool of yourself, you had better keep quiet now.
3. He had spoken too frankly, and he felt rather ashamed.
4. Talbot had not taken the money. He denied it.
5. I have interrupted you. Forgive me.
6. We have told you our story, and are waiting to hear yours.
7. I have never been asked to speak in public before, and feel very nervous.
8. We have been obliged to close your account with us, we regret.
9. My clients are complaining. They have been spoken to very rudely.
10. They had been refused permission to stay and left on the next plane.

'PLEASE EXPLAIN. WHAT IS THE EXPLANATION?'

Converting verbs into abstract nouns

141 Look again at Section FIVE. Now see how a complex verb can be split up into a construction consisting of a simpler verb plus an abstract noun. For example, instead of *'explain* something accurately' we can *'give an* accurate *explanation* of it'. Other examples:

Come to an agreement, a conclusion, a decision
Do (or *conduct*, or *carry out*) an experiment; *do* damage (to), do one's duty, do harm (to), do right, do wrong (*Note*).
Draw (or *make*) a distinction.
Enter into an argument, into competition.
Find a cure, a solution.
Give a description,   a definition,   encouragement,
    permission,   support,   trouble,
Have (a) desire (for), (an) effect (on), (an) influence (on).
Keep something under control

Make	an accusation	an agreement	an allowance
	an appearance	an application	a calculation
	a comment	comparison	a connection
	a contribution	a correction	a criticism
	a decision	a discovery	an investigation
	an observation	a proposal	a recommendation
	a reduction	a reference	a reservation

Offer an explanation, one's resignation, a suggestion.
Put emphasis (on), stress (on)
Reach an agreement, a conclusion, a decision.
Take an interest (in), a measurement, trouble.

Further examples:

Adopt or *Follow* a procedure.

Note: For the difference between *do* and *make*, see the author's *English as a Foreign Language*, paragraph 220. Notice also the fixed expressions with *do* and *make* in 43 and 141 of the present work.

'PLEASE EXPLAIN. WHAT IS THE EXPLANATION?'

Grant admission, or permission.
Submit an application, one's resignation.

142 EXERCISE. *Using a dictionary if necessary, give abstract nouns corresponding to the verbs below. Check the pronunciation:*

accuse	choose	educate	increase	recognise
admit	depend	enjoy	introduce	reduce
allow	describe	entertain	invite	refer
apologise	destroy	examine	occur	refuse
appear	develop	except	offend	repeat
apply	disappoint	express	omit	resign
arrange	discover	extend	practise	satisfy
associate	distinguish	fail	prefer	solve
behave	disturb	hesitate	prepare	treat
believe	divide	imagine	receive	try

143 EXERCISE. *Re-phrase the following, using a simpler verb plus abstract noun instead of the verb in italics and making the necessary changes, but without changing the meaning of the original:*

1. What have you *contributed* to your country?
2. I hope we shall be able to *agree* at our meeting today.
3. How shall we *proceed* in the circumstances?
4. Scientists tend to *emphasize* their own subject most.
5. Dr. Robinson did not *describe* the situation in the same way as you.
6. It is not always easy to *distinguish* clearly between fact and fiction.
7. I could *explain* the difference quite simply.
8. Dr. Norman *suggested*, among other things, that our reports should be *standardized*.
9. People have *used* DDT on a large scale, and this has led to many diseases being *eradicated*.
10. The number of deaths from malaria has *decreased* enormously.
11. The speaker last night *referred* (*Note*) favourably to our work, and *proposed* something very sensible about it.
12. We must do something to *control* this noise.
13. No doubt we shall *solve* the problem eventually.
14. Yesterday's storm severely *damaged* all our fruit trees.

Note: 143 (11). Refèr, refèrring, refèrred. *But* rèference, occùr, occùrring, occùrred, occùrrence.

15. How has radio *influenced* our lives most?
16. I want you to *support* me wholeheartedly.
17. Try to *criticize* constructively and tactfully.
18. When you have a new suit made, the tailor has to *measure* you.
19. That's very expensive. Can you *reduce* the price?
20. Stay where you are. Nobody has *permitted* you to leave.
21. I don't know what to *suggest*. I can't *recommend* anything definitely yet.
22. Do you like doctors *experimenting* on you?
23. These two substances *differ* from each other completely. One cannot *compare* them in any way.
24. After carefully *observing* how the animal *behaved*, Peterson *discovered* something very important.
25. No person will be *admitted* to the College unless he has first *applied* formally in writing.

Converting verbs into adjectives ending in -able or -ible

144 i. Many verbs can be converted into adjectives in the following way:

We can *drink* this water : it is *drinkable*.
We can't *drink* that : it is *undrinkable*.
This disease can't be *cured* : it is *incurable*.

ii. Adjectives ending in *-able* are normally formed from the stem of the verb, and keep the same stress as the verb. Note:

Verb	Noun	Adjective
imàgine	imaginàtion	imàginable

iii. The ending *-able* is freely added to make new words in English; e.g. *steer, steerable*. However, a closed group of adjectives end in *-ible*: these adjectives are usually formed not on the stem of the verb but on the stem of the abstract noun:

Verb	Noun	Adjective
respond	response	responsible
admit	admission	admissible
divide	division	divisible
destroy	destruction	destructible
neglect	negligence	negligible

iv. Note: solve — solution — soluble.

v. Note also: audible, incredible, edible, eligible, flexible, indigestible, inexhaustible, legible, reducible, visible.

145 EXERCISE. *Say and spell the adjectives associated with the following verbs:*

advise	comfort	not forgive	not reduce
agree	not comprehend	manage	regret
argue	count	note	rely
not believe	not cure	notice	not resist
not calculate	debate	permit	solve
change	demonstrate	prefer	not tolerate
charge	not fail	reason	translate
collapse	not forget	not reconcile	not use

146 EXERCISE. *Re-phrase the following, using an adjective instead of the verb etc. in italics, and making other necessary changes:*

1. This coat is made of linen *that can be washed*. It is guaranteed *not to shrink*.
2. These books *cannot be used. They cannot* possibly *be sold*.
3. Savings certificates *can be obtained* at any post-office.
4. We hope our proposals *can be accepted*.
5. Only people who *can* really *be relied on can be elected* as members of our Club.
6. Oysters *can be eaten*, but I find them *difficult to digest*.
7. If you are going to England, *I advise you* to take plenty of warm clothing. A heavy overcoat is very much *to be desired*.
8. Many people *prefer to* go to England in the spring, though the weather is *likely to change very often*.
9. The question you ask *cannot be answered*, I'm afraid.
10. *Nobody will ever solve* the problem before us.
11. The difficulties sailors had to overcome *cannot be imagined*.
12. The benefits that penicillin has brought to mankind *cannot be calculated*. It has enabled thousands to recover from illnesses that formerly *could not be cured*.
13. This machine *can easily be managed* if you follow the instructions properly.
14. *It is to be regretted* that so few people pay their subscriptions without being reminded.
15. Churchill's energy *could not be exhausted*.
16. It seemed that *nothing could destroy* his powerful physique.
17. Some of his sayings *will never be forgotten*.
18. During an eclipse of the sun, stars *can be seen* in the daytime, and many interesting phenomena may be *observed*.
19. Speak up! *No one can hear* your voice *at all*.
20. Now please be quiet. The noise you are making *cannot be tolerated*.

PART FOUR

VERBS IN SUBORDINATE CLAUSES

NOUN, RELATIVE, TIME, CONDITIONAL AND OTHER CLAUSES

Compound sentences and co-ordinate clauses

147 a. **Time and tide wait for no man.**

i. A sentence should have a finite verb and a subject: see 10. It may have more than one subject, as in the example above. Or it may have more than one finite verb, e.g.:

b. I walked up to the captain and shook him by the shoulder. He opened his eyes, but did not move (*Joseph Conrad*).

Notice that in b., the subjects (*I* and *he*) are not repeated (*Footnote*), although they could be repeated for emphasis.

ii. A sentence may also be composed of two simple sentences joined by a conjunction, *and, but, yet*, or *or*:

c. Take care of the pence and the pounds will take care of themselves (*Proverb*).

d. Sticks and stones may break my bones but words can never hurt me.

e. I see him every day, yet he has never once said good morning to me.

f. Put up your hands, or I'll shoot.

In such cases, the individual sentences that make up the longer, compound sentence are called clauses. A compound sentence may have more than two clauses, as in:

g. The wind howled, the waves rose higher and higher, but the good ship held firmly to its course.

Notice that if a verb is the same in each clause it need not be repeated, as in:

h. Some books are to be tasted, others to be swallowed, and some few to be chewed and digested (*Francis Bacon*).

Footnote: This applies to co-ordinate clauses only. See footnote to 159, b.

Complex sentences and subordinate clauses

Noun clauses

148 **One half of the world does not know/how the other half lives.**

i. In that proverb there are two clauses (separated by the oblique stroke). One is dependent on the other, the second clause acting as the object of the verb in the first. In this case, the first is the main clause, the second is a dependent or subordinate clause, which could be replaced by a noun.

ii. Noun clauses may be either reported (or indirect) questions, as in the example above, or reported (or indirect) statements, as in:

    b. Some say / the world will end in fire (*Robert Frost*).

Indirect commands are formed with an infinitive, thus:

    c. Go! I told you to go. I told you not to come here again.

Indirect statements

149 i. *Statement:* The style of broadcasting should be conversational.
Complex sentence containing a reported statement:

    a. I have always felt that the style of broadcasting should be conversational (*Sir Harold Nicolson*).

Notice the conjunction *that* (given a weak pronunciation in fluent speech). This conjunction is often absent, especially in short sentences: see 148, b. It is included in sentences containing more than one reported clause, in order to make it clear that both clauses are dependent on the same main verb:

    b. Does it mean that broadcasting will have a bad influence on our literary style, and that in a few years even the greatest of stylists will merely write as they talk? (*Sir Harold Nicolson again*).

ii. Indirect statements can also give details of feelings and thoughts, without being the object of a transitive verb in the main clause:

    c. I am sorry (that) you had all that trouble for nothing.

150 EXERCISE. i. *Form a sentence with a dependent noun clause, using each of the following verbs in the main clause:*

add	assure you	consider	expect	find out
admit	believe	decide	explain	gather
agree	comment	declare	fancy	guess
announce	complain	determine	fear	hear
answer	confess	doubt	feel	hope
assume	confirm	dream	find	imagine

inform you	notice	realise	report	suppose
know	observe	recommend	say	suspect
learn	persuade you	remember	see	tell you
move	pretend	remind you	show	think
(=propose)	promise you	repeat	state	trust
mention	propose	reply	suggest	wish

EXERCISE. ii. *Form sentences with a dependent noun clause, using the following in the main clause:*

be afraid	be disappointed	be pleased	be sorry
be careful	have a feeling	be positive	be sure
be certain	have an idea	be satisfied	be surprised

We can either say

a. George told me he failed all his examinations, or
b. George failed all his examinations, he told me.

That could introduce the noun clause in *a.*, but would not introduce the first clause in *b.*

EXERCISE. iii. *Form sentences, on the pattern of* b., *in which the following occur in the second clause:*

am afraid	expect	guess	notice	am sure
assume	fear	hear	am positive	see
believe	feel	hope	observe	suppose
am certain	gather	imagine	say	tell you
decided				

In these sentences, pronounce the second clause with a low, level intonation, except when using certain, sure, positive: *then the clause should have a rising-falling intonation.*

Indirect questions

151 Indirect questions are of three types (see 37).

A. Who spoke? — I asked you who spoke.
B. Is it raining? — I asked you if it was raining.
Are you coming with us or not? We want to know whether you are coming with us or not.
C. Why did you say that? — Tell me why you said that.
In type B, use *whether*, not *if*, after a preposition:
a. Are you coming? All our plans depend on whether you're coming or not.
b. It's a question of whether you've made up your mind.

c. As to (=with regard to the question of) whether you take your own car, that's entirely up to you (=for you to decide). But note *It looks* (*seems, appears*) *as if* (or *as though*) as in:
d. Is it raining? It looks as if (*or* as though) it's raining hard.

152 EXERCISE. i. *Form a sentence containing an indirect question, beginning with if or whether, using each of the following in the main clause:*

ask	find out	want to know	say
decide	hear	prove	tell you
doubt	inquire	remember	wonder

ii. *Form sentences, containing indirect questions beginning with* how, what, when, where, which, who *or* why, *using the following in the main clause:*

believe	hear	remember	tell you
decide	imagine	remind you	think
explain	know	say	understand
find out	want to know	see	wonder
guess	realise	suggest	

153 An indirect question may begin a sentence. In that case, indirect questions of the Yes-No type must begin with *whether*. Examples:
a. Whether there's any point in going on, I very much doubt.
b. How you ever expect me to read this writing, I can't imagine. Pronounce the second clause with a rising-falling intonation. Note that the word order in the first clause is that of an indirect question. But the order of the *direct* question is usually retained when *wonder* comes in the second clause, e.g.:
c. Can you tell me the time, I wonder? (intonation rises on *wonder*).
d. How shall we get home, I wonder? (intonation falls on *home* and *I wonder* is pronounced on a low level tone: see Note).

EXERCISE. *Form sentences, beginning with an indirect question, using each of the following in the second clause:*
I want to know. We'll have to ask. We shall decide later. You must find out. I can't imagine. I'd like to know.

Noun clause as subject

154 i. So far, we have been studying the noun clause as an object of the verb in the main clause. It can also act as the subject, thus:

Note: 153, d. The question in example c is the Yes–No type (36, B). The question in d is of type 36, C.

Indirect questions

   a. (We think he's guilty, but) *whether we shall ever be able to prove it* is another matter. (Begin with *whether*, not *if*.)

   b. *What word you should use* often depends on exactly what you have in mind.

Indirect statement

   c. *That our company is going bankrupt*, gentlemen, is now all too clear(*That* cannot be omitted in such a case: compare 149).

ii. Sentences of type c. belong rather to formal English. The following type of sentence is commoner:

   d. It is clear that our company is going bankrupt. (*That* can be omitted in this construction.)

   e. It seems (*or* appears) that we are going bankrupt. (*That* can be omitted.)

   f. It is doubtful whether we can save the situation now.

EXERCISE. *Form sentences on the pattern of* d., *beginning with* it + seems, appears, *and* it + *a part of* be + *one of the following:* certain, doubtful, fortunate, a good thing, impossible, necessary, nice, a pity, possible, regrettable, true, unbelievable.

155 EXERCISE. *Form one sentence from each of the following pairs or sets of sentences:*

1. Is Mr. Hall in yet? I'll go and see.

2. I have an appointment with him. At least I think so.

3. You made an appointment for me. You remember.

4. How do people live in other countries? I'd like to find out.

5. Can you write a good English essay? It remains to be seen.

6. Can you work hard enough on your own? Your progress depends on it.

7. What do universities teach? Whom do they admit? That is for them to decide.

8. Your father's condition is very serious. Do you realise it? I hope you do.

9. I want to ask two questions. First, what is wisdom? Then, what can we do to teach it?

10. In some ways, wisdom can be taught. Certain philosophers think so.

11. Good faith is the foundation of all human society. Let us always remember that motto.

12. Where have we gone wrong? I don't understand.

13. What causes influenza? Why does it come every so often? Let us consider these questions.

14. Smoking has something to do with cancer of the lung. Doctors often suspected that. But they had no definite proof.
16. 'I will have quite enough money. I hope so.' That was George's answer.

Noun clauses expressing plans, proposals, wishes, etc.
156 *I propose that our next meeting takes place on March 20th.*
In that example, the noun clause is an indirect statement not of fact but of a proposal about an event that has not yet occurred. The verb *takes* could be replaced by *shall take* (see 77), or *should take* (86), or even by *take* (171).

EXERCISE. *Use the above construction with the following verbs in the main clause:*
agree   arrange   ask   command   determine   recommend request   suggest.

Relative Clauses

157 Subordinate clauses can also act as adjectives, relating to a noun in the main clause. In this case, they are called relative clauses. Note the following kinds of relative clause:
i. *Defining clauses*, necessary to complete the sense of the main clause:
   a. Everything comes to the man *who waits* (*Proverb*).
(The sense of the main clause, ending at *man*, would not be complete without the relative clause answering the question, what man?)
   b. Many things grow in the garden *that were never sown there* (*Proverb*).
(The main clause would have a different meaning if it ended at *garden*. The relative clause answers the question: What kind of things?)
   c. Nothing costs so much as *what* (=the thing that) *is given us* (*Proverb*). What thing?
   d. Money speaks in a language (*that*) *all nations understand* (*Proverb*). What kind of language?
Notes: 1. *Who* and *that* (used in this way) are called relative pronouns.
   2. To avoid ambiguity, put the relative pronoun as soon as possible after the word it relates to (its antecedent). In b., the plural form *were*, as well as the sense, makes it clear that the antecedent is *things*.
   3. Use *who* when the antecedent refers to a person, *that* when it refers to a thing *or* a person.

4. *Which* is commonly used instead of *that* when the antecedent is a noun referring to a *thing*. But use *which* only, when the relative pronoun is preceded by a preposition:

    e. Old age is a disease which (*or* that) all must suffer from.

But

    f. Old age is a disease from which all must suffer.

In examples a, b, and c. above, the relative pronoun is the subject of the verb in the relative clause: *the man* waits, etc. In d., the relative pronoun is the object: *all nations* understand *that language*. In e. and f., it is the object of a preposition (i.e. from). The relative pronoun, *when it is the object*, is usually absent in short sentences: it may be included for the sake of rhythm, and should be included when there is more than one relative clause relating to the same antecedent.

ii. *Non-defining clauses*, not necessary to complete the sense of the main clause but adding something to it:

    g. Nothing could annoy my Uncle Tom, who was the most patient man alive.

    h. Many things grow in my garden, which is a perfect paradise at this time of the year.

    i. Many things grow in my garden, which I love.

    j. John lost his temper completely, which was most unfortunate for him.

Notes: 6. Only use *who* (whom, whose) or *which*, but not *that*, for non-defining clauses.

    7. Do not omit the relative pronoun in a non-defining clause, even if it is the object.

    8. Notice example j., where the antecedent is the whole main clause.

    9. Notice the comma separating the main clause and the non-defining clause.

    10. In speaking, begin the non-defining clause with a new intonation phrase.

158 EXERCISE. *Read the following sentences; then identify the relative clauses and their antecedents, and say when a relative pronoun could be changed, or omitted, or inserted:*

    1. This is the house that Jack built (*Nursery rhyme*).
    2. He looks like a dog that has lost its tail (*Common saying*).
    3. The nicest child I ever knew
       Was Charles Augustus Fortescue (*Hilaire Belloc*).
    4. Don't believe all you hear or tell all you know.

5. The world which I entered was a strange one (*Somerset Maugham*).

6. The room, which we entered without a sound, was pitch dark.

7. I never regret the five years which I spent on the farm.

8. My father was acquainted with men who had been very famous in their day.

9. All the articles which are on display are for sale.

10. Will the people who are sitting at the back of the hall come a little farther forward?

11. Everything that has been bought abroad should be declared at the Customs.

12. Everything that you have bought abroad is liable to duty.

13. All passengers who have just arrived should wait here for their baggage.

14. Visitors who wish to stay another night should notify the office before mid-day.

15. Anyone who wanted tickets for the theatre could have got them last night without any trouble.

16. Experience is the name everyone gives to their mistakes (*Oscar Wilde*).

17. One should never trust a woman who tells one her real age (*Oscar Wilde*).

18. He lay like a warrior who is taking his rest
With his martial cloak around him (*Charles Wolfe*).

19. Politics is perhaps the only profession for which no preparation is thought necessary (*Robert Louis Stevenson*).

20. The greatest pleasure I know is to do a good action secretly, and to have it found out by accident (*Charles Lamb*).

Time Clauses

159 **A son's a son till he's married a wife,**
But a daughter's a daughter all her life (*Proverb*).

i. A subordinate clause of time (e.g. *till he's married a wife*) indicates to what point of time or to what period the verb in the main clause (e.g., *a son's a son*) refers. A time clause may be introduced by one of a number of expressions, e.g.: *when, before, after, until, since, while, as, as soon as, immediately, every time, the moment, the day*, etc.

ii. Notice the tenses used in the following types of sentences:
Time clauses referring to future time
    a. Don't cross your bridges before you get to them (*Proverb*).

b. I'll come when I'm ready. (*Footnote.*)

c. I will write you a cheque as soon as my salary is paid into my bank.

d. Don't start writing until I tell you.

Time clauses referring to the pre-future

e. Please wait till I've finished speaking.

Time clauses beginning with 'since'

f. There have been a lot of changes in the world since I was a boy.

Note: 1. the use of the Present Tense in the time clauses in examples a., b., c. and d. and of the Pre-present in e.

2. the difference between example b. and:

g. Please tell me when you'll be here next time.

This is a noun clause, indirect question: see 37, type C.

3. the use of *since*, which marks the beginning of the pre-present period: see Note on 22. Thus, *there have been changes since a point of time in the past*: at that point of time, *I was a boy* (Past Tense: see 23).

160 EXERCISE. *Combine each of the following pairs of sentences to make one sentence containing a time clause:*

1. We shall meet on Thursday. Let us discuss our plans then.

2. Don't try to cross the bridge yet. You will come to it later.

3. The doctor will come soon. Then call me immediately.

4. I will give you instructions. Don't start until then.

5. We shall start a new book soon. We shall have finished this one in a short time.

6. To make a good cup of tea, don't pour the water on to the tea leaves yet. The water must have boiled first.

Conditional Clauses

161 **If you must fly, fly well.**

You'll hurt yourself, if you're not careful.

Conditional clauses are introduced by *if*: but see also 151, B.

The combination of tenses in a sentence containing a conditional clause depends on the meaning in each case: see 32. Many combinations are possible, but the following frequently occur:

i. *Main clause and conditional clause both referring to present time or to all time:*

a. If people try to hide anything from their doctor, he soon knows.

Footnote: 159 b. The subject must be repeated in any *subordinate* clause.

Use the Present Tense in both clauses.

ii. *Both clauses referring to future time:*
   b. The doctor will soon find out if you try to hide anything from him.

Use the Future Tense in the main clause, the Present in the if-clause.

   c. The doctor will soon know if you have hidden anything from him.

Use the Pre-present in the if-clause, if the verb refers to Pre-future time.

iii. *Supposing something that does not really happen:*
   d. You do not try to hide anything. But if you tried to hide anything, he would soon find out.

Use the Past Tense form in the if-clause, the Conditional (see 82) in the main clause.

Supposing something that did not happen:
   e. (You did not try, but) if you had tried to hide anything, he would have found out very soon.

Use the Pre-past Tense form in the if-clause, the Past Conditional in the main clause.

Note that the Pre-past of *can* (*do*) is *could have* (*done*), see 112. Hence the verb forms in the common saying:
   f. If a lie could have choked him, that would have done.

See also Section FIFTEEN

162 Conditional clauses can also be introduced by *unless, provided* (*that*), *as* (or *so*) *long as, supposing, in case.* Use the same combination of tenses as in 161. Examples:
   a. Unless you try (*in the future*) to hide anything, you will have nothing to fear.
   b. Provided (that) you keep very still, nobody will notice you.
   c. As long as war is regarded as wicked, it will always have its fascination. When it is looked upon as vulgar, it will cease to be popular (*Oscar Wilde*).
   d. Our meeting is on Friday, at 3.30 p.m. Make a note in your diary in case you forget. (i.e. you might forget, so make a note in your diary.)

Do not confuse *in case* + *verb* with *in case of* + *noun*, as in the example:
   e. In case of fire (i.e. if there is a fire), ring the alarm bell at once.

163 EXERCISE. *Combine each of the following pairs of sentences to make one sentence containing a conditional clause:*
1. I mustn't eat too much. I get violent indigestion.
2. Call me up tomorrow. I will give you the answer then.
3. Take the new road. You will be in Rome in two hours.
4. You are not taking the new road. You will not be there in two hours.
5. You did not take the new road. You did not arrive in time.
6. You did not listen to me. You lost your way.
7. We may need you at our meeting, In that case, I'll phone you.
8. I'll take an umbrella with me. It might rain.
9. There may be an urgent telephone call. Otherwise, don't disturb me.
10. You may borrow my typewriter, on one condition. You must bring it back this evening.
11. Will you meet me at seven? You will probably have finished your work by then.
12. It is a pity you did not answer all the questions. As a result you did not pass your examination with distinctions.

Other Clauses

164 i. *Expressing cause or reason*

    a. We had to move house, *because* we needed another bedroom for the children.

    b. *As* (or *since*) you are so interested in science, you ought to study it properly.

ii. *Expressing purpose*

    c. *In order that* (or *so that*) everybody could understand, the lecturer spoke very slowly.

iii. *Expressing result*

    d. The lecturer spoke very slowly, *so that* everybody was able to understand.

Note this distinction between *could* and *was able to*, see 109.

iv. *Stating one thing* in spite of *another*

    e. *Though* (or *although*) you have tried very hard, I am afraid you haven't done well enough yet.

(This can also be expressed: You may have tried very hard, but I am afraid, etc.)

    f. *However* hard I try, I cannot keep upright on skis.

g. *Whatever* (or *no matter what*) I say, you will never believe me.

h. *Whether* you believe me or not, I am telling the truth. (*Compare this with* 153, a.)

i. *Even if* one produces definite evidence, some peopie will never face an unpleasant fact.

NOUN CLAUSE, INFINITIVE, OR -ING

165 A. **I propose to stop   for a few minutes**
B. „   „   **stopping** „ „ „   „
C. „   „   **we stop** „ „ „   „

i. If you refer to 116, 131-4, and the Verb List on page 149, you will see that some verbs fit into pattern A above, some into B, some into C, some into two of them, some into all three.

ii. When you have a choice, *use Pattern A* when the person who *proposes* (for example) is the same who is to *stop*, and when stop refers to a new act in the course of events (see 125). Thus you can say, *I hope (or hoped) to meet him again* instead of *I hope (or hoped) I will (or would) meet him again*; but you cannot use the infinitive construction instead of *I hope he will come* or *I hope I said the right thing*.

iii. *Use Pattern C.* (if the verb will fit into it) when you wish to say precisely *who* will stop, and when the person who is to stop is different from the person who proposes.

166 C. I expect (that) he will be there.
D. I expect   him   to be there.
C. We believe (that) the prisoner is innocent.
E. We believe   the prisoner to be innocent.
C. I will arrange that you will have a quiet room.
F. I will arrange for you to have a quiet room.

i. See the List on page 149 to make sure whether a verb can fit into the patterns above.

ii. There may be a difference in meaning between one pattern and another. For example, *I expect he will be there* means *I think he probably will be there*; but *I expect him to be there* can mean either the same thing or *I want him to be there*.

167   *Noun clause*   *Infinitive Construction*
I don't know what I must do   *or* what to do.
            who(m) I should see   *or* who(m) to see.
I wonder   where I can go today   *or* where to go today.

Please tell us how we can answer this *or* how to answer this.
    when we should stop *or* when to stop.
    whether we should stay *or* whether to stay here
     here or not   or not.

The infinitive construction can be used when the person who has to do the action referred to in the second part of the sentence is the same person who is referred to by the subject or the indirect object in the first part. The infinitive construction cannot be used, therefore, instead of the following examples:

 Please tell me what we have to do next.
 I wonder what the speaker can say on that subject.

168 EXERCISE. *Make up sentences, using one or more of the patterns in* 163, 164 *and* 165 *from the following material:*

1. The Minister will attend our meeting tomorrow. He has agreed.
2. Can we start the meeting half an hour later? He hopes so.
3. We should wait for him. He expects that.
4. His car will bring him straight here. His secretary will arrange it.
5. Where should the driver go? Does he know?
6. The secretary should make a note of our address. Please remind the secretary.
7. We shall expect the Minister at 7.30. Please remind the Minister.
8. Can he stay till 9 o'clock? We shall try to persuade him.
9. Could we offer him a drink first? Do you suggest that?
10. Will he want to make a speech? I suppose so.
11. He is a good speaker. People consider he is.
12. When should one stop talking? Some speakers have no idea.

'IF I WERE YOU'

169 a. You haven't gone yet: **it's time you went.**
   b. I can't swim: **I wish I could.**
   i. You have not gone, I cannot swim: your going and my being able to swim are *non*-facts, which the speaker imagines to be *actual* facts. Notice that in these cases the non-fact, which the speaker imagines to be actual, is stated in the past tense. This special use of tense forms may be regarded as an example of the subjunctive, an old form of which a few examples survive in modern English. Notice also:

   c. I'm not enjoying myself: I wish I was.
      I'm working today: I wish I wasn't.
   d. I don't feel well: I wish I felt better.
      I feel tired: I wish I didn't (feel so tired).
   e. That's not true: I wish you were telling the truth.
   f. I did not see that book: I wish I had seen it.
   g. I'll send it to you: I wish you would (send it to me).

   ii. Compare the tenses following *wish* (examples b-g) with those following *hope*:

   h. A. I'm enjoying myself. B. I hope you are.
   i. A. I feel better now. B. I hope you do.
   j. A. That's my story. B. I hope you are telling the truth.
   k. A. I enjoyed that book. B. I hope you did.
   l. A. I'll send it back tomorrow. B. I hope you will.

170 *I wish I was enjoying myself* states a non-fact that *could* be true.
   Instead of *was*, we could use *were*—for all persons, singular and plural—to express something highly improbable, or impossible:

   a. *If I were you,* I should not worry about the subjunctive, except in examples such as these.
   b. Difficult do you call it, sir? *I wish it were* impossible! (*Samuel Johnson* on a violinist's performance.)
   c. *Were I in your place,* I would keep quiet. (Use only *were* in this construction.)

171 Other surviving examples of the subjunctive are:
a. If the grate *be* empty, put coal on (*see* Note).
b. The Committee recommended that a further sum *be* invested in Government stocks. (In such a case, *be* for all persons, singular and plural, may be used instead of *should be*.)
c. The Committee also recommends that the Secretary *receive* a regular salary. (Here, *receive*, for all persons, singular and plural, may be used instead of *should receive* (which is safer in modern English), see 156.

172 *If* can be followed by the normal tenses, like *hope* (169, ii) when the speaker assumes something to be a *fact*. *If* can be followed by the 'subjunctive' tenses, like *wish*, when the speaker refers to a non-fact and imagines it as an actual fact. These two uses of *if-* clauses are shown in table 6 on page 132. Note:
i. After *hope*, future time can be expressed by the Present Tenses, or by the Future Tense to emphasise the fact that an event has not yet taken place but will take place in future time. Examples:
a. Good-bye. I hope you have an easy journey.
b. Our newspaper hasn't arrived yet. I do hope they'll send it soon.
ii. After *if*, future time is normally expressed by the Present Tense, as in 161, b. But the Future Tense is possible, if the speaker wishes to give particular emphasis to the idea that the future is uncertain:
c. I'll close the window—if that will be any help (whether it will be or not remains to be seen).

173 Examples of TABLE 6:
Column 1
a. If you tell the truth, people trust you.
b. If you are telling the truth, we have no time to lose.
c. If you have studied all this book, you must know a lot.
d. If you have been walking in this heat, you must be very thirsty.
e. If we told Father the truth, he never punished us.
f. If you were walking all day yesterday, no wonder you are tired today.

Note 171a: This is part of an old riddle:
What does this mean? If B mt put: If B. putting: ?
Answer; If the grate be (great B) empty, put coal on (colon).
If the grate be full, stop putting coal on.

TABLE 6

	I HOPE and IF assuming a FACT	II WISH and IF imagining NON-FACT to be actual fact

PRESENT	a. I hope⎫
	   If ⎬ he tells the truth
	
	b. I hope⎫
	   If ⎬ he is telling
		m. I wish⎫
		    If ⎬ **he told**
		
		n. I wish⎫
		    If ⎬ **he were telling**

**PRE-
PRESENT**
	c. I hope⎫
	   If ⎬ he has told
	
	d. I hope⎱ he has been
	   If ⎰ telling
		o.

PAST	e. I hope⎫
	   If ⎬ he told
	
	f. I hope⎫
	   If ⎬ he was telling
		p. *For these three tenses,*
		use the same form:
		
		  I wish⎫
		    If ⎬ **he had told**
		
		  I wish⎱ **he had been**
		    If ⎰ **telling**

PRE-PAST	g. I hope⎫
	   If ⎬ he had told
	
	h. I hope⎱ he had been
	   If ⎰ telling
		q.

FUTURE	i. I hope ⎧ he tells (*Note 1*)
	        ⎩ he will tell
	    If he **tells** (*Note 2*)
	j. I hope he will be telling
	    If **he is telling**
		r. I wish he would tell
		   If he told
		
		          —
		s. If he were telling

**PRE-
FUTURE**
	k. I hope he will have told
	    If **he has told**
	        (161, c)
		—
		t. If he had told

**FUT. IN
THE PAST**
	l. I hoped he would tell
	(He said that) if **he told**
		u. —
		   (He said that) if he had
		   told

g. If you had met John before, why didn't you speak to him last night?

h. If you had been swimming before breakfast yesterday, no wonder you ate such a lot.

i. If you tell the truth (*Future*), you will be quite safe.

j. If you are playing tennis tomorrow, we shall not be able to go for our usual walk.

k. If you have read this report by next Friday, you will be able to discuss it at our meeting on Friday afternoon.

l. Didn't I say that if you told the truth (*Future in the Past*) you would be quite safe?

Column II

m. (You don't tell the truth.) If you told the truth, people $\begin{cases} \text{would} \\ \text{might} \end{cases}$ trust you more.

n. (You're not telling the truth.) If you were telling the truth, you would be looking me straight in the eye.

o. (You have not told the truth.) If you had told the truth, you wouldn't have blushed like that.

p. (You did not tell the truth.) If you had told the truth, you would not have been punished.

q. (You had not met John before I introduced him to you.) If you had met him before, I am sure he would have recognised you.

r. (We shall not go out in this rain.) If we went out, we should only get soaking wet.

s. (We shall not be playing tennis tomorrow.) If we were playing tennis, we shouldn't be able to finish our work.

Notes: 1. For the present of BE, one can say, in Column I, *if it is true* (or, more rarely, *if it be true*); and in Column II, *if it were true*.

2. In Column II, the emphatic form of the verb (see 8) is often used after *wish* and *if*. Thus:

If he *were* telling the truth.
If he *had* told the truth.
If he *did* tell the truth. (Present or Future.)

174 EXERCISE. *Put the verbs, in brackets, into a suitable tense form:*

1. *Motorist A at Sutton:* Am I on the road for Epsom? *Policeman:* Yes, sir. If you (go) straight on, you (be) there in twenty minutes. But wait. If you (go) to Epsom, will you take my mother-in-law too?

2. *Motorist B at Sutton:* Am I on the right road for Epsom? *Policeman:* No, sir. If you (follow) the road you are on now, you (be) going in the opposite direction.

3. *Friend, at Epsom, to Motorist A:* You got here without any difficulty, I see. If you (ask) the policeman at Sutton to direct you, you (be) very wise.

4. *Friend, at Epsom, to Motorist B:* You were on the wrong road. If you (take) *that* road, you were going right out of your way; and if you (go) on in that direction, you (never, get) here.

5. *Motorist B to Motorist A:* Why didn't you wait for me? If you (wait) I (not taken) the wrong road. How did you find the way so easily?

6. A to B: Well, for one thing, I follow the sign posts. If I (do) that, I seldom get lost. Then if I (be) in doubt, I ask a policeman. If I (be) you, I (follow) the red buses on your way back.

7. If all the good people (be) clever, the world (be) nicer than ever (*Elizabeth Wordsworth*).

8. If I (be) present at the creation (i.e. the creation of the world), I (give) some useful hints for the better arrangement of the Universe (*Alfonso the Wise, King of Castile*).

ECONOMIZING ON FINITE VERBS

175 In learning to use a language efficiently, the learner passes through three stages in the construction of sentences:

1. *He composes a series of simple sentences. Examples:*

   a. We are going on holiday next week. We shall finish this book by then. At least, we hope so.

2. *He puts these sentences together so as to form a complex sentence:*

   b. We hope we shall finish this book before we go on holiday next week.

3. *He reduces the complex sentence to make a more condensed one, with fewer finite verbs,* thus:

   c. We hope to finish this book before going on holiday next week.

Avoiding noun clauses

176 See 165, 166 and 167, and the Verb List on page 149.

Avoiding relative clauses

177 i. Relative clauses, of certain types, are frequently avoided, especially in journalism, by the omission of the relative pronoun *subject* (157) and the verb *be*, full verb or auxiliary. This applies to both defining and non-defining clauses. Thus, in 158, examples 9, 10 and 11 could be simplified to:

   a. (9) All the articles on display are for sale.

   b. (10) Will the people sitting at the back of the hall come a little farther forward?

   c. (11) Everything bought abroad should be declared at the Customs.

Those were originally examples of defining clauses. An example of a non-defining clause reduced in that way is:

   d. The west wing of the palace, built in the 16th century, was destroyed by fire twenty years ago.

ii. Note also that instead of examples 14 and 15 in 158, we can say:

e. (14) Visitors wishing to stay another night should notify the office before mid-day.

f. (15) Anyone wanting tickets for the theatre could have got them without any trouble.

iii. *Instead of* — *we can say*

g. I want a book that I can read — I want a book to read

h. Here is something that you can do — Here is something for you to do

i. You are the first person who has said that to me — You are the first person to say that to me

j. He is not a man whom you can trust — He is not a man to trust

k. He is not a man who can be trusted — He is not a man to be trusted

Avoiding other clauses

178 When the subject of a subordinate clause is the same as that of the main clause, the subordinate clause can be reduced to a phrase in the following circumstances:

i. The subject and the verb *be* can be omitted in the subordinate clause. Thus:

a. When you are in Rome, do as Rome does *becomes* When in Rome, do as Rome does (*Proverb*).

This frequently happens when *be* is an auxiliary.

b. While John was waiting for his turn at the dentist, he finished a whole crossword puzzle *becomes* While waiting . . ., John finished . . .

ii. Time clauses, introduced by *when, before, after, since, while* can be reduced to a phrase containing a present participle, thus:

c. Take two of these pills before you go to bed *becomes* Take two . . . before going to bed.

d. Since I spoke to you yesterday, I have re-read your report *becomes* Since speaking to you yesterday . . .

e. When I was opening that packing case, I tore my finger on a nail *becomes* Opening that . . ., I tore . . .: *see g. below.*

iii. Note the use of the present participle in the phrases *by* (*go*)*ing, on* (*go*)*ing, in* (*go*)*ing:*

f. If (or when) you mix blue paint and yellow (the result is that) you get green *becomes* By mixing blue paint and yellow, you get green.

g. When I opened the packing case, I found every piece of china in it broken *becomes* On opening (or simply *Opening as in 126, ii*) the packing case, I found . . .

h. While you are writing out these exercises, be careful you spell all the words right *becomes* In writing out, *etc.*

iv. A time clause can be reduced to a phrase containing a preposition plus noun, thus:

i. When you arrive at your hotel, go straight to the reception desk *becomes* On arrival at, *etc.*

j. When we had completed the experiment, *etc. becomes* On completion of the experiment, *etc.*

k. As soon as I received your letter, *etc. becomes* Immediately on receipt of your letter, *etc.*

v. A clause of purpose beginning with *in order that* (or *so that*), can be reduced to a phrase containing an infinitive:

l. The lecturer spoke very slowly, *in order to* (or *so as to*) make himself fully understood.

179

Instead of	*we can say*
a. We had to move house, because there was so much noise.	We had to move house, *because of* (or owing to) the noise.
b. As you are so interested in science, you ought to study it properly.	*In view of* your interest in science, you ought, *etc.*
c. Although you have worked so hard, you haven't done well enough yet.	*In spite of* (or *despite* or *for all*) your hard work, you haven't, *etc.*
d. If you are ignorant of the law, that does not excuse you.	Ignorance of the law does not excuse you.

180 EXERCISE. *Reduce each of the following compound or complex sentences, if possible, to a sentence containing only one finite verb:*

1. I hope I shall see you on Friday.
2. I hope Jim and Dave will be there too.
3. I now regret I spoke to the boy so sharply.
4. We believe that Robert is thoroughly honest.
5. I don't pretend that I am as clever as you are.
6. The detective noticed that a shoe was sticking out from under the curtain.
7. I'm afraid I might have an accident.
8. We are sorry we are so late.

9. The children decided they would go home to bed.

10. Have you any idea how one can make this machine work?

11. Please tell us whether we should wait for you or not.

12. Some people never know when they should stop talking.

13. Remind me that I have to go for my medical examination tomorrow.

14. Be careful you don't drop that bottle.

15. The thought that she might lose all her money haunted the old lady day and night.

16. None of the prisoners can complain that they have been badly treated.

17. But they insist that they are innocent.

18. I cannot understand why you behaved so foolishly.

19. He promised he would buy me a bunch of red roses.

20. Do you suggest that we should start this again?

21. When I began this talk, I did not intend that I should speak for more than half an hour.

22. Anyone who wishes to take a photograph of the view may do so when we come to the next stop.

23. Goods that have been in any way damaged in transit must be returned to the factory at once.

24. The meeting that was arranged for next Tuesday will now be held the Tuesday after.

25. The Hotel cannot accept responsibility for any valuables which are left in the bedrooms and which are then lost.

26. Can you find something that will stop that door banging?

27. I have never been to India, so I can't answer that question.

28. You seem to have changed your mind about Joe since you met his mother-in-law.

29. One can make rapid progress with a new language if one listens to recordings of it regularly.

30. Passengers must go through the Customs before they embark.

31. When I receive your application, I will deal with your case at once.

32. All sailings have been cancelled because there is thick fog in the Channel.

33. There will be time to discuss that after you have been elected.

34. There is no difference between these two photographs that anyone can notice.

35. If I may speak frankly, I didn't like the way you described my paintings at all.

36. Smuts was a lawyer by training, but when he was forced to be a soldier he was a very good soldier.

37. I don't wish to criticize, but I must draw attention to the fact that some of your remarks are inaccurate.

38. Jackson was asked if he could explain why he was absent on Monday, but he could give no answer that was satisfactory.

39. Do not forget you must deposit your key at the reception desk when you leave the Hotel.

40. If you work through this book systematically, you can learn how you can use the English verb more efficiently.

ANSWERS TO CERTAIN EXERCISES

WARNING: Other answers may be correct. If in doubt, adopt the answers given below.

Br. = British English   Am. = American

13a 1. I've brought one, *etc.*   2. I've bought some, *etc.*   4. I've cleaned them, *etc.*   6. I've done it, *etc.*   13. I've picked one up   14. We've put them down

13c 41. is   42. are   43. wants   44. the crowd was (*or* were), the police were   45. Do   46. has   47. come and sit   48. were   49. is   50. is

16 1. quarrels   2. bite   3. sucks, sucks   4. likes   5. flock   6. begins   7. alter   8. comes   9. eat, dig   10. must   11. catches   12. want, must   13. make   14. comes, waits   15. has   16. does, does   17. does not know, lives   18. excuses   19. ought   20. may, cannot

20 *Note:* beginning, covering, die/dying, dye/dyeing, entering, forbidding, forgetting, hindering, kidnapping (Br.) kidnaping (Am.), occurring, offering, omitting, panicking, preferring, quarrelling (Br.) quarreling (Am.), referring, regretting, signalling (Br.) signaling (Am.), tying, travelling (Br.) traveling (Am.), visiting

21 1. accept   2. is (*or* are) advancing rapidly and attacking   3. are behaving, are being, behave   4. believe, know, are telling, are, tell   5. buy, borrow   6. cannot, am carrying   7. have, are shivering, think, are catching   8. charges, does yours charge   9. don't know, 'm still checking   10. contains, has   11. bear, complain   12. is always complaining   13. is doing, is only trying   14. do you do, depends   15. 'm, 'm having, 'm enjoying   16. expands, rusts   17. 's expanding, 's making   18. do you explain, don't remember   19. extends   20. provides   21. flows   22. do not grow, keeps   23. 's happening, are you slowing, 're running, 'm looking   24. happens, put   25. CRASHES, JUMP

24 *Note:* died, gassed (*but* gases, *plural noun*), limited, occurred, offered, omitted, permitted, preferred, profited, quarrelled (Br.) quarreled (Am.), referred, signalled (Br.) signaled (Am.), travelled (Br.) traveled (Am.), wondered

26 1. Have you had, arrived, haven't answered, received, accepted, haven't seen, 've had, arranged, came   2. has caught, 've been

watching, has caught (*or* caught), threw, Have you ever tried, tried, had   3. stole, went, was, didn't see, took, 've already spoken, spoke, admitted, had been, swore, didn't touch (*or* hadn't touched). believe, was telling   4. 's been, Has anyone sent . . . or called, happened, came, didn't notice, crashed, was, had only just bought, was driving, wasn't, Was he looking, he was going, Wasn't he exceeding, staggered, thought, had been drinking, had not been drinking, has never touched   5. discussed, decided, were, has done, met, have drawn up . . . and made, dealt, elected, Has the Secretary written, have all paid, spent, pointed out, were spending, cost, cut, have saved   6. was staying, was sleeping, arose, woke up, looked, saw, had become, were breaking, was drifting, had lost, could   7. has given, was, was, died   8. were, did you live, were   9. was, invented, died, had made   10. planted, reached, found, had arrived

31 Note that *will* and *would* can be used instead of *shall* and *should* in all of the following: 1. Shall not (*or* are not going to) be able   2. should not (*or* were not going to) be able   3. shall not (*or* am not going to) be; am going (*or* shall go *or* shall be going: see 79)   4. shall (*or* am going to) be   5. shall accept   6. should accept (*but* would *avoids the ambiguity mentioned in 89*)   7. are going to (*or* will) catch   8. are going to (*or* shall) have   9. was going to (*or* would) snow   10. are you going to (*or* will you) do   11. shall not take *or* am not going to take *or* am not taking; am playing (*or* shall be playing: see 79)   12. Because he was playing   13. leaves *or* is leaving *or* will leave   14. shall give; am seeing *or* am going to see *or* shall see.   15. are moving *or* are going to move *or* shall move; are you doing *or* are you going to do *or* will you do; shall sell *or* are going to sell *or* are selling   16. was doing *or* was going to do *or* would do

32 Other verbs are possible, but note the tenses:
1. has got, is running, will have *or* will be having   2. has been, he has been running, He has not had   3. sits, begins, will work *or* will be working   4. he has been working, has read, he will have finished   5. will he be doing *or* is he going to do, he has been working, is   6. is going, has, he has been working   7. had, has not had, he is going to (*or* will) have   8. was working, had been, had had, had been working   9. was, had been working, had not had   10. was, had read, was, would (*or* was going to) finish   11. will get up (*or* will be getting up: see 79), will be running, will, will have finished   12. he used to, he used to, used to, He has become

33 1. packed, had, left, walked   2. have been, shall probably stay

3. have been living, are still living   4. went up, was, is   5. had gone up, had been, became   6. had lain, fell, dreamt, had sailed (*or* was sailing), would never see *or* was never going to see   7. am, has gone, knows, will be   8. was, explained, had gone, knew, would be   9. died, had gone, left, hoped, would return, realized, would be   10. are flying, takes, have been travelling, will be travelling

35   1. had had, were   2. seemed, was going   3. they would reach   4. they had been climbing   5. to bring   6. he had built   7. not to be angry with her   8. she had only wanted   9. they had both suffered   10. they would never be   11. he had tried, but had had   12. he still didn't know who had taken   13. at their last meeting they had discussed, had decided, would be made   14. they were spending, would have to   15. had lost, had been searching

42b 2. am   4. did   5. don't   6. do   7. haven't you?   8. have   9. will he?   10. won't   12. does   14. they are   16. didn't   17. would   18. wouldn't   20. can, do   22. Is there?   24. wasn't   25. could

43   1. Take a deep breath. Take hold of my arm.   4. give my shoes a polish and have a wash   14. May I make a request?   15. you put a question and I'll give the answer

45   1. I   2. my glasses   3. sticks, stones   4. tyres   5. shops (*or* shopkeepers)   6. my pen   7. cattle   8. aeroplanes (*or* men) can fly, pigs can't   9. sheep   10. eggs   11. our pictures   12. the dentist *or* my tooth   13. ice   14. oil and water   15. dancers *or* their limbs   16. every visitor *or* the bell   17. tree-trunks   18. secondhand books   19. broken limbs   20. the table (*or* somebody)   21. these fish   22. cars   23. these screws   24. Jack *or* his new pen   25. that suit (*see 67, a*)

52   See 48-51 and the Verb List on page 149.

53   See Verb List on page 149.

57   1. Man was formed for society.   2. New opinions are always suspected and usually opposed.   3. Many things grow in the garden that were never sown there.   6. An old fox is not snared easily.   7. Penicillin was discovered by Sir A . . . F . . .   8. Jewels worth $100,000 were stolen . . .   9. Was the thief caught? Yes, a man was arrested and charged.   22. Man's environment is being ruined . . .   *Add 'by (the agent)'* in numbers 7, 10, 12, 14, 18, 19, 22, 24.

58   1. It was agreed that . . .   2. It is assumed by everyone in the capital that . . .   3. It has been decided (by the Committee) that . . .   4. It is expected that . . .   5. It is hoped that . . .   6. It

has been proved that ... 7. It was announced that ... 8. It was taken for granted that ... 9. It is thought that ... 10. It will be understood that ... 11. It has been shown that ... 12. It has been found necessary to ...

59 1. Our position must be held ... 2. ... what can be done today. 3. These plans ought to be taken back and done again. 4. This ought to have been made clearer. 5. ... children cannot be admitted ... 6. Your tickets must be shown ... 7. A man's life may be shortened by over-eating. 8. I needn't be told ... 9. This must have been known ... 10. Atomic physics might be applied ... 11. The bird ... can never be caught but perhaps some ... can be found. 12. This ... might have been prevented by (*or* with) a little more care.

60 1. Have all ... been accounted for? 2. I think my bill has been added up incorrectly. 3. All ... must be cleared away ... 4. Your teeth ought to be seen to (by a dentist). 5. I was brought up to believe ... 6. What is a ... used for? 7. What has all ... been spent on? 8. We mustn't let ourselves be carried away by ... 9. New possibilities ... are opened up by ... 10. The prolongation of life may be thought of as a ...

61 1. What a pity these ... are never looked at. 2. He was looked on as ... 3. This ... hasn't been looked after properly. 4. This ... has been gone over ... 5. ... a man who will always be listened to. 6. ... as soon as it is sat on. 7. I was spoken to very rudely ... 8. Has any decision been come to yet? 9. ... a man who can always be relied on. 10. ... his bed has not been slept in.

62 1. The patient must be kept ... 2. ... They can never be proved ... 3. All ... will be set free. 4. He was found working ... 5. ... can't be kept waiting.

63 1. This ... is called ... 2. A lot of questions will be asked. 3. You will be asked a lot ... 4. What else shall we be asked for? 5. ... or you may be charged too much. 6. Good translators are paid five ... 7. 500 dollars will be paid for ... 8. You will be made our ... 9. When will a new P. be nominated? 10. Prof. Hill was elected President ...

64 Note that in 2, 3, 4, 5 and 6, *to* can be omitted, i.e. when the indirect object is a personal pronoun.

65 1. I am tired of being told ... 2. I hope you don't mind being asked ... 3. I am not accustomed to being spoken to ... 4. ... how to avoid being held up by ... 5. ... afraid of being laughed at.

66 1. Half the inhabitants ... are known to be ... 2. Roberts is

known to have left home . . . 3. All northern Italy is reported to be . . . 4. This drug is thought to have . . . 5. Caesar is believed to have crossed . . . 6. Students . . . are assumed to have covered . . .

71 1. . . . get your hair cut? 2. . . . get this tooth taken out. 3. . . . need your garden dug? 4. . . . to make his presence felt. 5. Can we get this rubbish swept up? 6. You must get that letter written . . . 7. . . . have a new agreement drawn up . . . 8. Do you want your neck wrung? 9. . . . you will find yourself ignored by everyone. 10. . . . or you will have your licence taken away.

72 Use Pattern b. in 2, 4, 6, 8 and 9. *In 4, say*: Invited to speak first, he held . . . 8. Severely damaged . . ., the house had to be . . . 9. Painted blue, the walls looked . . . *Note that in 3*, we could say: Having taken off our shoes, we went . . .: see 139.

78 1. will; shall (*or* will) 2. will *or* shall 3. will 4. will; will 5. will; shall (*or* will) 6. will *or* shall; will 7. will; won't 8. will; shall (*or* will) 9. shall (*or* will) 10. will; shall (*or* will) 11. shall; shall 12. shall; will 13. Will (*or* shall) 14. shall 15. will

81 1. will arrive, will be, shall (*or* will) go 2. will you ask . . .? 3. If you will, shall (*or* will) be 4. shall (*or* will) be enjoying 5. shall (*or* will) know, shall (*or* will) have finished 6. will be, Will you introduce . . .? 7. Won't (*or* Will) you sit down? 8. will have met 9. Will you allow . . .? 10. You will all have heard . . ., shan't (*or* won't) repeat 11. will tell 12. will carry out 13. will do 14. shall do 15. You shan't 16. will have 17. shall have 18. will die 19. shall be, shall die, will be 20. Will you . . .? 21. Shall I . . .? 22. I *will* press 23. will lie 24. shall live, will continue 25. Shall Miss J. go, or shall she wait? 26. *will* have, shall (or will), will 27. Will you be staying . . . 28. shall leave 29. shall (*or* will) 30. will (*or* shall)

92 1. would 2. should resign, would 3. if I would lend, would lend, should (*or* would) have, would (*or* should) 4. would press, wouldn't 5. would sit, we should, wouldn't 6. should be, should go (or should be going) 7. wouldn't discuss, Would you 8. should have, should have had 9. should apologize 10. would allow, should (*or* would) be 11. would explode 12. I should do, would do 13. would (*or* should) have been 14. would take place 15. would do, should never do 16. wouldn't, shouldn't have faded 17. would be, should (*or* would) like, Should it be, would your secretary give 18. would expand, should never put 19. Would you see, should be,

would be 20. would have had, should try, would (*or* should) like, would cut, should not be 21. would sweep, should have (*better than* would have)

103 1. ought to 2. ought, mustn't *or* oughtn't to 3. oughtn't to, must, have to 4. must, must, mustn't 5. needn't 6. must, must have, needn't 7. 've had 8. had to, had to, didn't have to 9. needn't have 10. must *or* shall have to, must 11. mustn't, needn't have 12. must, shall have to 13. have to 14. should (*or* would) have to 15. needn't, should (*or* would) have had to

104 1. You ought to inform, you ought not to delay 2. Ought we to disturb him, oughtn't we to let him sleep? 3. You ought to have woken me, you ought not to have let me sleep 4. You ought to have been writing it, you ought not to have been doing 5. you must sink or swim, you mustn't struggle, you must keep still 6. I had to jump. But I needn't have done 7. You mustn't tell, she must never know. His father needn't know, but . . . he will have to keep it a secret 8. We have had to, we have not had to 9. You have to take. You need not stay in bed, but you must not stay up late. 10. the patient had to take. He did not need to stay (*or* needn't stay), but he was not to (*or* must not) stay up late 11. I had to, didn't have to, wasn't to 12. You are to report. Then you are to remain. You are not to reveal. You need not (*or* do not have to) 13. he need not have done. We was to have reported at 1900 hours.

113 a. Can, may, can, cannot, might be b. may, may, may, you can, Some of you may not like . . . and may feel unable to, may (*or* can), may soon be, could give, was able to, could not, could have done so c. the world population may have doubled, can, may be useful, cannot, may

126 1. Arriving at the station, we found . . . 2. We watched the train disappearing . . . 3. Standing up here, you can . . . 4. You can just see our house standing . . . 5. We saw herds of splendid cattle grazing . . . 6. Wearing rubber gloves, one can handle the wires . . . 7. Tearing up his letter, she said . . . 8. Considering how hot it is outside, this room . . . 9. The explorers were astonished to see hundreds of monkeys hanging . . . 10. Turning on the light, we were immediately attacked by . . .

137 1. make, breaking 2. Pouring, to quench 3. to please 4. to pull down, to build 5. to quarrel 6. going 7. Saying, doing 8. to speak, to be silent 9. doing, doing 10. lose, to catch 11. never to begin, never to make 12. eating 13. go round 14. Reading, avoiding 15. to enjoy being 16. to fetch 17. to

be, borrowing 18. to keep, to go 19. to read, to distinguish, reading 20. to corrupt 21. to give up, trying to study, learning 22. to be able to follow, taking 23. studying, working 24. avoid promising to take

138 1. to decide on acting, to begin making 2. Change 'to cross' to 'at crossing'. 3. Say 'in order to increase'.

140 1. Not having seen . . ., I have no idea . . . 2. Having made a fool of yourself, you . . . 3. Having spoken too frankly, he felt . . . 4. Talbot denied having taken . . . 5. Forgive me for having . . . 6. Having told you our story, we . . . 7. Never having been asked . . ., I feel . . . 8. We regret having been obliged . . . 9. My clients are complaining of having been spoken to . . . 10. Having been refused permission . . ., they left . . .

143 See 141. Note: 4. . . . put most emphasis on . . . 5. . . . give the same description of . . . 6. . . . make a clear distinction . . . 7. . . . give a simple explanation of . . . 8. Dr. Norman's suggestions included the standardization of . . . 9. People have made great (or widespread) use of . . . led to the eradication of . . . 10. There has been an enormous decrease in the number . . . 11. . . . made a favourable reference to . . . and made a very sensible proposal . . . 12. . . . to keep this noise under control. 13. . . . we shall find a solution to the problem . . . 14. . . . did severe damage to . . . 15. What is the greatest influence that radio has had on our lives? 16. . . . to give me wholehearted support. 17. Try to make constructive and tactful criticisms. 18. . . . has to take your measurements. 19. Can you make a reduction in the price? 20. Nobody has given you permission . . . 21. . . . what suggestion to make (or offer). I can't make any definite recommendation yet. 22. . . . making experiments on you? 23. There is a complete difference between . . . One cannot make any comparison between them. 24. After making careful observations of the animal's behaviour, Peterson made a very important discovery. 25. No person will be granted admission to . . . unless he has first made (or submitted) a formal application in writing.

145 advisable, agreeable, arguable, unbelievable (or incredible), incalculable, changeable, chargeable, collapsible, comfortable, incomprehensible, countable, incurable, debatable, demonstrable, infallible, unforgettable, unforgivable, manageable, notable, noticeable, permissible, preferable, reasonable, irreconcilible, irreducible, regrettable, reliable, irresistible, soluble, intolerable, translatable, unusable

146 1. washable linen, guaranteed unshrinkable 2. These books are

unusable. They are quite unsaleable. 3. . . . are obtainable . . .
4. . . . are acceptable. 5. Only really reliable people are eligible
. . . 6. . . . are edible, very indigestible. 7. . . . it is advisable
to take . . . overcoat is very desirable. 8. It is preferable to go . . .
weather is very changeable. 9. . . . is unanswerable. 10. The
problem before us is quite insoluble.

155 1. I'll go and see if Mr. Hall is in. 2. I think I have an appointment with him. 4. I'd like to find out how people live . . .

160 1. Let us discuss our plans when we meet on Thursday. 3. Call
me immediately (or as soon as) the doctor comes. 5. We shall
start a new book as soon as we have finished this one. 6. . . .
don't pour the water . . . until the water has boiled.

163 1. If I eat too much, I get . . . 2. If you call . . ., I will give . . .
3. If you take . . ., you will be . . . 4. If you took . . ., you
would be 5. If you had taken . . ., you would have arrived . . .
6. If you had listened . . ., you would not have lost . . . 7. I'll
phone you if we need you . . . 8. I'll take . . ., in case it rains.
9. Don't disturb me unless there is an urgent . . . 10. You may
borrow . . ., provided you bring it back . . . 11. Will you meet
me . . ., if you have finished . . . 12. If you had answered all . . .,
you would have passed . . .

168 1. The Minister has agreed to attend . . . 2. He hopes (that) we
can start . . . 3. He expects us to wait . . . 4. His secretary will
arrange for his car to bring . . . 5. Does the driver know where
to go? 6. Please remind the secretary to make . . . 7. Please
remind the Minister (that) we shall expect him . . . 8. We shall
try to persuade him to stay . . . 9. Do you suggest (that) we
offer . . . 10. I suppose he will want . . . 11. People consider
he is (or him to be) a good . . . 12. Some people have no idea
when to stop talking.

180 1. I hope to see . . . 2. *No change* 3. I now regret speaking *or*
having spoken . . . 4. We believe R. to be . . . 5. I don't
pretend to be as clever as you. 6. . . . noticed a shoe sticking
out . . . 7. I'm afraid of having . . . 8. We are sorry to be . . .
9. . . . decided to go . . . 10. . . . any idea how to make . . .
11. . . . whether to wait . . . 12. . . . know when to stop . . . 13.
Remind me to go . . . 14. Be careful not to drop . . . 15. The
thought of losing . . . 16. . . . can complain of having been
badly treated. 17. . . . insist on their innocence. 18. . . . understand your behaving . . . 19. He promised to buy . . . 20. Do
you suggest (our) starting . . . 21. At the beginning of this
talk, I did not intend to speak . . . 22. Anyone wishing to
take . . . 23. Goods in any way damaged . . . 24. The meeting

arranged for next Tuesday . . . 25. . . . responsibility for the loss of any valuables left . . . 26. . . . something to stop . . . 27. Never having been to India . . . 28. . . . since meeting his mother-in-law. 29. . . . by listening . . . 30. . . . before embarkation. 31. On receipt of your . . . 32. . . . because of (or owing to) thick fog. 33. . . . after your election. 34. . . . no noticeable difference . . . 35. To speak frankly, I didn't like your description of . . . 36. A lawyer by training, when forced to be a soldier, Smuts was . . . 37. Without wishing to criticize, I must draw attention to the inaccuracy of . . . 38. Asked to explain his absence . . ., J. could give no satisfactory answer. 39. Do not forget to deposit your key . . . on leaving the Hotel. 40. In working . . ., you can learn how to use . . .

VERB LIST
with a key to commonly used patterns

Explanations

1. stg = something; sby = somebody; ∼ = head-word repeated; intr. = intransitive.
2. Numbers refer to paragraphs in this book.
3. *apologize* (*to sby*) (*for sby, or for doing*) indicates that we can say *I apologize*, or *I apologize to somebody*, or *I apologize for something*, or *for doing something*, or *I apologize to somebody for something*.
4. Absence of brackets, as in *enjoy stg;* ∼ *oneself;* ∼ *going* indicates that the verb requires a complement, which cannot be omitted.
5. ∼ *that* indicates that the verb can be followed by a noun clause, as in 156; ∼ (that) indicates the same except that the conjunction *that* can be omitted, as in 149.
6. A, B, C and D refer to the four patterns in 54, thus:
   A = call on somebody
   B = go on
   C = call up a friend, call a friend up, call him up
   D = get on with your work.
7. Note *talk of stg* (=refer in speech to that subject); *talk about it* (=say various things related to it); *talk on it* (=treat it systematically, as in a lecture). Similar differences apply to *think of, dream of, think about, dream about,* etc.
8. Brief notes on meaning are given only to indicate which construction is referred to. For more precise meaning, consult a dictionary.

abandon stg or sby; ∼ oneself to stg
abide (by a decision)
absorb a liquid; be ∼d in stg
abstain from alcohol, from smoking
accord (=grant) sby stg, 49; stg ∼s (=agrees) with stg else
account for stg; give an ∼ of it
accuse sby (of stg, of doing)
acquaint sby with a fact; be ∼d with sby (=know him)
adapt stg (to stg else)
add stg (to stg else); ∼ (that)
address a letter (to sby); ∼ sby as Mr. X.
adhere to stg

admire stg; ~ sby (for stg)

admit (=confess) an error; ~ doing, *or* having done stg; ~ (that); ~ sby (=let him enter)

adopt stg; ~ a child

advance, intr. (=go forward); ~ (=give) sby some money, 49

advise sby (to go); ~ sby on *or* about stg

affect stg or sby; have an *effect* on it or him

afford stg; ~ to go

agree (with sby) (on *or* about stg); ~ to go, *or* to your going; ~ to a course of action (=approve); ~ (that) 149 or 156

aim at going, *or* to go

allow sby to go; ~ sby stg, 49; ~ for something (=take it into account)

amount to a total

announce stg (to sby), 48; ~ (that)

annoy sby; be ~d (with sby) (about stg)

answer (a question); ~ sby; ~ (that); ~ (sby) back (=argue against authority); ~ for stg or sby; ~ to a description (=conform with it)

appeal (to sby) (for stg); ~ against a decision

appear, intr; ~ (=seem) to go; it ~s (that); ~s as if, *or* as though

apologize (to sby) (for stg, for doing stg.)

apply, intr. =be true; ~ stg (=put it close) (to stg else); ~ oneself to a task; ~ (to sby) (for stg)

appoint sby (to a post); ~ sby (stg) 47; ~ sby to go

approach (stg or sby); make an ~ to sby

approve (of stg or sby); ~ of your going

argue (with sby) (about stg); ~ for stg (=in support of it); ~ sby out of going (=persuade him not to go); ~ (that)

arrange stg (with sby); ~ (for sby) to go; ~ (with sby) for stg to be done; ~ that, 156

arrive (at a point, on a surface, in a space)

assert stg; ~ (that)

ask (sby) (stg), 47, h; ~ sby for stg, 47, h; ~ sby about stg; ~ sby a favour, or ~ a favour of sby; ~ after sby, A (=inquire about his health); ~ sby in (out, up, etc.) = ask sby to come in; ~ to go; ~ sby to go; ~ for sby to go; ~ (sby) if (whether, how, etc.); ~ that, 156

assume (that)

assure sby (that)

attack (sby or stg); make an ~ on sby or stg

attempt a task; ~ to go

attend (=be present at) a meeting; ~ (give medical attention to) a patient; ~ (= pay attention) to sby or stg

avail myself of an opportunity

avoid stg or sby; ~ going

await sby or stg

back, intr. = go backwards; ~ (support) sby or stg, or ~ sby up; ~ out, B (=withdraw)

bargain (with sby) (for stg)

be, Section ONE; am to, 99; ~ away (in, out, etc.), B; ~ up to stg (=capable of it); ~ up to sby (=be his responsibility)

bear (=carry, endure) stg; ~ to go, or ~ going, 132, ii; ~ (tolerate) sby; ~ stg in mind (=remember it); X ~s on Y (=relates to it); ~ out, C (=prove to be right); ~ up, B (=not collapse)

become a lawyer, ~ wiser

beg for money; ~ sby to go

begin work; ~ to work, or working, 132, ii

believe sby, 19; ∼ a report; ∼ (that); ∼ (=have faith) in sby; ∼ sby to be honest

belong to sby or stg

blame sby (for stg); ∼ stg on sby

blow, intr. (e.g. The wind ∼s); ∼ out, B or C (=extinguish); ∼ up, B or C (=fill with air, or explode)

boast (of or about stg); ∼ (that)

boil, 44, c

borrow (stg) (from sby)

bother (sby) (with, or about stg)

break, 44, c; ∼ down (in, off, up), B or C; ∼ out (=escape, begin suddenly), B

bring stg to sby; ∼ sby stg, 49; ∼ about, C (=produce, cause to be); ∼ up, C (=educate sby; or introduce a subject)

build stg (for sby); ∼ sby stg, 51

burn, 44, c

burst, 44, c; ∼ out laughing; ∼ into tears

buy stg (for sby); ∼ sby stg, 51

call (sby); ∼ sby or stg a name, 47; ∼ stg for sby; ∼ sby stg, 51; ∼ off, C (=cancel); ∼ on sby, A (=a visit); ∼ up, B or C (=telephone)

can, 105–112

care =take trouble (about sby); ∼ for stg (=like it); I don't care for dancing (=I don't like it); ∼ (=like) to go

carry stg; ∼ on, B or C (=continue); ∼ out, C (=perform)

cause trouble (to sby); ∼ sby trouble, 49; ∼ stg to go

catch stg; ∼ up, B or C (=reduce the gap between oneself and people ahead); ∼ up with stg or sby, D

cease to go, or ∼ going, 132, ii

change, 44, c; ∼ stg for stg else

charge sby (=make him pay) (for stg); ∼ a price; ∼ sby with a crime (=accuse him of it)

choose stg; ∼ between X and Y; ∼ to go; ∼ stg for sby; ∼ sby stg, 51

claim stg; ∼ (money) for damage; ∼ to be

clear, 44, c; ∼ away (out, up), B or C

close, 44, c; ∼ down (or up) B or C; ∼ with sby (=agree on a deal)

come, intr.; ∼ across stg, A (=find it by chance); ∼ down (in, out, up, etc.), B; ∼ to, B (recover, consciousness)

command sby (to go); ∼ (that), 156

comment (on stg); ∼ (that)

commence, 44, c; ∼ to work or ∼ working

communicate with sby; ∼ information (to sby)

compel sby to go

compete (with sby) (for stg)

complain (to sby) (about the noise; *but* ∼ of feeling unwell); ∼ (that)

compliment sby (on stg, or on being stg, or on having done stg)

concentrate (on stg, *or* on going)

concern sby (e.g. This ∼s you); ∼ oneself with stg; ∼ed (=worried) about stg; ∼ed (=worried) to see; ∼ed in or with stg (=engaged in it)

confess (stg) (to sby); ∼ (that)

confirm a statement (to sby); ∼ (that)

congratulate sby (on stg, *or* on winning)

connect X and Y; ∼ X to, or with, Y

consider stg; ∼ going; ∼ (that); ∼ sby to be honest

consist of stg (=be made up of it); ∼ in stg, in being (=be an element of it)

consult sby (about, or on, stg)
contain stg; X is ~ed in Y
continue (going, or to go), 132, ii
consult sby about *or* on stg
control stg or sby
convince sby (of stg)
co-operate (with sby) (in stg)
cost (sby) stg, 49
could, 108–112
count (units); ~ (=rely) on sby
cover stg (with stg else); ~ed
with stg
credit sby with stg, with doing
cut (stg); ~ down (off, out), C
cry (about stg); ~ out, B
cure sby (of an illness, of being)

dare (to) go, 114, 122; ~ sby to go
deal cards; ~ (=do business)
with sby; ~ with business
debate a subject, *or* ~ about *or*
on it
decide an argument; ~ about *or*
on a subject; ~ to go *or* on
going; ~ (that)
declare war; ~ (that)
defend one's honour; defend sby
(from going)
delay stg or sby; ~ going
delight sby; ~ in seeing; ~ed to
see *or* at seeing
demand stg (of, or from, sby); ~
(that) 156
deny going, or having gone; ~
(that)
depend on stg; ~ on sby (for
stg); ~ on going
describe stg (to sby)
deserve to go; ~ shooting, 134
desire stg; ~ to go
desist from going
despair (of (sby's) going)
determine to go, or on going; ~
(that), 156; X ~s Y (is the cause
of it)
die (of an illness, from injuries);
~ away (down, out), B

differ from stg
disagree (with sby) (about *or* on
stg)
discourage sby (from doing stg)
discover stg; ~ (that); ~ sby to
be a thief
discuss stg (with sby)
dislike sby or stg; ~ going
distinguish between X and Y; ~
X from Y.
divide X by Y; ~ X into Y parts; ~
Y into X
do 5, 6, 8; ~ (stg) (for, or to,
sby); What shall we ~ about it?;
~ away with stg, D (=abolish
it); ~ up, C (=repair);
redecorate); ~ without stg, A
(=manage without it
doubt (stg); ~ that (before a
statement); ~ if, or whether
(before a question)
dream (of *or* about stg); ~ of
going
drink (stg); ~ up, B (=go on
drinking); ~ up, C (=drink all)
drive 44, c; ~ sby to do stg
drop 44, c; ~ in, B (come
unexpectedly); ~ in on sby, D;
~ out, B (=withdraw)

earn money
eat (stg); ~ up, B (=go on
eating); ~ up, C (=eat all)
effect (=produce) a cure
encourage sby (to go)
end 44, c; ~ in going, by
going; ~ up with stg, D (=have
it left)
endeavour to go
endure (stg); ~ seeing stg
engage sby (as an employee); ~
sby to do stg; ~d in (=busy)
doing stg
enjoy stg; ~ oneself; ~ going
enquire see *inquire*
enter (a room); ~ into a
conversation, an agreement

152

entrust stg to sby
envy sby (his good fortune); ~
sby for having stg
equal stg; X ~s ZY
equip sby (with an instrument, for
a purpose)
excuse sby; ~ sby for saying stg
that he has said; ~ sby from
doing stg, so that he need not do
it
expect stg (of sby); ~ (sby) to
go; ~ (that)
experiment (on stg)
explain stg (to sby), 48; ~ (to
sby) that

fail to go; ~ in an attempt
fall, intr.; ~ back (down, in,
out), B; ~ back on stg, D; ~
off, B (=decrease); ~ in love,
into decay; ~ in with a plan, D
(= accept it)
fancy stg (=imagine, or like it);
~ doing that! (=imagine it);
I don't ~ (your) doing that (=I
don't like it); ~ (that) =imagine
(that)
favour, stg or sby; ~ going
fear (stg or sby); ~ to go, or ~
going; ~ for your safety; ~
(that); I fear not (6, iv)
feed sby; Cows ~ on grass
feel (stg); ~ about stg or sby; ~
for sby (=sympathise); ~ stg go
or going, 132, i; ~ (that)
fetch (=go and bring) stg; ~ stg
for sby; ~ sby stg, 51
fight (sby); ~ with, or against,
sby
fill, 44, c; ~ stg with stg else; ~
in (out or up) a form, C
find stg (for sby); ~ sby stg, 51;
~ (that); ~ out, B or C
(=discover); ~ out (that); ~ sby
out (=discover him to be at
fault)
finish (stg); ~ doing; ~ by going

(=do that last)
fix stg; ~ up, C (=arrange)
fly, 44, c
follow, 44, c; X ~s Y, so Y is
~ed by X
forbid stg; ~ sby to go
force stg; ~ sby to go
forget (stg); ~ about stg; ~ to
go (=not go); ~ going, having
gone (=go but forget the event),
134; ~ (that)
forgive sby (for) an offence; ~
sby (for) doing wrong
form, 44, c.

gather stg; ~ (that) =understand
(that)
get stg (for sby); ~ sby stg, 51;
~ wet, intr; ~ stg wet; ~ across
(away, back, down, in, off, out,
through, up) B or C; ~ at stg, A
(=reach it); ~ away with, D
(=escape without punishment);
~ to a destination, A (=go there
and arrive); ~ on, B (=make
progress); ~ up a play, C
(=arrange it)
give stg (to sby); ~ sby stg, 49;
~ away (back, in, out, up), C; ~
in or up, B (=surrender); ~ sby
away (=betray them)
go, intr.; ~ away (back, down, in,
out, through, up), B; ~ on, B
(=continue); ~ back on a
promise, D (=withdraw it); ~ in
for sports, D (=take part in
them); ~ through with, D
(=finish); be going to do stg, 28
grant stg (to sby); ~ sby stg, 49
guess (the answer); ~ (that)
grow, 44, c; ~ up, B (=become
adult)

had better, 115, ii
hand stg to sby; ~ sby stg, 49; ~
back (down, in, out, over), C
hang 44, c; ~ on stg (=be

supported by it); ∼ from stg (emphasizes the downward fall of what is hanging); ∼ about or around, A or B, (=wait); ∼ on B (=hold tight); ∼ on to stg, D (=keep it)

happen (to stg or sby); ∼ to go; ∼ (that)

harm stg or sby

hasten to go

hate stg or sby; ∼ to go or going, 132, ii, iii and iv

have, 3–5, ∼ to, 97, 102

hear (stg of sby); ∼ stg or sby go or going, 132; **heard** to go, or going

help (sby) ∼ sby go or to go, 122; cannot ∼ going, 131

hesitate to go

hinder (sby) (from going)

hide, 44, c; ∼ stg from sby

hold stg or sby; ∼ off, B or C (=keep away); ∼ on, B (=wait); ∼ out, B (=survive); ∼ up, C (=stop, delay)

hope (for stg); ∼ to go; I ∼ not, 6, iv; ∼ (that); For tenses commonly used with *hope*, see 172

imagine (stg); ∼ (sby or sby's) going; ∼ (that)

increase: an amount ∼s; or we ∼ an amount

influence sby; have an ∼ on or over him

inform sby (of or about stg); ∼ sby (that)

inquire (about stg); ∼ after sby's health; ∼ into, A (=investigate); ∼ whether

insist (on stg); on sby's going; ∼ (that)

instruct sby (to go)

intend to go or going, 132, ii; ∼ sby to go; ∼ (that), 156

interest sby (in stg, or in going); I was ∼ed to hear stg (=I heard it

with interest); Are you ∼d in listening to music (=Do you take an interest in it?)

introduce sby or stg (to sby)

invite sby (to go)

join X to or with Y; ∼ in an activity, A (=take part in it); ∼ up, B (=enter the army)

joke (about stg) (with sby)

judge (sby or stg); ∼ by or from evidence, to reach a conclusion; ∼ (that)

jump, intr.; ∼ at an opportunity (=accept it at once); ∼ for joy; ∼ to conclusions (=arrive at them too quickly)

keep stg (for sby); ∼ sby stg, 51; ∼ quiet, intr.; ∼ sby quiet; ∼ away (back, down, in, off, out, up) B or C; ∼ (on) (talking) = continue; ∼ up, B (=don't proceed too slowly); ∼ up with the others, D

kneel intr.; ∼ down, B

knock (stg); ∼ on or at the door; ∼ over, C (=cause to fall); ∼ off (work) =stop; ∼ out an opponent, C

know (stg or sby) 19, ∼ of or about stg or sby; ∼ (that); ∼ if, or whether; ∼ how, etc.

lack stg; X is ∼ing in Y

last: How long does this term last? Can you ∼ out? (=continue)

laugh (at stg or sby)

lay stg, 44, a; ∼ down (in, out, up), C

lead (sby) (to a place). What does all this lead up to? (=What is the result?)

lean (stg) on stg else

learn (stg); ∼ of or about stg (from sby); ∼ to dance; ∼ (that); ∼ how, etc.

leave (=go away from) (sby, or a place); ~ sby alone; ~ stg to sby, ~ sby stg, 49; ~ this to me (=let me do it); ~ off (working) =stop; ~ out, C (=omit)

lend stg to sby; ~ sby stg, 49

let sby, or stg, go; (Passive =be *allowed* to go); ~ in, or out, C; ~ down, C (=lower); ~ sby down (=disappoint him); ~ sby off (=not punish him)

lie, intr.; ~ down, B

like stg or sby, 19; ~ (sby) to go, or ~ sby (going), 132

listen (to sby, or stg); ~ to sby sing *or* singing

live (at, or in, a place); ~ on (food), A; ~ up to a standard, D

lock a door; ~ up, B or C

long (for sby) to go

look (at stg); ~ for stg, A (=try to find it; ~ after sby, A (=take care of him); ~ into stg, A (=investigate it); ~ on sby, A (=consider him) as a father; ~ out, B (=watch); ~ out for sby, D; ~ up to sby, D (=respect him); ~ down on sby (=not respect him); It ~s (to me) as if (*or* as though) it is going to rain

love sby, 19; ~ (sby) to go *or* going, 132

make stg (for sby); ~ sby stg, 47 & 51; ~ sby, or stg, go; (Passive = be made to go); ~ for a place, A (=go towards it); ~ off, B (=escape); ~ out, C (=understand, compile); ~ up, C (=invent) a story, (or =end) a quarrel; ~ up for, D (=compensate for)

made: X is ~ of the substance Y; or is ~ from (more directly) the object Z; or is ~ up of various elements

manage (stg); ~ to go

may, 106, 112

mean stg, 19; ~ (=intend) to go; Does this ~ (=signify) starting again? ~ (that)

meet sby; ~ with approval

mention stg (to sby); ~ (that)

might, 110, 112

mind stg (=take care of it, be careful of it); Do you mind (my) going? Do you mind if I smoke?

miss stg or sby; ~ going

mistake sby for sby else

mix X and Y, or ~ X with Y; ~ up, C

move, 44, c; ~ in (out, up), B; ~ on, B (=go forward); ~ =propose (that)

must, 95–102

name sby; ~ sby stg, 47

need go, 100–102; ~ to go, 116; ~ cleaning, 134

neglect stg or sby; ~ to do stg

note stg; ~ (that)

notice stg; ~ stg go *or* going, 132, i; ~ (that); ~ whether

obey sby; ~ the rules

object (to stg); ~ to going; ~ (that)

oblige sby to go; be ~d to go

observe stg; ~ (that)

offend sby; ~ against the law

offer stg (to sby); ~ sby stg, 49; ~ to go

omit stg; ~ to go *or* ~ going

open, 44, c; ~ up, B or C

oppose sby; be ~d to stg, to sby's going

order stg (for sby); ~ sby stg, 51; ~ sby to go

ought to go, 93–94

owe stg (to sby); ~ sby stg, 49

own property; ~ that (=confess that); ~ up, B (=confess); ~ up to a misdeed, D

reply (to sby, or to a letter); ∼ that

report stg or sby; ∼ on stg or sby; ∼ (that)

represent stg or sby

request stg (of sby); ∼ sby to go; ∼ (that), 156

require stg; ∼ sby to go

rescue sby (from stg, from drowning)

resemble stg. *Avoid passive*

resent stg; ∼ going

reserve stg (for sby)

resign (from) a post

resist stg or sby; ∼ going

respect sby (for stg, for doing stg)

restore stg or sby (to a state)

result (from a cause) (in an effect)

retire (from work) (to rest)

return (from X to Y); ∼ stg to sby; ∼ sby stg, 49

reveal stg

revenge a wrong; ∼ oneself on sby

reward sby; ∼ sby for (doing) stg; ∼ sby with stg

rid sby of trouble

ring (=call); ∼ up, B or C (=telephone)

rise 44, a; ∼ up, B

risk one's life; ∼ losing

roar, intr.; ∼ with laughter

rob sby (of stg)

roll, 44, c; ∼ down (up), B or C

rub, 44, c; ∼ out (up), C; ∼ up, C (=polish)

run, intr.; ∼ stg (=organize); ∼ down, C (=criticize); ∼ out of stg, D (=exhaust one's stock of it)

satisfy sby; ∼ied with stg

save sby (from drowning); ∼ stg for sby; ∼ sby stg, 51; ∼ up, (money), B or C

say stg (to sby), 48; ∼ 'Thank you'; ∼ one's prayers; ∼ (that); ∼ (if or whether); ∼ how, etc.

search (a place) (for stg); ∼ through a place, A; ∼ out, C (=search a place thoroughly, or succeed in finding)

see (stg), 19; ∼ (=make arrangements) about stg, or about doing stg; ∼ sby off (=go with him to say good-bye); ∼ to stg, A (=be responsible for it)

seem to be; ∼ (that); ∼ as if, or as though

sell stg (at *or* for a price); ∼ stg to sby; ∼ sby stg, 49; ∼ off, C (=sell cheaply); sold out, (=all sold); These sell well, 67

send stg (to sby); ∼ sby stg, 49; ∼ for sby, A (=tell him to come); ∼ in an application, C; ∼ stg on, C, to sby (=send it to him after he has gone)

separate X and Y; ∼ X from Y

serve sby; ∼ a purpose; ∼ on a committee

set, intr. (e.g. The sun ∼s); ∼ stg on, or in, a place; ∼ sby some work to do; ∼ about your business, A (=start it) ∼ down (out, up) C; ∼ in, B (=begin, e.g. The rains set in); ∼ off, or ∼ out, B, (=start); ∼ off, or out, on a journey; ∼ to work (=begin)

settle, 44, c; ∼ down, B; ∼ down to work; ∼ up, B (=pay a bill)

shake, 44, c; ∼ off (out, up), C

shall, 76–80

share stg (with sby); ∼ stg between both; ∼ it among all

shelter (from the storm)

shield sby (from danger)

shoot (at a target) (with a weapon)

should, 85–93

shout (at sby)

show stg to sby; ∼ sby stg, 49; ∼ me; ∼ off, B or C (=display); ∼ up, B (=appear)

157

shut, 44, c; ~ down, (in, off, out, up), C; Shut up! (=be quiet)

sit, intr.; ~ down (up), B

smell, 19; This ~s of soap

smile (at sby)

spare stg (for sby); ~ sby stg, 51

speak (to sby) (of, about or on stg); ~ a language, ~ the truth; ~ up, B (=more loudly); ~ out, B (=boldly)

spread, 44, c; ~ out, C

stand (stg); ~ losing or to lose, 134; ~ for, A (=represent); ~ out, B (=be prominent); ~ up, B; ~ up for sby, D (=defend him); ~ up to sby, D (=defend oneself against him)

start (stg); ~ to go or going, 132, ii; ~ off or out (on a journey)

state stg; ~ (that)

stay (at, on or in a place); ~ (=remain) talking

steal (stg) (from sby)

stop (sby) talking, 134; ~ sby from going too far

stretch, 44, c; ~ out, B or C

strike (stg or sby); ~ at sby (=try to hit); ~ out, B or C

struggle (with or against sby or stg)

study (stg)

succeed (in doing stg); ~ (=follow) sby

suffer (pain); ~ fools gladly; ~ from an illness; ~ with one's nerves

suggest a plan; ~ (that); ~ (sby's) going

supply stg (to sby); ~ sby with stg

suppose (that); He is ~d to be rich

suspect sby (of stealing); ~ (that)

swear (at sby); ~ to be true; ~ (that)

sympathize (with sby)

take stg (from sby); ~ away (back, down, in, off, out, up), C; ~ after one's father, A (=be like him); ~ (=mistake) sby for sby else; ~ in, C (=deceive, or receive); ~ on, or over, C (=undertake responsibility); ~ to, A (develop a liking for); ~ sby up on that, (=challenge him on it)

talk (sense); ~ of, about or on a subject (to or with sby); ~ over, C (=discuss)

taste, 19; This ~s of soap

teach (sby); ~ stg (to sby); ~ sby stg, 49; ~ sby to do stg; ~ (sby) (that)

tell stg to sby; ~ sby (stg), 49; ~ me; ~ sby to go; ~ sby (that)

tempt sby (to do stg)

tend to make; ~towards stg

thank sby (for stg, for doing stg); ~ sby to keep quiet, 134

think (of or about a subject); ~ over, C (=consider carefully); ~ of going, or to go, 134; ~ (that)

threaten sby with stg; ~ to go

throw stg (at sby =to hit him); ~ stg to sby =in his direction; ~ away, (back, down, in, out, up), C; ~ up, C (=abandon)

tie a knot; ~ up a parcel, C

touch stg or sby

translate stg (from one language) (into another)

trouble (sby or oneself) about stg; Don't trouble to write

trust sby (to do stg); ~ sby with stg; ~ in stg, A

try (stg); ~ to do (=attempt); try and do, 125; ~ doing (=experiment), 134; ~ on, C (=see if it fits, see if you can succeed); ~ out, C (test)

turn, 44, c; ~ away (over, round), B; ~ away (down, out, over, round), C; ~ on (off) a light, C

understand (stg or sby), 19; ∼
sby to say; ∼ (that)
undertake work; ∼ to do it
urge sby to go
use stg; ∼ up, C (=exhaust); ∼d
to (3, 5, 6); I am used
(=accustomed) to going)

vary, 44, c

wait (for sby or stg); ∼ on, A
(=serve)
wake, 44, c; ∼ up, B or C
walk, intr.; ∼ about (along), A
or B
want stg, 19; ∼ to go; ∼
mending, 134; ∼ sby to go or
going, 132, ii
warn sby about stg; ∼ sby not to
go; ∼ sby (that)
wash (oneself or stg else); ∼ up,
B or C (=clean the dishes); ∼

away (off, out), B or C
watch (sby or stg); ∼ sby or stg
go or going, 132; ∼ for sby, A;
∼ out, B (=watch carefully); ∼
out for sby or stg, D
wear, 44, c; 67; ∼ away (down,
out), B or C
will, Modal verb, 73–75
will, Full Regular Verb; ∼ stg
win (a race, a prize)
wish (for stg); ∼ sby a Merry
Christmas; ∼ sby to go; ∼ you
would go, or you had gone, 169
wonder (if, or whether)
work, intr.; ∼ stg (=make it
work); ∼ out, B (=solve itself);
∼ out, C (=solve)
worry (about stg or sby)
would, 82–92
would rather 115, ii
write (a letter to sby); ∼ sby a
letter, 49; ∼ about or on stg; ∼
(to sby) that

ADDITIONAL NOTES FOR TEACHERS AND ADVANCED STUDENTS

The numbers refer to paragraphs in this book.

1, iv　　There is a difference between *cànnot* and *can nòt* in examples like the following:

You must stay here. You cannot go yet.
You can certainly nòt go yet.
You need not go. You can nòt go if you don't want to.

5, i &　Practice may be needed when the subject is a noun group made
ii　　up of several words, e.g.:

Have all those noisy people gone?
Does everyone in your party know what to do?

5, ii (Footnote)　There may be a difference between *I usually didn't go* and *I used not to go*. The former may emphasize my *not* being in the habit of going; the latter, my *being* in the habit of not going.

Questions can also be formed by retaining the word order usually given to statements, but ending the sentence with a sharply rising intonation:

You've eaten all that apple pie alréady?

This form is often used when the speaker asks, with surprise, for confirmation.

6, iii　　*Be* can follow the full verb pattern in cases like:

Why don't you be more careful?, meaning *Why don't you act more carefully?* See 19, i.

9　　*Be* and *have* can follow all these forms of the imperative; e.g.

Do be quiet. Don't be silly. Do have some more tea.

11　　*Bet, wet* and *quit* commonly follow the pattern of *set* and *hit*.

12, Table 2　*Mayn't* is found, but is more likely to occur in the sense of 106 a–c than of 106 d–j.

Let's commonly occurs before a verb, but not in an expression like *Let us alone*.

13 (43)　We can use *their* or *his* with *every* (*one*), though *his* is safer in formal composition. In any case, the verb takes the singular form.

18, Note 1　One can compile a list of verbs which are seldom, if ever, found in the continuous form. The list would include *belong, consist, contain, deserve, matter, own* and some of the verbs in 19. But see *English as a Foreign Language*, 146–152.

19, iii　For the distinction between *see* and *look* (*at*), and between *hear*
& iv　and *listen* (*to*), see *English as a Foreign Language*, 149–150, and *A Linguistic Study of the English Verb* (F. R. Palmer), section

5.3.4. This distinction is not made by using two different words in the case of *feel*, *smell* and *taste*. With each of these three verbs one can safely use the continuous form when the word corresponds to *look* (*at*) or *listen* (*to*).

21   In making the choice, much depends on exactly what one has in mind and wishes to emphasize. See *English as a Foreign Language*, 141–2.

34   This treatment follows the line that there are no special rules for tenses in reported speech.

50   This pattern, rather than the pattern in 48, is necessary to avoid ambiguity in a case like:
He explained to the police why she had gone.

56, f   'One should make little birds that can sing but won't sing, sing' sounds absurd. Prefer 'If little birds that can sing won't sing, one should make them sing'.

67   The passive would have to be used if 'by (the agent)' is added:
This book is sold by our local bookseller.

70, a   Other participles used like *tired* include *amused, annoyed, confused, determined, exaggerated, limited, pleased, satisfied, worried*.

70, b   *Bended, drunken, lighted* are likely to be found only as attributive adjectives.

73, v   In this case, *will play*, etc. can be replaced by *play*, etc. in the Ordinary Present Tense, as an example of 15 a. or c.

100   *Need* and *dare* do not adopt all the features of a modal verb. For example:
We can't wait—nor can you; *but*
We needn't wait—nor do you.
We dare not say so—nor do you.

105   In a., *can* is replaceable by (*are*) *able to*; in b., by zero; in c., by (*are*) *able to*; in d., by (*am*) *able or free to*; in e. and f., by *may*; in g., by *will*; in h., by *may*; in i., by (*is*) *often*; in j., by *may*; in k., *can be* is replaceable by *is*.

106   In a., b., c., and d., *may* is replaceable by *can*; in b., also by *might*; in e., *may be* by *is perhaps* or *could*; in f., *may* by *perhaps*; in g., *may be* by *is perhaps*; in h., i., and j., *may* by *will perhaps*.

117   Other verbs that fit into the pattern *I advise you to go* are *command, forbid, intend, lead, mean, teach, train. Warn* is most likely to fit into the pattern *I asked you not to do it.*

124   If we imagine No. 16 to mean 'It seems to me, from the evidence I see before me now, that this window was forced open, at the time when it *was* opened', then we must say 'This window seems to have been forced open'.

161, ii   *If you will* is found when *will* means (*are*) *willing*: see 73, d. But see also 172, ii.

169   Other verbs that fit into the pattern *It's time you went* are *suppose* (or *supposing*), and *would rather.*

Suppose (or supposing) you failed, then what would you do? I would rather you didn't mention that possibility.

172   A variation for example r. in Table 6 would be *If he were to tell* (future).

GEORGE ALLEN & UNWIN LTD

Head Office:
40 Museum Street, London, W.C.1
Telephone: 01-405 8577

Sales, Distribution and Accounts Departments
Park Lane, Hemel Hempstead, Herts.
Telephone: 0442 3244

Athens: 7 Stadiou Street, Athens 125
Barbados: Rockley New Road, St. Lawrence 4
Bombay: 103/5 Fort Street, Bombay 1
Calcutta: 285J Bepin Behari Ganguli Street, Calcutta 12
Dacca: Alico Building, 18 Montijheel, Dacca 2
Hornsby, N.S.W.: Cnr. Bridge Road and Jersey Street, 2077
Ibadan: P.O. Box 62
Johannesburg: P.O. Box 23134, Joubert Park
Karachi: Karachi Chambers, McLeod Road, Karachi 2
Lahore: 22 Falettis' Hotel, Egerton Road
Madras: 2/18 Mount Road, Madras 2
Manila: P.O. Box 157, Quezon City, D-502
Mexico: Serapio Rendon 125, Mexico 4, D.F.
Nairobi: P.O. Box 30583
New Delhi: 4/21-22B Asaf Ali Road, New Delhi 1
Ontario: 2330 Midland Avenue, Agincourt
Singapore: 248c-6 Orchard Road, Singapore 9
Tokyo: C.P.O. Box 1728, Tokyo 100-91
Wellington: P.O. Box 1467, Wellington, New Zealand

ENGLISH AS A FOREIGN LANGUAGE

R. A. CLOSE

In English, one can use words and forms which are correct by themselves, without being able to put them together in an intelligible or idiomatic way. This difficulty confronts the advanced student, especially in the use of articles, tenses, the infinitive, gerund, prepositions, the placing of adverbs, etc. Rules governing these features of the language are very hard to formulate and the rules of thumb which help the beginner may only obstruct the more advanced student's recognition of underlying distinction and meaning.

Taking examples of generally-accepted, modern English usage as the only reliable guide. Mr. Close offers criteria by which these problems can be more satisfactorily explained, and then applies the criteria to the student's and teacher's practical difficulties. His scheme fits the facts of natural usage remarkably well, and the chapters on the articles, on the prepositions, on aspects of activity and of time, contain much that is quite new.

Mr. Close sets out to help teachers and advanced students to *understand* usage with which they may already have become vaguely familiar in the course of their studies, and his human approach and long experience make him very successful. He also establishes the principles for A *Grammar With Exercises*—with simple instructions, without abstract explanation and suitable for beginners and less advanced students. This is now in preparation.

QUALIFYING IN ENGLISH

JANET J. SCOBIE

Qualifying in English deals with examinations from the examiner's point of view, as well as from that of the candidates. It points out the things that give an examiner a bad impression, and the things which please him, and cause him to award high marks.

The book will also be most useful to Teachers, who find the normal English textbook inadequate as a source of exercises for the correction of errors, and it will also be found invaluable by clerks and typists in the course of their work.

It is indeed a book that no prospective candidate should be without.

ENGLISH FOR TODAY

J. SCOBIE AND W. O. WILLIAMS

Many foreign students of English pass from the elementary to the more advanced stages and then find their ability to express themselves in good accurate English is not what they thought. In the earlier stages they have, no doubt, concentrated on difficulties one at a time, and when required to overcome a number of difficulties at the same time, for their employers or for examination purposes, they make bad mistakes. It is to remedy such mistakes in expression that this book has been written.

Its aim is to help students to express themselves clearly and accurately in the English they may have to use in the course of their work and to pass examinations in English, especially those conducted for, foreign students by the University of Cambridge.

The types of mistakes most commonly committed by foreign students are pointed out, and exercises on how to correct errors in usage, in vocabulary, in grammar, in punctuation and spelling are given to help eradicate such errors.

GEORGE ALLEN & UNWIN LTD